WOMEN
OF THE
WALL

WOMEN
OF THE
WALL

CLAIMING SACRED GROUND
AT JUDAISM'S HOLY SITE

Edited by Phyllis Chesler and Rivka Haut

JEWISH LIGHTS PUBLISHING
Woodstock, Vermont

Women of the Wall:
Claiming Sacred Ground at Judaism's Holy Site

Library of Congress Cataloging-in-Publication Data
Women of the wall: claiming sacred ground at Judaism's holy site / edited by Phyllis Chesler and Rivka Haut.
        p. cm.
Includes bibliographical references.
ISBN 1-58023-161-6
1. Women in Judaism. 2. Women of the Wall (Organization : Israel) 3. Feminism—Religious aspects—Judaism. 4. Jewish women—Legal status, laws, etc.—Israel. 5. Western Wall (Jerusalem) 6. Jewish women—Religious life—Anecdotes. I. Chesler, Phyllis. II. Haut, Rivka, 1942–
BM729.W6 .W67 2002
296.4'5'082—dc21   2002006658

10 9 8 7 6 5 4 3 2 1

Manufactured in the United States of America

Published by Jewish Lights Publishing
A Division of LongHill Partners, Inc.
Sunset Farm Offices, Route 4, P.O. Box 237
Woodstock, VT 05091
Tel: (802) 457-4000   Fax: (802) 457-4004
www.jewishlights.com

for the State of Israel

CONTENTS

PART I   Women Who Pray at the Kotel: In Their Own Words

PART II Legal and Political Analysis

PART III Denominational Views

PART IV Halakhic Theory and Ritual Objects

Contents

Prayer for Women of the Wall

MAY IT BE YOUR WILL, our God and God of our mothers and fathers, to bless this prayer group and all who pray within it: them, their families, and all that is theirs, together with all women's prayer groups and all the women and girls of Your people Israel. Strengthen us and turn our hearts to serve You in truth, reverence, and love. May our prayer be as desirable and acceptable before You as the prayers of our holy foremothers Sarah, Rivkah, Rahel, and Leah. May our song ascend to Your Glorious Throne in holiness and purity, like the song of Miriam the Prophet and Devorah the Judge, and may it be as a pleasant savor and sweet incense before You.

And for our sisters, all the women and girls of Your people Israel: let us merit to see their joy and hear their voices raised before You in song and praise. May no woman or girl of Your people Israel or anywhere else in the world be silenced ever again. God of Justice, let us merit justice and salvation soon, for the sanctity of Your name and the restoration of Your world, as it is written: Zion will hear and be joyful, and the daughters of Judah rejoice, over Your judgments, O God. And as it is written: For Zion's sake I will not be still and for Jerusalem's sake I will not be silent, until her righteousness comes forth like great light and her salvation like a torch aflame.

For Torah shall go forth from Zion and the word of God from Jerusalem. Amen, *selah*.

—RAHEL JASKOW

Preface

WE, THE WOMEN OF THE WALL, are engaged in a lawsuit against the State of Israel and the Ministry of Religion and in a grassroots struggle on behalf of Jewish women's religious rights. As a group we remain poised between opposing realities. Some think that we are unacceptably religious and therefore reactionary. They do not understand why we care so much about prayer, the Kotel, or God. Jewish fundamentalists think that we are unacceptably radical, secular, and heretical; they believe we want to overthrow religious Judaism.

We do not want our readers to think that we are anti-Israel or anti-religious Judaism. On the contrary. Most of us are quite religious. We are also feminists who are committed to tolerance, modernity, and democracy. We are also Zionists who dearly love the State of Israel. We want Israel to fulfill its potential as a haven for the Jews of the world, so that all, including Jewish women, may find in Israel a true spiritual home, a holy place where all who wish may approach God and pray in peace.

How we present our struggle for religious freedom remains an abiding tension. On the one hand, we hesitate to criticize Israel as a theocracy, since it is far more enlightened than the rest of the

Middle East. In fact, for this reason, we expect justice to ultimately prevail in this matter of women's religious freedom. Since Israel has always been harshly and unjustly judged by anti-Jewish forces in the world, it is emotionally wrenching to present our grievances in the court of public opinion. Despite these misgivings, we have chosen to tell our story because it constitutes an important chapter in the evolution of Jewish history and Jewish justice. We also want to preserve the story of women's heroism and faith, which might otherwise remain unknown as has much of Jewish women's spiritual history.

The world has changed dramatically, perhaps even completely, since we began work on this volume. Islamic terrorists have declared war on America and on the Western world. Western values—including freedom of religion and women's rights—are under deadly attack. Violence in Israel is a heartbreaking, daily occurrence. Our hopes for peace have not yet been realized. Hate speech against Israel and against Jews has increased alarmingly, as have anti-Semitic acts all over the world. Like all nation-states, Israel is imperfect. Nevertheless, it still remains a lone voice in the Middle East for modernity and democracy.

Although we have sued the State of Israel, we also understand that Israel is the only country in the Middle East where individuals could actually bring such a lawsuit, live to tell the tale, and prevail in Israel's Supreme Court, as we have done. Comparable lawsuits probably do not exist in the Muslim and Arab world, where any radical criticism of the state religion is unthinkable.

Post-9/11, the world is no longer the same; it may never return to "normal." The safety and peace of mind that Americans and Westerners once took for granted are no longer ours. Now, we are all Israelis, targeted for suicidal and homicidal terror by those who resent our very existence, despise our way of life, and are ready to sacrifice their children in God's name—the very act that God stopped our forefather Abraham from committing, which established an ethical norm.

The Midrash (*Yalkhut Shimoni,* Pinchas 27) teaches that when the five daughters of Tzelafchad approached Moses to demand their inheritance, the Israelites had not yet entered or conquered the land. These daughters chose a moment of national collective doubt and fear to inspire courage and faith in the people by demanding their future rights to a land not yet conquered. As daughters, and in the absence of sons, they insisted on their inheritance rights; God informed Moses that their demand was justified.

We too believe that the State of Israel will survive and will achieve peace with its neighbors. That is why we choose to stake our rightful claim now, to ensure freedom of religion and a just future for our children and grandchildren and for the coming generations. To that end, we dedicate this book and this struggle to the State of Israel.

Acknowledgments

WE WOULD LIKE TO THANK Gavriel Z. Bellino for his invaluable assistance and support. The Midrash (*Yalkhut* 234) teaches that when the children of Israel left Egypt and reached the Reed Sea, the angel Gavriel stood with them and "protected them like a Wall." He held back the turbulent waters and prevented the Israelites from drowning. So too has our Gavriel held back the waters of chaos and endless detail from engulfing us. His sturdy, devoted presence, his standing with us, enabled us to complete this volume. In addition to his advice and superior technical expertise, he sustained us with *divrei Torah,* wonderful Jewish music, and a sweetness of spirit.

Rivka: I would like to thank Phyllis Chesler, my co-editor, my friend, and *chevrutah,* for being at my side during my husband's illness and for extending a warm and helping hand after his death. Phyllis had to take over my work on this volume for many months when I was unable to work, and she did so with kindness and grace.

My wonderful daughters and their husbands, Sheryl Haut and David Rosenberg, and Tamara Weissman and Seth Weissman, were always with me during a time of great sadness for us all. I am eternally grateful to them for everything. To my grandchildren, Ariel Pesach Rosenberg, and Ayelet Medka Rosenberg, and Esther Eleanna Weissman, all my work is for you.

To my Yitzhak, I hope this volume would please you.

Phyllis: I would like to thank Rivka Haut, who is far more than my co-editor. She is also my teacher and my guide, whose learning, wisdom, integrity, and kindness have blessed and elevated my soul and my life. Our studying Torah and working together partakes of the miraculous in that it was utterly unexpected and yet now seems inevitable.

I would like to thank my beloved son, Ariel David; my dear friend and companion Susan L. Bender; and my wonderful friend Merle Hoffman, who have each supported this work in every way. To my parents, Lillian and Leon, *z"l*, I hope this work returns to you the daughter whom you thought you had lost. I would also like to thank the Park Slope Jewish Center in Brooklyn for providing me with a religious, God-centered community.

We gratefully acknowledge Dr. Shula Reinharz, director of Hadassah's International Research Institute on Jewish Women at Brandeis University, and Phyllis Deutsch, of the University Press of New England, for their strong support and enthusiasm for this project in its initial phase.

We also gratefully acknowledge the board of the International Committee for Women of the Wall (ICWOW) for its very generous funding of this volume. That we could turn to each other for what we needed was a great joy. A special thanks to board member Rabbi Gail Labovitz, who gave us Stuart Matlins' card and told us of his interest in this project. We also thank photographer Joan Roth, both for her ecstatic support over the years and for donating her wonderful photos to this volume.

The following people, among others, have also donated funds, led us to donors, and given their time, energy, and expertise to this anthology: Ti-Grace Atkinson; Susan L. Bender, Esq.; Dr. Paula J.

Caplan, in memory of William Herschel Karchmer; Ellen Chesler; The Diana Foundation; Karen Feit; Alan Ferris and our board treasurer, Rabbi Helene Ferris; Gila Gevirtz; Gail Hammerman; Francine Klagsbrun; Jennifer A. Migueis; the Honorable Ann W. Richards, former governor of Texas; Marcia Riklis; Rachel Josefowitz Siegel; Diane Troderman; and Henny Wenkart. We also wish to acknowledge our Torah study partner Necha Sirota. ICWOW's treasurer, Rabbi Ferris, may be contacted at 215 Hessian Hills Road, Croton, NY 10520. Checks should be payable to ICWOW, Inc.

It was our great good fortune to be able to work with Jewish Lights Publishing. Stuart Matlins, publisher of Jewish Lights, was always available, no matter where in the world he actually happened to be. He never pressured us, and he really listened to our ideas. Polly Mahoney and Emily Wichland of Jewish Lights were efficient, persistent, clear, and exceedingly patient and pleasant. We are glad that they were part of our team effort. Our thanks to Elisheva Urbas for her erudition and her professional editorial skills. We are grateful to our copy editor, Judith Antonelli, for her careful attention to every word, and to our design coordinator, Bridgett Taylor. Our volume is enriched by the contributions of all these people.

PHYLLIS CHESLER AND RIVKA HAUT

Introduction

> Rabbi Acha said: "The Shekhinah never leaves
> the Western Wall."
>
> —*SHEMOT RABBAH 2*

THIS VOLUME IS THE HISTORY OF Women of the Wall, the story of our struggle, at least in its beginning stages. We are a group of Jewish women who have gathered together to pray at the Kotel, the Western Wall in Jerusalem. It is also the story of those who wish to deny us this religious right.

The Women of the Wall have been the subject of countless articles and news reports. Too often, the group has been mischaracterized as Reform, Conservative, political, or as attempting to challenge the rule of Halakhah (Jewish law) at holy sites in Israel. Many have misrepresented us out of ignorance, not malice. This volume is our way of presenting ourselves to the world as we really are.

Our history began on the morning of December 1, 1988, when a multidenominational group of approximately seventy women approached the Kotel with a Torah scroll to conduct a halakhic women's prayer service. As no provision for Torah reading exists in the women's section, we brought a small folding table with us, upon which to rest the *sefer Torah* (Torah scroll). We stood together and prayed aloud together; a number of us wore *tallitot* (prayer shawls).

Our service was peaceful until we opened the Torah scroll. Then a woman began yelling. She insisted that women are not permitted to read from a Torah scroll. This alerted some *charedi* (right-wing fundamentalist) men, who stood on chairs in order to look over the *mechitzah* (the barrier separating men and women). The men began to loudly curse us. Despite the jeers, curses, and threats of many onlookers, we managed to complete our Torah reading. We were not stopped by the late Rabbi Yehuda Getz, *z"l*, who was then the Kotel administrator. In fact, a woman who happened to be standing near Rabbi Getz heard him tell the female complainer: "Let them continue. They are not violating Halakhah."

Since that first group service, our struggle has consisted of an attempt to relive that first service; to once again pray together at that holy site, wear *tallitot*, and read aloud from a Torah scroll. We have endured violence, spent many years in court, and raised many thousands of dollars to this end.

At one point, as a result of intense legal and political pressure to "compromise," we narrowed our vision and limited our demand to be permitted group prayer with a Torah to a mere eleven hours a year, provided that the government would recognize and enforce our right to pray together at the Kotel without our need to further pursue our claim in court.[1] Nevertheless, despite several decisive legal victories, as of this writing we are still not permitted even to stand together and pray aloud as a group at the Kotel.

The story of Women of the Wall is an important chapter in Jewish history. Whether we win our legal battles or not, we have already achieved an important victory. We are a unique example of religious pluralism in action and of Israeli-diaspora relationships. The Talmud (*Yoma* 9b) teaches that when Jews are not united, tragedy results: "In the Second Temple period, people occupied themselves with Torah, mitzvot, and deeds of lovingkindness, so why was it destroyed? Because there was baseless hatred." It was not our foreign enemies who destroyed us, but our incessant internal conflicts. At a time of denominational and political strife, the Women of the Wall are proving that Jews can work and pray together and transcend our differences in a tolerant, even loving, way.

The Torah (Exodus 35:25) teaches that the wise and skilled women of the desert generation wove a cover for the ark, creating a cloth of various hues that blended into a harmonious whole. We view our services as a similar offering to God, utilizing all our talents, all our differing theological views, to create a united service.

It has not been easy for a group composed of educated women, from all religious and ideological streams of Judaism, to form a united prayer group. Serious differences had to be dealt with; compromises had to be made. Our challenge is to remain within the confines of Halakhah, with all its various interpretations, while including those who do not accept Halakhah as binding. We are a work in process. Yet, despite our many and deep philosophical conflicts, we have learned to work together. Remarkably, since our inception no splinter group has emerged. We remain the only women's group presence at the Kotel.

In our view, therefore, our mandate is clear: We represent the Jews of the world who support women's group prayer at the Kotel.

The Jews in the Torah marked their sacred encounters with God with stones. From our earliest history, stones indicated locations of significant encounters with holiness. Jacob marked the place where he dreamed of the angels by erecting a stone monument (Genesis 28:18). Later, he returned to the site and "set up a pillar at the site where God had spoken to him, a pillar of stone" (Genesis 35:14). Even today, when Jews visit cemeteries to pray for the souls of the departed, we leave small stones on top of the engraved headstone. God is sometimes referred to as *Tzur*, our "Rock" and Redeemer. Rocks signify solidity, timelessness, and eternity and symbolize our relationship to God. So does the Kotel.

The Kotel is a huge wall composed of ancient, massive stones. Some of the newly uncovered stones date from the First Temple period.[2] Most of the stones date from the later Herodian era and are identified by their unique borders.[3] There are tufts of moss and grass growing in the clefts of the stones. People stuff hand-written prayers addressed to God into the crevices between the stones. Birds nestle, hover, and flutter among the stones, peering down at the worshipers below.

The Kotel is a surviving remnant of the ancient Temple Mount complex, where the First and Second Temples once stood. The Temple Mount has been considered holy since antiquity, as it is deemed to be the place where the binding of Isaac took place, and also where Muhammed ascended to heaven. The Kotel was not part of the Temple building itself but merely part of the Second Temple's outer retaining wall, built by Herod in the first century B.C.E. Since the destruction of the Second Temple, in 70 C.E., the Kotel replaced the Temple Mount as the most important area for Jewish public prayer. It alone remained, a solidly imposing remnant of Israel's glorious past. The Midrash (*Shemot Rabbah* 2) teaches that the Shekhinah, God's immanent presence in the world, has never left the Western Wall, but remains there to welcome back the exiled and persecuted Jews. It therefore acquired a special holiness.[4]

There are serious halakhic issues concerning the Temple Mount area. According to many rabbis, Jews today are forbidden to walk upon the actual site where the Temples once stood. In ancient times, and under Jewish law, only people who were ritually pure were permitted upon the Temple Mount. The presence of many *mikvaot* (ritual baths) close to the Mount attests to the fact that in antiquity these rules were strictly followed. Today, although we do have *mikvaot*, we lack the other rituals necessary to become ritually pure.[5] Thus, we are halakhically not permitted to stand in that area. However, the exact area where the Temples stood is subject to dispute.[6] The Temple Mount itself has no uncovered remnants of the ancient Temples.[7] Instead, it is now a Muslim prayer area containing two large mosques, al-Aksa and the Dome of the Rock.

For years, under Arab rule, the Kotel was literally a rubble-strewn garbage dump. During the years of Muslim control, Jews were forbidden to pray at the Kotel or allowed to do so only at special times. After the Six Day War, a war of self-defense in 1967, Jews flocked to the newly liberated area. A large plaza was built around the Kotel area, and a *mechitzah* was erected. The Kotel became a focal point for Jewish worshipers as the most sacred area for Jewish prayer. Jews from all over the world, as well as those in Israel, approach the Kotel to speak to God, to whisper their most personal requests, to place notes to God between the welcoming, ancient stones.

Many public ceremonies take place at the Kotel. Israeli soldiers are sworn in there. Foreign dignitaries are brought there. Bar mitzvah boys receive their first *aliyot* (being called to the Torah) there. At all hours of the day and night, there are male minyans (prayer quorums) gathered there. On Shabbat and holidays, yeshiva boys approach, singing aloud and dancing, praying together in groups. The Kotel has become the most precious treasure, the heart, of the Israeli state.

In recent times, the entire Temple Mount area, as well as the Kotel, has been the scene of horrific battles. In 1967, in the Six Day War, Israeli soldiers bravely fought through narrow streets, house by house, in hand-to-hand combat, and with many casualties, to redeem the Old City of Jerusalem from centuries of domination by other nations. Many Israeli soldiers died. Miraculously, they succeeded in recapturing Jerusalem for the Jewish people. After two thousand years, Jerusalem was once again part of a sovereign Jewish State. At the heart of the Old City, the Kotel, whose ancient stones were beloved images engraved in Jewish hearts for centuries, awaited the newly returned Jews.

In 1967, the Temple Mount once again became part of the Jewish State. However, under Moshe Dayan's orders, the area was placed under the control of the Muslim council known as the Waqf, which immediately prohibited Jews from praying there and has continued to do so ever since. This exclusion has provoked much opposition. A group known as the Temple Mount Faithful regularly appeals to the Israeli Supreme Court, asking to be permitted to pray atop the Mount on Passover and Tisha B'Av (the day when Jews mourn the destruction of both Temples). To date, the Israeli Supreme Court has refused all their pleas, citing the danger of Muslim riots. On Tisha B'Av in 2001, this group was again denied permission to ascend the Temple Mount to pray. However, it was granted permission to have a ceremony in the parking lot outside the Dung Gate, just yards from the ramp leading to the Mount. The ceremony involved a huge stone that the group had designated as the cornerstone for the Third Temple, yet to be built. Ashkenazi Chief Rabbi Yisrael Lau denounced the ceremony, which led to Muslim riots on the Mount. Stones were thrown from atop the Temple Mount platform down on worshipers at the Kotel below, and Jews had to be evacuated from the Kotel plaza for almost an hour.

Interestingly, the administrator of the Kotel on this Tisha B'Av expressed dissatisfaction with the fact that Jews worshiping there were evacuated for a while because of stone throwing from above. According to *The Jerusalem Post* (July 30, 2001), Kotel administrator Rabbi Shmuel Rabinovitz "blasted the police's decision to evacuate Jews from the Wall during Tisha B'Av, saying that security officials should have been better prepared for Palestinian violence and should have come up with alternatives. . . . This is harmful and painful. It did not have to come to this."[8]

Sadly, the Women of the Wall have been dragged from the Kotel on their previous Tisha B'Av observances. Undoubtedly, the State of Israel would have been able to protect the women from *charedi* attackers and harassers if the administrator in charge had so requested.

Another conflagration arose between Jews and Muslims over the area known as the Western Wall tunnels. In the late years of the twentieth century, Israeli archaeologists dug under the Kotel, along the western part that lay buried under the ground. They exposed large, ancient stones, some from the Second Temple, and some dating back even earlier, to the First Temple period. After a few years, the site was opened to supervised tour groups. A highlight of the tour is the opportunity to stand and pray in the spot that is thought to be exactly opposite the site where the Holy of Holies once stood. Prime Minister Ehud Barak decided to open an exit from the tunnels to the Muslim Quarter of the Old City. Up until that point, it had been necessary to retrace one's steps in order to exit the narrow tunnels. The opening of this exit was followed by Arab rioting, and people on both sides were killed. Since then, when a tour group exits the tunnel, it is accompanied by armed Israeli soldiers, in front and behind, protecting people until they return to the Kotel plaza itself.

Another terrible conflict arose on the day before Rosh Hashanah in 2000. Ariel Sharon, not yet prime minister, set off a huge outcry when he asked for and received permission from the Barak government to visit the Temple Mount area. In the aftermath of his visit, what has become known as the al-Aksa *intifada* broke out; there were riots and demonstrations on the part of Muslim militants, resulting in loss of life. There is strong evidence that the Arab violence was planned long before Sharon's visit. However, this incident marks the beginning of the recent conflict that threatens the safety of the region and the Jewish State.

In 2001, the Temple Mount became the focus of yet another sort of conflict. Archaeologists claimed that the Muslim authorities were permitting large-scale construction on the Mount, resulting in the destruction of priceless and irreplaceable antiquities, some dating from First Temple times. The Supreme Court of Israel has been appealed to, but as of this writing the Court has not intervened to stop the destruction. In the United States, a bill has been introduced in Congress to protest this desecration.[9]

In this already embattled zone, we, the Women of the Wall, have precipitated yet another dispute; however, our case is vastly different from the others. Our struggle is not halakhically problematic, nor does it involve other nations, nor does it threaten to cause international trouble. It is the struggle of Jews within Judaism, the struggle of women who wish to claim their rights, as the daughters of Tzelafchad did. It is a battle about what direction the State of Israel will take; it is a struggle for democracy against misogyny.

Let us be clear: Women are certainly able to pray at the Kotel. The women's section, on the right side, is smaller than the men's section. The two are separated by a *mechitzah*, a barrier about five feet high. The Wall area is always open and always accessible to women. Women may approach the part of the Wall in the women's section, walk right up to the huge stones, touch them, lean upon them, and put notes into their crevices. Women may pray there as individuals and read from *siddurim* (prayer books). Indeed, women are always praying there, at all hours of the day and night.

However, women cannot engage in the following activities: praying aloud in a group; singing prayers; wearing *tallitot* (prayer shawls); wearing tefillin (phylacteries); blowing a shofar (ritual ram's horn); carrying or chanting from a *sefer Torah* (Torah scroll).

These activities are all prohibited to women by Israeli law but not—and this is critically important—by Halakhah. Although women are not *obligated* to perform such religious acts, under many Orthodox interpretations of Jewish law they are also not *prohibited* from doing so. In fact, in most modern Orthodox communities throughout the world (e.g., the United States, Israel, England, Canada, Australia, and Sweden), Orthodox women regularly gather in women-only groups in which they perform exactly the same activities that are currently prohibited to women in Israel at the Wall.[10] It is these halakhically *permitted* activities that we seek to have legalized at the Kotel today.

While we do not oppose the claims of other denominations to pray at the Kotel in their own way, Women of the Wall (WOW) is not challenging the existence of the *mechitzah*, the barrier that separates men and women. We wish to conduct services in the women's section. Moreover, the group is not constituted as a minyan, which most (though not all) Orthodox rabbis maintain is forbidden to women. The services are non-minyan services, so that all Jewish women, including the strictly Orthodox, may feel comfortable joining the group in prayer.

The initial group service in 1988 left overwhelming impressions on many of the women who participated. Its impact reverberates still.

After that *tefillah* (prayer service), a group of Israeli women decided to continue, following the model we had set. From the first, they were met with violence. They were cursed, threatened, pushed, shoved, spit upon, and bitten. Heavy metal chairs were thrown at them over the *mechitzah*. *Charedi* women tried to pull *siddurim* out of their hands. Women were physically injured and rushed to hospitals. WOW members—rather than the violent *charedim*—were arrested by the state. Yet, there was no Israeli law forbidding our prayer services. By the summer of 1989, the Israeli WOW group appealed to the Supreme Court for protection from the serious violence that continuously erupted whenever members prayed together.

The court accepted our case but ordered us to cease and desist from group prayer with a Torah at the Kotel while they considered the matter. WOW thus began its prayer service at the Kotel but conducted the Torah reading at a nearby location.

In 1989, a group of diaspora women who had formed the International Committee for Women of the Wall (ICWOW) decided to raise monies for a Torah scroll to be donated to WOW. The response was extraordinary. *Klal Yisrael* (Jews) sent small personal checks; so many checks came in that the Torah was purchased very soon. We traveled to Israel in November 1989 with the Torah. With us were many women who had attended the first service. We again attempted to pray with the Torah as we had done in 1988. We were stopped at the security checkpoint and informed that we were forbidden to enter the Kotel plaza with a Torah scroll, and that even without the scroll we could not enter if we wanted to pray together as a group. Indeed, less than two months later, a new regulation was passed by the Ministry of Religion (*Kovetz Takanot* no. 190) that prohibited our group prayer. Reading from the Torah, wearing a tallit, and praying aloud in a group were all now illegal in the women's section and punishable by a six-month prison term and/or a fine. We chose not to violate this regulation and instead sought justice through legal means. Thus a new lawsuit was born. ICWOW joined with WOW in its attempt to win the legal right to conduct women's halakhic prayer services at the Kotel.

The state's brief against us was shocking. It contained rabbinic accusations that we were "doing the devil's work," "neglecting our husbands and children," "using birth control to avoid having children so that we could spend our time praying in women's minyans." We were also accused of being "misled by feminism."

In 1994, we received a split decision from the Supreme Court. Justice Shlomo Levine ordered that we be permitted to pray as we wished; Justice Menachem Elon, who is also an Orthodox halakhic scholar, wrote a very long opinion in which he upheld the halakhic permissibility of women's prayer groups. However, Elon claimed that conducting such halakhic services at the Kotel "offends the sensibilities of the worshipers" and leads to *charedi* violence. Instead of condemning the perpetrators of violence, he condemned us for provoking it. He said that the violence emanates from a very deep place in their hearts. The third judge, Justice Meir Shamgar, wrote that our matter was too weighty for the Supreme Court and required a political solution. Thus, we were sent to a series of Knesset commissions. The Court informed us that "the door would always be open for us to return."

At first, ICWOW and WOW were separate groups with their own attorneys. The Israeli group hired two young and enthusiastic attorneys. The international group turned to Arnold Shpaer, an experienced civil rights attorney who had argued before the Supreme Court many times. WOW's brief argued that women's civil rights were being violated. ICWOW's brief relied heavily upon halakhic material, and, indeed, the Court's decision in 1994 accepted that our practice is halakhic, which is a major victory. However, the decision stopped short of permitting us to actually pray together with police protection; instead, it bounced us into the political arena, where we languished for years, first before the Hollander Commission, then before the Ne'eman Commission.

Years passed with no legal progress. We contemplated engaging in civil disobedience, but ultimately, after much international discussion, both groups reached a consensus to continue our struggle within the courts. In 1995, in response to pressure from many supporters who insisted that we have a feminist attorney, both groups decided to hire one very distinguished attorney: Frances Raday, who conducted the case together with attorneys Jonathan Misheiker and Nira Azriel.[11] ICWOW member Miriam Benson, who is also an attorney, serves as ICWOW's legal liaison with Raday. Our legal team won a unanimous decision in the Supreme Court in May 2000, which declared that Women of the Wall have the right to pray in their manner in the women's section at the Kotel and gave the state six months to enforce their decision. The attorney general requested an additional hearing that, as of this writing, is still pending before nine judges.

Our appeal of the 1994 decision took years. We prepared papers and waited. During this time services continued, and they continue still. The group meets every Rosh Chodesh at 7:00 A.M., at the Kotel. The Torah is brought each time, camouflaged in a portable *aron* (ark), which is actually a green duffel bag made expressly for this purpose. (How sad that Jewish women, in the State of Israel, must hide a Torah scroll in this way!) The group prays together, sometimes aloud, sometimes in whispers, depending upon the climate and mood of the worshipers there. They sing *Hallel*, then repair to another location, far from the Kotel but within sight of it, where they unwrap *tallitot*, tefillin, and the Torah itself, and the service continues.

As we await a decision, our situation has become more complex. In 2000, the Masorati (Conservative) movement decided to accept another site, an extension of the Kotel known as Robinson's Arch,[12] in which to conduct their mixed-gender prayer services without a *mechitzah*. This group had been attempting to pray in the Kotel plaza, the large open area at a distance from the Kotel where both men and women congregate. They had been seeking a location near the Kotel for egalitarian prayer services and, like us, had been met with violence. The Reform movement, however, has decided to support our struggle by refraining from advancing their own interests at the Kotel at this time.

As for us, we categorically reject any alternative to the Kotel as unacceptable and unnecessary. We pray within the women's section, with women only, and do not require any physical changes or accommodations in that area. We wish to pray together with our sisters, with *Klal Yisrael;* we do not wish to be isolated in a separate area. Nevertheless, the fact that the Masorati movement negotiated for, and ultimately accepted, another site made us appear unreasonable and unwilling to compromise, in the eyes of the Court. In order to avoid making a decision on the merits of our case, the Court has continually held up the Conservative movement's choice to us as a model of reasonable compromise.[13]

For example, in February 2000, just before issuing their decision, the Supreme Court judges (Eliahu Matza, Dorit Beinish, and Tova Strasburg-Cohen) embarked on an extended tour of the Kotel and surrounding areas. Some of us accompanied them, together with our attorneys. Our first stop was Robinson's Arch; archaeologist Einat Mazar explained that this is the only archaeological site in the vicinity of the Temple Mount that remains exactly as it was since the destruction of the Temple in 70 C.E. It has not been tampered with in any way. It should remain as is, she stressed; opening this closed area to the public at large as a prayer area would adversely affect it as an archaeological site. Mazar pointed out that the Kotel stones cannot be touched at that location, because large boulders, which fell during the destruction and have been allowed to remain exactly where they fell, block physical access to the huge Kotel stones themselves. Moreover, the area is inaccessible to wheelchairs and baby carriages.

The group moved on to Hulda's Gate, and from there to the southeastern corner, where the representative of the Ministry of Religious Affairs pronounced that this was the best site for us. We stood stunned, as the site, besides being extremely difficult to reach, overlooks a cliff and is quite dangerous. "No problem," the representative declared, "we will make it safe and even build a parking lot!" Einat Mazar again intervened and explained that this site was actually used as a Christian burial site; crosses were discovered there. She tried to dissuade the judges from even considering the place. One of the judges, exhausted and panting from the difficult walk, was overheard whispering to another judge that even considering this area was ridiculous, as it was so hard to get to, and mothers and children could not possibly get there.

From there, we all moved to the parking lot near the Kotel plaza. The site is quite far from the Kotel. We stood there aghast, as the area is full of gasoline fumes and is not near the Kotel itself. The state's representative declared this area to be a perfect place for us to pray.

Finally, as we stood in the parking lot, two of our women managed to walk to the Kotel area where the group regularly stands, near the back, far from the men's section, and demonstrated to the judges how and exactly where we pray.

The official tour had ended. We began discussing how we would handle a negative decision.

In May 2000, we were informed that a decision had been reached. To our great surprise, it was a unanimous decision in our favor! We were totally unprepared for this victory. The Court agreed that we have the legal right to pray according to our custom, and it gave the state six months to make the necessary arrangements to guarantee our safety as we exercised our rights. However, despite our (seeming) victory, the end was not yet in sight. Attorney General Elyakim Rubinstein requested an additional hearing. The Court granted his appeal and added six judges to the existing panel. Now nine judges, including Chief Justice Aharon Barak, would hear the appeal.

In June 2001, the nine judges decided that another tour was in order. This time, they visited only Robinson's Arch and the Kotel. This tour took place at high noon on a blistering hot day. Again the Arch was presented by our opponents as the appropriate site for us. As of this writing, and despite an October 31, 2001 hearing on the merits, we still await the judges' decision.

We have experienced high points and low points. The worst incidents were when we were physically attacked and, indeed, some of us were actually dragged away from the Kotel. These incidents can be seen in the photographs included in this volume. More important, some of our high points are also documented here: a bat mitzvah, a female soldier reading from a Torah scroll, lovely moments of prayer. In February 2002, on Rosh Chodesh Adar, we actually experienced what we have longed for—WOW prayed aloud and read from a Torah scroll at the Kotel, before the ancient stones. We have included participants' impressions of this extraordinary prayer service. This was a milestone and a hopeful sign for the future of women's collective prayer at the Kotel.

However, we know that there is much work yet ahead. Many have challenged us. Some have viewed our commitment to Halakhah as old-fashioned and antifeminist. They have been critical of the fact that we follow Orthodox guidelines. Some have opposed the idea that the Kotel deserves the unique importance that has been assigned to it. Some have criticized us for pursuing a feminist agenda when the Jewish State and Jews everywhere are endangered. Always, where women's rights are concerned, women are told to step aside for more important national, military, and economic agendas. Some view our struggle as an attempt by outsiders to transplant Western feminist values into the Israeli body politic. We have taken such factors into account and have nevertheless remained steadfast in our decision to forge ahead.

In addition to dealing with the various opponents of women's group prayer, we have challenges within our own ranks. We are two groups separated by a vast distance. Overcoming geographical distance has been an ongoing issue. Half of our board members are Israeli, and half are diaspora women from North America. ICWOW considers itself an auxiliary of WOW. Because WOW conducts services and faces physical danger each time its members pray, it is WOW's right to make certain decisions, because it bears the brunt of the consequences.

Sometimes the two groups have major disagreements. For example, in 1994, after the Court rendered its first decision, a conflict arose. ICWOW believed very strongly that we must appeal the decision; WOW wished to leave the legal arena and focus its efforts on the political and educational spheres.[14] A crisis ensued because we had only fifteen days in which to institute legal proceedings. The deadline was upon us. After much debate, we arranged a transatlantic conference call for about ten women. It was a rather long and very intense call. WOW no longer expected swift legal justice and was frustrated by the constraints placed upon it by the Court. Some members wanted to commit civil disobedience; others wanted to lobby the Knesset and the Israeli public. Everyone was given a chance to speak. Finally, ICWOW convinced WOW to appeal. This meant that WOW would have to "behave" for the duration—no civil disobedience, no illegal activities. To turn to the Court, one must have "clean hands."

Time-zone differences (before widespread Internet access) made instant communication quite difficult. Many Court hearings occurred while diaspora women were asleep, yet ICWOW has always insisted that we be consulted for on-the-spot decisions. ICWOW has spent many sleepless nights worrying about WOW's safety, particularly when violence was threatened. ICWOW members have slept with our phones beside our beds, ready to be awakened in the middle of the night. We have gotten up before dawn to check our phone machines and e-mail about what happened at a WOW 7:00 A.M. service at the Kotel. Although we are far apart geographically, we remain very close.

Over the years, ICWOW has conducted a number of solidarity services across North America to coincide with WOW's prayer services.

Despite the natural strains that arise when two groups are situated so far apart, we have managed to remain a cohesive group, even sharing information about health concerns and family events (births, deaths). When WOW members give birth or adopt children, word goes out over the Internet. When Rivka's late husband was ill, the members of WOW regularly prayed for him. When one of WOW's attorneys, Jonathan Misheiker, lost his son Gilad in an Israeli military helicopter crash, ICWOW shared in the pain. Of course, when ICWOW members visit Israel, they attend WOW's planning sessions as well as visit privately.

WOW has become a community, a feminist sisterhood, and a spiritual home for many of its members. WOW members get together not only to pray once a month but also to study Torah together. WOW has read aloud from *Megillat Esther* on Purim and *Eikhah* on Tisha B'Av and has been joined by many women. WOW also conducts bat mitzvah ceremonies for Jewish girls at the Kotel. WOW has sponsored seminars, lectures, and retreats. Currently, it is engaged in a major, ongoing campaign to educate Israelis and the world about religious possibilities for Jewish women.

WOW has spoken openly about its struggle to the secular world media. It has also been the subject of several documentaries. ICWOW has been more constrained about how we present our lawsuit in the non-Jewish media.

We have an e-mail list for board members only. Here we discuss issues of Halakhah (e.g., which prayers to say and which to omit, whose halakhic authority to follow), updated legal reports, and other issues that arise. Reports of the prayer services are also sent over the Internet. One of ICWOW's board members, Rabbi Gail Labovitz, regularly sends out e-mail notices of WOW's prayer schedule and activities to thousands of people from around the world.

We are essentially a grassroots organization, without an office or a paid staff until quite recently, when WOW hired a part-time coordinator.

While ICWOW remains WOW's sister organization, neither group has ever become affiliated with any other organization in the Jewish world, either in the diaspora or in Israel. Our historic prayer service was organized in Jerusalem at an American Jewish Congress conference. We have had support from a number of friendly organizations. In the beginning, the New Israel Fund assisted us enormously in financial and organizational ways. The Reform movement assisted us politically in Israel and continues to do so. Many organizations—Artza, Hadassah, National Council for Jewish Women, Rabbinical Assembly, US/Israel Women to Women, Women's League for Conservative Judaism, and the World Jewish Congress—wrote letters to both Knesset commissions on our behalf.[15] Many representatives of these organizations have prayed together with WOW. The Israel Women's Network testified on our behalf before the Sheves Commission. However, despite our concerted efforts, no Jewish organization submitted an amicus brief on our behalf or undertook to legally represent us.[16] No Jewish organization or major philanthropist ever funded us in a major or ongoing way.

Some organizations have awarded us small grants, as have some individuals. On the whole, we have raised funds ourselves in various ways. We have gone on speaking tours, held parlor meetings, sold WOW-related ritual articles. We have struggled to raise large sums for our legal expenses. We have received support from some religious groups,[17] but we have maintained our independence from any specific stream of Judaism. Most of our donations have been from individuals—small amounts, sent in one at a time, in response to newsletter requests.

Our struggle has received enormous grassroots support. When we mention that we are part of Women of the Wall, many Jews literally become radiant with pleasure and pride. For example, in 1989, as we have noted, we decided to raise funds for a Torah scroll to be used by WOW. With little publicity, money flowed in, and we soon had enough to purchase the Torah, a gift from diaspora women and men, to the women of Jerusalem. This is the Torah that is still read by the group. In addition to organizational letters, many individual letters of support were written on our behalf to the Israeli government. Rabbis from every denomination wrote letters of support.

Few Orthodox rabbis or Orthodox women's groups have supported us, but the ones who have are well known and special. Rabbi Rene Sirat, former chief rabbi of France, mentioned us in a speech in which he noted that despite the enormous educational accomplishments of Jewish women in the modern world, at the Kotel they still "cannot hear anything, see anything, or participate in any religious ceremony." Rabbi Sirat called on Jewish men to do *teshuvah* (repentance) for their behavior toward Jewish women. The late Rabbi Shlomo Carlebach, *z"l*, joined us at the Torah dedication ceremony. Finally, the Jewish Orthodox Feminist Alliance (JOFA) congratulated us in a newspaper ad upon our May 2000 legal victory.

One may ask the following: What cause could unite twenty-five women, radical feminists and Orthodox feminists, lawyers and professors, housewives and mothers, Conservative and Reform women, rabbis and *rebbetzins*, from different parts of the world? How could they continue, for thirteen years, to endure physical violence, verbal curses, ridicule, accusations of heresy, and setback after setback—not for monetary gain, or personal fame, but for an ideal to which they cling and that they will not abandon? What drives them to spend hours lecturing, educating, raising funds? Why must they pray at *that* place and not accept a substitute site? Why can't they pray like the other women there; why do they need to pray in groups, with tallit and *sefer Torah?* Why is this cause so important?

Each writer in this anthology deals with these questions and answers them in her own way.

Some of our members are North Americans who regularly visit Israel. Some are Israelis, including both sabras and Jews who have made *aliyah* from other countries such as the United States, Canada, France, England, and Morocco. Some members spent a year or more in Israel, where they became active members of WOW, and then joined ICWOW when they returned to the United States. Some are Israeli and have remained there.

Some of our members have dropped out for various reasons; to our knowledge, no one has ceased being a supporter. Some active board members have not written essays for this anthology. One of us died trying to rescue an Israeli child who was drowning. Her name is Barbara Wachs, *z"l*. She is in our photographs.

Our contributors are Orthodox, Conservative, Reform, Reconstructionist, unaffiliated, and secular. They are rabbis, *rebbetzins*, politicians, lawyers, professors, scholars, feminist activists, artists, writers, a religious singer, a dance therapist, and a filmmaker.

We, the co-editors of this volume, symbolize the different backgrounds and diversity of beliefs that the group encompasses. We first met at the Kotel, at the first *tefillah*. Rivka, while organizing the first service, had designated women who would lead prayers and read Torah but had left open some Torah honors, to be given out on the spot. When the time came to uncover the Torah scroll, which had been placed on the folding table we had brought with us, Rivka looked around at the assembled women. One woman caught her eye. Despite the threatening sounds that had begun emanating from over the *mechitzah*, this woman seemed oblivious to any danger. She seemed to be in another world, focused on what we—and not our opponents—were doing. Her eyes were so dreamy, so happy, so otherworldly. Rivka invited her to open the Torah for us. This was how we first met, at the Kotel, before the Torah.

After the conference, we discovered that we both lived in Brooklyn, New York. Phyllis gave Rivka copies of her books. Rivka took Phyllis to demonstrations on behalf of *agunot* (women denied religious divorces). Despite major differences in our lifestyles, and after some serious disagreements, we became close friends. Phyllis, a much-traveled radical feminist author and psychologist, is involved in many feminist causes. Rivka, who leads a traditional sheltered Orthodox lifestyle, is involved in Orthodox women's issues, including women's prayer groups. Our collaboration on WOW has led to a real friendship. We have celebrated Jewish holidays together, we have shared sad times, and our families have become friendly. We engage in weekly Torah study together. We hope that this book, our first published work together, will be followed by others.

The Torah teaches that when the Israelites crossed the Reed Sea, they were surrounded by walls: "and the water was a wall for them, on their right side and their left side." We, the writers of this volume, also feel that, since December 1, 1988, our lives have been surrounded by walls. The Western Wall, the Kotel, looms large in our lives, as do the walls of prejudice and discrimination that surround us and threaten to hem us in. Our souls yearn to pray, in peace, in the sacred place, to read from our holy Torah, together with other Jewish women. This volume is the story of our efforts to attain that goal.

It is our hope that after you have read this volume, you will have a greater understanding of Women of the Wall; its history, halakhic underpinnings, legal struggle, and philosophy; and the personal stories of many in the group. The ark in the desert Tabernacle had a cherub placed on each side. Some commentators say they were actually figures of winged children, one male and one female. They faced each other. Their presence in the Tabernacle may have been to teach and remind the people of Israel that both men and women are necessary, and desired, in the worship of God; that both men and women are to be invited into the most innermost precincts of worship, where humanity encounters the Divine. Until and unless this becomes reality, as long as women are excluded from sacred space, there can be no complete worship of God.

PART I

Women Who Pray at the Kotel: In Their Own Words

BONNA HABERMAN

Drama in Jerusalem

THE ROOSTERS IN THE OLD CITY of Jerusalem were still crowing as women streamed through narrow passageways, under archways, pouring down stone steps, finally collecting in a pool outside the entrance to the Dung Gate. Each month for the first tumultuous year I prepared a group of women for our morning prayers with these words: "Let us search our hearts for our deepest and purest desire to pray to God, to sanctify God at the sacred place, as a collectivity of women among the people of Israel."

The movement Women of the Wall had its genesis in the first International Conference for the Empowerment of Jewish Women, held in Jerusalem under the auspices of the American Jewish Congress in December 1988. On Thursday of the conference week, seventy of the women went down in a group to pray and read the Torah together, aloud, in the women's section at the Kotel. Rabbi Meir Yehuda Getz, the administrator of the Kotel, offered his commentary after the service: "Although the women have done nothing against Halakhah, religious law, what they have done is not accepted in the community of Israel."

At home later that evening, I was distraught over the contradiction between the *kavanah* (spiritual emotion, concentration) experienced by the women who participated and the negativity and misogyny expressed by the authority who observed us. I sought to affirm the validity of our claim to the sacred ground. I was anxious

3

to install women at the central territory of the Jewish people and insistent that women should be a visible Jewish image there. This was to symbolize the historic entry of Jewish women into the spiritual, intellectual, and political center of the Jewish people. I resolved to organize a group of Israeli women to pray on Rosh Chodesh at the Western Wall.[1] I intended that we would read from the Torah scroll, adorned in our prayer shawls, persisting until it is "accepted in the community of Israel"—to borrow Rabbi Getz's formulation.

Among my portfolio of teaching commitments during the winter semester of 1989 was a Talmud class at a women's yeshiva in Jerusalem. At the session after the conference, I proposed that we inaugurate a monthly prayer celebration of Rosh Chodesh at the Wall.

Anxious to welcome the exiled Shekhinah back into the neighborhood, the students agreed to gather at the entrance of the women's section at 7:00 A.M. on Rosh Chodesh Tevet. In addition to some women who had prayed at the Wall on December 1, I also recruited some members of an evening Rosh Chodesh group to join the Talmud class for prayers at the Wall. I borrowed a Torah scroll from an Orthodox learning institution. On Rosh Chodesh Tevet (December 1988), "Women of the Wall," as we came to be known in the Israeli and diaspora media, was born.

Twenty-five women arrived in the plaza of the Western Wall as the morning mist was still clearing. I had brought the Torah in a lovely Guatemalan backpack. We gathered in the middle of the women's section, placed the Torah upon a table piled with prayer books, and respectfully began our prayers.

From the moment that we were identified as an autonomous group of women praying, in possession of a Torah scroll, a commotion began. Ultra-Orthodox women whispered to men through the partition that separates the sexes. One of my companions drew my attention to a mass of black-attired ultra-Orthodox men that was assembling at the rear of the women's section. "Bon, they're coming," declared Gila, with a tremor in her voice. I reassured her that they would never touch us, observant as they are of the prohibition against touching women to whom they are not married.

Nevertheless, the men began to infiltrate the women's section, encircling us in the midst of our prayers. Still others broke through the back section of the partition and swarmed around us. They began to jeer at us, then to tug at our clothes and prayer shawls. Some women were thrown to the ground. "The Torah belongs to men," shouted some ultra-Orthodox women as they sought to wrest the holy scroll from our custody. A puppetlike, black-hatted, white-bearded figure popped up and down from behind the partition, shaking his long finger at us and proclaiming, "I denounce, I denounce"—a technical usage denoting halakhic disapproval. The female assailants laid their hands directly upon our bodies, a gesture usually reserved for blessing, and instead intoned curses that we should never bear children and that we should die young, in traffic accidents. There were catcalls: "whores," "Nazis," "dogs," "witches."

Jolted from the vulnerable moment of prayerful intention into a defensive deployment, we closed in around each other in tight concentric circular formation, arms supporting each other, delineating and protecting. We gripped one another as one mass. I was in the center, arms wrapped around the Torah, which I had grasped in time before the table on which it had rested was overturned by the disrupters. Prayer books spilled onto the ground; pages printed with God's holy Name scattered in the commotion. I stood, frozen, gripping the Torah. Acts of desecration shattered and dispersed the sacred letters; women's bodies and prayers were routed from holy space.

Proceeding out of the Kotel plaza with dignity and trembling, the women sang together a liturgical verse about the Torah: "She is a tree of life for those who hold on to her" (Proverbs 3:18). We were not sure whether we were protecting the Torah or whether she was protecting us. I envisaged the Shekhinah suffering the same exile—a collectivity of Jewish women longing for a sacred celebration of our people, banished from the Temple site by senseless hatred.

Enduring the attack together, we had coalesced in shock, fear, and the rhythm of our prayer. We assembled elsewhere to debrief. Who are we? Why are we here? What next? Our group ran the gamut from radical feminists to Orthodox observers of Halakhah, Jewish law. Coming from different places, experiences, and lineages, each woman told the story that had brought her to the sacred ground of the Jewish people and to this moment. We were a gathering of sparks hopeful for redemption.

We were absolutely clear that violence is unacceptable to us and that we would have no part in it. Our peaceful approach derived not only from the incompatibility of prayer with any form of violent response but also from our consciousness of the violence that has pervaded Israel since the 1980s, during the Lebanon War and the two *intifadas*. The goal of Women of the Wall was to contribute to the sanctity of a very dear place. We were determined to demonstrate peaceful methods, exercising the institutions of democracy to effect the changes we envisioned. We were hopeful that, ultimately, women's full participation in the public religious life of the Jewish State would be upheld, protected, honored, and perhaps even welcomed.

We vowed to convene for prayers every Friday and Rosh Chodesh at 7:00 A.M. in the women's section at the Kotel. The Friday morning prayers continued for three and a half years, until the birth of my fifth child; they were an oasis of spiritual sustenance, a quiet respite from the monthly confrontations that ensued. At a smaller weekly gathering, we quickly began to establish a comfortable niche in the Kotel landscape. We were a tight knot of regulars, with frequent visitors, often positioned very close to the Wall. We came to be respected among many of those who frequent the site; we were even recognized and anticipated. We sang our prayers and wordless meditative melodies with confidence and even abandon. There were often expressions of appreciation for our songfulness and joy.

The only truly nasty incident on a Friday involved a woman in a green dress. We had often seen her there and had nicknamed her after the color of her dress. One Friday morning, in the midst of our prayers, and with no advance warning, the woman in the green dress rushed at us, grabbed us, cursed us, and flailed. She took hold of Barbara, a slight, middle-aged, gray-haired woman, and bit her arm. Millie, one of our regulars, always carried a camera in her bag. She pulled it out to photograph the woman, who became even more infuriated. She lunged at Millie, who was flanked by her terrified children, struggling to wrest the camera from Millie's hands. I gripped the arm of the woman in green as her whole body writhed with malicious intent. No official came forth to intervene. Finally exhausted, the woman ceased her attack as suddenly as she had begun it, and fled.

We all filed reports of our injuries to the police and submitted the photos. Persevering to determine the identity of the mysterious assailant was not a high priority for the officials. The response from the Old City police department to most of our reports was a notice in the mail that the case was closed "due to lack of public interest."

The situation on Rosh Chodesh was radically different from that on Fridays. The volume of worshipers at the Kotel is generally much higher on Rosh Chodesh. Many yeshiva communities gather in the plaza for celebrations, as do individuals who come to mark the semifestival. We ourselves were a larger group than on Fridays.

Those who frequent the Kotel derive from a variety of cultural backgrounds and experiences, from Morocco to Iran, from New Delhi to Los Angeles. We were investigating the possibility of a common discourse of the Jewish people, one that would include the voices of women joined together from a representative spectrum of the Jewish world. We imagined a radical pluralism enacted through prayer at the Wall.

So often the momentum to conduct a revolution is powered by harnessing fear and fiery anger against opponents and oppressors. In Jerusalem, people are prepared to argue at every corner, in every shop, in every queue. Views about religion, politics, education, peace, and spiritual beliefs are diverse and are invested with extraordinary emotional intensity. Between those who hold the most extreme positions, tensions smolder just below the surface, ready to erupt. The secular media and politicians often demonize black-attired men and wig-wearing women, whereas bareheaded Israelis are ridiculed by many of the religious as empty materialists. "Religious" and "secular" Israelis and their representatives compete for power, resources, and control of the life and destiny of Israel in many sectors.

Women of the Wall (WOW) might easily have joined the culture of dispute that pervades Israel, pitting ourselves against the intolerable "other," identifying ourselves and mobilizing support against our opponents. The ultra-Orthodox were responding violently to what they perceived as our insurgence into their territory and an affront to the Torah. We had so many justifications for anger. We had suffered violating curses and abuse during the sensitive moments of prayer, and forceful eviction from the holy site of our people. Instead, however, we chose to seek ways to press our convictions with courage and peace. We had no intention of degrading ourselves by participating in cursing and shoving. Our vision was to share the sacred space, honoring the dignity and beauty of multiple Jewish communities of prayer.

For me, prayer is a journey toward the sacred, enveloped in awe and divine glory, a delicate and sublime endeavor. I cannot envision violence as having any relation to prayer. How can we proclaim praises of the Divine and utter supplications while cursing Her creatures and harboring hatred?

During the first year, we assembled weekly in the evening to study the halakhic sources that deal with women's prayer, quorum, Torah reading, tallit, and women's voices. Our findings supported our practices. Our firsthand knowledge of the sources was critical to sustaining the strength of our own conviction about the appropriateness of our practice. It was also invaluable in our constant educating function, explaining the halakhic basis of our practice to so many who have inquired. Ultimately, we chose to accept the halakhic guidelines established by the Orthodox Women's Tefillah Network, the umbrella organization of halakhic women's prayer groups.

This learning was the infrastructure for the network of WOW that has evolved over so many years. We have helped, and continue to help, hundreds of women become initiated into the methods of

leading prayer and in the cantillation of the Torah and *Megillot.*
Indeed, the experience of our prayer as a form of activism has
enticed many women to choose careers in the rabbinate and other
leadership positions in the Jewish community. I have personally
been inspired to research and teach text study classes on the experience of prayer in biblical, rabbinic, mystical, and Hasidic texts to
people in Jerusalem and throughout America.

Meanwhile, we were extending our outreach toward officials to
enable some resolution of the violence. Although Rabbi Getz had
refused to meet with us when we first contacted him because, to
quote his assistant, "he does not meet with women," he did appear
at joint sessions in the office of the Ministry of Religion when he
was summoned by Minister Zevulun Hammer. At one such meeting,
on March 12, 1989, he explained his revised position in relation to
the halakhic status of our prayer. Initially he had declared outright
that women reading from the Torah scroll, wearing *tallitot,* and praying collectively did not constitute an offense against Halakhah. He
now ruled that our practice was halakhically unacceptable. He
admitted forthrightly that his personal view had not altered but
that the chief rabbis had overruled his opinion with their own. They
held our prayer to be a sacrilege, a breach with thousands of years
of tradition. Because Rabbi Getz derived his rabbinic authority from
them, he was obliged to annul his views in order to adopt theirs.

His old face, framed by the white of his beard and the black of
his hat, looked resigned and remorseful as he offered this confession. We will never know if he genuinely regretted the policy he had
been forced to adopt. Every time I had occasion to see him, he certainly bore the marks of anguish about the strife among Jews. Yet
he did not assert his position as an appointee of the government
to defend our claims.

His conflict of interest is symptomatic of the chaotic intersection of "church and state" authority in Israel. Later, in our submissions to the Court, we challenged this problem of the unaccountability of the "Official of the Wall" to the democratic institutions of Israel and to his public constituency. I insisted from the beginning that we refer to Rabbi Getz as the "Official of the Wall" because this is the wording in the state's Laws Governing Holy Sites. There is no requirement that this person be a rabbi or a man, and we look forward to the day when an official is appointed who values religious pluralism. Perhaps it will even be a woman.

Into a Tunnel

In an apparent gesture of reconciliation, Rabbi Getz offered us the use of his private synagogue deep in the recesses of the enclosed northern segment of the Wall. He proposed to give us a tour of the site. When we arrived on the morning of March 15, 1989, at the meeting place, we found that Rabbi Getz had sent his assistant, Rabbi Zvi Hersh, in his stead to lead our tour. No explanations or apologies were offered for this substitution.

It was a damp, drizzly morning. We huddled together under umbrellas and waited for Rabbi Hersh while he procured the keys from Rabbi Getz's yeshiva overlooking the plaza, then we began the excursion into the dark tunnels, the bowels of the remains of the ancient Temple. The first passageway, a massive arch-ceilinged hallway, was dotted with sacred arks filled with Torah scrolls. Clustered around some of them were groups of men, wrapped in their prayer shawls. The chants of morning psalms echoed in the damp hollowness. Some of the men turned toward us, their eyes both curious and excluding.

11

As we went farther into the interior, the hallway opened into a larger space organized by a central platform into a traditional Sephardic synagogue. Silver adornments glimmered under the tiny electric light. Attendants were arranging the prayer books for the next minyan. They too looked at us quizzically, acknowledging our guide, deferring to his privilege to bring in "foreigners."

We were led down steep stone steps and across a bridgeway against the exposed lower face of the Western Wall, moving in deeper in the direction of the most inner sacred enclosure. The huge old stones, some layers etched with a smooth collar—the trademark of Herod, who had restored the Second Temple during the first century of this era—massive with the weight of centuries, witnessed our presence. At the end of this passage, Rabbi Hersh unlocked a heavy wooden door that led into a well-appointed synagogue enclosure. Carved wooden benches were arranged in concentric horseshoes facing the Wall. This was the private synagogue of Rabbi Getz. He had appropriated the spot shortly after the Israeli army had captured the Old City during the Six Day War in 1967. A mystic from France, Rabbi Getz bolstered his claim on the fact that two of his own sons had been killed in the Israeli battalion that had captured the Jewish Quarter and the Kotel.

According to our guide, we were standing directly opposite the Holy of Holies. Just on the other side of the massive stones was the historic dwelling place of the Divine Presence on earth. Struck by the moment, we fell silent. I breathed in the pulse of generations, their presence and their exile. I felt embraced at the boundary of awe and fear. I fingered some of the holy books scattered on tables, lost in a reverie of the Shekhinah's wandering, hoping to welcome Her home. "We have seen it," Hersh announced, abruptly ending a sacred moment.

On our return route, I was more aware of the labyrinthine maze of interconnected tunnels, passageways, and crisscrossing levels. We moved purposefully out of the damp darkness toward the hazy light.

After the official tour was over, Rabbi Hersh delayed in one of the cavelike enclosures. He turned to offer his private advice "off the record." We huddled together while he spoke in a deep, hollow whisper. He emphasized to us that our opponents were violent and formidable. As soon as the ultra-Orthodox community learned of our intention to pray within the holy tunnels, he said, "they would bus in thousands of people bearing knives." Keys to the passageways were easily procured. We would be trapped inside the tunnels and massacred, he warned. We would be much safer outside.

He made one further attempt to dissuade us from accepting the offer of the synagogue. If we established our precedent of women praying together with the Torah and *tallitot,* a radical innovation in practice, then we could expect all of the non-Orthodox denominations to follow suit. These groups would defile the sanctity of the site with their profane practices. He could not have fathomed the idea that we represented all of these movements, and that we welcomed the fuller participation of many strands of the Jewish people at the Wall.

We discussed the offer of the underground synagogue. The expert opinion of a member of WOW who is a police security officer was that it was easier to protect an interior enclosed space than an open exposed one. This judgment, however, depended upon the will of the police to actually protect us, and of this basic premise we had no conclusive evidence. On the other hand, we did have evidence of malevolent intentions on the part of our antagonists. On more than one occasion, the streets of Mea

Shearim, an ultra-Orthodox neighborhood, had been plastered with posters inveighing against WOW. Admittedly frightened by the horrific image drawn for us by the dubiously benevolent assistant, we were nevertheless inclined to accept the offer of Rabbi Getz's private synagogue.

We calculated our opponents' obvious interest in discouraging us from accepting. The state would thereby appear to have made a serious conciliatory offer in good faith that was rejected by the women. Although we were terrified, we nevertheless hovered close enough to willingness to call this bluff. Before there was any opportunity to communicate our acceptance, however, we were notified that the offer was rescinded. Again there was no explanation or apology.

That the excursion was reduced to an impossible fantasy was met by us with no small sense of relief at having escaped facing the ugly threat. However, we were also genuinely disappointed at not having a chance to be so close to the Holy of Holies.

We returned to our clarity of purpose: to claim our place in the public sacred space of the Jewish people. Visibility was actually quite important to us. However inviting the prospect of the inner privacy inside a holy enclosure, one of our goals was to alter the popular image of a Jew, often figured as a man praying before the Western Wall. Our presence asserts a compelling image of Jewish women at prayer. We wanted to be out and in the open.

Violence

Meanwhile, our Rosh Chodesh prayers were met with more strenuous opposition. On Rosh Chodesh Shevat, January 1989, before the lenses of television and newspaper cameras, dozens of ultra-Orthodox men assaulted us, sending metal chairs as projectiles over the partition. Police protection was not forthcoming. Although a number of bystanders were concerned with our safety and intervened against the assailants, we were terrified. No one was physically injured, however.

There was massive coverage of the event in all of the media. Both secular and religious reporters portrayed us as provocateurs, the cause of the disturbance. Making little attempt to comprehend us or our motives, they quickly labeled and denounced us as "Reform women," which was an attempt to dismiss us, as Reform Judaism is anathema to most Israelis. Women of the Wall, according to Ronit Campf, who wrote her master's thesis on the subject at the Hebrew University, grew to become the most covered women's issue in the Israeli media, though often the least understood. Reporters began to call our homes regularly to get the inside scoop on our plans. We were an enigma, intriguing, and unquestionably news. Foreign reporters contacted us and ran major stories in both Jewish and secular media. North Americans seemed to grasp our struggle and eagerly identified with us.

My telephone was ringing with the queries of curious reporters anxious for a lead about our intentions. In spite of all of the publicity, the police were singularly unresponsive to the obvious need for intervention on our behalf in the face of repeated violent aggression against us during the first months of 1989. We endured difficult discussions with high-level officials in the Ministry of Religious Affairs. Fearful of the escalating violence, we intended to return to the Wall with police protection.

Compromise

On the eve of the Fast of Esther, 1989, our overtures to all the relevant officials in an effort to negotiate a resolution to an intolerable situation culminated in the receipt of an ultimatum. We had convened to finalize our strategy, overflowing one of our members' living room. Now a foreboding ambiguity hung over us. Finally, I had the crucial telephone conversation with the Minister of Religious Affairs, Zevulun Hammer, and Rabbi Getz. They were speaking from their car phone, stationed at the back of the Kotel plaza. In exchange for their personal guarantee and official undertaking to deploy police in order to ensure our safety, they demanded that we arrive the next morning with neither the Torah scroll nor our prayer shawls.

Conscious that this was a devastating compromise of our practice, we agonized about our choice. We were striving for an outcome that would not betray our convictions and the justice of our claims to wear prayer shawls and chant from the Torah scroll, but we also wanted to demonstrate sincerity and some modicum of conciliation. After an agonizing night of deliberation, we achieved what we used to refer to in the feminist movement as "consensus by exhaustion." Ultimately, we accepted the conditions.

Our relief at the prospect of safety offset, to a small extent, our discomfort with the compromise. We nonetheless ached with the concern that we had betrayed ourselves and were setting a precedent for our acceptance of prayer without the holy scroll and our *tallitot*. As I reflect on it now, that fateful decision might, ironically, have determined the form of our practice for the next decade. We regretfully and somewhat naively established our willingness to pray without the sacred instruments of Jewish prayer communities. We stripped ourselves bare for the sake of a promise of safety.

I realize more fully now how frightened and desperate we must have felt. Having suffered the violence that was allowed and even condoned by these men, we had been humbled to accept the terms by which we compromised our spiritual yearnings. Repression by the threat of violence is a recurring theme in women's struggles for liberation. In retrospect, might we have challenged the authorities? Would they have behaved differently if we had refused to capitulate to the ultimatum? I have no answers.

The memory of the fear is still vivid in my consciousness; the faces of rage impaling us are still in my dreams. Some of us were nursing mothers of infants and very young children, justifiably reluctant to take more risk.

As powerful as that fear was, however, it was matched by the emotional intensity with which we invested every choice with the significance of the historic moment. Our going together to the Wall epitomized our vision of Judaism. The simplicity of the symbol was gripping: a wall, massive stones holding the prayers and tears of thousands of years of longing. Our feet retraced the same pathways as our ancestors from the time of Abraham and Sarah. We were marking our footprints among those of the collectivity of the Jewish people throughout time, imprinting the public sacred space with women's soles and souls forever.

Betrayal

We arrived the next morning at the plaza, numbering approximately 150 women and 100 male supporters. As we approached the Kotel, a dense wall of ultra-Orthodox people blocked our passage. A police contingent cleared a path and escorted us to the Wall. Rows of ultra-Orthodox men who lined the passageway shouted curses and spat as we walked through the sea of black. My husband, Shmuel, stood at the back, our baby on his chest, our two other young children gripping his hands. Their consciousness will forever be imprinted with the images of what transpired.

Soon after we began our prayers in the women's section, men began to hurl objects in our direction, over the partition. Metal chairs and even a table were flying toward us. In the mayhem, many of our male supporters rushed to join and help protect us. Reform and Orthodox male rabbis stood alongside one another, catching chairs in midair, one after another, sliding them across the stone paving out of range of the assailants. In the melee that ensued, one woman was injured. A chair had landed on her head; she was bleeding from the neck. One of us rushed her to the hospital, where she was treated briefly. The daughter of a rabbi, she lay in her hospital bed and committed herself to a career in the leadership of the Jewish community.

Meanwhile, onlookers desperately called upon the border police stationed at the rear of the plaza to assist, but they refused to even descend from their vans. Assembled on the back steps of the plaza was the contingent from the Ministry of Religious Affairs, the chief of police, and Rabbi Getz. They were watching as we endured our roles in the macabre, bitter drama unfolding against the backdrop of the old stone wall on the eve of Purim, the festival of masquerade.

Finally, the police issued instructions. Two shiny silver tear gas canisters were hurled toward the crowd at the Wall. People dashed recklessly, fleeing from the dispersing clouds of gas. Soon the Kotel and plaza were engulfed in a thick smoky mist. One man wearing a black suit, with phylacteries on his arm and head, masking his face with his tallit, picked up one of the canisters and pitched it directly into our midst. His form—racing across the plaza, gripping the can, his tallit billowing behind him into the smoke—was captured on the front page of *The Jerusalem Post*.

I recall my first inhalation of the scorching gas, the burning in my throat, nose, and eyes. Clutching my shirt and hat to my face, I regretted not having my tallit to enshroud me. Coughing and gagging, we retreated, horrified. We had been utterly betrayed.

Lawsuit and Eviction

Four of us proceeded directly from the Kotel plaza to the offices of our attorneys to prepare a Supreme Court petition. Our lawyers, Uri Ganor and Herzl Kadesh, were young and relatively inexperienced but affordable, having cultivated their careers in the field of civil rights. Anat Hoffman, Judith Green, and I met with them for many hours to discuss our principles and strategies at every stage. We exchanged drafts with comments and corrections, and they amended them accordingly. This process enabled me, as a social activist, to have astoundingly direct input into the legal system. We buttressed our arguments with a network of sources, ranging from the Israeli Declaration of Independence, to feminist theory, to relevant halakhic responsa, to Israeli court precedents. Using the Supreme Court as a tool to induce change, we constructed a form of strategic activism fueled by confidence in the inexorable momentum of women moving into the public core of Jewish experience.

In April 1989, WOW petitioned the Supreme Court of Israel on behalf of all Jewish women. In addition to the right to pray together, we called upon the Ministry of Religious Affairs to provide a Torah scroll and a covered area adjacent to the Kotel where we would be sheltered during inclement weather. The interior portion of the men's side of the Wall, as we had seen on our foray into the tunnels, is stocked with dozens of Torah scrolls, each in its ark and niche, ready for any men's quorum.

Right-wing religious parties speedily petitioned the Court to align themselves with the state against us. Later, the chief rabbi of Jerusalem and other officials joined the list of opponents to our petitions.

The ensuing process revealed the state's unwillingness to assert the rule of law to protect the rights of female citizens, or to indict or even decry the criminal assailants. Indeed, not a single Israeli official has ever condemned the violence against Women of the Wall. Instead, there was a concerted campaign to demoralize us, erode our conviction, and break us down. By Rosh Chodesh Av 1989, we had been praying for a number of months without *tallitot* or the Torah in the women's section. The discussions in Court seemed to have permeated the atmosphere at the Wall. Some ultra-Orthodox women had been considerably aggressive during our prayers, and this culminated on Rosh Chodesh Av 1989.

The Ministry of Religious Affairs had hired female security guards to remove us from the Kotel were we to "sing." In view of the somberness of Av, the month in which we commemorate the destruction of the Temple, we had opted to sit together on the paving stones in the event that action was taken against us. Very quickly after we had begun our initial prayers, the guards swooped in on us, two struggling to remove each one of us. We seated ourselves, arms linked, attempting to persevere with our prayers. Our ultra-Orthodox opponents seized the opportunity of our low posture to spray us with dirt and water, hurl curses, grab our prayer books, and snatch our hats. These events were fully filmed and broadcast on Israeli television.

Solidarity

After these extreme incidents, a different dynamic gradually emerged in the women's section of the Kotel. Over the course of the months of our consistent presence, engaging in sensitive and even ecstatic prayers, the hostility and resentment of many of the ultra-Orthodox women who were "regulars" began to erode. From the beginning, I had always made a point of greeting with the blessing "Good month!" even those women who had cursed us. At first, some of them just muttered under their breath. The turning point was when I returned after one month's absence, having given birth to my fourth child. I wore the baby strapped onto my chest in a carrier. One of the women approached me to congratulate me and offer a blessing. A few others followed suit. From then on, we became accustomed to exchanging greetings, connecting at what they considered to be a female concern. Whenever I rarely happened to miss a month, they would ask about the well-being of my children, or if I was expecting another child. One woman even inquired about my husband.

After our first round of Supreme Court appeals, a contingent of North American women, many of whom had attended the original conference in December 1988, formed a nonprofit organization, the International Committee for Women of the Wall (ICWOW). Visiting Israel to present us with a Torah scroll, the American women were prohibited, on the basis of the new law, from conducting their prayer service at the Wall. The American group joined its Supreme Court petition with ours and took on a major burden of supporting our struggle—particularly the legal expenses. They have also provided extraordinary moral encouragement and support of every kind.

I cannot express enough gratitude to those who conceived and fulfilled this dream of a Torah scroll for the women of Jerusalem. Hundreds of women have chanted from this scroll, including many bat mitzvah girls and dozens of women who have never before had the opportunity to say the blessings.

Another initiative of our American sisters was to finesse an audience with Ashkenazi Chief Rabbi Avraham Shapira. "Let's assume that you are right. Still, it infuriates the Jews," Rabbi Shapira had said during the ICWOW session with him in New York City. ICWOW secured a promise from him to meet with us in Israel.[2]

Having brushed up on the protocol of formal address befitting an audience with an extremely honored individual such as a judge or a monarch, we ascended to the rabbi's office. His message to us was clear: Peace among the people of Israel at the holy site, and everywhere, was the highest priority. We were obviously the provocation, the cause of tremendous disturbance. Therefore, we must desist from interfering with the order and quiet of the site, which has known no violation, in Rabbi Shapira's view, except the ones we had instigated, since its capture by the Israeli army in 1967.

We authoritatively cited verses, rabbinic and legal sources in support of our practice of reading from the Torah and wearing prayer shawls, including a decision rendered by a former chief rabbi, Rabbi Shlomo Goren, endorsing women's group prayer. Although Rabbi Shapira could summon no halakhic obstacle or prohibition to support his position, he nevertheless insisted on the utter unacceptability of our group prayer at the Kotel. The status quo was to be upheld, even though it excludes us. For the sake of eliminating unnecessary dissent among the people, it was incumbent upon us to desist. Indeed, he said candidly, it would be preferable for us to remain at home. His wife, after all, prays happily at home and never feels any lack.

Our initial project of demonstrating the sincerity, knowledge, and commitment that motivated us to stake our claim among the Jewish people degenerated as the exchange proceeded. As a result of this encounter, the chief rabbis solidified their opposition.

From various such encounters we gleaned information about our opponents and gained insight into their worldviews. We chose meetings strategically to attain the maximum leverage in proportion to the energy we spent, because we never had enough time. Every hour was stolen from our work schedules and childcare responsibilities; every shekel was the product of hard-earned grant proposals, parlor meetings, and fundraising lectures.

Our limited resources were dwarfed by the massive state machine. We perceived that relatively huge amounts of time and money were invested toward our defeat. We also suffered some attrition because some women were demoralized by the compromising prayer arrangements that prohibited us from wearing *tallitot*, reading from the Torah, and even singing our prayers aloud.

Nonetheless, we were able to reinforce each other's hopefulness through our sharing of monthly prayers, our learning, and the intermittent meetings. In the face of so much opposition, we managed to maintain a balance between the joy of our practice and the inevitable frustration with the snail's pace of the Court and the methods it recommended.

As the effort progressed, ICWOW seemed more inclined to reject the committees and commissions proposed to us by the state as diversions from the straight and narrow Supreme Court strategy. ICWOW was cynical about the possibility that such political mechanisms would yield any fruit. Overall, ICWOW seemed to us to put too much emphasis on the legal endeavor. We understood this preoccupation, as it was the only means by which ICWOW members could take an active role and feel part of a cause so dear to their hearts. Late-night, multiple-party phone conversations, often attempting to persuade or dissuade us about a particular course of action, were common during the first few years. This was the means by which we conquered the separation of distance and felt the commonality of our struggle.

I view the connection between WOW and ICWOW during the first years as a microcosm of Israel-diaspora relations. There was no question that the risk, the action, and the danger were all in Jerusalem. We were the ones who experienced the events firsthand; we put ourselves on the line. ICWOW experienced the events vicariously through us. This dynamic was similar to the Israel-diaspora mode during the years of war and insecurity. Whenever there was cause for disagreement about strategy or policy, it was we who made the ultimate decision, for we would experience the consequences.

The dynamic of counterinclinations between WOW and ICWOW created a system of checks and balances. There were occasions when we, the Israeli women, were ready to conduct an act of civil disobedience, defying the Court order to desist from our prayer practices in the Kotel, thereby jeopardizing the legal case, when ICWOW preferred to forge ahead in Court. There were also occasions when ICWOW was extremely impatient with Court delays, anxious to intervene in an aggressive manner, while we preferred to demonstrate as much good faith as we could muster, exercising the system maximally at each opportunity.

Learning from the Process

Our persistent, continuous presence at the Kotel has been the mainstay of our activism throughout these many years. Prayer in the presence of opposition has been a tremendously challenging as well as strangely enlightening experience. We are puzzled about how Jews who derive their worldviews and commitments from the same Torah, the same Talmud, and the same Shabbat and festivals have come to such incompatible conclusions about how to live a Jewish life in the holy land.

I have personally developed a heightened awareness of the methods, assumptions, and agendas that inform the study and interpretation of sacred sources and of how interpretation is an instrument of power. I have become more sensitive to the tremendous ethical implications of study, to my own responsibility to infuse with social activism my role as a scholar and teacher of Jewish texts, and to being a model for prayer and Jewish practice.

The Kotel has become a symbolic opportunity to strive to fulfill some of these visions. The Kotel represents an ingathering from the four corners of dispersion. Returning to the ancient site, Jews have been bringing customs and costumes, chants and experiences, integrating years of exile. Jews have also been creating new customs and rituals to respond to the contemporary historic moment of Jewish access to the Temple remnant. Swearing-in ceremonies of Israel Defense Force soldiers, celebrations of Independence Day, and commemorations of the Holocaust are examples of such innovations. The participation of women in the public sacred arena is a movement toward which the Jewish world of North America has made serious strides. Securing the ongoing presence of Women at the Wall will be a symbolic inclusion of women among the full spectrum of the Jewish people.

In our situation, we have been conscious of the intensity of the commitment of many of our members to egalitarian practice, whereby women do constitute a prayer quorum and utter the communal parts of the prayer service. Most Orthodox opinions reserve these special utterances only for a quorum of ten Jewish men. Halakhic strictures that limit the status of our prayer because we are women were unacceptable to many of our members. With tremendous sensitivity and compassion we nevertheless engaged in a process of creating a practice that we could share.

We were all convinced that there would be little chance of success without halakhic support for our practice. If we proved the halakhic integrity of our prayer, we reasoned, there would be more likelihood that we would be accepted by the right-wing authorities who control the site. A women's "minyan," we reasoned, was too radical for the context. Furthermore, a number of us, affiliates of the Orthodox community, would not allow ourselves to participate if the group performed what are considered prohibited religious acts. Those who held the opposite view, that we should perform them, accepted the strategic argument as long as we promoted maximum freedom for individual variation in the practice of the community.

During the first year of Supreme Court hearings, a ruling was made that the status quo was to be upheld until such time as a conclusive decision was rendered by the Court. The status quo meant that for the time being, Rabbi Getz was charged to determine what was the accepted practice at the Kotel. He decided that we were not to read from the Torah, wear *tallitot,* or, later, sing aloud. We challenged the ruling that a single official could be empowered to unilaterally decide what was the acceptable practice at the most sacred site for the entire Jewish people. Nevertheless, having initiated the proceedings, we were committed to seeing the legal process through to its end. Our practice of beginning with the morning service and the special prayers of thanksgiving, *Hallel,* at the Wall, and then retiring to another site overlooking the Kotel for the Torah reading, blessings, and additional prayers, evolved from the legal strictures imposed upon us.

There is also a subliminal awareness of our fear of the violence that might ensue if we were to open the Torah scroll at the Kotel. The preliminary songs at the Kotel, therefore, have often been a source of anxiety due to our awareness of the censoring glares and the not-infrequent interrupting remarks, arguments, and disdainful "shh's." Nonetheless, we have usually managed to tap our joyous spirit, at moments achieving exquisite and intense harmonies. Indeed, during these psalms, we have often attracted many random women and sometimes even entire groups to participate with us.

I am inclined toward a strategy of revolution, of creating new facts on the ground. Many times I have donned my tallit at the Kotel and encouraged others to do so too. Sometimes we have suffered the humiliation of being ordered by a guard to remove our *tallitot.* Since my tallit is not the usual white with black or blue stripes, the guards often do not identify mine as a tallit. This is a creative strategy, indeed. We achieve our purpose while no one feels offended.

There is rarely a month that passes that a number of ultra-Orthodox women don't rebuke us for singing. Some do it with sensitivity, presuming that we are simply ill-informed about the alleged prohibition of singing near men. Others are aggressive and nasty. In spite of distractions, we usually manage to complete the entire *Hallel* service with prayerful songs of great joy.

The Kotel can be an alienating and lonely site for some women. Many women respond to our invitation to connect with prayer at the historic sacred core of the Jewish universe by participating with us. I glimpse the fulfillment of my initial conception of Women of the Wall as an enduring monthly Rosh Chodesh celebration, a time sanctified for Jewish women to convene for public festive prayer.

Upstairs, where we come to read the Torah overlooking the Kotel plaza, some of us wrap ourselves in *tallitot;* some bind ourselves with the leather straps and sacred boxes of tefillin, while many do not. Many women say the full blessing over the chanting of the Torah reading, whereas others choose to substitute an alternate utterance.[3] The liturgy of the silent private "standing" prayer, the *Amidah,* is open to the individual discretion of the participants. One of our native Israeli members created her own *siddur* (prayer book). Others have created songs and supplications.

Our arrangement of dividing the service between the Kotel itself and the "Archaeological Gardens," though somewhat awkward, has enabled us to preserve our ongoing presence at the Wall and to fulfill our need to read from the Torah and wear *tallitot* and tefillin. As we ascend toward the upstairs location, we can feel the weight of the excessive prohibitions lifting, our freedom to pray un–self-consciously restored.

Bat Mitzvah

Sunny Korda's parents called me one day to tell of their daughter's dream. She wanted to be the first to celebrate her bat mitzvah at the Kotel. Sunny was steadfast through months of preparation, coming weekly to my home to study the text of her Torah portion and learn the cantillation. She prepared meticulously for the spectacular day, acknowledging the risk of possible violence with the open naivete of a twelve-year-old. Women of the Wall convened specially to celebrate with Sunny. She began by leading the morning prayers in a thin and sweet voice. We were captivated by the power of her youth, the symbol she represented of a vision transferred to the next generation with so much conviction. Only a few of her classmates had been brave enough to join us. We experienced no interruption that day; we were encased in a shell of innocence.

Sunny carried the Torah scroll and led the procession upstairs to the Archaeological Gardens. Calling her up to bless and read from the Torah was one of those holy moments, like a kiss of heaven and earth. Her mother beamed at close range while her father stood off in the distance, absorbing the joy. We danced her to exhaustion, circled and blessed her. Hers was the first bat mitzvah at the Kotel. We had broken new ground. There will be no turning back from that bright young face blazing ahead with faith and confidence.

The Ne'eman Commission

In the summer of 1998, residing in Boston, I joined the WOW contingent to the Ne'eman Commission. In an effort to reduce the animosity over proposed Israeli legislation to progressively exclude non-Orthodox denominations from defining who is a Jew, Yakov Ne'eman had formed a commission. He had gathered representatives of the Conservative and Reform movements to meet with government officials from the Ministry of Religious Affairs and the chief rabbinate to conduct a "civil discourse." The goal was to ease the unbearable tension and animosity that threatened to drive an irreparable wedge between Israel and diaspora Jewry. The deliberations had culminated in a series of resolutions to form a joint institute for conversion to Judaism in which rabbis from all of the denominations would participate. The Supreme Court later propounded its view that a more broadly constituted committee should convene to address the social, political, and religious challenges posed by Women of the Wall. This became the mandate of the Ne'eman Commission during the summer of 1998: to advance recommendations about how to enable Women of the Wall to pray at the Kotel.

The Commission met in the offices of the Finance Ministry, around an enormous oval table. Black *kipot* topped the heads of the contingent from Religious Affairs, who occupied one part of the table adjacent to Minister Ne'eman. Opposite him sat secular archaeologists, who represented the interests of the Ministry of Antiquities, with their claims to protect the historical remains of the sacred sites. The police commissioner and his aide were present to provide insight and advice about security and public order. Among the police were seated the Reform and Conservative representatives, as well as a few miscellaneous advisors whose entitlement to membership on the Commission was ambiguous at best. Together, these men held the deed to the sacred real estate that we, the women, were contesting.

Yakov Ne'eman conducted these meetings with a strong hand. His body language indicated the extent to which he excluded us from the deliberations. He often spoke with his back to us and motioned with his hands toward the other five-sixths of the table. To us he directed patronizing and castigating remarks. After the second meeting, it was clear to me that we needed to adopt a new tactic. (I published a letter in *The Jerusalem Post* expressing this.)

In my view, it was time for some creative strategy to alter the dynamic of the conversation that degraded and excluded us. I felt that we should attempt to enter the conversation by quoting a biblical text to open the meeting. We had one last meeting to discuss our strategy. Even though we all agreed that the Commission was not sincere and that the process was demeaning, there were differences of opinion among us on how to proceed. One woman argued that the Commission was a powerful assembly that we needed to respect by following through with due process. We needed to be "good girls" and not disrupt. In view of the briefness of my sojourn in Israel at that time, I was unwilling to try to prevail over the locals, who would continue with the day-to-day responsibility for WOW after I left. Thus I deferred to the "good girl" opinion. I entered the large, hollow room burdened with sadness, resigned to endure the humiliation of another meeting.

One of our preoccupations at that final meeting, an issue strenuously emphasized by our attorney, was to discover who was to be included as voting members of the Commission, in order that we could determine who would formulate the final recommendations. There was a tacit assumption that a consensus was required. Judging from the way Yakov Ne'eman had conducted the meetings up to that point, it was impossible to imagine how we could achieve any shared conclusion. When we posed the question directly, he responded with rage, "Whoever is present!"

Representatives of the Ministry of Religious Affairs had already conveyed their decision (in quite a demeaning letter) to boycott the meetings, and it was clear that a recommendation made without their active support would have no chance of success. We were also aware that we were not being treated properly as members, although our consent was a sine qua non of success. Ultimately, it seemed to us, Yakov Ne'eman himself was the only relevant member; he unilaterally intended to control the outcome. Surely he also grasped the futility of our gathering, for indeed there was no possible compromise that could satisfy the mandate as each interest understood it. Perhaps this was a source of his frustration and rage. In any case, it was evident that his problem-solving powers were somewhat less than advertised.

Quickly we saw that our minimalist proposal of one protected hour per month in the women's section at the Kotel was not even to be included among the options under discussion. Yet there was one fanciful possibility that we had saved until the last hour. Anat Hoffman had masterminded a plan for a rooftop balcony enclosed with tinted Plexiglas overlooking the Wall. The architects who were under municipal contract to design a series of shelters for the perimeters of the plaza had collaborated with us to include a very modest elevated area for Women of the Wall in their plans. Although we had considered this proposal to be excessively compromising, enclosing us on a high, narrow plexiglassed rooftop, we humbled our expectations and submitted it in good faith because we believed that it satisfied the criteria of the Commission so fully. It enabled us to pray close to the Wall, albeit in a restricted manner, while minimizing possible offense to the other worshipers. Much to the chagrin of Anat, who had worked so enthusiastically to enable this plan to come to the table, the Commission refused to even contemplate it, to even look at the documents and drawings.

The only options Yakov Ne'eman was willing to consider were outside the Kotel plaza: in the corner where the buses and taxis enter, at the southern wall, among the archaeological remains beneath Robinson's Arch, and in a patently insecure area inside the Muslim Quarter. It was our considered opinion that this slate of available options defied the entire mandate of the Commission: to enable us to pray at the Kotel.

We had stressed many times how we needed no special arrangements or Supreme Court appeal to pray at alternate sites. Yet the Commission detained itself with conversations about a dispensation to waive the standard entrance fee to the archaeological excavations at the southern wall. The southern wall was already accessible for alternative prayer services; my family had celebrated our daughter's bat mitzvah there the previous year.

The Commission concluded by reviewing each of the options on the list. We had no choice but to reject them all, since none enabled us to fulfill our goal of prayer among the ingathered people of Israel at the symbolic site.

As people were dispersing, a small group clustered around Minister Ne'eman. I overheard them exchanging jokes about the new drug for male impotence. "What blessing do you say on Viagra? The blessing for the resurrection of the dead." I slipped out of the room as these powerful men chortled and snickered together at their crude repartee. At that instant, the gap between our hope for serious engagement and the attitude of our partners was quite explicit. These last words were a discouraging confirmation that the Commission was incapable of addressing the weighty issues at hand with justice and grace.

Reflections

After six years of leading WOW, I left Jerusalem and became one of the overseas supporters. Still, I frequently return to the group in Israel. I have had the opportunity to reevaluate my position with the benefit of the perspective of North American Jewish life. Each time I perceive the context anew, I am conscious of my evolution.

Reflecting retrospectively about our choice to follow the halakhic guidelines of the Women's Tefillah Network, I now feel a certain ambivalence. A decade ago, there was no doubt in my mind that the halakhic consensus was critical to our struggle. Now I question that decision. My critique is directed more at myself than at anyone else. It is the confession of a social activist whose position has evolved through the processes of trial and error, the unfolding of experience, intensifying research and continual analysis, and, most of all, the inspection of my faith.

I have come to identify myself more and more as a Jew and less as a "Jewish woman" or "female Jew." It is with tremendous awe and fear that I have come to take upon myself more of the obligations of the Torah from which rabbinic Judaism has exempted, and thereby excluded, me. My desire to share and participate fully in the covenant of the Jewish people has unfolded gradually and with increasing intensity as I study and teach the more sublime discourses of the Torah.

My experience with the early history of WOW demonstrates some of the challenges inherent in the multiple processes of feminist social change in Israel. I strove to achieve and foster a tolerable, if not inspired, level of integrity even while our opponents abused us with tremendous affronts to dignity, indescribable humiliations, and violations of body and spirit.

Among the many faces of the social-change movement that WOW has become, the actual prayers are the most gratifying. Having been away for a number of years, returning frequently for visits, I am moved to witness the continuation of this initiative, the strengthening of the core group with the addition of knowledgeable and talented new members, and the fervent commitment to sustaining the vision of women's participation in the public sacred service of the Jewish people.

One of our foremost strategies has been to alter the "facts on the ground." WOW has undertaken not only legal but also social, educational, and political activist efforts. In my initial and developing strategies, I intentionally sought to direct our efforts toward the intersection of secular and religious jurisdiction and to propose new mappings of Israeli sacred space that are germane to both religious and secular Zionism. WOW has been exercising the instruments of a fervently democratic society: the courts, the media, the Knesset, organizations, and schools.

I have been seeking to nurture a spiritual momentum of women toward the symbolic public Jewish center. We have begun the process of sanctifying the inner holy space of Jerusalem with the prayers and songs of women. Our strategy has been intentional and adamantly nonviolent. As our husbands, brothers, fathers, and sons were called upon to serve the systems of war, we conceived and pursued change by peaceful means.

Many are inclined to dismiss gender inequalities during times of crisis and war, appealing to the need to present a united front against the enemy. Women have long been oppressed by the doctrines of power that serve militarist priorities. A premise basic to my feminist analysis is that the everyday relationships among men and women are a barometer of the moral caliber of society. Relationships that express dignity and mutual respect, that care for the needy and vulnerable, are prerequisites for a healthy and peaceful society. Acceptance by both sexes of the sanctity of the service of *all* members of the Jewish people, women *and* men, is not a distraction from, but a prerequisite for, attaining peace—both among the people of Israel and with our neighbors.

My desire is for a society imbued with respect for and recognition of the wholesome plurality of human conceptions of the sacred. Women of the Wall has been engaging and persevering in a peaceful process of cultivating holiness while reconciling intense differences. May its initiative inspire and empower change throughout the world.

SHARON PIKUS

Encountering Fear

ON THE FIRST DAY OF AV, 5749 (August 2, 1989), my husband and I had the privilege of attending a Rosh Chodesh service at the Kotel in Jerusalem. This should have been as uplifting and wonderful as any experience one could have, particularly in Israel. It was, however, marred by what I consider to be a blight on the concept that all Jews are free to practice their religion in Israel, the Jewish State.

What I actually wound up experiencing was the oppression of a group of Jews who came to the Kotel and were persecuted for "singing" aloud. The women wore no prayer shawls or *kipot,* thereby complying with previous requests not to do so. However, after about three minutes into a mellow service, these women had rocks and sand thrown at them. They were then pushed, shoved, and eventually dragged along the floor away from the Kotel by mostly female security guards who were hired particularly for this event.

I initially attempted to participate in the service at the Kotel, but when the going got truly rough, I removed myself for fear of personal bodily harm. I was ashamed of myself for being a coward, but I truly did not feel prepared physically or emotionally for the discrimination, violence, and abuse that was heaped upon a group of reverently praying women by other "observant" Jews.

RAHEL JASKOW

A Personal Account

DURING THE BRITISH MANDATE, Jews were not allowed to read the Torah at the Kotel. They would pray at the Kotel, go up to their synagogues for the Torah reading, and then come back down for the rest of the service. As everyone knows, the British Mandate ended fifty-four years ago, and we got the Kotel back thirty-five years ago—but this restriction still exists for Jewish women.

I've been an active member of Women of the Wall for about five years. Actually, I'd been active before that and stopped briefly. It was a Shabbat with Rabbi Shlomo Carlebach in Ein Karem that inspired me to go back.

People are very curious about who we are and what we do, so I'd like to give my own personal account of a typical Rosh Chodesh with Women of the Wall. We meet at the women's section of the Kotel every Rosh Chodesh at 7:00 A.M., rain or shine, always on the first day of the Hebrew month. (That means that if Rosh Chodesh is two days, we meet on the second day, unless it's Shabbat. If Rosh Chodesh falls on Shabbat, we don't meet.)

The group stands near the guard station at the women's section. There we daven *Shachrit,* led sometimes by women who live in Jerusalem, sometimes by women who come to visit from abroad. The *baalat tefillah* (prayer leader) stands in the middle so that everyone can hear her and say "amen" at the proper time. Women drift in and join us, looking over our shoulders to find out where we are in the *tefillah,* then open their *siddurim* and join in. Others who are less familiar with the *tefillah* look on with their neighbors. Still other women look at us from a distance, some with curiosity, a few with suspicion. Sometimes I find myself wanting to say, "What's the big deal? The *Ashrei* I'm saying and the *Ashrei* you're saying are exactly the same."

Sometimes people ask me, "But don't you get chairs thrown at you?" Not anymore, thank heaven. Folks are used to us by now. Chair throwing hasn't happened for years, and we pray for everybody's sake that it never will again. Our group is always different. The members who live in Jerusalem come every time, but there are always new faces: young college students who are here for a year, teachers on sabbatical, young sabra women, bat mitzvah girls and their families. We've had families come to us to celebrate their daughters' coming of age from as nearby as Haifa and as far away as the United States, Australia, and New Zealand.

Because we don't consider ourselves a minyan, we don't say things that would normally be recited only in a minyan. That means no Kaddish, no *Barkhu,* no repetition of the *Amidah.* In this we are no different from most Orthodox women's prayer groups, although our members are Orthodox, Conservative, Reform, Reconstructionist, and everything in between. We are proud and happy that all these women come to us to pray, that many of them give up their own, more liberal, interpretation of a women's service for the sake of unity. With open hearts they accept the restrictions we've imposed upon ourselves. Once again I'm reassured that, as women, we can overcome our differences, find our own voices, and make our own way.

After *Shachrit* we go into *Hallel,* and each time, our leader cautions the others about getting carried away. Singing full-voice here could get us into trouble, even though by this time there's more than enough noise from the men's section and the neighboring construction to drown out any sound we make. The group moves inward, tightening up its edges, as we offer our praise and thanks to the Holy One for the renewed month.

After *Hallel* we leave the women's section of the Kotel. There's a last-minute replacing of *siddurim;* some women go close to the Kotel for a moment and then rejoin the group as we walk to a site in the Jewish Quarter for the Torah reading. Under the open sky we spread a specially made silk cloth over the raised stone structure that we use as a *bimah,* and we place the Torah upon it, wrapped in its woven cover and a tallit. It is there that many women get to see the inside of a Torah scroll up close for the first time. Our *gabbai* asks the group, "Is there anyone here who has never received an *aliyah?*" Five years ago there were several in each group; now there are almost none. Once, when no one in the group answered in the affirmative, one of the women exclaimed, in joyful disbelief, "You mean everyone here has had an *aliyah* at one time or another?" Everybody had. She yelled, laughing, "I think this deserves a *shehecheyanu* all by itself!"

Once during the Torah service I was standing near a young woman who had the current *aliyah.* The reading was finished, and she began the blessing that is recited afterward. Suddenly she stopped, and I leaned forward to help. As I opened my mouth to prompt her with the words of the blessing, tears spilled from her eyes and she started to cry.

"I never had an *aliyah* before," she sobbed. "I never saw an open Torah." And I stood silent, not daring to say a word. She never completed the blessing, but how could I interfere? Her soul-deep reaction to her first chance to get close to the Torah, I thought, must mean so much to the Holy One, maybe even more than the proper blessing. As Rabbi Shlomo Carlebach used to say, "What do we know? What do we know at all?"

The Torah reading progresses, and as with Rabbi Shlomo's davening, the *Mi Sheberakhs* are personalized. The *gabbai* makes sure to find out a little bit about each *olah* and asks for appropriate blessings for her. We respond with an enthusiastic *"Amen."*

Now it's time for *Musaf,* Psalm 104, *Alenu.* Then we greet friends, meet new people. One member passes around a mailing list. We hear *divrei Torah,* updates on our Court case. We make plans for future activities: this is the third year that we're reading *Megillat Esther* on Purim at the Kotel, and *Eikhah* on Tisha B'Av, with great success.

Then we disperse, going our ways into the Jerusalem morning. The high of *tefillah* is slowly replaced by more mundane concerns. Is anyone going into town? To my neighborhood? Who's bringing back the Torah? *Chodesh tov, l'hitra'ot.* Until next month.

Last Sukkot, I went to the Kotel with my colleagues of WOW with the *lulav* and *etrog,* which constitute the *arba minim,* or "four species," as is our custom every year during *chol hamoed.* We finished *Shachrit* and took out our *arba minim* to make the blessing. A number of women noticed what we were doing and approached us, asking to borrow our sets so that they could make the blessing as well.

An older woman told us she was from the Syrian Jewish community. We gave her a set and, prompted by one of our group, she made the blessing with great devotion. When she had finished waving the *lulav,* she handed it back and said wistfully, "I wish I could get my daughter more interested in her Judaism."

A woman of our group said, "So get her an *arba minim* set of her own and teach her how to make the blessing on it."

She replied, "It's not the custom in our community for women to take the *arba minim.*"

I watched this exchange and thought sadly that in our day, this woman and others like her have a choice: they can consciously elect to forget such customs, or they can forget about passing Judaism on to their daughters.

There is a tune I sing at every bat mitzvah celebration I attend, whether or not it takes place as part of WOW. It is Rabbi Carlebach's *Hashmi'ini et Kolekh,* "Let Me Hear Your Voice," and I sing it to every bat mitzvah girl with all my heart and soul. I've led it in the Jewish Quarter where we do our Torah reading, as we dance after the bat mitzvah girl's *aliyah.* I sing it as a prayer that the young woman coming of age will speak and sing out proudly and with joy throughout her life, never to be silenced, neither by her own spiritual leaders nor by anyone else. In a widely quoted interpretation of this passage from the Song of Songs, God is saying to the Jewish people, "Let me hear your voice, for your voice is sweet!" That is God speaking to all of us, sons and daughters alike. Dare we contradict?

Interview with Anat Hoffman

Anat Hoffman, a longtime member of the Jerusalem city council, is currently the head of the Reform movement in Israel.

THIS DIALOGUE TOOK PLACE in a transatlantic telephone call.

Phyllis: Has this struggle changed your life?

Anat: It changed the way I understood feminism. I thought that the marginalization of women was related to women's being seen as unclean. Women of the Wall has taught me that the most important thing is for women to be heard and that being heard is even more important than being clean.

P: How biblical! As Jews, perhaps we do have a special relationship to listening, really hearing: the *Shema*, the Torah reading, the sounds of Sinai, and the still, small voice within.

A: Yes. The real issue is voice and being heard. For example, I actually did a study on the mayor of Jerusalem in terms of how he silences women. I wanted to understand how women have been silenced historically in Jerusalem, and today, in the city council where I am.

P: Give me an example of how the mayor silences women.

A: He silences women by complimenting women—or not saying anything! We have these long six-and-a-half-hour meetings. He says to one woman, "Thank you for being here. I'm so proud to have you here." And she has said nothing. He noticed that she hardly spoke, and at the end of every meeting he complimented her for that. Another way he has of silencing women is by making comments about women's voice. Some men growl and some men bark, but the mayor never comments on the quality of the sound. Nurit Yardeni Levi from Labour has a very high voice. The mayor says, "Why are you screaming? Why are you screeching? Why are you attacking? I can't listen to this hysteria." Note how he "hears" a high voice as hysterical. The mayor allows one of my colleagues, an older woman, to speak the most. He rewards her for being self-deprecating. "I'm a dumb speaker, I don't understand anything, I don't remember anything, I'm senile." This woman actually gets to speak the most, because when she says, "I'm dumb and stupid," he responds with "No, you're not." She averages the most talking time.

P: That's quite a love duet.

A: Right. These are all modes of silencing women. He rewards women who are quiet or self-deprecating. In my case, he calls me names in Yiddish: *catchke, platchke, yenta.* Or we are told that we are immodest, that our voices show a disregard for modesty. Understanding how modesty has been defined in modern Israel, we see that it has been defined way above and beyond what has been called for by tradition.

Being seen is also a problem for women. I am a founding member of Women of the Wall. We were always told that one of our big problems is that we're too visible. People always like to photograph us rather than interview us. The idea that women might have a voice on a political or military-security issue is absolutely new in

Israel. Women have always been there to be looked at. We are the decoration, the accompaniment. To use our voice or our bodies to make a political or religious statement of our own—that's new.

P: Women's voices are not yet synonymous with public authority. Our voices are not heard as powerful voices that can save someone's life, or intercede with God for you.

A: Exactly. Look, until that moment [December 1, 1988], I was a political person. I just read feminist literature and I was inspired by it. I read about sisterhood but I hadn't experienced it until Women of the Wall. They were wonderful words, but I understood nothing until I experienced and really saw women do it. I thought there was nothing more passive than an Orthodox woman on the outside, but inside she's not passive at all. Sisterhood is amazing. It can really bridge our denominations, language problems, cultural differences, even across oceans. For example, Barbara Sutnick [a WOW member] is a settler, and I am a leftist who opposes such settlements, but we are both sisters and Women of the Wall. I'm proud of her. She brings people from Efrat with her to daven with us.

In 1988, Bella Abzug and Letty Cottin Pogrebin invited me to their table and treated me like one of the gals in five minutes. Letty has become a friend. At the time it was very empowering to be included. These very famous, important, women, whom I had only read about, had no problem inviting me over. I've tried to emulate them any way I can. I try to invite others to my table. I remember telling Bella that it was too hard to choose between many different, urgent issues: Women in Black, fighting for peace, women's economic and legal rights. She took off her hat, which took some doing because she had a lot of hair, and she said, "Anat, you're gonna have to learn to walk and chew gum at the same time."

P: Why do you think WOW has not been overwhelmed by differences or destroyed by infighting?

A: Maybe because we are not a dialogue group. We don't meet once a month and discuss. We *pray* together. I don't know of any other group in the Jewish world that actually prays together and is multidenominational. We've done this for more than thirteen years.

P: There is no other group. Would you say that there's something unique about a women-only prayer group?

A: We are oppressed. The texts are unfriendly. The environment within which we operate is unfriendly. Despite our huge denominational differences, we can still pray together. I'm sure that as Israel develops and progresses and becomes more woman- and freedom-friendly, we will start seeing our differences more clearly. Right now we see common denominators. There is so much in common between the others and myself, but the fact that I'm a Woman in Black [Peace movement] and she's a Woman in Green [Settler movement]—that is a small thing.

P: This is so important. It suggests that praying together and being in political battle together may allow women to productively work together despite incredible differences. How has the group evolved and matured? Where is it now?

A: I'll start with the bad things. One bad thing is that the group has not grown much. We have many visitors, but the leadership of the group has not grown much. To be a leader in the group, you have to have a commitment to live in or near Jerusalem and come to meetings. We have some very committed women, but very few are willing to attend many meetings. In addition to Rosh Chodesh, we meet quite a bit.

The strength of the group is that we've learned to respect and relish the great gifts that some of us have. We all feel comfortable with our weaknesses, too. We all know what Chaia can't do, we all know what Chaia *can* do. Chaia can do great things. We all know what Betsy can do and what she can't do. Same with Jessie, same with me, same with all our leaders. What we do is allocate roles according to our different talents.

P: Psychologically, this is quite revolutionary. Among oppressed people, there is usually a *kotzer ruach* problem, a shortness of spirit that often destroys the leaders, leadership qualities, and the group itself [Exodus 6:9: "And Moses spoke to the children of Israel; and they did not listen to Moses out of shortness of spirit and hard labor"].

A: I am amazed that the group is able to share media attention. The other Israeli women's organizations—Israel Women's Network, Kol Ishah, Bat Shalom, there are quite a few Israeli women's organizations—none of them compare to Women of the Wall in terms of the ease and harmony with which decisions are made. Usually, feminist groups fight when the few goodies are being handed out, be they funds or media attention.

P: Are you saying the Women of the Wall don't mind it when one member gets most of the media attention?

A: The one time I see the women riled up is when we are discussing a *d'var Torah*, which someone gives at the beginning of each meeting. Then Nira remembers that this rabbi said this, and Chaia and Betsy are willing to eat her alive because, according to them, this is not true. On issues of Torah they can tear each other apart. Immediately, books are brought in and someone has to be called and some man has to be discussed and consulted until this point is eventually cleared.

P: *(laughing)* I think you are saying that Women of the Wall is not a secular group. A secular group is primarily concerned with secular, worldly goodies. A religious group—at least this one—may have other concerns.

A: This is exactly true. On the issue of Torah text, and on what happens within the prayers, this is a very rigid group. But when it comes to the other goodies, this group is different. Someone resigned from the Israel Women's Network over media attention. I've seen women cry when they are not mentioned in an article. Some of the Women in Black are so afraid that the media attention will go to them that they are not willing to be interviewed by name. They are so afraid of jealousy. The writer Ephraim Kishon used to spell *Eretz Kana'an,* to mean the Land of Jealousy. There is a tremendous envy problem.

P: We know that tremendous wrong can be done in the name of religion. Still, would you say that in this instance, establishing and being part of a prayer community has led to harmony, ethical behavior, and sisterhood?

A: I like how you said it before. *Yediot Acharonot* [an Israeli newspaper] is not the text WOW cares about. There are so few goodies to go around to the other women's organizations. With other organizations I am always so careful to quote other people and reluctant to be interviewed because I have been burnt so often. With us, whenever there was a media profile of one of us, we all rose to the occasion and weren't envious.

P: I can only repeat myself. Psychologically, this is revolutionary.

A: For me, it's a *chavaya mitakent,* a corrective experience. It's wonderful to encounter this after being burnt so many times by other groups.

P: As I understand it, WOW has been wrestling with remaining halakhic but also with the reality of not wanting to dishonor or insult a woman at the Kotel whose prayer *minhag* is not Orthodox.

A: This is a question for Betsy or Chaia. This is out of my turf. One more thing about sisterhood. It consists of more than just knowing what another person's talent or point of view is. We're involved in each other's lives. We meet in each other's homes. We're involved in everyone's babysitting arrangements. We know each other's husbands. We're inside each other's biographies.

P: So, you're saying that sisterhood exists partly because you're *not* a secular group and partly because you all live in the same city, meet often, pray together regularly, and are part of a larger struggle. These are all factors in the creation of a community of spirit.

A: That's it, that really is.

P: A community of spirit.

A: Yes. Also, we're all reading the same texts; we know what we're thinking about. I also know who's trying to get pregnant, who's traveling to the Ukraine or to South America to adopt a baby, who's going to the fertility clinic, who has a functioning organ or a grossly malignant growth. It's not only the text that comes alive. We do, too.

P: You're describing an Ovarian group. What is it about having so many ovaries together in one place?

A: For the past ten years, we were all in our reproductive stage. Either things were going right or going wrong, our uteruses were growing or they were not. These were our issues, and these are also the issues in Jewish women's prayer. Our focus has worked well with the text, which fortified us for our own battles. And also, we allowed each other in. Men who have served in the army or who do reserve duty together will often be lifelong friends even when they have nothing in common. But because they've been in a life-threatening situation together, faced frightening experiences together, it bonds them, it makes for group cohesion. It can turn a guy into a very special person and friend. The Women of the Wall have shared an intense experience for the last thirteen years.

P: In other words, there is a heightened, battlelike intimacy, a life-transforming intimacy.

A: In all candor, I can say to you I'm not sure that anyone would choose me as their mate, friend, or sister in regular circumstances.

P: And you might not choose them.

A: I might not choose them. It's hard for me to even say this, because it's so unlikely, unthinkable, now. We've been ironed together into one garment, one tallit.

P: There are exceptions, but few secular feminists anywhere in the world would describe themselves as woven together into one tribal or antitribal garment. What is different about WOW?

A: We are fighting an issue that is so much bigger and greater than any other thing. Say we were dealing with something smaller, like working on a fairer representation of women in commercials, or on a campaign to have the first woman captain of a combat ship. The issue could be interesting and important and yet not be enough to keep us working together. This struggle gets to the heart of so much of our culture. It's so huge; it really is a huge issue. I think that's why I can't write about it. Every page I write ends up in the garbage in a minute because what we do will affect people for generations. What if I don't choose the right words?

P: As a writer, I'm used to writing books by myself. I knew that I could not write about us on my own, not until I'd first arranged for us to write this book together. The story is bigger than any one of us, bigger than all of us.

A: It deals with territory and compromise and peace, the men and the women, the Arabs and the Jews—there's so much here. Here we are dealing with the most important issues of feminism and democracy in Israel. The group has been able to iron out all our differences very harmoniously.

P: You're a political person. Meretz, your political party, is known as the "antireligion" or pro–civil and secular rights party. How did you come to pray with us the first time?

A: I was a reluctant participant. I was invited by Rivka. As practical as she is, she had immediately thought about where she would put the Torah. She couldn't rent a table from the hotel. She needed a native with a folding table. Rivka saw I was a native. I came holding my folding table. Within one second, the *charedim* at the Kotel knew that we—"these women"—had to be stopped. As if all their lives they'd been trained to know that this was a combat call.

P: Has political support for WOW grown?

A: In America, yes; in Israel, no. In Israel, we have never mattered. We have always been the least important item on the agenda. I don't think things have changed much.

P: Has Meretz, your own party, supported you and WOW—your issue?

A: Not really.

P: But they of all parties should understand that religious freedom is as important as the right to not be religiously coerced.

A: This idea is just now dawning on my colleagues.

P: Has the Labor Party supported us?

A: Not really. They paid no attention when our opponents were trying to pass the bills that would have had us jailed for either six months or seven years for praying.

P: Winning our legal and civil rights in court is one thing; mustering the political will to enact the law is something else. Does WOW have any political allies in this next phase of the struggle?

A: We are a society under siege. The major issues are still "male" issues. Women and children are still lumped together, to be protected by men. We are infantilized. After the May 22, 2000, court decision, we had a variety of wonderful women praying with us at the Kotel. We had women with babies, we had a young soldier in uniform, we had women of all ages and sizes, we had really marvelous visuals. Yet, at two different newspapers, two different editors chose to run the exact same photo, that of a very tall women who looked almost like a man. That's fine, but that's not who we are. It's like they were saying to their female readers, "Do you want to be one of the guys? Do you want to *look* like a guy?"

P: Tell me about WOW's relationship to the police. We were so frustrated when the police refused to arrest anyone who threw rocks, chairs, or teargas at you; who dropped bags of water and dirt on you; who spit, pushed, bit, and cursed you. I know you filed many police reports.

A: One problem is that the police refused to arrest anyone. They would not even arrest *us*, or our opponents. In 1992 or 1993, when the government passed some regulation that would send us to jail for six months for "disturbing the feelings of others by praying," we wanted them to arrest us. We thought that arresting women for praying would rock the Jewish world. It'd be a major wake-up call. At the time, we were brilliant enough to figure out that this regulation would probably lead to worse legislation. And now it has. Now, Shas has proposed jailing us for seven years for praying. The police are practical. They refused to enforce a ridiculous regulation. What does it mean to "disturb someone's feelings"? We will never enforce this. Now, if you disturb the peace in any way, we will detain you for disturbing the peace. Disturbing the peace is a much more widely used regulation.

The other problem was that the police would not arrest violent men and women who *were* disturbing the peace by physically assaulting us. The only person we were ever able to have arrested was one older woman. She couldn't disappear into a yeshiva like the men did. They seemed to operate inside there. She couldn't blend in like that. In 1995 or '96, she did admit cursing and disturbing us. I testified against her in court. The court told her not to bother us anymore, and she didn't.

P: So, only one woman, and no man, was ever forced to stop their violence.

A: Look, I'm not proud about this. I remember having really ambivalent feelings about testifying against her. On the other hand, I knew she would not be fined or jailed but only reprimanded and warned to stop. That was good enough.

P: How do you handle the *charedi* women in the women's section at the Kotel?

A: We have a whole different attitude toward the women. Women who say that our presence disturbs their silent or private prayers—this disturbs us. We really respect their right to pray according to their *minhag*. But when a woman interrupts us and says she's worried about her husband who's praying three hundred yards away, on the other side of the partition, we don't respect this view. We have found that, overall, the men cannot be disturbed by the women. We are unheard on the other side of the partition.

P: Well, the sky is so high.

A: And the general noise level is also very high. There are church bells, the muezzin's call from the mosque, and enormous "noise" from many competing religious services, including many different *minyanim* of Jewish men. You have to work hard to be disturbed by Women of the Wall. But, you know, the "disturbance" we create is the symbolic invasion of territory. "We don't want you there because this is men's turf."

P: It's the ultimate boys-only club.

A: Right. We want to reclaim this symbolic turf.

P: In 1954, an African-American woman, Claudette Colvin, refused to sit at the back of the bus in Montgomery, Alabama. Soon afterwards, Mary Louise Smith also refused to do so. Finally, the NAACP decided to back Rosa Parks, who, on December 1, 1955, was arrested for refusing to move to the back of the bus. Parks and the NAACP were, symbolically, challenging the Jim Crow segregation in the American South.

A: We are the same. Rosa Parks wasn't only about a bus issue. We are in the back of the bus, and we want to move to the front of the bus, and people are telling us this is unacceptable.

P: Actually, we are also different, because WOW is not seeking integration but a separate-but-equal prayer option. You are a Reform Jew, yet as part of WOW you have refused to accept Robinson's Arch as an alternative prayer site. The Masorati movement has done so.

A: The Conservatives have, and I think they made a mistake. If you want to get our group riled up, just say "Robinson's Arch." Watch us erupt. We see accepting it as accepting second-class citizenship. Look, I don't need the government's permission to let me pray next to any other wall in Jerusalem. There is just this one Wall, and, unfortunately, at that Wall I do need government permission in order to pray [in a group].

P: Has the Masorati decision hurt us?

A: I think so. The government official who helped this happen, Chaim Herzog, is the grandson of a chief rabbi and the son of a general. He's very proud of brokering an achievement that is seen as "positive" by all. The Conservatives are not seeing this as a permanent solution but only as an experiment. And their experiment is going pretty well. They have a spiritual feeling; it doesn't feel like an archaeological site to them. However, they have used it only on holidays, when the archaeological site is not open for work. I wonder how they will feel when there are a thousand Japanese tourists gawking at them as they are praying, or there are archaeologists there, moving things up and down. Also, as we know, it is not accessible for the handicapped.

Symbolically, they have accepted being away from the rest of Israel.

P: Let me play devil's advocate for a moment. You've found the Archaeological Gardens to be a beautiful place to daven; it's also a respectable, spiritual place. . . .

A: So is my living room! Andy Sacks, the Masorati leader, is politically naive. In politics, there are no temporary solutions. Temporary solutions are the ones that last the longest.

P: The Reform movement has been very supportive of us and very principled, both behind the scenes and visibly.

A: The Reform movements in America, Australia, Canada, and England have been very supportive. The Israeli Reform movement—that's another story. For example, on May 23, 2000, Jonathan Livni, its chairman, said that he didn't feel that Women at the Wall was "his struggle." Seven years ago, Gloria Berish, then chairwoman of the Israeli Reform movement, also said that Women of the Wall was not her struggle.

P: Uri Regev has refused to accept Robinson's Arch or to approach the Court until the matter of Women of the Wall has been resolved.

A: Uri Regev is my candidate for the Jerusalem Religious Council. He and the Religious Action Center, the political arm of the Reform movement, have always been a great help to us, both in terms of lobbying and the media. I'm personally part of the Religious Action Center. My work with Uri will definitely improve the climate of opinion about us.

P: As much as WOW needs all the allies we can find, as I understand it, WOW is also endangered by support from groups, including this one, that would only add us to a long list of other very different kinds of issues and would, in our name, control our political and media lobbying and our access to independent funding.

So at this moment, our political allies are very few. A few Meretz members have begun to support us—Naomi Chazan, for example. But modern and liberal Orthodox Israelis do not have a high opinion of Meretz and may not join a coalition with Meretz on our behalf. Do you place your trust in the Supreme Court? Do you believe that the nine-judge panel will ultimately confirm our May 22 legal victory?

A: I've learned that you can win and lose at the same time. The May 22 decision helped us "win" in the media. But then the Court very quickly decided to allow the government to appeal the decision. In other cases, the Court took a much longer time to make such a decision. When our case came up, the Court was in turmoil over some other controversial decisions they had made, such as the jailing of Shas's Aryeh Deri. Some Supreme Court judges have bodyguards because of death threats. The Court is trying to walk a very thin line. It is very sensitive about entering the arena of religion. The Court was begging us to accept a compromise and was not ordering the government to immediately enforce our rights. The Supreme Court won't do anything that would put the Court at risk. They are part of the political process, not totally above it. They will sell us down the river if they have to.

P: May I quote you on this?

A: Sure!

P: What, then, are our political options? Civil disobedience?

A: We have a lot of hard work ahead of us. We in Israel have a huge task. We must grow. You in America have to muster all the political links that you have—and you do have them. We will both have to do it. I'm not afraid of the political work. We're going to succeed in that.

P: I think so, too.

A: We have the tenacity, we have the cause. We haven't done all of the legwork. We haven't made sure that every Jewish woman and every Jewish man knows about us and understands why our struggle is important. We need them to catch our enthusiasm.

P: We'd have to grow, both in Israel and in the States. We would have to get ourselves seriously funded—something that has never happened. But we might also have to go outside both the legal and political system. Would women be willing to do civil disobedience, get arrested?

A: Absolutely! We are hoping that Shas actually passes the bill that would put us in jail for seven years.

P: You would sit in jail for seven years?

A: We have quite a few women who are willing to become prisoners of conscience.

P: Prisoners of conscience . . .

A: If the police weren't ready to arrest us for six months, do you think they'd arrest us for seven years? If they did, it would be very good for us, both legally and in terms of media support. Imagine what Amnesty International will do with this!

P: Thank you, Anat. We'll end here for now.

RABBI GEELA RAYZEL RAPHAEL

Sacred Tears

THE KOTEL HAS ALWAYS BEEN a very magical, powerful place for me. It contains the energy of thousands of Jewish prayers throughout time and space. The site is a vortex for sacred tears and heart openings compiled through centuries. The presence of ancestors long gone are palpable, the veils between the worlds lift, and the energy of the Shekhinah radiates to all who attune to Her.

HARRIET KURLANDER

Torah Dedication Ceremony

WEDNESDAY MORNING, still thoroughly unaware that the next day we would all make history, I joined Rivka and her husband, Rabbi Irwin Haut *(z"l)*, for breakfast. When Rivka went to the buffet, Rabbi Haut leaned over the table and, in a hushed voice, asked if I thought the American Jewish Congress should arrange for some men to be at the Kotel Thursday morning to protect the women.

"What are you suggesting?" I asked him. "Why would they need protection?"

"I don't think you understand, Harriet," he quietly explained. "This has never been done before and the *charedim* will not approve. They could react violently."

I was thoroughly shaken. The American Jewish Congress was responsible for the safety and security of hundreds of women from around the world. So much effort, time, and money had been invested in this conference. Would violence be its legacy? It was unthinkable. We could not allow that to happen.

I immediately left the breakfast table and rushed to the American Jewish Congress office in the hotel. On the way, I met Henry Siegman, our executive director and an Orthodox rabbi. "Henry, the women are taking a Torah to the Kotel tomorrow morning. Is this historic? Will there be violence? What must we do to protect the women?" Although clearly he was surprised, he calmly replied, "This is historic, but do not worry, we will make certain that the women are safe."

Listening to the heated discussion and different opinions expressed by the women most directly involved in the decision making (many strongly opposed going, others were just as passionately in favor), I was torn by my own conflicting emotions. At that time I was a member of the Stephen Wise Free Synagogue in New York, the synagogue that hired the first woman rabbi, Sally Priesand. What a powerful image on our *bimah*—Rabbi Helene Ferris and Cantor Ellen Math leading services! As a Reform Jew, I have always had all the synagogue, prayer, and Torah I wanted and needed. The Kotel is my historic place; I always go there first when I enter Jerusalem, to pay my respect. I am drawn there at sunset on Shabbat, because the images before my eyes allow me to step back into time. However, the Kotel is *not* my synagogue, and this is *not* my fight.

On the other hand, what could be more passive and benign than women praying? Why should anyone feel menaced by women's spirituality? Or, was the opposition merely symbolic of a deeper and more fundamental fear: the fear of women's fuller participation in the broad range of human experience? Furthermore, if I profess to be a feminist and want to have every opportunity to realize my dream, don't I have an obligation to help other women realize theirs, whatever that dream may be, even if it is not one I share? I knew that Orthodox women were on the verge of realizing their dream, but they needed our help. That was all that really mattered.

For me, the prayer service at the Kotel is a paradigm for the future: Women from all parts of the world, reflecting different feminist perspectives and representing every denomination of Judaism, will put aside these differences, and by helping Orthodox women to empower themselves, we will also empower each other.

A movement was born.

Almost a year later, in November–December 1989, the American Jewish Congress joined the International Committee for Women of the Wall (ICWOW) in its mission to donate a Torah to the women of Jerusalem. The Torah was bought with contributions from hundreds of Jewish women and men around the world.

The scheduled Torah dedication ceremony at the Laromme Hotel was to follow an evening outdoor prayer service at the nearby park and a candlelight procession back to the hotel. The Jerusalem rabbinate threatened to revoke the hotel's kashrut certificate and impose a ban on the hotel if the ceremony took place on its premises. The hotel informed the American Jewish Congress that not only was the Torah dedication ceremony canceled, but a scheduled women's Shabbat Torah service would be canceled as well.

The Jerusalem Hotel Association strongly protested the interference of the rabbinate in matters unrelated to kashrut laws, maintaining that the rabbinate has no right to dictate what sort of functions hotels may host, and claiming that millions of dollars of income are lost annually for fear of the revocation of kashrut status.

The American Jewish Congress filed a lawsuit against the Laromme Hotel, to compel it to fulfill its contractual obligations, and against the Jerusalem rabbinate, for causing the breach of contract. Although the court upheld the hotel's action in canceling the dedication ceremony, it ruled that the hotel must provide the women with a place to hold their Shabbat morning service.

Several days later, when the ICWOW tried to pray at the Kotel with the Torah, as many had done exactly one year earlier, they were prevented from entering the area by Ministry of Religious Affairs officials. This refusal became ICWOW's grounds for lodging a lawsuit in the Israeli Supreme Court. The group prayed instead at a magnificent site overlooking and facing the Kotel.

When we had completed our service and were making our way out in semiprocession with the Torah, a group of tourists, North African Jews on their way to the Kotel, approached us. One by one, they reached out to reverently kiss the Torah, unconcerned that it was being carried by a woman, clearly unaware of any controversy surrounding this fact.

Now, so many years later, I still consider myself fortunate to have been there, to have seen history unfold before my eyes. I am surprised at how swiftly emotions surface, and I am grateful that my memories are sharp and clear. I continue to be inspired by the courage and determination of a small band of women who had a dream and made it come true. I will always stand in awe of the Women of the Wall, who, despite violence and ridicule, would not be deterred from their quest to secure the right of all Jewish women to pray communally at the Western Wall.

HAVIVA NER–DAVID

Tzitzit and Tefillin
at the Kotel

IT'S 8:00 A.M., and I am at the Archaeological Gardens, where we, Nashot haKotel[1] (Women of the Wall), read from the Torah scroll each month on Rosh Chodesh, the celebration of the new moon. We read from the Torah scroll here, away from the Kotel itself or even the plaza behind it, because we have been forbidden by Israeli law to read from a Torah at the Wall. This was not always the case, but almost ten years ago, when a group of women came with a Torah scroll to the Kotel to pray, they were attacked by a group of *charedim*, ultra-Orthodox Jews. Since then, there has been an ongoing case in the Supreme Court, which, once decided, should determine whether or not a group of women can pray aloud together using a Torah scroll, wearing *tallitot*, at the Kotel. In the meantime, the Court has forbidden all of the above.

I am standing in an alcove made of Jerusalem stone, beside a hole in the stone that creates a glassless window, and I am looking out at the gray sky over the Kotel plaza. Only ten minutes ago, we were praying down there, on the women's side of the seven-foot-high *mechitzah* that separates the women from the men in front of the Wall. I was with a group of women, huddling together against the cold. Winter has just arrived here in Jerusalem, and with it a chill that the ancient stones surrounding the Kotel plaza seem to soak up. To warm both our souls and our physical bodies, we swayed and rocked and hugged ourselves closely. We were a mass of women, praying aloud, which is a rare occurrence at the Kotel. The *charedim* have monopolized this historical sacred space that should belong to the whole Jewish people, and the Israeli government has allowed them to do so.

In *charedi* society, women do not pray collectively, nor do they raise their voices in prayer. Women, according to this interpretation of Judaism, should be quiet, private beings. Modesty, as they define it, means being internal and silent; modesty, as they see it, is a woman's trait and virtue. If you are a woman, and you are not silent, you are, they believe, going against the purpose for which you were put on this earth by God. You are a rebellious, provocative, and even dangerous woman.

It has been three months since my husband, two children, and I made our big move, our *aliyah*, to Israel. It is the first day of Kislev, the month in which we celebrate the holiday of *Hanukkah*, when the small group of Jewish Maccabees defeated the large and strong Greek army. It is a month to contemplate modes of empowerment aside from physical strength, and to remind ourselves that a struggle for what one believes in, no matter how seemingly hopeless, is worthwhile.

I come here each month with these women on Rosh Chodesh, which, according to rabbinic literature, was the holiday given specifically to women as a reward for not having donated jewelry toward the building of the golden calf. Each month, we come to this Wall—the place that modern Jews around the world have implicitly chosen as our most holy spot—to pray as a group of women. Coming from various religious communities and backgrounds, we join into one cohesive unit for this prayer service, to be uplifted and empowered by our collective presence. This monthly gathering is one of the things I enjoy most about living here in Jerusalem. I feel privileged to be part of this sincere and intensely spiritual group that is committed in a very deep sense to *tikkun olam*, the repairing of the world.

This month's service, however, was terribly disturbing. Within two minutes of beginning our *tefillah* (prayer service), we heard shouting from the other side of the *mechitzah*: "*Goyim!* [Gentiles!], *T'meot!* [Impure!], *Naziyim!* [Nazis!], *Asur!* [Forbidden!]." The hatred in these voices made me shudder. At first I pretended to myself that they were not yelling at us. Then I realized that those men in black-black hats, black coats, black suits, and black shoes were throwing objects at us over the *mechitzah*: metal chairs, tables, and whatever else they could find. They might well have killed us in the name of the same God to whom we both came to the Kotel to pray.

Immediately, a security guard ordered *us* to leave the premises—not those who were attacking us, who were causing the violence, but rather, us, the victims of the violence. They were breaking the law, but we, who had hushed our voices in order *not* to break the law and disturb those who are offended by our voices, were banished.

"*HaKotel shelanu!* [The Kotel is ours!]" one *charedi* woman yelled out to me in triumph as we left, and I felt a heaviness bear down on my heart. Even ultra-Orthodox women feel threatened by our presence. It is not enough for them to restrict themselves so extensively; it is not enough that they have chosen for themselves a Judaism that represses their voices. They feel the need to force their own stringencies and narrow interpretation of what constitutes a Jewish lifestyle upon us. They join the men of their community in claiming public Jewish space as their own.

Now, with that experience behind me, I am up at the Archaeological Gardens, still processing the hatred I have just encountered. I have mixed feelings about being here. On the one hand, I feel safer away from those who are hostile to our presence. On the other hand, I am angered at being banished from the Wall. My hope is that someday we will be able to pray down there at the Wall with the same comfort, ease, and joy that we can up here.

I drape my tallit, my prayer shawl, over my head, and suddenly it is dark. I block out all distractions for a completely private moment with God. I inhale a deep breath of clean morning air, thinking about life and light and the kindness that God has bestowed on me, and say in Hebrew:

> How precious is Your lovingkindness, O God! The children of humanity take refuge in the shadow of Your wings. May they be sated from the abundance of Your house; and may You give them to drink from the stream of Your delights. For with You is the source of all life—by Your light we shall see light. Extend Your kindness to those who know You, and Your charity to the upright of heart.

I remember when I first decided to start wearing *tzitzit.* I had already taken upon myself the mitzvah of wearing tefillin each morning while praying, a practice that only men are obligated to perform by traditional Jewish law. I had been praying with tefillin for months and had been contemplating taking upon myself another traditionally male mitzvah, tallit, but I had not yet taken that step. Somehow, I was not yet spiritually ready. Yet on that one particular morning, I was praying the morning service with my tefillin and reciting the *Shema.* In that prayer, which Jews (or, according to Halakhah, Jewish men) are supposed to recite three times each day, the third paragraph says that God commanded us to wear fringes, *tzitzit*, on the corners of our garments. When we say the word *tzitzit*, which appears three times in the prayer, we are supposed to kiss the fringes on our *tallit katan* (four-cornered undergarment with ritual fringes at the four corners) or *tallit gadol* (four-cornered prayer shawl with ritual fringes at the four corners) to highlight the fact that we are indeed performing this mitzvah. This paragraph is a direct quotation from the Book of Numbers.

Although a woman is not halakhically required to recite the *Shema*, I was never told or made to feel as a child that I should not recite it (which was not the case with doing the mitzvah of *tzitzit* itself). Girls and boys alike were expected to recite this paragraph as part of our daily morning prayer service. Somehow it never seemed strange to me that I was saying that God commanded us to wear *tzitzit* when everything else around me indicated that not only wasn't I commanded to wear *tzitzit*, but I should not wear them.

This one particular morning, however, as I recited the *Shema*, the words jumped out at me. The irony of what I was saying aroused me from years of empty recitation. For twenty-two years I had been reciting this prayer without meaning what I was saying, and I knew that I could never again recite that particular paragraph during morning prayers unless I too was wearing *tzitzit* and could kiss the fringes while I said the word *tzitzit*, just as I had seen the men and boys around me doing since my childhood.

Since that moment, I have felt personally commanded by God to wear *tzitzit*, no matter what I have been told by teachers and rabbis throughout the years about a woman not being obligated to perform this mitzvah. The traditional rationale behind a woman's exemption from this mitzvah is that it is a positive timebound commandment (we are required to wear *tzitzit* only during daylight hours, when they can be seen by natural light, although there is no prohibition against wearing them at night), and women are exempt from most positive timebound commandments. However, I cannot find a reason that women as a class today should be exempt from performing this mitzvah, which to me feels related to sanctifying our bodies and the clothing with which we cover our nakedness. It is also a constant reminder of what is expected of us as Jewish people bound by the mitzvot. The essence of the mitzvah itself has no relation to time. It seems as though women are missing out on the power of performing this mitzvah because of a technicality. Performing this mitzvah in no way interferes with one's daily schedule, which one could argue that donning tefillin does. I imagine that God is waiting for Jewish women to reclaim this mitzvah, to say, "It is ours, too! How dare you take it away from us?!"

I am not insisting that all women take on this mitzvah, although obviously I think it would be a fine idea. Performance of this mitzvah—as well as the others from which women are exempt—must stem from a desire within the woman. I understand that there are many women who feel comfortable in the ritual role that Halakhah has thus far carved out for them. My hope is that some day masses of women will see the beauty in these mitzvot enough to set aside their exemption, as they have already done with other timebound mitzvot, such as shofar (hearing the blowing of the ram's horn on Rosh Hashanah) and sukkah (sitting in a temporary hut on Sukkot). Until then, I am asking only that the small number of women who today feel this deep desire to don tefillin and wear *tzitzit* not be discouraged from doing so.

The Rema, Rav Moshe Isserles—the Eastern European legal codifier from the sixteenth century whose gloss to the *Shulchan Arukh*, the Code of Jewish Law, is probably the most influential Ashkenazi compilation of Halakhah—gives the following reason to discour-age women from taking upon themselves this mitzvah: *yoharah,* pride or boastfulness (see *Shulchan Arukh, OC* 17:2). The commandment in the Torah is to place *tzitzit* on the comers of a four-cornered garment, and because today we do not wear four-cornered gar-ments, men especially put on a four-cornered garment in order to perform this mitzvah, to which they are obligated. There is an inter-pretation of *yoharah* that claims, therefore, that it would be a show of excessive pride if women too performed this mitzvah, since they are not obligated to the mitzvah altogether.

Yet I wonder, if a woman wears her *tallit katan* beneath her cloth-ing, with no one even seeing it, is that a show of boastfulness? And even for women who, like myself, also wear a *tallit gadol* when they pray in the mornings, it seems to me that this act is also a very personal one, between the woman and her Creator. All the women I have spoken to who have taken upon themselves this mitzvah have described it to me in very personal terms. The tallit enhances their *tefillah,* they tell me; it gives them more *kavanah,* more ability to concentrate. In fact, they tell me, it helps them to feel more private in their prayers, because they can use the tallit to create a kind of personal prayer tent. The Rabbis' fear of *yoharah* seems to me to be a projection of their own feelings upon women. They were suspi-cious of the motivations of a woman who would want to adopt a mitzvah that she was not obligated to perform, assuming she was driven by exhibitionism.

I also wonder, did the Rabbis' discomfort with a woman per-forming this mitzvah have more to do with their view of women as inferior, as less holy in some ways, and therefore not worthy of plac-ing this sacred garment on their bodies? It is interesting that the major-ity opinion in Halakhah does not take issue with women performing other mitzvot from which they are exempt. It is only tefillin and *tzitzit*, holy objects or garments that must be worn, that cause the problem. I know that as a woman, I find these mitzvot especially meaningful, because they help me to see my body as worthy of sanctification—an idea that many women, including myself, may find difficult to internalize after years of being bombarded with messages to the contrary.

Besides, don't women too need to be reminded of the mitzvot? *Tzitzit* are a visual reminder of God's will and God's presence in our lives at each and every moment of the day, and I know that I need such a reminder. Even when I am spending the entire day sitting and studying Torah, it is easy, for example, to forget to pray the afternoon prayer service before sundown. When I am spending the day with my young, demanding children, it is even easier to forget to perform certain mitzvot, especially those that must be performed at a certain time. I realize that this is one of the arguments for exempting women from timebound mitzvot, but the mitzvah of *tzitzit* is not an act that comes and goes as the hands of the clock turn. On the contrary, it serves as a reminder to perform mitzvot!

My *tzitzit* remind me all day of what I would like to be, even when I cannot live up to the image I see in the fringes before me. They remind me that my body is holy and that I was created in the image of God. This is why I wear *tzitzit*, despite the criticism and even the berating I receive, and despite the fact that it sets me apart from virtually every other religious (and nonreligious) Jewish woman.

With my white and gray tallit now wrapped around me, I take my tefillin out of their blue velvet bag. Wearing tefillin is not a prohibition for women. Influential legal codifiers such as the Rema and Hafez Hayyim, the author of *Mishnah Berurah*, discourage women from performing this mitzvah, however. The latter quotes an idea raised by the Tosafot, a group of medieval commentators on the Talmud, that a woman should not don tefillin because of the issue of *guf naki,* the requirement that one's body must be clean while performing this mitzvah. Traditionally, only men have worn tefillin, except for a few exceptions recorded throughout Jewish history: Michal, King Saul's daughter and King David's first wife, wore tefillin, the Talmud tells us. There is also a tradition that the three daughters of Rashi, the eleventh-century French scholar who wrote the most commonly studied commentary on the Bible and Talmud, wore tefillin, as did Chana Rochel Werbermacher, the Maiden of Ludomir, a Hasidic woman who had a large following in the nineteenth century.

Although I know that there have been other women throughout the ages who have chosen to wear tefillin, they have been anomalies and could probably fit into one room. In the past two decades, since women have been given the opportunity to become rabbis in the Conservative movement and must, as a requirement for ordination, wear tefillin every morning when they pray, there have been more women taking on this practice. However, I cannot think of more than twenty women who are not Conservative rabbis or rabbinical students who wear tefillin.

Having donned both my arm and head tefillin, I recite the following verse, meditating on my personal *brit,* or covenant, with God: "I will betroth you to Me forever, and I will betroth you to Me with righteousness, justice, kindness, and mercy. I will betroth you to Me with fidelity, and you will know God."

I wonder! How will I strive to fulfill my side of the *brit* today?

The tefillin remind me that my obligation to help bring God's divine plan into the human world is through the actions of my hands and the thoughts in my head. By praying at the Kotel each month with this group of women, I believe that I am enacting God's plan. We are working for justice, our vision of a diverse yet unified Jewish nation, and an open, progressive Judaism that is about inclusion rather than exclusion.

It saddens me that I cannot wear my tallit and tefillin at the Wall. My *tefillah* would be so much more enhanced. I feel so uplifted, so much a part of Jewish history, when I pray at the Kotel, and yet I cannot pray the way in which I am accustomed. I feel religiously oppressed by my own people.

When I come here to pray each month, I do not kiss my *tzitzit* fringes when I recite the *Shema.* Instead, I can only keep them in mind as I say the words "And God said to Moses: Speak to the Children of Israel and tell them to make for themselves *tzitzit* on the four corners of their garments for generations." I imagine myself kissing the fringes that are beneath my shirt, praying that some day I won't have to feel like a Marrano here in the Jewish homeland.

People ask us, the Women of the Wall, why we care so much about praying at the Kotel. If we want to pray as a group of women, sing aloud together with *tallitot* and read from a Torah, we can do so somewhere else. No one can object to our doing so in a private home, for example.

This question surprised me the first time it was asked of me. I assumed that most Jews, especially religious ones, felt the way I do about the Kotel. The Kotel has always symbolized for me the Jewish people's return to Zion in the twentieth century. It was one of the retaining walls of our Second Temple. The feeling I have when standing there about the history of the place is so powerful. The fact that we are so privileged to be able to pray there, and that only thirty-five years ago we could not, is reason enough to feel pulled to the site. When, as a child, I came to visit Israel, the Kotel was our first stop and last stop. For me, the question seems ridiculous. Why the Kotel? "Why not the Kotel?" I would ask.

The year after my bat mitzvah, the boys in my grade began, one after another, to turn thirteen, the age at which a boy becomes responsible for his own deeds, the age of bar mitzvah.

I had witnessed my older brother's bar mitzvah and the enormous preparation that went into it. The party itself was much more lavish than my own, but that was not what bothered me most. The few months I spent preparing the speech for my bat mitzvah paled in comparison to the year Jonathan spent in preparation for his bar mitzvah. After all, not only did he have to deliver a *devar Torah*, but also he had to chant an entire portion from the Torah scroll without any punctuation or vowels, all with the correct musical notes, as well as lead the *tefillah* (prayer service) and chant the *haftarah*, a reading from the Prophets, also according to the correct musical notes. The thought of performing this enormous one-person show was frightening; so when my brother prepared for his bar mitzvah, I was more relieved than jealous that I would not have to do the same.

Once I saw my male peers reaching bar mitzvah, however, reading from the Torah and leading the service, I suddenly awoke to the inequity of the religious laws. All the boys in my class managed to pull it off, even those who received much poorer grades than I did in the religious subjects in school. I began to feel that I was cheated by not even being allowed to try. This was a rite of passage that all boys went through to prepare them for the challenges of adulthood as responsible and active members of our religious community, and it appeared that I and my female peers were not expected to live up to such challenges. Chanting from the Torah was not a skill that an Orthodox Jewish girl needed to learn, because when would she use it? Women did not get close enough to touch the Torah, let alone read from it.

In addition, as the boys in my class became of bar mitzvah age, they began to show up for morning prayer at school with their tefillin, which are worn during morning prayers on weekdays. The boys had worn their *tzitzit* and *kipot* since they were three years old, whereas the girls did not. At that point in my childhood, this inequity was merely a sociological gender difference, comparable to the boys wearing pants and the girls wearing skirts and dresses. It was more of a dress-code disparity and didn't hold great religious significance for me at the time, perhaps because it was introduced at such a young age. However, when those same boys, who had for years been wearing their *kipot* and *tzitzit*, showed up in seventh grade with their blue velvet bags containing their shining new leather tefillin, I was bothered terribly by the fact that they had something tangible to show for their new status as adults in our religion, and I had nothing. Coming of age for my male peers meant taking on more mitzvot, whereas for me it meant being excluded from them. This was a harsh and poignant awakening to my place as a young woman in Jewish religious life.

I watched from the other side of the *mechitzah* as the boys in my class wrapped the leather tefillin straps around their forearms and placed them on their heads—the boxes containing the sacred *Shema* between their eyes and on their biceps as a reminder of how this proclamation of God's oneness should always be on their minds and integrated into their actions—and I longed for some tangible ritual to draw me closer to God at this turning point in my life as a Jew. There was nothing. At the close of my first year as a newly initiated responsible member of the Jewish people, I was beginning to get a taste of the alienation that would plague me as a religiously observant Jewish woman. In order to be an insider, I would have to remain outside.

Today, as I pray at the Kotel, I feel the same way. Although I have taken upon myself the obligation of praying with tefillin and a tallit each morning, when I am at the Kotel I cannot do so. Although my practice is within the bounds of mainstream Jewish law, here I am forced to abide by the strict interpretation of the ultra-Orthodox community. I have studied the texts, and I know that no one can claim that what I do is forbidden. Away from the Kotel, I have found a way to integrate my feminist and traditional selves, and yet when I pray at the Kotel I feel as though I am thrown back to my childhood, sitting behind the *mechitzah*, looking longingly over at the men and boys, who are reading from the Torah, wrapped in their *tallitot* and tefillin, uninhibited, singing so joyously and familiarly to God. I, and other women like me, have worked hard to create a space for ourselves within the tradition. Nevertheless, at the Kotel we are still on the sidelines looking in, outsiders in our own religion.

There is no explicit reason given in the Talmud for women being exempt from positive timebound commandments, but theories abound among medieval and modern religious thinkers alike. A common view that is bandied about, although I could not find it published anywhere, is that the exemption is due to the fact that women are busy raising children, so their time is left more flexible to devote to the erratic schedule of child rearing, an equally important task to davening. Another popular explanation, suggested by Rabbis Emanuel Rackman and Norman Lamm, for instance, is that women are innately more aware of the sanctity of time due to their bodily cycle, so they do not need these timebound mitzvot, which are designed in part to make us aware of time and its cyclical nature, and to sanctify time by devoting it to mitzvot. They add that if and when a woman marries and keeps the laws of family purity, that mitzvah will serve as a substitute for the timebound mitzvot. Still others, such as Rabbi Jacob Anatoli of the thirteenth century, say that a woman should be serving her husband, so the Rabbis didn't want to obligate her in mitzvot that might take her away from her God-given role. Rabbi David ben Joseph Avudraham, of the fourteenth century, offers a similar explanation, but he does not declare that women *should* be subservient to their husbands. Instead, he points out that women are in fact subservient to their husbands, so the Rabbis did not want to create a situation in which her husband would be asking her to do one thing when God was asking her to do another (e.g., lay tefillin). In order to preserve the peace in the home *(shalom bayit)*, they exempted women from some of the mitzvot that must be performed at a specific time. (The idea behind this view is that God would be more understanding than her husband!)

Still another theory is that the category of positive timebound mitzvot is descriptive and not prescriptive, because there are many positive timebound mitzvot that a woman *is* required to perform. Rabbi Saul Berman, a contemporary modern Orthodox rabbi, one of the proponents of this theory, prefers to use the categories of public mitzvot and private mitzvot. He writes in his article "The Status of Women in *Halachic* Judaism" that it is public ritual from which women were exempt, perhaps because women are innately more private beings or perhaps because the Rabbis were sending the message that women should be more private than men.

Rabbi Samson Raphael Hirsch, of nineteenth-century Germany, suggested that women are spiritually superior to men (both innately and due to their more cloistered existence away from the temptations and distractions of the world outside the home) and therefore do not need these mitzvot.

Although there are many theories, the actual reason for the exemption remains a mystery. No one theory includes all of the mitzvot from which women are exempt. For instance, women's exemption from wearing *tzitzit* is not explained by any of these theories. If it is a public-private issue, *tzitzit* are not a public ritual, so why are women exempt from wearing them? If the Rabbis were worried about children, wearing *tzitzit* does not interfere with the hectic life of a full-time mother. Although *tzitzit* are required only during the day, one can choose to wear them also at night. Moreover, the mitzvah does not require any time commitment whatsoever. Nor do *tzitzit* remind us of the cyclical nature of time.

These theories also do not jive with the historical reality of the time in which the exemption originated. A woman in talmudic times lived with her husband's family, so she would have had a number of people around to care for her children while she performed a mitzvah. Moreover, her husband would have been equally as busy with household chores as she was, unless they were of the upper class of society, in which case they would both have had servants to perform household and childcare duties, and both husband and wife would have been free to perform mitzvot. As for the idea that women do not need these mitzvot, because women are obligated in many positive timebound mitzvot—such as Shabbat candlelighting, general prayer, and the Grace after Meals—the notion that they are in some way above performing these mitzvot does not make sense. This is especially so because the general attitude of the Rabbis in the

Talmud toward women seems to put them on a lower spiritual level than men, not a higher one.

In addition, these theories are no longer applicable today, at least not in the world in which I live. Fathers, for the most part, are beginning to take on substantial parenting responsibilities. If women are exempt from timebound mitzvot because of their parenting responsibilities, then men who are caring for their children full-time also should be exempt. (My view is based on the assumption that greater paternal involvement in child rearing is a positive societal development; I realize that not all communities accept this as a given.) Furthermore, what about women who are not mothers, or women who are no longer involved in the daily care of children because their children are grown?

In addition, women are active in the public sphere today, so unless we advocate returning women exclusively to the private sphere, we should not perpetuate an exemption from what Berman calls the public mitzvot.

Although I can speak only for myself, my experience is that menstruating and even keeping the laws of family purity do not replace the need for mitzvot such as tefillin, shofar, or sukkah. I don't understand how one can substitute for the other; they are such different experiences. Praying with tefillin each morning adds an element to my spiritual life that is not fulfilled through menstruation or even the mitzvot associated with menstruation, such as immersing in the *mikvah* each month seven days after my bleeding stops. All of these are important mitzvot in my life, filling very different functions.

Our lives are radically different than women's lives were during the time of the Talmud. Women today, just as much as men, are active in a world that is very much governed by the clock. Even with menstruation as a reminder of the cycle of the moon, we still live our daily lives by clock time, not lunar time. Whether we are working or even mothering full-time, there are schedules to keep, which often can seem as though they have taken over our lives. Even women need to stop and remind themselves that there is a higher power more important than the clock, that time actually is in the hands of God.

Most important, perhaps, this theory does not apply to post-menopausal women, and with the majority of women today living many years after menopause, this is a serious oversight. The theory that I find most convincing, therefore, is the one that Judith Hauptman posits in her book *Rereading the Rabbis: A Woman's Voice.* She defines the category of positive timebound mitzvot as mitzvot that will come your way no matter what the circumstances of your life. Hauptman posits that women were exempt from performing this category of mitzvot, "the highest form of ritual act," in order to restrict their performance to men, to heads of household. The Mishnah, where this exemption first appears in halakhic literature, categorizes it with the *mishnayot* that deal with the acquisition of a wife and the hierarchy of society in mishnaic times. In these *mishnayot* we find that slaves, like women, also were exempt from certain mitzvot. From the context of this *mishnah*, it seems clear that women's exemption stemmed not from women's higher spiritual level but rather from their lower social status. There is no doubt that men were of higher social standing than women in the time of the Mishnah; therefore, it is easy to understand why the Rabbis would have placed women on a lower rung on the ladder of religious worship.

No matter what the reason for this exemption, it is interesting to note that most mitzvot in this positive timebound category are performed by women today with no objection from contemporary rabbis. In fact, I'd say that often they are encouraged to perform them. Take, for example, the blowing of the shofar on Rosh Hashanah. It has become the practice in most Orthodox synagogues to have a special shofar blowing for women who missed hearing the blasts because of a conflict with their responsibilities at home. Although women are not required by the letter of the law to hear the shofar, they are encouraged to perform that mitzvah nevertheless. Until I learned the Halakhah on this matter from the original sources, I had always assumed that women were required to hear the shofar. Tefillin and *tzitzit* both fit into this category of positive timebound mitzvot. Tefillin are worn only during the morning prayers, and *tzitzit* are worn only when it is light outside. Women are neither obligated to wear tefillin and *tzitzit* nor encouraged to take these mitzvot upon themselves even if they feel able and willing.

Mochin b'yadan—literally, "we prevent their hands"—the Rema writes about women wearing tefillin. He based his opinion on the writings of the Tosafot, who were worried about *guf naki*, bodily cleanliness. It is unclear whether they thought that a woman's body was less clean than a man's. Two explanations of *guf naki* appear in the Talmud (*Shabbat* 49a and 130a): one should not flatulate or sleep while wearing tefillin. Accordingly, women must pass gas and sleep more than men, or at least have less control over these two bodily functions than men have.

Another explanation of *guf naki* is given by the Maharam of Rothenberg, of the thirteenth century (see *Tashbetz*, paragraph 270, and *Kol Bo*, paragraph 21). He connects it, understandably, with menstruation, as that is the one bodily function that is unique to women that could be considered unsanitary. Another explanation would posit that women are no less clean than men, but that since a woman is not obligated to wear tefillin, she should not take the risk of sullying these holy objects, whereas a man is obligated and must therefore take the risk, although his body too may be unclean.

Or perhaps, as the Magen Avraham (*Shulchan Arukh, OC* 38) asserts, because women are not obligated in this mitzvah, they might not be as careful in the proper performance of it as are men, who are obligated. However, in the Babylonian Talmud, the discussion of this issue includes the example of Michal, who, we are told, "wore tefillin and the Sages did not protest her action" (*Eruvin* 96a). (The Jerusalem Talmud, which is considered less authoritative for halakhic purposes than the Babylonian Talmud, says that the Sages did protest.) Even in the minds of the Babylonian sages, there was room to stray from the norm.

Women are discouraged from wearing *tzitzit* for similar reasons. The commandment in the Torah is to wear fringes on any four-cornered garments; because people today no longer wear four-cornered garments, technically no one is obligated to wear *tzitzit.* However, we want to preserve this central mitzvah, so the custom is to wear a separate four-cornered garment beneath one's clothing all day long, as well as a four-cornered prayer shawl during the morning service. The Rema considered a woman who decides to take on these extra obligations guilty of *yoharah,* or pride, a "holier-than-thou" attitude (*Shulchan Arukh, OC* 17). She is, in effect, doubly taking upon herself a mitzvah that she is not required to perform: once because she is a woman, and once because (unlike a man) she wouldn't normally be wearing a four-cornered garment.

This exemption was created, however, by male rabbis living in a period when women had little autonomy or power and few rights, and most women had little or no education. Therefore, one should understand the Rabbis' fear of *yoharah* in relation to women and mitzvot—which are considered an obligation but also a privilege and an honor—in its social context. Perhaps it did seem incongruous for women, who were of a lower social standing than men, to be taking on mitzvot that they were not even required to perform.

Do we usually see pious people as guilty of hubris when they take upon themselves additional obligations? Men who go beyond the letter of the law are called Hasidim ("pious") in the Gemara. There is the story of a woman, Kimchit, in the Talmud (*Yoma* 47a), who was so righteous that she didn't let even the beams in her house "see" a strand of her hair. So, we might ask, when a woman wants to take upon herself additional mitzvot, is she guilty of *yoharah?* It appears that it is appropriate for a woman to take upon herself extra stringencies when it comes to modesty, but when it comes to prayer ritual and touching holy ritual objects, a woman who wants to go beyond the limits of her obligations is considered unseemly.

We need to read these sources with a critical eye as we make contemporary decisions about women and mitzvot. Surprisingly, or perhaps not, the Rabbis themselves leave us room to disagree with them. Even with the strong language of *mochin b'yadan*, no one actually forbids a woman from doing these mitzvot. If the Rabbis had wanted to forbid it, for all times and all women, they would have done so—with no qualms. The Rema discouraged, but discouraging is not forbidding. It is as if the Rabbis were saying, "We will try to prevent you, but in the end, it is your decision. If you must, go ahead. If a woman wants to draw closer to God, if she reads God's words in the Torah and says, 'Yes! God's will is my will. What God is commanding, I will do. That is how to sanctify my life!' could we completely forbid her? How could we tell her no?"

Perhaps, we might even imagine, the Rabbis could envision a

future in which large numbers of women would take upon themselves these mitzvot. The sages did relate the story of Michal, after all. The compiler of the Gemara could have left her out. Perhaps even then they could foresee a time when more women would follow in Michal's path, a time when women taking on previously "male" mitzvot would be considered a positive development. Whether or not the Orthodox rabbinical establishment wants to recognize this fact, we have already reached that time today in regard to some of these mitzvot. Many women have already taken upon themselves the obligations of Torah study and formal prayer, as well as shofar, *lulav* (the palm branch waved on the holiday of Sukkot), and sukkah. Although it is unlikely, perhaps the Rabbis even had a sense that women's full inclusion, in its time, would be part of *tikkun olam.*

It is Purim, the holiday when we celebrate the fact that the Jews of Shushan were saved by Queen Esther and her cousin Mordechai from the hands of Haman during the Babylonian exile. I am at the Kotel, where we, Nashot haKotel, are reading from the Scroll of Esther. We are in costume, and at the reading of the name Haman, we shake our noisemakers to blot out his name. My three children are with me—Michal, my five-year-old daughter; Adin, my three-year-old son; and Meira, my three-month-old daughter. After about half an hour, the older kids lose interest and start to climb on the rocks next to the women's section. Adin is dressed as Peter Pan, and Michal as Wendy, and they are each wearing a *tallit katan* beneath their clothing, as they do regularly. From down below the rocks, where the women pray, we have a perfect view of their *tzitzit* fringes. There is no hiding the fact that Michal is wearing a *tallit katan.* I am nervous about what the reaction of the *charedi* women might be, and I am glad that it is Purim, a holiday of merriment, masquerade, and general anarchy. Perhaps the women there will assume that the *tzitzit* are part of her costume. I do not, after all, want to provoke any violent reactions.

Michal, who does not look boyish in any way, has been mistaken for a boy numerous times because she wears a *tallit katan*. It is fascinating to me that even when Michal is wearing a ribbon in her hair or a feminine outfit with flowers, people assume that because she is wearing *tzitzit*, she is a boy. Once, a woman even made the mistake when Michal was wearing a dress. She looked confused when she noticed the *tzitzit* poking out of the hemline of Michal's dress, but she quickly decided that someone like myself, who appears to be an observant Jew (because of my head covering), would sooner put a dress on my son than *tzitzit* on my daughter.

I am torn about my decision to give Michal *tzitzit*. Although I have adopted for myself practices that cross gender lines in the community in which I live, I am not sure it is fair for me to put Michal in that position before she is old enough to understand the implications of what she is doing. For the same reason, I have not pushed her to wear a *kipah* all the time, although she does own one and wears it often when she prays. On the other hand, I do not want her to feel that these practices are off-limits to her because she is a girl. I believe that it is my responsibility as a Jewish mother to introduce my children to Torah and mitzvot with love, enthusiasm, and careful thought, but with a daughter this job becomes more complicated. How can I best prepare Michal to make the decision of what her role will be as a Jewish woman? Social norms give her a bias in one direction. Is it wrong for me to balance the scales, to show her that there is an alternative to the status quo?

I do not want her to grow up feeling resentful, marginalized, and irrelevant, as I often felt as a child. Even if it means that she will be different, and perhaps even feel alienated at times, I hope that the fact that she grows up experiencing the entirety of her tradition—all the mitzvot—will outweigh the difficulties she encounters.

I do not force Michal to wear *tzitzit*. The decision is her own. However, she sees me wearing them; she sees her father, Jacob, wearing them; and we strongly encourage her to follow in our path. When she first turned three, and we cut her hair for the first time and gave her her first *tallit katan,* she was thrilled to wear it and to say the blessing each morning when she put it on; the joy and pride that I saw in her eyes when she kissed the fringes was enough to reinforce my decision. Nevertheless, there are some days when she tells me she doesn't want to wear her *tzitzit,* and on those days I let her go without them. At first this decision seemed whimsical and unrelated to her gender. Sometimes she said they itched her, and sometimes she said they made her hot—perfectly understandable reasons. Then she told me she wanted to wear her *tzitzit* only on Shabbat. When I asked why, she said that the boys in her kindergarten were making fun of her. I asked what they were saying.

"They laugh at me and tell me that girls don't wear *tzitzit,*" Michal said, her round face in a pout.

"Did you tell them that girls don't have to wear *tzitzit,* but they can if they want to?"

"I told them that," she insisted, "but they don't listen. They still make fun of me."

"Well, I will speak to your teacher about it," I said, giving Michal an assuring hug, "and you don't have to wear them if you don't want to. When you feel ready to start again, you tell me. Just because these boys don't know that girls can wear *tzitzit* doesn't mean that you should have to stop. Okay?"

Since then, Michal has not gone back to wearing her *tzitzit* every day. She rarely wore them to kindergarten anymore. And that is a shame. It was sad and disheartening to see her naive and pure enthusiasm wane as she was exposed more and more to the world outside our home, but I knew I would not be able to shield her from the stares and fingerpointing of strangers, or the comments such as, "Why is she wearing *tzitzit*? Girls don't wear *tzitzit!*" I knew the day would come when she would discover that none of the girls around her, even the religious ones, were wearing a *tallit katan*. Now that the reality is out in the open, I will not force her to wear *tzitzit*. I do not want to make religious issues a point of argument between us. I want Michal to have positive experiences and associations with her Jewish practices, not negative ones.

I do the same with Adin, even with issues such as *tzitzit*, which for a boy are obligatory. He too was enthusiastic about the *tallit katan* when he first started wearing it at age three, and then, when my third child was born a few months later, he rebelled and refused to wear it. A few months later he started again and has been wearing it with pride. I feel bad that he was praised by others upon adopting this mitzvah while Michal was subjected to scorn and criticism. It hurts me to witness this, and I will understand if Michal decides to drop the mitzvah entirely for now. No matter what, however, I am glad that the message she receives at home is that this is her mitzvah, too.

When we complete the reading of the Scroll of Esther, we sing the song *Shoshanat Yaakov*, which customarily is sung at this time, and begin, spontaneously, to dance. We women have never danced at the Kotel, always being afraid to stir up trouble, but today we sense that the other women praying here actually approve of our service. Some have even come over to listen.

When the dancing starts, Michal and Adin notice and come down from their rock climbing to join us. One of my Nashot haKotel sisters takes Michal's hand and pulls her into the circle. I hear her say to Michal, "I see you are wearing your *tallit katan* today. You're doing a mitzvah. Good for you!"

Thank God for my Kotel sisters!

Women of the Wall has decided to branch out. We think that the only way we can win our case will be to gain public support and sympathy. We decide that we need to go out into Israeli society and get our message across to people. We need to start an education campaign to explain our position to the public. One woman in our group, Anat Hoffman, comes up with a brilliant idea. "Why not set up a table in the center of town, teaching women how to put on a tallit?" she suggests at one of our long nighttime meetings. "Chabad does it. Why can't we?"

That is how we ended up at Zion Square, standing behind a folding table covered with an assortment of *tallitot* and some halakhic material outlining the laws of women and tallit, approaching women as they pass. "Would you like to wrap yourself in a tallit?" we ask them in Hebrew. "It is a mitzvah."

Some women look at us as though we are crazy. Some take a peek, seem to ponder the idea for a moment, and then move on. Others even stop to engage us in conversation but then decide that they are not interested or just not ready yet. Finally, there are the women who decide to give it a try. We show them how to put the tallit on and teach them how to recite the *berakhah* (blessing). It is amazing to watch the expressions on these women's faces as they perform this mitzvah for the first time. Some are older women, gray and wrinkled, and some are young teenagers, moving in packs, giggling, and wearing the latest trends.

After about an hour, a *charedi* man comes over to our table. He tells us that what we are doing is a transgression. We tell him that it is not. He insists that it is. He will not leave us alone. He continues to debate, and we tell him that he is disturbing us. He begins to harass the women who come over to our table. He tells them that what we are doing is forbidden. We continue to explain that it is not. We ask him politely to leave. He refuses.

I am pregnant with my third child, and I have brought my other two children with me. They are sitting happily behind the table, eating their falafel dinner. Suddenly I see this man swipe his hand across the tabletop, scattering all of our papers and *tallitot* to the floor. Then, with the other hand, he slams the metal table down to the ground. My son starts to cry; he was hit by the table. I pull him away and check his wounds. He is only scratched, thank God. By now my daughter is crying, too. I hug them both to me and watch the man run away. Another man, wearing a knitted *kipah*, starts off after him.

"Why did that man do that?" Michal asks between frightened sobs.

"Because he doesn't like what we are doing," I answer, holding both children in my arms.

"Why not?" she asks, wiping her eyes.

"He doesn't think that women should wear *tallitot*," I explain.

"But it's a mitzvah," she says. She has stopped crying, but my son is still in tears. As I hold him close, I answer, "Yes, but he thinks women shouldn't do all of the mitzvot."

"But that's not fair," she argues, her hands on her hips.

"He has different ideas than ours," I say.

"But that doesn't mean he should hurt us," she so wisely and naively says.

I tell her I agree, and that is why we will try and find the man and bring him to the police. I also know that even if we do find this man, and even if we do press charges, he will go free. Might will win out over right once again. Nevertheless, we will be back. The faces of those women, tears in their eyes, reciting the blessing over the tallit for the first time, will draw us back.

It is 1999, Rosh Chodesh Tamuz, the month when the siege on the Temple began, the initiation of our current exile. This is not usually a joyous month, but a month of mourning, during which we begin the "countdown" to the destruction of the Temple. This time, however, at the Kotel, we are celebrating. We have a woman with us who just the day before converted to Judaism. This morning she will have her first *aliyah* to the Torah. I look over at her. Her lips are moving, her body swaying. She is seriously engrossed in her *tefillah*.

One woman, a core member of our group, has decided this month to wear her tallit. It has been relatively peaceful here at the Kotel for the past several months, and some of us feel that the time is ripe to push a bit more. This woman, Jessie, stands in the back of the group, surrounded by women, in her cream-colored, lace tallit. One would have to look quite carefully to notice it.

With Meira, my six-month-old, in a sling on my hip, I am standing on the outer rim of our group, closest to the *mechitzah*, though certainly not close, as we always stand as far away as possible from the men. A woman dressed in long stockings, long sleeves, and a *sheitl* (wig) with a pill-box hat over it, approaches me. "Don't join those women," she whispers to me in Hebrew. "They are evil."

I tell her that they are not, that in fact I am part of the group, and that we pray here every month on Rosh Chodesh.

"What are they?" she asks with a smile, continuing to assume that I can't be one of them. "*Reformiot?* I heard they read from the Torah."

"Yes, that is true that we read from the Torah, but not here at the Kotel."

"But that is forbidden!" she says, keeping a smile plastered to her face. She thinks she is saving me.

"No, it is not," I say. "Ask your rabbi. He will tell you."

This woman gives up on me. She walks over to the two security guards who stand nearby, points at us, and shakes her head. I see them shake their heads back at this woman, and she walks away. I am surprised to see the guards on our side this time. Reassured and feeling safe, I look back into my *siddur.*

When the time comes for us each to say our silent *Amidah*, I put Meira down on a blanket on the ground, and she plays happily with her toys as I pray. I feel at peace.

When one by one we finish praying the *Amidah*, we huddle around Rahel, who will lead us in the *Hallel*, a joyous prayer sung only on certain holidays, such as Rosh Chodesh, Passover, and Yom ha-Atzmaut (Israel Independence Day). She begins to sing. Her voice is a breeze flowing through me and up to the ancient stones of the Wall, through the cracks in the stone and the weeds that have grown in those cracks. I see the breeze rustling the weeds and then flowing upward, upward. Our voices are getting louder as more women come to join the singing and as we are each energized and uplifted by one another.

Suddenly, I hear men yelling, and then a crash. I look over to the men's side of the *mechitzah.* There are metal chairs flying over the *mechitzah* at us! I quickly scoop Meira off the ground and hold her on my hip, blocking her with my body, and continue to sing.

There is more yelling, and more chairs come flying at us. Although I have been attacked numerous times with my children at the Kotel, it still amazes me each time that these men don't seem at all inhibited by the fact that they are attacking women with children.

One of the guards, who has been watching us since the beginning of our service, rushes over to the *mechitzah* and climbs over it. I am shocked! Never before have I seen a guard or police officer actually try to protect us by restraining our attackers. Usually, they tell us to leave. Now this police officer was actually attempting to calm the *charedi* men, and surprisingly, succeeding! We are able to finish the *Hallel* and head up to the Archaeological Gardens for our Torah service.

As I walk up the steps, I discuss with some of the other women what happened at the Kotel. We wonder why the men attacked us today. We were not any louder than usual, nor were we an especially large group. "Probably one of the women pointed us out to the men," one woman suggests. Often it seems that it is the women who feel most threatened by us, although they don't use violence themselves. They go to the men for that. It occurs to me now that the woman who was trying to pull me away from the service earlier this morning is a likely candidate. If she couldn't stop us with words, she may have decided to resort to physical force.

Once we are up at the Archaeological Gardens, I feel the tension dissipating and the mood changing. Women are taking out their *tallitot* and wrapping themselves in them like a collective sigh of relief. I take out my tallit and put it on, saying the *berakhah*, and then put on my tefillin. After the Torah is carried around, and I kiss it, I make my way up to our makeshift stone *bimah*, where the Torah scroll is now lying. I am going to be reading the Torah for my newly converted friend's first *aliyah*. What an incredible honor!

I read from the Torah, Meira in a sling at my hip. I hope that she feels the closeness to the Torah scroll that I never felt as a child. When my friend Veronica, her face beaming, recites the concluding *berakhah*, "Blessed are You, our Lord, our God, King of the Universe, Who chose us from among all of the nations and gave us the Torah," my eyes fill with tears, for Veronica too has chosen us and our Torah from among the nations. Despite the divisiveness that exists among our people, she has chosen us. Knowing that reminds me that although there is hatred, there is also passion, and sometimes even love.

As Veronica finishes her blessing, we all break out in song and dance around the *bimah*. "*Siman tov u'mazel tov y'hei lanu ul'khol Yisrael!*" we all sing, wishing upon us and all of Israel good luck and fortune. As I dance, I think about the words we are singing. Good fortune for all of Israel. What does that mean? If we are successful in our struggle, it will be at the expense of the *charedim*. Is there a way for us all to be happy? I wonder.

Then it occurs to me: If we can get along, it will be to the benefit of all of us in the long run. The Second Temple was destroyed because of *sinat chinam*, senseless hatred among Jews. Perhaps we can find a way to dissipate that hatred now, before it is too late.

A beggar woman, who comes each month to our Torah service to ask for money, walks into our service to panhandle as usual. She walks past the *bimah* and kisses the Torah.

"*Chodesh tov*," we say to her, wishing her a good month.

"*Chodesh tov*," she answers back, as always. But this time, when she asks for money, we tell her to wait until the end of the service. "Please join us," we say in Hebrew. When Batyah, our *gabbait*, begins to recite the prayer for the sick and asks for names of people in need of healing, the beggar comes forward and gives her own name. When Batyah calls upon people to lift the Torah and dress it, she calls upon Veronica to do the lifting, and then asks the beggar to do the dressing.

"But I don't know what to do," she says.

"We'll show you how," Batyah insists, and so the woman accepts the honor. After all these years of watching us, this woman seems to have finally learned not only to tolerate us but to appreciate us as well—enough to want to join our *tefillah* and do as we do. Her joining us has acted as a *tikkun* for what happened earlier this morning with the woman down at the Kotel. The hatred has been transformed into love. There is hope for us yet, for all of Israel.

DANIELLE BERNSTEIN

The Kotel and Me

MY RELATIONSHIP WITH THE KOTEL has quite a complicated history. It is not easy for me to talk about it. Faith, like love, is an intimate experience, and I feel shy about sharing it publicly.

I remember my first walk through the *shuk* (Arab market) to the Kotel. I had been in Israel for three months before I dared to travel to Jerusalem. Then it took me three days of walking the streets of Jerusalem before I dared to enter the Old City. On a late afternoon in September 1968, I went down from the Jaffa Gate through the *shuk.* A right turn, a few steps on the left, and there was the Kotel on the other side of the wide plaza.

In 1968, the plaza was still a large space of dirt with a single tree standing in the middle. The only sign of institutionalization was the *mechitzah,* the barrier dividing the area close to the Wall into a large section for men and a smaller section for women.

I remember the stones being surprisingly smooth and warm. I did not pray; I just stood there. I looked, listened, and smelled.

During the following years I learned the way to the Kotel from the many neighborhoods of Jerusalem in which I happened to live; through the different gates. Sometimes I forgot my way and got lost. I went there in any season, at any hour, alone, or with friends.

I sat there, watching, resting, meditating. I never prayed.

Gradually, so gradually that I was unaware of the process, changes took place. A higher and steadier *mechitzah* enforced the separation between men and women; more stone fencing isolated the prayer area from the plaza; the tree that used to welcome me disappeared. There also were personnel changes. Two groups claimed special rights at the Kotel, the ultra-Orthodox and the religious nationalists. Because I could not identify with either group, I started feeling like a stranger at the Kotel. I remember one of my last visits, on Shavuot in the early 1980s. The exaltation of the two-and-a-half-hour nighttime walk from the remote neighborhood of Gilo, joining at each intersection the ever-growing human stream flowing toward the Old City, the silent climbing of Mount Zion, ended up in the anticlimax of a three-hour wait, standing in the acute morning sun, unable to grasp anything of the services taking place on the men's side.

I stopped going to the Kotel.

When seventy women gathered for the first time to pray and read from a *sefer Torah* at the Kotel in December 1988, I was not there, either physically or spiritually. I was in France, where my mother had just passed away. I had also grown completely alienated from the Kotel.

Still, when I heard about the first gatherings, all my sympathy went to the Women of the Wall. Their prayer gave me a clue that there might be an answer to the growing dissatisfaction that I felt in my own spiritual life. I could not quite understand them: Why should they trouble with the Kotel? How can a woman wish to pray at this unfriendly site?

A few months later my family and I moved to the Negev. In the town of Yeroham, identified with the site of Hagar's well (Genesis 21:19), I found friends with yearnings similar to mine. I joined a group of women who met to study and to celebrate holidays and private events. A prayer group emerged. Having a community in which I could actively pray and study was a new and extraordinarily fulfilling experience. So, a few years later, when we moved back to the Jerusalem area, the loss of this community was painful. I found myself completely isolated. I had lost my House of Learning and Prayer.

When a friend invited me to join the Women of the Wall (WOW) for the next Rosh Chodesh service, I did not hesitate; I went. I came to WOW's *tefillah* almost in *spite* of the fact that the group met at the Kotel, not *because* they did; I needed a community with which to pray. From the first moment, I felt spiritually at home with WOW. I found the same warmth, the same welcoming quality, as in the Yeroham group. It is what makes the prayer in a women's prayer group such a spiritually nourishing experience.

For the first time, I actually prayed at the Kotel. What I had been unable to do alone, I did with WOW. And for the first time in maybe ten years, I felt at home at the Kotel. WOW had given me back the Kotel.

I immediately became an active member of WOW. I often reflected on the nonhierarchical structure of our group, which enabled me to participate fully in the prayers, the meetings, and the decision making from the very beginning of my involvement. I believe that this cooperative quality makes WOW a truly feminist group. Our strength is based on openness, acceptance of one another, sharing, and listening.

I was also very enthusiastic about the pluralistic nature of WOW. I find the animosity between the different branches of Judaism distressing. I have always sensed that women may be able to overcome the barriers between the different denominations—

naming, or labeling, was Adam's job, not Eve's (Genesis 3:20)! Being able to join women different from me in prayer gives me a sense of accomplishment and hope. True, sometimes *minhagim* (customs) that are not mine seem strange and awkward, but I am sure this is true for others as well, maybe even more so because the core of WOW's prayer is Orthodox, which is my *minhag*. I am ready to accept this strangeness, for I want what we have in common to take precedence over what divides us.

If one were to ask me, "Why try to achieve such a goal at such a controversial site?" I would answer as follows: According to our sages, the Temple was destroyed because of *sinat chinam*, because of the "hatred without a cause" that existed among the Jews. Shouldn't the *tikkun*, or repair, of this senseless hatred take place where the Temple remains are?

I can easily relate to the reservation that some people have about the Kotel because of the nationalism that colors most references to this site. I have been there! True, there are prayers that are more political than religious. I witnessed the slow institutionalization, or reduction, of the Kotel to an ultra-Orthodox, nationalist site. It doesn't have to be so, and we ought not to accept the situation. By reclaiming the right for women to pray at the Kotel aloud, with tallit and *sefer Torah*, WOW is fighting for openness and fluidity, without which no spiritual life is possible. Through the pluralism we practice in our group, we advocate for pluralism and tolerance around us.

At a Jewish women's conference, I presented a paper in which I tried to understand why WOW is the target of so much criticism, even from other religious Jewish feminists. My feeling is that we are not really different from any other women's *tefillah* group, but because of our constituency, of the place we meet, and some other circumstances, we reveal (as chemicals "reveal" the picture on the paper) unanswered questions and fearful tensions that are part and parcel of any women's *tefillah* group but that many women think it's good policy to downplay.

Sometimes I wonder if WOW-bashing is a way to get a *teudat hekhsher* (kosher certification—i.e., legitimacy) for one's own group. As a WOW member, I really feel sometimes like a *seir l'azazel* (scapegoat). Before the issue of whether we constituted a minyan came up, WOW conducted *Shachrit, Hallel,* and *Hakafot* at the Kotel—with our *sefer Torah*—in a peaceful and festive atmosphere, but this got little media attention.

We have a vision. We try to find old and new ways to express our love for and commitment to Torah. We want to find a way for Jewish women of all denominations to pray together. Because we are praying next to the remains of the *beit hamikdash* (Temple), we are more sensitive to the issue of *sinat chinam.* (Having chairs thrown at us from time to time is also a pretty good reminder!)

We have no model for what we are doing. Maybe we are wrong, and maybe we are right. I do not know the answer; maybe our grandchildren will. Are women falling into the trap of the either-or, patriarchal thinking that in order for one side to be right, the other has to be wrong? Even if you do not agree with all that we do, it is important to work toward our common goals in a respectful manner.

KAREN ERLICHMAN

Reawakening

WE LANDED IN ISRAEL AND HEADED by bus for the hotel. As I unpacked, I made a vow to myself that I would be open to any new experiences this trip had to offer me. I knew that I would be meeting other lesbians, feminists, and activists. I also promised myself and God that I would make a conscious effort to talk with women who were different from me in many ways. At that time in my life I had a broken Jewish heart; I had experienced a shattering disillusionment in working for a major Jewish organization, and this was not my first betrayal.

In 1971, at the age of nine, I knew that I wanted to become a rabbi. I lived one block from my shul and used to attend services alone or tag along with friends. My parents were highly assimilated and had no interest in God or spirituality. I used to come home from school on Friday afternoons and insist that my parents make Shabbat dinner. They would snicker at me as I lit the Shabbat candles, bringing the light into my eyes as I sang the blessing. Unlike my defiant peers, I loved Jewish ritual and prayer, felt at home in Hebrew school, and was hungry for more. My friend and I went to talk to our rabbi, to tell him of our decision to grow up and be rabbis, and to seek his counsel and guidance. I was devastated when he told us that because we were girls, we couldn't be rabbis, but perhaps we could one day marry rabbis.

As a young Jewish woman, I searched desperately and unsuccessfully for role models beyond the egregious and repulsive caricatures of the Jewish mother and the "Jewish American Princess." Finding nothing, I decided to sever my connection to Judaism. When people asked me if I was Jewish, I said no. As my radical politics evolved, I became a devout atheist.

Later, I came out as a lesbian in 1983 in a small community where the most important role models for me were proud, powerful Jewish lesbians. They invited me to Friday night Shabbat dinners; we observed the holidays together and took a visible role in campus activism. I was still denying God, but I was returning to my cultural and communal identity as a Jew.

This trip to Jerusalem was a significant milestone on my spiritual journey. I had not attended a religious service in years. I could still stumble my way through prayerbook Hebrew. Something was reawakening in me.

There was some discussion of the idea of organizing a group of women to hold a prayer service at the Kotel. I decided that if I was awake that morning, I would join them, but I wasn't sure if I would make it. I was very blasé about the whole idea.

I awoke that morning quite early. It was *bashert* (predestined) that I even ended up on that bus to the Kotel. I hadn't set an alarm clock; I unexpectedly woke up early and said to myself, "Well, since I'm awake, I might as well go." I dressed quickly and headed to the lobby to join the group of women who were about to board the bus for the Kotel. There was a palpable energy in the group as Rabbi Deborah Brin reviewed our organizing strategy with us for safety reasons. We would stand in a circle at the Kotel. If we were targets of violence or harassment, we would link arms and form a very tight, close circle. If necessary, we would leave quickly and board our bus.

We began quietly, in a circle, very close to the Wall itself. Women took turns reading and singing *Berakhot* (blessings). When we sang in unison, we did so gently and quietly, which gave our service a mystical feeling. Soon we were noticed by one of the elderly Orthodox women. She began to pace frantically behind us, calling out in Hebrew that we were doing something that was unnatural, wrong, dangerous. Her voice became louder, and then I remember hearing an animal-like noise from the other side of the *mechitzah.* The men had become aware of our presence and had begun to protest in rage. They rattled the *mechitzah* that separated them from us. They screamed and shrieked in beastly voices. Several women, their faces pressed to the Wall, rocked their bodies as they too wailed and cried that what we were doing was *treyf* (unkosher, forbidden). The men shook their fists and waived their *siddurim* at us in horror. We continued to sing, we linked arms and embraced, the Torah protected inside the circle like a womb. For our safety, we decided to complete our prayer and head back to the bus. We filed back to the bus peacefully, singing *Oseh Shalom,* the prayer for peace.

When we got back on the bus, I began to cry. The woman next to me embraced me, stroking my hair and continuing to sing. To pray together at the Kotel as women was an amazing act of courage and righteousness. It was also a holy event. Each one of us was sanctified by the experience. The men at the Kotel (and a few women) must have sensed the power we held, because they were visibly frightened. Of course, their fear was manifested as violent, threatening rage, whereas we were peaceful, loving, and steadfast.

I don't think I fully realized the impact that the experience of davening at the Kotel had on me spiritually, politically, emotionally, and religiously. Intellectually, I knew that women had not previously claimed their place at the Kotel, but until that day I hadn't felt it in my *kishkes* (insides).

We created our own *mishkan* (Tabernacle) in our circle that morning at the Wall. In that circle I felt righteous and powerful, connected to God and to myself and to each individual Jewish woman who was there with me. I didn't even know all of their names, but it didn't matter. The feeling of claiming our place at the Kotel, claiming the Torah, demanding that we hear our own voices aloud in prayer and in song, reaching for our right to pray together—all of this is still with me.

My Jewish identity and spiritual practice have deepened tremendously in the past fourteen years. I have a regular Jewish meditation practice and study. I have been a member of a synagogue for fourteen years. As a social worker, I address the spiritual dimension of health and healing in my work with people. In addition, I am now longing for more intense Jewish study and training. I am not sure what this will entail; perhaps I will fulfill my childhood dream of becoming a rabbi. I worry that if I don't fulfill that dream, it will be the most haunting regret of my life.

On a more tangible level, my regular spiritual practice recognizes God's love and presence in all things. Sometimes I use the traditional Hebrew language in my songs and prayers; at other times I change the language to be more gender-neutral or to reflect the feminine aspect of the Divine. Any and all of these options are open to me whenever I choose them.

BAT MELECH (PSEUDONYM)

With Strings Attached: A Jew Wears a Tallit to the Kotel

SOME YEARS AGO, I saw a picture of a *tefillin shel yad* (worn on the arm) from Inquisition times. The leather box was tiny and could fit easily into the palm of a hand. The caption explained that such a small size was essential at that time and in that place, for anyone suspected of even the slightest Jewish practice risked arrest and imprisonment, torture, and possibly a terrible death. I breathed a sigh of relief. How lucky, I thought, to be living in modern times, when most countries no longer behave so dreadfully. True, the world is far from perfect; there are still plenty of places where religious persecution exists. For the most part, however, a Jew does not have to fear for his life if he prays in public with tallit and tefillin.

Here in Israel, of course, there is no question of his safety—unless the Jew is a woman praying at the Kotel. I will not speak here of the halakhic decisions that allow women to take on the mitzvot of tallit and tefillin, along with the other timebound commandments that we have taken on, with halakhic sanction, throughout our history. Such a discussion is beyond the scope of this essay. I wish only to write about my own feelings as a committed, practicing

Jewish woman who nearly three years ago took on the mitzvah of *tzitzit* and began wearing a tallit for morning prayers shortly thereafter.

Last Shabbat I decided to go to the Kotel for morning prayers. As I prepared to go, I thought yet again how absurd it seemed that I had to put on my tallit beforehand and then take it off so I could go and pray. Then I got an idea: Suppose I were to wear my tallit to the Kotel? I would take good care to hide it, of course, but I wanted to say the *Shema* at the Kotel as I've become accustomed to doing for nearly the past three years: with my *tzitziot* between my fingers as I raise them to my heart and kiss them at each mention of this beloved mitzvah. So I put on my tallit, then put a long coat over it, making sure that it covered the *tzitziot*, for no matter how pure my own motives might be, I knew perfectly well what could happen to me if I were discovered. The best I could expect would be dirty looks, perhaps a few mutterings directed at the *Reformit* (a term applied indiscriminately to any woman who appears to deviate from accepted custom), perhaps a pitying look or two for the misguided feminist. Or perhaps an earnest *frum* (Orthodox) woman, experienced in *kiruv* (outreach), might approach and try to convince me that I was transgressing Halakhah, assuming that I had no knowledge of Jewish practice. At worst, heaven forbid, I could expect verbal and physical violence, the refusal of the police to protect me, and perhaps even arrest and a trial, ending in imprisonment or a heavy fine. It would not occur to many people that my motives might be pure, that all I wished to do was a mitzvah. "Judge everyone favorably," admonishes *Pirkei Avot* (a Mishnah tractate). If only it were so.

As I finished getting ready, a memory surfaced from long ago: a Shabbat meal at the home of a local family, and a rabbi's wife who made a disparaging comment about "those women who wear a tallit." This was years before I started wearing one, but the remark stung and I stuck up for those women, whoever they were. "Who are we to judge?" I asked. "Aren't we supposed to give people the benefit of the doubt?" The rabbi's wife replied, "I once knew a grandmother who wore a tallit when she prayed, always in a locked room. No one knew. This was in a very *frum* area, and she had been dead for several years before her daughter told me about it. That is how a woman should wear a tallit, if she chooses to do so at all— in modesty and privacy, as that grandmother did." I held my tongue, thinking that it was no wonder that the grandmother had hidden her fringes. Perhaps it was indeed from modesty, but I am more inclined to think that she simply wished to remain on speaking terms with her neighbors.

As I approached the stairs leading down to the Kotel, a young man passed me. He was wearing a spotless white tallit, and as I looked at it, I realized that it was exactly the same as mine, right down to the machine-brocaded pattern on the *atarah* (top piece). He walked serenely, confidently, even regally in his ritual garment, a true son of the King. I'm sure it would never have occurred to him that the woman walking behind him was concealing a tallit exactly like his beneath her long, dark coat.

God, I thought, *Your sons are free. What about Your daughters?* I tasted envy, then, and anger.

A second later I tried to put it out of my mind. I was, after all, going to the Kotel to pray, and Halakhah forbids praying while angry. Luckily for me, Halakhah does not forbid praying while frightened. I looked down constantly, anxious lest the ends of my *tzitziot* peek out from beneath my coat; but of course, no one was paying attention. I took a deep breath and chuckled softly at my fears.

At the Kotel, I arranged my coat and sat down, then undid a few of its fastenings and reached inside it, around behind me so that all four fringes would be available at the proper time. I reflected that if I did this often, I might become good at it. As it was, it took a few clumsy tries before I got all four of them hanging down where they were supposed to be, within my reach.

I davened then with a mixture of joy and apprehension—joy that I merited to pray at the Kotel enwrapped in a tallit, and apprehension lest anyone notice and raise the alarm. God sees into our hearts and discerns our motives, and I prayed that He keep mine pure: *V'taher libenu l'ovd'kha be'emet* ("Purify our hearts to worship You in peace").

And then it was time. This was the moment for which I had come. I reached inside, around behind me, first one hand, then the other, grasping each fringe on the second or third try. Finally, I got them all, wondering if my halting attempts to gather my *tzitziot* in this part of the davening might reflect the difficulties of gathering all of us from the four corners of the earth. I wrapped the *tzitziot* around my finger, put my hand over my eyes, and softly proclaimed God's Oneness.

Now I came to the third paragraph of the *Shema*, where we kiss our *tzitziot* each of the three times they are mentioned. How would I manage this without being seen? I stood, although it is not customary to do so at this time, and used my body to shield my left hand. I bent slightly, moved my hand away from the shelter of my coat, and brought hand and lips together. *God, please be with me*, I thought. *Save me from being seen and getting into trouble. After all, this is Your mitzvah I'm doing.*

Behind me, a woman was speaking in Yiddish. I thought I heard the word *shtut*, "foolishness," and I froze. Did she see, did she know?

Then I realized that in Yiddish, she would have said *shtus,* not *shtut.* I took a deep breath and kept on davening. The rest of my *tefillah* went by without event—almost. Shortly before I left, I met an acquaintance of mine. Around her neck she wore a charm that depicted the ten *sefirot,* or divine emanations, of the Jewish mystical tradition. At the bottom of the charm was tied a single set of *tzitzit,* open to the air for all to see. I wondered if I dared tell my friend what I had on under my coat. In the end I kept quiet, but I wondered whether that charm might not be my friend's way of doing what I had just done. It's said that ideas spread from one person to the other, even without our sharing them verbally. So who knows?

The second thing that happened just before I left the Kotel that day was that an older woman in a long skirt and dark wig approached me. "Oh, I know who you are," she said with a big smile. "You're from that group that comes here every Rosh Chodesh. I love to listen to your davening. Good Shabbos!"

I smiled, wishing her the same, and kept my hand on my coat's lower fastenings. *Well,* I thought, *maybe there's hope after all.*

CELIA SZTERENFELD

A Worshiper from Brazil

THIRTEEN YEARS AGO, while marching with other women carrying a Torah to be read at the Wall, sensing the tension that our presence built all around us, I had an acute feeling of the future. The startling aggressiveness of the local women called our attention to the amount of work ahead. At that moment I was fed with enough energy to work for the next thirteen years.

For ten years now, the Bat Kol Rosh Chodesh Group of the Jewish Congregation of Brazil has met on a monthly basis, stimulating hundreds of women to study their tradition, reflect on their condition as contemporary women living in Rio, share experiences and feelings, and meditate and pray. As a result, in my synagogue, women constitute more than half of the daily minyan and also of the board of directors (there were three female presidents in a row for the first time in Brazil). Women are able to conduct services on every occasion and to raise a new generation with an egalitarian outlook.

I can only thank you and all women who keep up the energy of transformation alive and circulating all over the world. I'm proud to be a link in this powerful chain!

REBECCA SCHWARTZ

Turning Point

MARCH 1989, TAANIT ESTHER. When I arrived that morning, I didn't know what to expect. A group of women, mostly young and English-speaking, huddled together just outside the Dung Gate, the main entrance to the Jewish Quarter. A Canadian woman, who seemed to be in charge, offered caveats about staying together and keeping track of the person next to you. A core of volunteers would stand around the outside of the prayer circle facing the crowds, watching for signs of trouble. Suddenly, I began to feel nervous. What the hell was I doing here?

We marched through the gate and down the plaza in two single lines, singing *Oseh Shalom,* a traditional Jewish song of peace. The men obviously had been forewarned of our arrival, for they waited in large bands stationed along the walkway. They looked almost military, in their matching uniforms of black suits and hats, long sidecurls and fringed shawls. As they shouted obscenities at us as we passed, I noticed how young some of them were, just schoolboys out for a field trip.

Once we assembled at the Wall, I opened my *siddur,* bought a few days earlier from a hole-in-the-wall shop on Jaffa Road just for the occasion. I struggled to follow the small Hebrew lettering and unfamiliar tunes. Just as I was getting into the service, the assault began. Over our leader's voice I had heard yelling and shushing from the beginning, but when objects started flying over the *mechitzah*, I realized how much trouble we were in. The young woman in front of me, whom I recognized from one of my classes at Hebrew University, collapsed at my feet as a chair crashed into her head.

A police officer tossed a canister of tear gas into the attacking mob, but an old man wrapped himself in his prayer shawl, picked up the canister, and threw it directly into our midst. We all ran, coughing and choking, trying to escape to the more open space above. My eyes burned and my throat stung, but I didn't catch the worst of it. The men were still screaming at us: "Whores, lesbians—go home!" They were yelling in Hebrew, the holy tongue, so I didn't understand all of it. For once, I gave thanks for my ignorance.

After the police chased everyone away and the smoke had literally cleared from my eyes, I rode a rickety bus, filled with shopping housewives, back to my apartment building, walked out onto the roof, and looked down on Jerusalem. For a woman who had not yet been to a Rosh Chodesh service or heard the name Shekhinah, it was quite a wake-up call.

On that day a Jewish feminist was born.

As I watched the changing color patterns of sun glistening on stone, I asked myself, Why would the sight of Jewish women praying and singing together at Judaism's holiest site cause offense to Jewish men? Why would they desecrate their own sacred space with verbal and physical violence? Did we, in our long skirts and head scarves, pose such a threat to their tradition? I didn't expect to be attacked for davening *Shachrit* in Jerusalem. What was really going on?

Upon returning to the United States, I began an annual tradition of hosting feminist seders, which have grown from a living room to an auditorium. Through this venue I heard stories from other women who have undergone similar transformations. I have found kindred spirits on my quest to merge the two sides of myself that I never knew were at odds. The "Jewish-feminist dichotomy," which I had never dreamed existed, now defines my life.

Not everyone can identify the turning point, a single fork in the infinitely branched road of our lives, that sets the stage for future dreams and passions, even a life's work. I can.

SUE POLANSKY

My Daughter's Bat Mitzvah

IN MAY 1996, my daughter Marni celebrated her bat mitzvah at our home synagogue in Longmeadow, Massachusetts. The experience lacked something significant—Israel. Our family had visited Israel numerous times before, but never in the context of a religious ritual. We wanted Marni and the rest of us to have the opportunity to claim our Jewish heritage in Israel as Jews, not as tourists. The Women of the Wall graciously provided us with that precious moment later that summer.

Although WOW's Kotel services normally were conducted only on Rosh Chodesh and holidays, our travel plans necessitated that our Torah service be held on an ordinary Monday or Thursday morning. No problem. Despite the very early hour on a workday, WOW came through for us. Our family was privileged to have our child welcomed as a Jewish adult at our most holy space in Jerusalem. Our daughters were the Torah readers, and the Women of the Wall provided the group and the service. What a beautiful shared experience it was for us! At the conclusion of Marni's *aliyah*, all of us danced the hora in her honor. It was truly a celebration. Thank you for making it happen!

PART II

Legal and
Political Analysis

FRANCES RADAY

The Fight against Being Silenced

THE ASPECT OF THE WOMEN OF THE WALL'S case history that I will present here is its struggle against private violence and public veto in Jerusalem, a struggle that has brought them to petition the Israeli Supreme Court repeatedly over the past thirteen years. It is a struggle in which I have represented them as counsel, together with my friends and colleagues Jonathan Misheiker and Nira Azriel. I am writing this not only as counsel but also as an ally who has participated in and wholly supported the cause. Mine is not a religious perspective but a human rights perspective. The Western Wall of the Temple, the Kotel, has been expressly recognized by the Supreme Court as a site of great symbolic significance, for both Jews in Israel and Jews in the diaspora. It is not just a holy place; it is also a historical, national, and cultural symbol. On this historic stage, the struggle between enlightenment and theocracy and between patriarchy and feminism is being acted out. Its outcome is important not only for the Women of the Wall themselves but also for the future of human rights in Israel.

WOW's manner of prayer is women's prayer in a group, wearing prayer shawls and praying aloud from the Torah scroll. They have called it the three Ts: tallit, Torah, *tefillah.* This manner of prayer is customary for men but not for women and is therefore a

115

subject of controversy among Orthodox Jewish authorities. It is considered by many Orthodox rabbinical authorities to be prohibited by Jewish law, or, even if it is not, to constitute an impermissible deviation from the custom of the place (the Kotel). However, it is also fully condoned by some well-respected Orthodox authorities, and in this it is distinguished from the mode of prayer of Reform and Conservative Jews. The distinction is that WOW does not pray in a mixed group of men and women, but prays separately from men in the *ezrat nashim*, the women's section, at the Kotel. Nor does WOW attempt to pray in a minyan, which is a group of at least ten men, required for certain prayers. WOW prays in a group that is not a minyan and does not read those prayers whose recitation requires a minyan.

In Judaism, interpretation is not monolithic. Judaism is not given to a single hierarchy of authoritative interpretation. The interpretation of the sources is a matter of dialectic; theological rulings are determined by the accumulation of conflicting rabbinical writings and responsa to questions from the community. Thus, because alongside the core of opposition there *is* Orthodox authority that supports the women's claim, it can be said that the status of this mode of prayer is not decided under Halakhah. Hence it is within the limits of Orthodox Judaism that WOW is seeking to pray in a group as men do, to wear ceremonial prayer shawls as men do, to hold the Torah scroll as men do, and to raise their voices in prayer as men do. The women seek the chance to pray as full partners in the Orthodox Jewish tradition and not as silent, passive shadows of men.

WOW's prayer in this manner has been greeted with violent opposition from other Orthodox worshipers, male and female. WOW members have been physically attacked and verbally abused.

Similar violence has met Reform and Conservative congregations of Jews that have attempted to pray near the Kotel in mixed prayer groups of men and women. Scenes of spitting and even the throwing of excrement at these groups have appeared on television screens around the world. The violence is orchestrated by small groups of fanatics, mostly yeshiva students who study and live in the vicinity of the Kotel. However, the importance of these groups far exceeds the number of perpetrators. Many people who do not identify with the fanatical violence nevertheless openly condemn the participants in a women's or a mixed prayer group as provoking the violence. Officialdom has not banished the violent fanatics from the Kotel; it has instead banished WOW and the Reform and Conservative congregations.

In an open letter, Judy Labehnson, one of the early members of WOW, reminisces about its initial encounter with violence and her own decision to abandon the group and leave the Kotel to the *charedi* fanatics. Subsequently regretting her decision to surrender, in the light of new manifestations of renewed violence, she argued that the Jewish people cannot allow the Kotel to be turned into a bastion of *charedi* intolerance and talked of her fear that, if this should happen, the words of Lamentations might become prophetically true for those Jews in search of a middle path: "How doth the city sit solitary that was full of people—all beauty so departed."

Why the violence against the Women of the Wall? Even though this is not the way every Orthodox Jewish woman wants to pray, why should it arouse opposition to the point of violence? What is so threatening about it? It is not an activity that directly threatens or even delegitimizes the right of others to pray in their own way. It is not a mode of prayer that clearly infringes basic halakhic prohibitions. Nevertheless, although there is good authority for its halakhic permissibility, WOW's attempt to pray in its manner arouses furious opposition and fanatical violence on the part of some other worshipers at the Kotel. The reason for the violence is that WOW's prayer threatens something deep in religious conviction that permeates and extends beyond the halakhic debate: patriarchal hegemony.

The violence against the Women of the Wall is a manifestation of the attempt of ultra-religious activists to preserve their patriarchal hegemony. This attempt is unique neither to Judaism nor to Jerusalem. The use of spiritual symbolism by traditionalist religious leaders to preserve patriarchy is no different from other forms of patriarchal politics. More than that, it is the most virulent form of patriarchal politics in this era. Religious fanaticism has the subjugation of women high on its agenda. Patriarchal hegemony was, of course, not invented by religion. Other forms of human thought, from the pagan and the political to the philosophical, have been patriarchal; in historical terms, religion merely assimilated into the prevailing patriarchal organization of human thought and society. However, at the dawn of the twenty-first century, the patriarchal hegemony of religion persists as an ideological core at the center of a growing egalitarian women's role in society. Religious institutions preach and proselytize patriarchy, fueling resistance to feminist change and legitimizing such resistance.

Jewish fundamentalism aims to exclude women from active participation in public religious life and to retain the husband's exclusive power of divorce. Christian fundamentalism aims for control of women's bodies by the Church; it opposes contraception and violently opposes the autonomous choice of abortion. It preaches a return to traditional family values, with wifely obedience and mothers educating their children at home. Muslim fundamentalism returns women to polygamy, obedience to their husbands in all social and sexual matters, and the veil, depriving them of both private power and public participation. Hindu fundamentalists have rallied to support reintroduction of the institution of *sati* (widow-burning). The fundamentalist religious communities are not only holding on to an internal ethos of patriarchy, but are also trying to reintroduce this ethos as a universal norm in pluralistic democracies.

WOW represents a new kind of activism struggling for feminist expression within the religious context. This struggle has also been carried on by women in Christianity, who have succeeded in some denominations in being admitted to the priesthood. It can be compared to the early days of the struggle to gain a voice in democracy. The attempt of women to gain a voice in Western democracies lasted more than a hundred years, from the time of the French Revolution. The struggle of the Seneca Falls feminists and the English suffragists against exclusion and silencing met with violent opposition from democratic governments. Their long struggle succeeded in achieving, for women in Europe and America, the right to vote. On the secular political level, women's participation and voices have become an accepted part of democratic discourse. The feminist struggle against exclusion from the public sphere and against silencing is now being reenacted in the context of religion.

All the aspects of WOW's mode of prayer—group prayer, wearing prayer shawls, and raising voices in reading from the Torah scroll—challenge the patriarchal hegemony of the religion. The reasons that each of these attributes is considered offensive are richly symbolic of patriarchy in feminist discourse. This explains the violent opposition by fundamentalist forces to their manifestation. In the eyes of the opponents of WOW, the different aspects of its mode of prayer are linked to public participatory prayer in a minyan and therefore (directly or indirectly) to the performance of active duties at fixed times *(mitzvot aseh she hazman geraman)*. Women are exempt from performing such duties, and there is conflicting opinion as to whether they may waive this exemption if the exemption is not to their advantage or to their disadvantage.

The objections to women's active participatory public prayer are ostensibly attributable to women's family role; it would seem as though the primary concern might be their traditional child-caring role. However, on closer examination, this turns out not to be the entire story. A medieval tract called the *Book of Abudraham* spells out for us the family functions that preempt a woman from carrying out *mitzvot aseh she hazman geraman:*

> And the reason why women are exempted from *mitzvot aseh she hazman geraman* is that the woman is bound to her husband to tender to his needs. And had she been obliged to do *mitzvot aseh she hazman geraman*, it is possible at the appointed time for the carrying out of the mitzvah the husband might order her to do his mitzvah. And if she carries out the Almighty's mitzvah and neglects his mitzvah, let her beware of her husband. And if she carries out her husband's mitzvah and neglects the Almighty's mitzvah, let her beware of her Creator. Hence, the Almighty exempted her from His mitzvot so that she would be at peace with her husband.[1]

Even for the skeptical, this tract portrays an unexpectedly patriarchal picture. It does not relate to women's childbearing role or even to child rearing, but concentrates solely on the competing duties that a woman has to her husband and to God. However, it would be wrong to leave the impression that there is, in Judaism, prevalent acceptance of the idea of subjugation of women to their husband's absolute power. Indeed, there are sources that deny that a wife has the duty to be submissive and obedient to her husband; in particular, it is clearly forbidden for a husband to coerce his wife to have intercourse with him. Nevertheless, in the context of *mitzvot aseh she hazman geraman,* the emphasis on wifely duty to her husband and the competition between her husband and the Almighty for the right to her obedience express patriarchal hegemony.

The objection to women's group prayer is actually an objection to official group prayer in a minyan or with tallit and Torah scroll, and not to the idea of a number of women praying together. There seems to be no real objection to women praying in a group, provided that the group has none of the trappings of "official" group prayer—that is, a minyan. The prohibition of women's public reading from the Torah, when public Torah reading is so central to Jewish culture and community, is a further manifestation of the exclusion of women from the public sphere and public functions. In this context, it touches on that aspect of public-sphere activity that is associated with the acquisition of power through knowledge and spiritual authority. A division between the public and the private spheres in which women are excluded from the public sphere is a well-worn theme of feminist analysis. In her book *Public Man, Private Woman,* Jean Bethke Elshtain summarizes the course of Western civilization starting from the Greeks:

> Truly public, political speech was the exclusive preserve of free male citizens. Neither women nor slaves were public beings. Their tongues were silent on the public issues of the day. Their speech was severed from the name of action: it filled the air, echoed for a time, and faded from public memory with none to record it or to embody it in public forms.

121

The objection to women wearing prayer shawls is also primarily attributed to the exemption from *mitzvot aseh she hazman geraman*. Relying on the writings of Maimonides in the twelfth century, Shiloh and Shifman, the halakhic experts for WOW in the Supreme Court, conclude that women may wear prayer shawls. Relying on the later writings of the Rema, Shuchetman, the halakhic expert for the state, concludes that they may not. He argues that although it might be theoretically permissible, it would be an exhibition of "arrogance" for them to do so. Arrogance, in this context, is "behavior which is vulgar and proud, shows contempt for others, and is unconventional in the community"; arrogant behavior by women even in private, but most certainly in public, is considered improper and impermissible. It need scarcely be said that this requirement for women's private modesty and public invisibility is another example of the patriarchal exclusion of women from the public sphere. Furthermore, Shuchetman points out that women's wearing of tallit is contrary to the prohibition in the Torah according to which "a woman must not take man's apparel." This prohibition calls to mind Naomi Wolf's analysis in her book *The Beauty Myth* of the role that the differentiation between male and female clothing has played in reinforcing male supremacy.

Perhaps the most emotive objection that has been brought to bear against the Women of the Wall is the argument that it is forbidden for men to hear women's voices in song. It is pertinent to quote the opinion of Shuchetman, the state's expert, on this issue: "An additional problem [to that of a women's minyan] . . . is that . . . women who seek to organize themselves into a separate minyan in the Kotel Plaza certainly might, by their singing, disturb the prayers of others—a thing which is absolutely prohibited." It is this objection that is most loudly heard in the fanatical denunciation of WOW.

The fear of the disturbing impact of women's voices first appears in the Babylonian Talmud, which states that Shmuel spoke of the need for modesty in women's dress, saying, "A woman's thigh is seductive," and admonishing women as follows: "If you show your thigh, you show your shamefulness." In this context, the Talmud reports, Shmuel also said, "A woman's voice is seductive, as it has been said, 'Your voice is sweet and your countenance comely.'" This saying of Shmuel's came to be taken as requiring women to preserve their modesty by not exposing their voices, in song, in public, analogously to not exposing their bodies. The requirement that women not raise their voices in song at the time of prayer later found expression as a prohibition in the *Shulchan Arukh*. However, the original source of the phrase referred to by Shmuel is the Song of Songs: "O my dove, that art in the clefts of the rock, in the secret places of the stairs, let me see thy countenance, let me hear thy voice; for sweet is thy voice and thy countenance is comely."

This etymological explanation of the "seductiveness" of women's voices is stunning evidence that the silencing of women is linked with the politics of patriarchal domination as well as with the psychology of the fear of women's sensuality. It is reminiscent of the sirens of Greek mythology, whose song lured sailors to their deaths. The move is from sensuality to silencing. This is indeed a fatal combination: silencing women's voices to implement the exclusion of women from participation in the public arena and silencing women's voices to protect men from women's sensuality. This objection to WOW's mode of prayer most clearly symbolizes the silencing of women throughout the history of patriarchy. The evolution of the prohibition in Judaism of women singing within earshot of men is a particularly revealing instance of the process of silencing and the reasons for it.

The accumulation of reasons for preventing Jewish women from praying in a group with tallit, Torah, and *tefillah*, embodies deep patriarchal fears of women's active participation and partnership in the public sphere of social life. The impact on women is, of course, marginalization. As Elshtain writes:

> Because women have throughout much of Western history been a silenced population in the arena of public speech, their views on these matters, and their role in the process of humanization, have either been taken for granted or assigned a lesser order of significance and honor compared to the public, political activities of males. Women were silenced in part because that which defines them and to which they are inescapably linked—sexuality, natality, the human body (images of uncleanness and taboo, visions of dependency, helplessness, vulnerability)—was omitted from public speech.

The traditional limitations on women's prayer all refer to patriarchy, and the current opposition to WOW is a reassertion of that patriarchal power. The site of the reassertion of patriarchy is the Kotel, the symbolic heart of Judaism. How, then, have the secular authorities in Israeli society dealt with these violent attacks on women's quest for active participation in prayer at the Kotel? In order to understand this, one has to remember that the legal stage on which the scene is being acted out is one of state promotion of religion rather than one of nonintervention. The promotion of religion, since its introduction under the Ottoman Empire and its adoption as the Millett system by the British Mandate, has been pluralistic regarding the major religions of Israel. The various communities have their own religious courts, which have exclusive jurisdiction over questions of personal status of the members of their communities (e.g., the rights to marriage and divorce), their own officially recognized days of rest and holidays, and their own holy places. Regarding the promotion of the Jewish religion, there is in most contexts a monopolistic preference given to Orthodox Judaism over the other branches of Judaism; this is indeed a highly contested matter over a whole range of issues, and, not least, in the context of the Kotel.

The Kotel is one of the sites governed by the Protection of Holy Places Law of 1967, which provides that the necessary measures will be taken to prevent desecration of holy places or behavior that is likely to obstruct the freedom of access or offend the sensibilities of the members of the religious communities to which they are holy. The implementation of the law is placed in the hands of an administrator appointed by the Minister of Religious Affairs, in consultation with the chief rabbis.

At the time of the initial violent reaction to WOW, the secular authorities responded by excluding WOW from praying in its own manner at the Kotel; the administrator of the Kotel, who is also an ultra-Orthodox rabbi, issued an order preventing WOW from praying in this manner. The police also intervened to prevent WOW's active prayer at the Kotel, claiming that this was necessary to prevent a breach of the peace and desecration of the Kotel. They intervened to prevent both WOW's women-only prayers and the mixed-group prayers of Conservative and Reform Jews. There are eyewitness reports that on one occasion the police roughly pushed the Conservative and Reform Jews, who were praying peacefully, away from the area of the Kotel even though the only activity of the *charedi* Jews there had been to call out cries of denunciation.

Journalist Gideon Summet observed that police reticence in dealing with religious violence in all its forms is a result of dual forces: the deference shown by the political leadership of the state to religious leaders of the ultra-Orthodox camp, and a certain mystical, if not religious, personal identification of the police themselves with Orthodox religious sentiment. To this analysis one can add the speculation that, in the case of WOW, the police have little sympathy with the women's cause, the struggle against silencing.

In reaction, WOW petitioned the Supreme Court. Its petition was based on the constitutional right to freedom of worship, the right of access to the Kotel, and, less emphatically, the right to equality as women. The group also claimed that the administrator had acted beyond the limits of his statutory powers, as determined by the regulations under the Holy Places Law. Upon submission of the petition, the Minister of Religious Affairs promptly amended the regulations under the law to expressly "prohibit the conducting of any religious ceremony which is not according to custom of the place and which injures the sensitivities of the worshiping public towards the place."

In 1994, the Supreme Court rejected WOW's petition. Nevertheless, the majority opinions of Justices Meir Shamgar and Shlomo Levine recognized in principle WOW's right of access and freedom of worship. Justice Shamgar, then president of the Court, held that the common denominator for Jewish worship at the Kotel should not be the most austere halakhic ruling but should be good-faith worship by all who wish to pray by the Kotel. Shamgar recommended that the government find a solution that would "allow the petitioners to enjoy freedom of access to the Kotel, while minimizing the injury to the sensitivities of other worshipers." He based his recommendation on the need for mutual tolerance between groups and opinions and on the need to respect human dignity. He did not mention the disempowerment of women and the need to guarantee their constitutional right to participate equally in the public arena. He was silent on the issue of equality, even though he noted, with the most tentative of criticisms, one of the primary manifestations of that inequality—the objection to hearing women's voices:

> The singing of the petitioners aroused fury, even though it was singing in prayer; and anyway is there any prohibition of singing by the Kotel? After all, there is dancing and singing there not infrequently, and it is unthinkable that the singing in dignified fashion of pilgrims, whether Israeli or foreign, soldiers or citizens, whether male or female, should be prevented. In view of this, it may be, and I emphasize, "may be," that the opponents are confusing their opposition to the identity of the singers with their opposition to the fact of the singing, and this should not be.

Justice Levine based his recognition of WOW's right to pray in its manner at the Kotel on his view that the Kotel has not only religious but also national and historical importance to all the different groups and persons who come there, in good faith, for the purpose of prayer or any other legitimate purpose. Although the struggle for women's right to participate in the full ceremonial worship of Judaism, their struggle for equality, is at the core of the conflict, the majority of judgments were devoid of any mention of this right. The judges based their recognition of WOW's right to pray on the right to freedom of worship but not of equality. They upheld the need to protect pluralism but did not address the issue of religious patriarchy.

It was only in the minority opinion, written by Justice Menachem Elon, who was then the religious-seat incumbent on the

127

Supreme Court, that the issue of equality for women was discussed. Justice Elon examined in depth the various halakhic opinions on women's prayer groups. He concluded the following:

> It is conceivable that the substantial change in women's status and position in the present century, in which religiously observant women are also full participants, will in the course of time bring about an appropriate solution to the complicated and sensitive issue of women's prayer groups. However, the area for prayer beside the Western Wall is not the place for a "war" of deeds and ideas on this issue. As of today, the fact is that a decisive majority of the halakhic authorities, including Israel's chief rabbis, would regard acceptance of the petition of the petitioners a travesty of the custom of a synagogue and its sacredness ... such is the case as regards the Western Wall, which is the most sacred synagogue in the Jewish religion.

Thus Justice Elon examines the issue of women's right to equality in the modern world, only to dismiss the possibility of addressing it at the site that is, in his view, the most central to Judaism—the Kotel.

Why should the secular judges ignore the issue of women's right to equality while the religious judge alludes to it as a problem? This apparently paradoxical motif in the Supreme Court becomes less strange and more significant when we try to analyze the reasons for it. The approach of the secular judges can be deconstructed in light of the secular ethos regarding the autonomy of religion. Among the secular, the ways of religion seem to be outside the framework of secular ethical analysis. The religious are a closed community whose members act according to their own norms. Religious communities are entitled to autonomy, and the Court will hesitate to interfere by imposing universalist values on their internal organization. This attitude rests on a freedom of religion, a multicultural conviction that abdicates responsibility for suppressed subgroups within the autonomous religious community. Subgroups that belong to the religious community are taken to have consented to its entire set of mores, including their own inequality. This being so, the issue of equality for women within the religion becomes, for the secular, a nonissue. The matter is otherwise for more progressive religious leaders like Justice Elon. For them, religion is a way of life that should provide solutions for current social problems. Justice Elon, in another case, has indicated his own conviction that religious institutionalism should not fail to take account of the change in women's status over the past two hundred years, and he hints at this view in the case of WOW. Nevertheless, he holds that the place is inappropriate for the conflict that will accompany change. Ironically and significantly, he holds that the Kotel is too important as a spiritual and religious center to be the site for a struggle over women's rights. The message is yet again the marginalization of women's issues, even by those who are the advocates of change within the Orthodox community.

In response to the Supreme Court's recommendation, the government set up a Committee of Directors General of various ministries. This committee, after deliberating for two years, finally made its recommendations: WOW could pray in its manner. However, this prayer was to be held outside the southeastern corner of the battlements of the Old City—well away from the Kotel. At the Kotel WOW could not pray in its manner for reasons of internal security (i.e., the threat to the breach of the peace). The government then appointed a ministerial committee, which, after taking a year to deliberate, went one better: WOW could not pray at the Kotel for internal security reasons and, in addition, could not pray at any of the alternative sites considered because of external security reasons. The third committee to sit on the matter was the Ne'eman Commission, which at the time was deliberating the issue of non-Orthodox conversions; this commission recommended Robinson's Arch as the most practical alternative.

After the conclusions of the first committee were issued, we retraced our steps back to the Supreme Court. The Court issued an order *nisi*—an order to show cause—on WOW's renewed petition, and the hearing was held on September 24, 1998. We argued that because the government has shown itself to be clearly incapable of implementing the recommendations of the Court and securing WOW's right of worship and right of access to the Kotel, the last resort was the Court itself. Only after the conclusions of the third committee did the repeated hearings before the Supreme Court and the repeated postponements requested by the government and conceded to by the Court culminate in a summing up and a decision in May 2000. Our arguments were heard by Justices Eliahu Matza, Dorit Beinish and Tova Strasburg-Cohen, who conducted a tour of the Kotel and all the alternative sites that had been considered by the various committees before rendering judgment. It is worthy of note that in the first decision, which I shall refer to as "Hoffman I," all the justices were male; in "Hoffman II" the Court was composed of two women and one man.

In Hoffman II, Justice Matza wrote the opinion of the Court, and Justices Beinish and Strasburg-Cohen concurred. The Court held that the majority in Hoffman I had recognized the right of WOW to pray in its manner at the Kotel. Hence it concluded that the recommendations of the various governmental committees, in seeking alternative sites, had all been contrary to the directions of the Court. Indeed, the Court held, on the basis of its own impressions from the tour of the sites, none of the alternative sites could serve, even partially, to implement WOW's right to pray at the Kotel. The Court directed the government to implement WOW's prayer rights at the Kotel within six months.

The decision was a groundbreaking and courageous opinion and constituted a significant step forward in the implementation of WOW's previously abstract right. It clarified that the Hoffman I decision bestowed full recognition of WOW's right to pray in accordance with its custom at the Kotel. It also transformed the Shamgar recommendation into a judicial directive and concretized the government's obligation to implement the right as an obligation fixed in time and place. However, the Court refrained from actively intervening and itself establishing the prayer arrangements at the Kotel. It held that it was, at this stage, refraining from doing so because the petition had been presented in the context of an expected government decision, but the government had not actually issued a decision. This somewhat evasive conclusion is probably to be attributed to the Court's defensiveness in the face of ongoing attacks by politicians, religious elements, and some academics that the Court is too activist, particularly in matters of state and religion.

The reactions in Israel to the decision in Hoffman II were aggressive. The religious parties immediately introduced a bill to convert the area in front of the Kotel into a religious shrine exclusively for Orthodox religious practices and to impose a penalty of seven years' imprisonment on any woman violating the current (Orthodox) custom of prayer at the Kotel. These bills were supported by a number of Knesset members from secular parties and are still pending at the time of this writing. The attorney general asked the president of the Supreme Court to grant a further hearing of the case and to overrule Hoffman II—a surprising move on the legal level, as the decision had been unanimous. The attorney general claimed, amongst other things, that the Court misunderstood Hoffman I. The decision of the attorney general is political, demonstrating the reluctance of the government to implement the human rights of WOW in accordance with the Court's directive. The president of the Court, Aharon Barak, granted the request and appointed an expanded panel of nine justices to reconsider the issue.

The popular reaction to the decision in Hoffman II has also been hostile. The religious right has been predictably vicious in its response. However, even academics, intellectuals, and journalists who are generally committed to a liberal point of view have demonstrated an overt hostility to the women. They have claimed in newspaper articles and public discussion that this was a "provocation." This claim is not as surprising as it may seem; it is consonant with the general perspective of the secular majority in Israel that the Jewish religion is Orthodoxy. The secular liberal community has no interest in women's struggle to open up Orthodoxy and make it more egalitarian, regarding it as irrelevant to human rights concerns. Political hostility to WOW probably stems from the perception that the issue may create an obstruction to the various coalition maneuvers that each of the political players conducts in order to gain the support of the religious parties for its agenda. (In Israel's coalition government system, the religious parties hold the political balance of power and exercise disproportionate power.)

The case of WOW is heavy with symbolism. The violent opposition to the group, condoned by the public will and officialdom, symbolizes the silencing of women through the ages; it epitomizes tradition and patriarchy at the heart of Jewish nationhood. The petition of WOW, condoned by the Supreme Court, represents a universalist and feminist ethic. In this confrontation, there is little option but to await the Court's verdict for the third time. The other organs of government seem to offer little hope for a solution. The government has demonstrated its unwillingness to act. The Knesset is most unlikely to provide a political option. The fate of the petition is greatly significant not only for religious women and men but also for the secular world and constitutional values. Its success would signify the victory of pluralism and tolerance over fundamentalism. Whatever the legal outcome may be, the Women of the Wall have placed the issue of women's full personhood within religion on the public agenda in Israel.

SUSAN ALTER

Scenes from a Courtroom

ON MAY 22, 2000, I was in the Israeli Supreme Court to hear a decision on an appeal made to that Court a number of years earlier. The Court had denied us the right to pray as a group of women at the Kotel and read from a *sefer Torah.*

At that time, the Israeli authorities had adamantly refused to respond to our numerous requests for a meeting. We wanted to explain our intentions to conduct a prayer service strictly according to Halakhah. Their intransigence led to the filing of our lawsuit as the only way to make our intentions known and, ultimately, our voices heard.

At 9:00 A.M., Peggy Cidor of WOW picked me up by cab in front of the residential complex where I was staying. We arrived at the Supreme Court building at 10:00 A.M. and went through security. We walked up the stairs and down a grand hallway that serves as an antechamber and common waiting area for all the courtrooms. There was not a soul anywhere. I was surprised and asked Peggy when the rest of the women would arrive. She stated matter-of-factly that she expected no one else except perhaps some Hebrew University students and, of course, Jerusalem city council member Anat Hoffman. Peggy explained that because the appeal was doomed to failure, there was no purpose in asking women to take time away from school, jobs, and family to appear in Court.

To my delight, at 11:00 A.M. Anat arrived, along with WOW members Danielle Bernstein and Stephanie Raker. Trotting behind were TV and print media reporters. Anat showed us a press release she had prepared to distribute to the media after the verdict, decrying the decision against us.

The four of us entered the courtroom and sat huddled together. We whispered half thoughts to each other about what should be done after our defeat. Suddenly, the courtroom became hushed as the three magistrates entered. The women slid back into their seats. The docket was called. Our case was first. We were settling in, expecting a long harangue about why our actions were not acceptable. Our mouths fell open; we moved to the edge of our seats. We stared ahead in total disbelief. Then we looked back and forth at each other, trying to capture from each other unspoken histrionics indicating the clear assurance that we had actually won our appeal. Indeed, the court's decision was that the Israeli women could, as was their custom, pray as a group and read from a *sefer Torah* at the Kotel.

MIRIAM BENSON

The Lawsuit: 1989–Present

SINCE 1989, a group of women has been trying to pray together at the Kotel, the Western Wall, in Jerusalem. This attempt has been thwarted by private and state-sanctioned violence. The legal and political systems in Israel have capitulated to *charedi* violence or the threat of violence. Awareness of the chronology of the legal procedures and some related events is critical in order to fully understand our shock and dismay at each step of the legal proceedings. Our treatment during this lawsuit amounts to a travesty of justice. Only through this awareness of each "small" delay, denial, rejection, and misrepresentation to the court can one fully understand the enormity of the travesty of justice perpetrated against us.

In December 1988, the First International Jewish Feminist Conference, entitled "The Empowerment of Jewish Women," took place in Jerusalem; while there, a group of Orthodox, Conservative, Reform, Reconstructionist, and unaffiliated Jewish women decided to pray at the Kotel, in the women's section. The prayer service took place with relatively minor disturbances. Subsequently, a group of Jerusalem women, Women of the Wall (WOW), attempted to pray together at the Kotel in January and February 1989. They were harassed, cursed, and beaten by ultra-Orthodox men, who even tried to steal the Torah scroll. The ushers and police refused to intervene at all; thus the acts of private violence gained sanction by the state. The prayers in March 1989 ended when the police intervened with tear gas.

Stage One of the Lawsuit

This intolerable situation led four members of the group to initiate stage one of our lawsuit. They submitted a petition to the Supreme Court asking for an order for the police, the Ministry of Religious Affairs, and the administrator, or *memuneh*, of the Kotel to allow the women to pray together as a group with a *sefer Torah* and wearing *tallitot*, and to protect them from violence. At this stage, the petition did not include the demand to be allowed to pray out loud, as this had not yet been denied us, and who could possibly have imagined that it would be? This would in fact be denied in July and August of 1989.

Meanwhile, WOW decided to pray together every Friday morning and Rosh Chodesh at the Kotel. April and May passed; there was more violence from ultra-Orthodox men and women. In one incident, heavy metal chairs were thrown by the ultra-Orthodox at our group. One woman was seriously injured with a deep cut on her head. She submitted a formal complaint to the police, but this file was closed by them for its alleged "lack of public interest."

May 1989 also marked the first hearing in the Supreme Court. The state was given six months, until December 31, 1989, to respond to our petition. Normally, the court mandates a response time of thirty or forty-five days, so six months was unusually long. When WOW protested such a long delay, the response of Justice Menachem Elon was, "You've waited two thousand years; you can wait six more months." This felt like an unbearable delay, but WOW had to play by the rules mandated by the Court. In this context, the Court issued a temporary injunction ordering that until the final decision is rendered, WOW may not pray with Torah and tallit. In return for this, WOW was promised protection by the state.

June came, and with it the next twist: WOW went to the Kotel, without tallit or *sefer Torah,* obeying the court's injunction. The attacking ultra-Orthodox women were now screaming that WOW may not pray aloud, because *Kol b'ishah erva*—"The voice of a woman is lewd." Police and ushers again refused to intervene.

In July, female guards hired by the Ministry of Religious Affairs were at the Kotel when WOW arrived. Naively, we thought they were there for our protection. We were wrong; they were there to physically and violently disband and eject us, because Rabbi Getz, the administrator of the Kotel, ordered them to do this. The guards were for the most part young Sephardic women; they had no idea who we were, what we were trying to do, and why. The guards' reaction to us—their ridicule and their lack of comprehension—seemed to indicate that on the surface this issue is marginal or irrelevant for native Israeli women. It is not truly marginal or irrelevant, however, because the spiritual empowerment of any women in this area could never be marginal or irrelevant.

In August, the same female guards again harassed us and threatened to remove us. This time we sat down and linked arms in order to finish praying, and we were dragged out one by one by these guards. We were bruised, beaten, cursed, and pelted with dirt.

Immediately, we returned to the Supreme Court to request that the date for the state's response be moved up from December 31 and that we be allowed to pray out loud. The court refused, again stating that we must observe the state's current definition of the "custom of the place." The representative of the state in this case was a woman, Nili Arad. She is an intelligent, articulate lawyer and she heads the Bagatz, or High Court of Justice Department in the State Attorney General's Office. The outrageous position of the state in this case forced her into the ironic, ludicrous position of having to get up before the Supreme Court on August 25, 1989, and declare that the state's official position is that *Kol b'ishah erva.*

More than thirteen years have now passed. WOW has stringently obeyed the court's rules, set down in the temporary injunction. The women do not chant their prayers, they recite them in a monotone. They are stifled and almost silenced. This situation brings to mind a passage from Judith Plaskow's book *Standing Again at Sinai: Judaism from a Feminist Perspective:* "The silence of women reverberates through the tradition, distorting the shape of narrative and skewing the content of the law. Only the deliberate recovery of women's hidden voices, the unearthing and invention of women's Torah, can give us Jewish teachings that are the product of the whole Jewish people and that reflect more fully its experiences of God." The events of the last thirteen years concerning women's prayer at the Kotel epitomize the attempt to silence women. We will, however, continue our effort to triumph over this attempt to silence us.

In the meantime, until such triumph, what transpires each Rosh Chodesh reflects the travesty of justice that has been perpetrated against us. In order to adapt to the Court's rules, WOW often conducts the morning service at the Kotel in a monotone, until the Torah service. The women then "retreat" to a courtyard in the Jewish Quarter, away from the Kotel, out of the jurisdiction of the *memuneh,* to conduct the Torah reading and concluding service. For many years they had to house the donated Torah scroll at a sympathetic synagogue all the way across town, causing terribly inconvenient logistical problems; they had to schlepp our precious Torah scroll in a duffel bag, by taxi, to and from the Kotel each month. Bear in mind that the Ministry of Religious Affairs purchases, maintains, and houses at least a hundred Torah scrolls on the men's side, all at the Israeli taxpayers' expense.

On December 31, 1989, a new regulation was promulgated by the Ministries of Religious Affairs and Justice that "prohibits any religious ceremony at a holy place that is not in accordance with the custom of the holy site and which offends the sensibilities of the worshipers at the place." The penalty for violating this regulation is six months in jail and/or a fine. The state submitted this regulation instead of answering our petition on the merits. In spite of this attempt to ignore, belittle, and dismiss our petition, the state was ordered by the Supreme Court to answer the petition on the merits.

Right before Passover in April 1990, the state finally filed its response, which was a 150-page compendium of some of the most antiwoman halakhic opinions on women's right to pray out loud as a group, to wear tallit, and to touch and read from the Torah scroll. The state could have chosen less vitriolic opinions in support of its position. It is in fact astounding that they chose such extremist, reactionary opinions to submit in opposing our lawsuit and that they got away with it with barely a peep of protest (except by our attorneys). We imagined, even assumed, that when we published excerpts from the state's brief in our 1991 newsletter, there would follow a worldwide outcry about the travesty of justice occurring in the Israeli Supreme Court. This travesty is immediately apparent upon reviewing the vitriolic misogyny of the state's brief. How could Nili Arad imagine that she could get away with adopting these halakhic opinions as part of the state's official position against our lawsuit? She could, and she did. To our total shock and dismay, we were met with a deafening silence, despite our exposure of the state's brief.

In August 1990, the Israel Women's Network submitted a motion to the court to allow them to join the Israeli women's lawsuit as a co-petitioner. This action was taken to demonstrate that there were even more women who were interested parties on our side, and to give our lawsuit more legal and political clout. The Court rejected the Israel Women's Network motion, saying that too much time had passed since the original petition had been filed, and that the joinder would complicate matters too much. This was an unjust, discriminatory, and baseless decision, particularly in view of the fact that two ultra-Orthodox political parties, Shas and Degel Hatorah, were allowed to join the respondents (i.e., the state) on their behalf in the case. The Court did not even raise an eyebrow in granting their motion. There was, unfortunately, no appeal available, according to the rules of the decision of the Court to reject the Israel Women's Network motion. The travesty of justice continued.

Concurrently with all the events described above, a group of women, based primarily in the United States and Canada, formed the International Committee for Women of the Wall (ICWOW). Our goals are, among others, to secure the right of all Jewish women to pray together at the Kotel; to encourage women's study and learning; and to enable women to function as religious authorities. I serve as the legal liaison from ICWOW to our attorneys in Israel.

We planned to go to Israel to give a Torah scroll to the Israeli women in December 1989 and to attempt to pray together on Rosh Chodesh at the Kotel. Until that time, the women had borrowed Torah scrolls from various sympathetic Jerusalem synagogues. We succeeded in raising the money for the Torah—quite a hefty sum— and dedicated it to the Israeli women. However, the dedication ceremony did not occur at the Laromme Hotel (a posh, five-star hotel) as planned, because the Jerusalem rabbinate threatened to revoke the hotel's kashrut license if the ceremony went ahead on the premises. Our attorneys submitted an urgent court motion to force the hotel to fulfill its side of the bargain, but the Court did not enforce the contract. We also did not succeed in praying at the Kotel, because Rav Getz, the administrator of the Kotel, prevented us from doing so.

Pursuant to these events, ICWOW decided to file its own lawsuit in June 1990. This issue is of critical importance not only for Israeli Jewish women but also for Jewish women in the entire diaspora. Just imagine tourism brochures that advertise celebrating your daughter's bat mitzvah at the Kotel! As an option in addition to Masada! Or imagine being able to conduct a woman's *aufruf* before a wedding at the Kotel! Why shouldn't these joyous occasions be possible? Significantly, the state never once, in the thirteen years of litigation, challenged ICWOW's "standing," or "right to sue," in the Israeli Supreme Court, despite the fact that ICWOW is unabashedly a diaspora-based group. Our standing was taken for granted, perhaps because Israel would not dare challenge the diaspora community's claim to the Kotel as a holy site for all the Jewish people. The authorities feign impotence in protecting those Jews who happen to be women and who want to pray as a group, out loud, with Torah and tallit, at the Kotel. Nonetheless, they did not dare to challenge our standing. This act of omission illustrates that the issue is a legitimate one for diaspora Jewry, so much so that our opponents never challenged our standing.

Soon after ICWOW filed its petition, the state submitted one sentence saying that their response to our petition was the same as the one they submitted in the Israeli women's case. At the suggestion of our first attorney, Arnold Shpaer, we hired our own expert to write an opinion on the issues of Halakhah and *minhag*. We also eagerly searched for one or more organizational co-petitioners in order to show that there are large numbers of women who are interested parties, and to add legal and political strength to our side, but unfortunately, we were completely unsuccessful in this effort. The Supreme Court heard oral arguments on the case on February 27, 1991. The court's decision was finally given on January 26, 1994. The three judges on the panel were Menachem Elon, Meir Shamgar, and Shlomo Levine.

The decision was 2 to 1 against us. Each judge wrote his own separate opinion, for a total of ninety-three pages (see *Piskei Din* 48, Vol. 2, pp. 265–358). In brief, Justice Elon (pp. 274–353), interestingly, found that our mode of prayer does meet halakhic requirements (p. 321, letter Dalet), but that it goes against *minhag hamakom*, the "custom of the place." He found that the Kotel is equivalent to a synagogue, and the custom of the place is determined by Rav Getz, the *mara d'atra*, or "halakhic decisor," of that "synagogue." Justice Elon concluded that we may not conduct these types of services at the Kotel. He also found that the regulations promulgated by the Minister of Religious Affairs were within his authority, and therefore they were upheld.

Justice Levine, in the minority, accepted our petition (pp. 356–358), with the proviso that there be a one-year delay in which time the public could get used to the idea of women praying at the Kotel, in a group, with a *sefer Torah* and wearing a tallit. Justice Shamgar, the presiding judge, said that in principle he was in favor of our petition, but he rejected it anyway (pp. 353–356) because the legal remedy we were asking for was premature. Rather, he recommended that we first fully explore the political process and that the government set up a commission to study the matter. He issued what we term the Shamgar Mandate, which we maintain binds the political and legal machinery to this day. Shamgar's mandate to the commission was "to find a solution that will ensure free access to the Kotel and minimize any offense to the worshipers' sensitivities."

In a vague, somewhat patronizing, but perhaps meant-to-be-com-forting statement, Justice Shamgar stated that if we were not satis-fied with the political process, the doors of the Court were always open to us (p. 356).

We were faced with a dilemma. We had only fifteen days from January 26 to decide whether to request an appeal, which would be heard before a panel of five judges (the same three plus two new ones, except that Justice Elon retired soon after the decision was rendered, so our panel would have been Justices Shamgar, Levine, and three others). This would have been an appeal by discretion, not right—that is, we had to *request* the right to appeal. There were those among us who preferred to file the request for appeal and those who preferred to continue the battle only in the political forum, with the commission. We decided, after intense discussion, to think big and fight on all fronts. We did file a request for an appeal, just in time.

Our request for an appeal was made on four grounds: (1) this was the first case regarding free access to holy sites where free expression was denied to members of the same faith (i.e., not a case of Jews versus Muslims or Muslims versus Christians, but of Jews versus Jews); (2) Elon's exclusive reliance on halakhic grounds is questionable; (3) the Ministers of Religious Affairs and Justice improperly exceeded their authority when they issued regulations that restricted free access even as they based the issuance of them on a statute that ostensibly *ensures* free access; and (4) the issues of the guarantees for women's rights and pluralism were not adequately addressed by the Court.

We simultaneously requested that the government set up a com-mission to study this matter, as Justice Shamgar recommended. In May 1994, the government appointed a directors' general commission to study the issue. The mandate for the Mancal Commission, as it became known, was to "propose a realistic solution that will guarantee free access to the Kotel while minimizing any offense to the sensitivities of the other worshipers at the site." This directly reflected Justice Shamgar's mandate. Not one woman was appointed to the Commission; only after pressure was Navah Arad, advisor to the prime minister on the status of women, named as an observer—she did not even have a vote. The Commission had six months—until November 17, 1994—to come up with recommendations.

Ten days later, the Supreme Court ruled on our request for an appeal. Justice Aharon Barak, currently president of the Court, rejected it, stating that the Commission had been set up and it was now the proper venue. According to Supreme Court rules, there is no appeal of the decision to reject the request for an appeal. However, the Court quoted Justice Shamgar's words—namely, that the doors of the court are always open to us if we are not satisfied by the political process. In this somewhat ambiguous atmosphere—request for appeal denied and no appeal available against the denial, coupled with a vague, patronizing, yet meant-to-be-comforting statement by Justice Shamgar (and quoted subsequently by Justice Barak) that the doors of the Court are always open to us—stage one of the lawsuit ended. The result: we were "thrown to the dogs" in the Mancal Commission.

The Commission Nightmare

We are certain that the Mancal Commission was set up only because we had requested the appeal—that is, we had used the leverage of further Court action.

As soon as the Mancal Commission was set up, we immediately began a massive lobbying campaign to encourage individuals and organizations to write letters of support to the Commission. At least six hundred individuals and organizations, representing the views of more than 3.5 million Jews, wrote letters to the Mancal Commission in support of our position. The organizational letters were from an impressive list that we hoped would influence the Commission to find a just solution: Hadassah, American Jewish Congress, American Jewish Committee, World Jewish Congress, and all the organizational bodies of the Conservative, Reform, and Reconstructionist branches, as well as the Academy for Jewish Religion (nondenominational). The denominational letters were from the Rabbinical Assembly (Conservative), the Women's League for Conservative Judaism, the United Synagogue for Conservative Judaism, the Central Conference of American Rabbis (Reform), the Union of American Hebrew Congregations, the Federation of Temple Sisterhoods, Hebrew Union College, the Reconstructionist Rabbinical Assembly, Reconstructionist Rabbinical College, the Federation of Reconstructionist Synagogues, and the Academy for Jewish Religion. There were many beautiful, moving letters that we fervently hoped would influence the Commission in our favor.

However, despite this outpouring of support for our position in response to our letter-writing campaign, the Commission took no action whatsoever. The Commission was granted a six-month extension by the government, so the new deadline was May 17, 1995. We opposed such an extension; we thought that six months should have been enough time to come up with any possible proposals for a solution. The government's request for an extension was especially outrageous, as the state had fraudulently misrepresented to the Court when we requested the appeal that the Commission would issue its report within the original mandated period—that is, six months. The Court denied our request for an appeal based on this fraudulent misrepresentation by the state.

Immediately after the Commission was established, we officially requested to testify before it, and after much back-and-forth correspondence about setting the date, whether our testimony would be before the entire Commission, and other contrived obstacles, we testified before the entire Commission on February 27, 1995. ICWOW sent one representative from the United States to speak on our behalf, and there were six Israeli women who have been active over the years, including a thirteen-year-old girl who celebrated her bat mitzvah with the group at the Kotel and a woman who celebrated her *aufruf* with the group at the Kotel. These seven representatives and our lawyers met with the Commission members for two and a half hours. It was apparent that the chairman, Shimon Sheves, had his mind made up in advance—he had marked the page of the Supreme Court decision where we were called "provocateurs" by the Court. The representative from the Ministry of Religious Affairs was quite hostile to us. The state's continuing lack of good-faith negotiation was never even criticized by the Court.

After our testimony on February 27, despite the seeming hostility of certain members, we still remained cautiously optimistic about the Commission. However, as the new deadline of May 17 approached and we heard absolutely nothing about the presumed report, we began to get more and more concerned. We began to prepare for the possibility of returning to Court—by this I mean fundraising, as this sort of litigation requires tens of thousands of dollars for legal fees and court fees. We were able to authorize our new attorney, Frances Raday, to file suit against the Commission for its inaction in late May 1995, immediately after the deadline expired, and to ask that the Court find a solution at the Kotel if the government did not.

Stage Two of the Lawsuit

Thus began stage two of the litigation, with the filing of the second lawsuit. The lawsuit asked that the Court issue an injunction against the government, prohibiting any further deadline extensions, and that the Commission issue its report immediately. Our attorney also demanded that until the Commission issued its report, we be allowed to pray out loud, as a group, with Torah and tallit, so that our rights of access, worship, assembly, religion, and equality would not continue to be violated. In October 1996, our attorney added another demand: if the government could not find a solution for us at the Kotel, the Court must do so.

We view this second lawsuit as a direct outgrowth of the first. It is essentially part and parcel of the same legal action. This is especially true in view of the fact that we were unjustly denied the right to appeal the first lawsuit, based on the blatant misrepresentation by the state that they would deal with us in good faith through the Mancal Commission by finding us a solution at the Kotel within six months of its appointment in May 1994, in accordance with Justice Shamgar's mandate. Therefore, while stage two technically refers to a separate lawsuit, it cannot be separated from stage one. In essence, we view stage two as our appeal of stage one, as we were denied the technical opportunity to appeal stage one directly.

Unfortunately, the Court rejected our request for an injunction preventing the government from further extending a deadline. In June 1995, predictably, the government decided on yet another extension, until November 17, 1995. Finally, in April 1996, the Mancal Commission recommended to the government that we be given an absurd site: at the southeastern corner of the Old City wall, entirely outside the Old City, near the Tower of Avshalom, adjacent to the Ophel Road. This site has no access through the Jewish Quarter at all. Despite the absurdity of the Commission's result, on April 21, 1996, the government acknowledged receipt of the report and appointed yet a new commission, made up of several ministers, to decide whether to approve, reject, or amend the first commission's recommendation. Elections occurred a month later, which led to Labor being ousted by Likud.

On a more positive note, at a pretrial hearing on October 24, 1996, the Court ordered the state to pay us five thousand shekels plus 17 percent tax in costs (approximately $1,800). On the one hand, this covered only a miniscule fraction of our legal costs; on the other hand, this award represented the Court's explicit lack of patience with the seemingly unending delay tactics of the state. Thus it symbolizes for us the small hope that justice will eventually be done. Furthermore, in the beginning of March 1997, the Court finally ordered the state to answer our petition on the merits in sixty days.

The day after the Court order, a bill proposed by the Shas Party passed the first of its two required votes in the Knesset, 25 to 8. The bill's essential purpose was to expand, through statute, the authority of the Kotel administrator, to be the final arbiter of all disputes and to make final decisions concerning the custom of the place. Shas hoped to circumvent any possible Supreme Court decision in our favor through this legislation. It is possible in Israel to overturn a Supreme Court decision by Knesset legislation, with a simple majority; as Israel has no written constitution, there is not even a requirement of a two-thirds majority. This ominous development prompted us to start yet another letter-writing campaign to Prime Minister Benjamin Netanyahu and all the members of the Knesset, demanding that they oppose the bill in all future votes. The identical bill has been resubmitted each year, most recently in May 2000, but it has not passed so far; we must, however, remain forever vigilant.

In a separate but related development, right before Rosh Hashanah, 1995, Rav Getz died. We sent letters to the appointing ministers, asking that a progressive administrator of the Kotel be appointed as his successor. Rav Getz had been the administrator of the Kotel since 1967. His successor would continue to affect the spiritual, legal, and political atmosphere at the Kotel; thus we went on record to request a progressive person. How wonderful it would be if the successor brought a different attitude to this position. Despite our letter-writing campaign, a very reactionary man was appointed: Rav Shmuel Rabinovitz. He was succeeded by Rav Maya and then by Rav Gamliel. There have been several new appointments to this position, none of whom have acted in a less misogynist, reactionary fashion.

We insist that the proper title be used for this person. This functionary is commonly referred to in the media and by the Court as *Rav ha-Kotel*, "Rabbi of the Kotel." The title *Rav ha-Kotel* appears nowhere in Israeli statute or regulation. Rather, the proper title is *Memuneh al ha-Kotel*, "Administrator of the Kotel." The misuse of the title is not merely a semantic error; it is more deeply problematic because it implies a religious authority to this functionary. Calling the administrator a *rav* imputes a power that we explicitly dispute. The Kotel is not, in our view, a synagogue; nor was Rav Getz or any of his successors the *mara d'atra* (halakhic decisor) of that place; nor may any of these rabbis have proper authority to ascertain the *minhag* (custom) of that place and prohibit all else. We were unjustly refused the opportunity to fully argue these points when we were denied the request to appeal to the Supreme Court. However, by accurately referring to this functionary as "administrator," we reasserted our position.

On June 2, 1997, in Decision "Jerusalem 14," the Ministerial Commission on Jerusalem decided that despite the fact that Israel recognizes freedom of worship and religion for everyone, the status quo at the Kotel must be preserved. This decision explicitly referred to a (secret) police report. The Commission stated that there will be danger to public order if any change is made in the status quo. Our lawyer requested discovery of this secret report. Nili Arad, the state's attorney, refused to turn it over.

At every stage of the lawsuit, in written and oral argument, the state has been permitted to argue this absurd and pernicious argument: "The Israeli police are impotent in protecting WOW in the women's section at the Kotel when they pray as a group, out loud, with Torah and tallit." This argument has been based on secret reports that we have been unable to refute because we have not been given copies. We argue that just as Jews and Muslims are afforded a time-sharing arrangement at the Cave of Machpelah, so too should women be afforded a time-sharing arrangement in the women's section at the Kotel. The arrangement at the Cave of Machpelah is viewed as important enough to maintain, at all costs, even after the Baruch Goldstein massacre. Are we any less important? Furthermore, a group of Conservative Jews was successfully protected by the police at the Kotel (at a spot slightly removed from the Kotel proper, not immediately adjacent to the Kotel but rather near the Dung Gate parking lot) on Shavuot 1998, despite two previous holiday prayer services where the *charedim* perpetrated acts of violence against this group (Shavuot and Tisha B'Av, 1997). We dispute that we are unprotectable. We are eminently protectable, if only the prime minister would order the Ministry of Internal Security to protect us, as he ultimately did for the Conservative group. At the minimum, we should have been given copies of the police reports to enable us to refute them factually. Otherwise, the Israeli legal and political system has entirely capitulated to *charedi* violence or threat of violence. We protest this capitulation with every fiber of our beings.

The lawsuit was set for a hearing on September 22, 1997. During the course of the hearing, WOW's attorneys were subjected to intense pressure by the judges to agree to attend meetings of the Ne'eman Commission, which was already convened to deal with the conversion issue. Our attorneys felt that we had to agree, as the Court would have viewed our refusal as bad-faith behavior. We attempted to impose conditions on our attendance, none of which were honored. We were ultimately not even voting members on the Commission! The Ne'eman Commission met several times to discuss our issue, and its members toured the Kotel area. On September 23, 1998, the Ne'eman Commission issued its report, in which Yakov Ne'eman (purportedly speaking for the Commission) concluded that we should pray at Robinson's Arch.

Robinson's Arch is an area along the western wall of the Temple Mount, south of the Kotel, and is currently an archaeological site. (The Conservative movement accepted this site as an interim arrangement for its prayer in May 2000.) It should be noted that several years ago, in the context of stage two of the lawsuit, both the Conservative and Reform movements in Israel signed affidavits stating that they do not wish their claims to in any way impede or delay a remedy for us. In his report, Ne'eman again repeated the absurd argument that we are unprotectable in the women's section at the Kotel. No serious attention was given by the Commission to a time-sharing arrangement in the women's section. Furthermore, WOW did not even get a vote.

The lawsuit was scheduled to be heard on the merits on February 17, 1999. The day before this hearing, the state submitted an affidavit by Jerusalem Chief of Police Yair Yitzhaki, in which he repeated the calumny that WOW provoked the violence.

> The Women of the Wall's prayer services agitate the regular worshipers at the site and cause disturbances to public order that necessitate police intervention. In the past, massive police intervention was necessary, including the use of tear gas. . . . Based on past experience and the situation today, especially in view of the sensitivity of the Kotel site and the deterioration in relations between the various Jewish denominations, I reiterate my position that I propounded before the Ne'eman Commission—namely, that the prayer services of WOW at the Kotel will cause serious disturbances of public order. Even WOW's minimalist proposal—namely, one prayer service per month according to their custom, on each Rosh Chodesh—will, with a high degree of likelihood, provoke the use of violent measures by the worshipers at the site and will cause huge riots and public disturbances, with a real risk of physical danger to the worshipers. . . . In my opinion, this scenario would occur not only in the women's section, but also in the parking lot site [where the Conservative and Reform groups have prayed in recent years]."

Yitzhaki's position clearly articulated the Israeli authorities' capitulation to *charedi* violence or threat of violence. His position represented, once again, the travesty of justice perpetrated against WOW and ICWOW by the Israeli legal and political machinery.

The February 17 bench consisted of Justices Eliahu Matza, Dorit Beinish, and Tova Strasburg-Cohen. This was probably one of the best judicial panels we could have gotten. However, we were very pessimistic about the outcome, based on various comments made by the judges during the hearings as well as during the tour of the alternate sites, which occurred in February 2000.

On May 22, 2000, the decision was handed down on our 1996 lawsuit. Although Judge Matza wrote a lengthy opinion (Judges Strasburg-Cohen and Beinish concurred) that explicitly recognized our rights in principle, he stopped short of awarding us a solution at the Kotel. Rather, by manufacturing the flimsy excuse that there had been no government decision in our matter (despite the tortuous legal and political proceedings that had resulted in the Mancal Commission's decision, the governmental decision that acknowledged receipt of the Shamgar report, the Ministerial Commission on Jerusalem decision, and the Ne'eman Commission report), he transferred the matter yet again to the government to find us a solution at the Kotel within a further six months. He did award us twenty thousand shekels to cover our legal costs—a symbolic, miniscule, drop-in-the-bucket sum compared to our true costs.

By explicitly declaring our rights in principle, Matza's opinion reiterated the tenor and wording of the Shamgar Mandate from January 1994 and, like Shamgar, insisted that the issue be dealt with by the government. On a practical level, Matza's opinion went not one iota further than Shamgar's. His wonderfully supportive statements concerning our rights in principle were enormously gratifying, but they constitute mere platitudes. He succeeded in persuading the media, our opponents, and even some of our supporters that we had truly won, thanks to his disingenuous reasoning and wording. The first twenty-eight paragraphs were enthusiastically supportive of our rights, but the operative paragraphs—twenty-nine and thirty—undercut the entire first part of the opinion by denying us an actual remedy. While we applaud the declarative recognition of our rights in principle, we decry the fact that the Court found it necessary to manufacture a loophole to avoid awarding us a remedy. Matza himself sharply criticized the entire legal and political process thus far as constituting *sachevet*, or foot-dragging bureaucracy. What is astonishing is that he himself perpetuated the *sachevet* by refusing to grant us any Court-imposed solution for our group, praying according to our custom, in the women's section at the Kotel. After all, Shamgar's six-month deadline from January 1994, issued with his mandate to the government to find us a solution at the Kotel, turned into more than six years, and still there has been no solution for us found at the Kotel. Matza's stance, together with the other two judges' concurrence, further constitutes the capitulation of the Israeli legal and political systems to *charedi* violence or threat of violence.

Now five out of six Supreme Court justices who have heard this case have declared our rights (Justices Shamgar and Levine in 1994, and Justices Matza, Beinish, and Strasburg-Cohen in 2000); despite this, the state filed a request for an appeal on the May 22 decision on June 6, 2000. On July 13, Justice Barak granted the request, despite our opposition and despite the fact that he had denied *our* request for an appeal after the January 1994 decision.

Our Claims

We deny the following points, which currently represent the status quo according to the January 1994 and May 2000 Supreme Court decisions. We protest each of the following findings, and pray that we have the funds and fortitude to continue the court battle until we reverse each one.

We deny that the 1989 regulation, which outlaws women's group prayer, out loud, with Torah and tallit, in the women's section, punishable by six months in jail and/or a heavy fine, is legal.

We deny that we provoke the violence.

We deny that we are unprotectable by the Israeli police and border police.

We deny that criminal thugs who perpetrate or threaten to perpetrate acts of violence against us should be immune from arrest and prosecution and should be permitted to dictate Israeli legal and political policy.

We deny that the state has done justice by capitulating to *charedi* violence or threat of violence.

We do not concede that we are less important than the Jews and Muslims who pray at the Cave of Machpelah according to a strict time-sharing arrangement, which has been enforced and upheld even after the Baruch Goldstein massacre.

We do not concede that the Kotel is a *beit knesset* (synagogue) with the *Memuneh al ha-Kotel* (Administrator of the Kotel) as *mara d'atra* (halakhic decisor) of that synagogue.

We do not concede that the *memuneh* has authority to determine what is the *minhag hamakom*, the custom of the site.

We do not concede that alternate sites—any sites other than the women's section at the Kotel—were, are, or will ever be satisfactory.

We will not rest until each of these assertions has been successfully refuted.

General Analysis

How could a modern democratic country have allowed each piece in this injustice to occur? Israel's politics, society, women's movement, and legal system are all implicated.

Politics. The ultra-Orthodox parties in Israel wield a great deal of power, disproportionate to their actual size, and they are having a real field day flexing their muscles, literally and figuratively, by keeping us silenced and excluded. In addition, the major political parties are far from supportive. This is evident in Dan Meridor, the former Minister of Justice, who is an avowed Likudnik and who signed the restrictive December 1989 regulation into effect.

Society. The Israeli public trivializes and dismisses this issue, as it does many women's issues. The religious or Orthodox sector claims that we are *Reformiot,* or Reform Jews, and the secular sector pretends not to be concerned with spiritual matters at all. The left-wing or liberal sector claims that we are "crazy feminists" and demonstrates that even this sector does not truly understand, care about, or fight for women's issues.

Women's movement. The various components of the women's movement in Israel have not consistently supported us, for a variety of reasons. Most recently this phenomenon has been apparent on the Internet discussion group Israel Feminist Forum, but it has been true throughout the entire decade. One commonly stated reason is that this is a marginal or irrelevant issue for Israeli women. However, the spiritual empowerment of women can never be viewed as marginal or irrelevant. Another basis for criticism has been our willingness to respect the *mechitzah,* and to omit the prayers that require a minyan. We obviously are convinced that our goals are legitimate, powerful, and feminist. However, the lack of support from the women's movement resulted in our failure to obtain an additional co-petitioner for our "second" 1995 lawsuit. The lone organization that has responded to our pleas for a co-petitioner was the Israel Women's Network, which requested to join the first lawsuit. The Court unjustly rejected their request.

Legal system. Israel has no written constitution, so the principles of freedom of worship, freedom of assembly, freedom of speech, and equal protection under the law are not codified in any such binding document. These principles do exist in Israeli jurisprudence, based on the case law that has developed over the last fifty years. However, these principles are more likely to be overridden in Israel than in the United States by considerations such as the protection of public order, especially at places like the Kotel that are designated by law as "holy sites." The amount of discretion that the administrators of the Kotel have been allowed to exercise has been excessive, and they have done so in a discriminatory fashion.

We fervently hope that our strategy brings about change and improvements in Israeli society by ensuring spiritual empowerment for Jewish women, and that we succeed in resisting the oppression of an enforced silence. We intend to expose and reverse the Israeli political and legal systems' policy of capitulation to *charedi* violence or threat of violence, and to prove that we are eminently protectable at the Kotel. Until that time, each passing day perpetuates the travesty of justice, as justice delayed is justice denied.

Stone Song

Seven stones build 5,040 houses.
From here on go out and think what the mouth is
not able to express, and the ear is
unable to hear.

—*TANYA, IGGERET HAKODESH*, 4:10.[1]

ONE BY ONE THEY CAME, and one by one they began to build. They came alone and they sang alone, and the prayers they offered were silent, as if a woman must approach her Creator carrying a stone, alone. It is what each had been taught, what each dared to hear. From all parts of the world they came to this sacred place, and with each soundless letter from their lips, one by one, alone, they prayed in their silence and in their tears and in the comfort they could feel standing close to the women beside them. For ages, women wept and prayed and indeed were building a dwelling with the stones of faith they kept hidden against their breasts, an invisible temple whose holy walls were held erect by sighs, breathed through closed eyes, built of wish-stones sent to the heavens with the private faith of countless women of valor.

Cold, G-d, it is cold here, sighs one of the women one of the days she has come to pray, alone, cold, and distant. She looks around at the other women bending their heads and huddling in their coats and blowing steam in the chill. She stretches her arms alone to place a stone-prayer atop the wall. *Maybe You want we should sing some together, maybe You want we should lift our heads, and hold the women's hands, maybe, maybe You want that some of us should try, just some, some, G-d, who never know and cannot learn to carry the stones silent inside their pockets, the weight of those elder-rocks causing a droop and a stoop that mutes the cry and the joy and kills the soul to Your word? Maybe You want that we shouldn't all be alone? Maybe You want a sacred change and maybe You are asking, G-d, that we should help? You've given us the stone-block, G-d; we've got the chisels and hammers, and maybe we've got the song as well?*

One by one, each in her way, the women came to this Wall and heard the question, muted by winter's wind and whispers of the ages, but when they listened hard and sometimes even when they tried not to hear, the women heard and had to admit they knew. They did not have to build alone. They did not have to be ashamed. *We can sculpt our words together, this is how the Temple will be reborn.* One by one they found this thing out, and the secret grew like a winter bloom inside their breasts.

This is a recounting of numerous women house-building in Jerusalem. These stories actually happened, in the holy city during 1988 and 1989, or 5749. This is a story sung stone by stone, still incomplete.

Part One: Moonstone-Gathering

In the houses of the fathers, the daughters, sisters, and mothers seek past chants. They suckle at Torah's ample breast and nest in the rest of Shabbat. They smell challah, and the trope of words, and growing, each in her way, builds her Jewish dwelling. But the swelling chokes her lungs, she suffocates on thick, sharp, deeply inscribed stone. She tries to sing and is told to stop, lest she disrupt the thoughts of the men worshiping loudly beside her. She implodes.

She squats on the edge of the fields of the fathers, gleans grapes from the corners of the harvest. She remains ravenous despite her repeated readings of the texts. Rocks crack her teeth as she chews. She asks the rabbi where the women were, how the teaching speaks to women, who were the priestesses and what were women's visions, why she should give thanks for being made something she is not. Silence. After so many patient nods of bearded heads and so many dismissals of the intuition guiding her spirit with subtle finesse, she turns away, alone.

From the fathers' houses she roams, and for a time she is sad and feels hopeless, and she wonders where her G-d might be found (not seeing the holy breath from her lips, her soul's question a precious prayer). Maybe in her wanderings she dares to dream that G-d, too, knows of this exile from the dwelling and longs, like her, to rest again in a sacred center.

The hurt carves deep in her soul and chisels notes of iron through her throat. She sings, maybe, when she is alone, and prays—without words, only melodies—to the One. It is enough to keep the soul alive. She alights in Jerusalem, walking its streets with tiny granules of stone lining the hems of her skirt or pants. They scratch against her knees, constant, rhythmic, rubbing, questions clunking; she doesn't yet know she carries seeds for the stone-song prayer of the building.

This one has always sung aloud and could never understand why other women didn't raise their voices to the heavens or at least to the rooftops and praise the Lord; they were such beautiful creatures of strength and power. She has seen how the traditions of the world keep the sisters apart and silent, and she knows better, and she'll be damned if she wastes time cramping in to fit their ideas about who she is. She knows this is a veil between herself and her Creator. She sniffs sacred winds that she knows, the Shekhinah's embrace.

She feels a holy counterhistory in that white around the letters; it is this instinct that brings her to Jerusalem. Around and through and sometimes in spite of what tradition has revealed, hers is the inheritance of the sacred secrets. She knows her mission is to renew the not-yet-born. So she is here, juggling sacred stones freely in her palm so she stands squarely looking the fathers right in the eye, and moving on.

(Sometimes she visits the Kotel late at night and stills her voice and listens hard, and sometimes the aging stones whisper to a very private part of her. Ancient winds catch against her blouse and burrow deep; lately they chant of the sweetness of unification, they pulse harmony in female tones, and they lodge very close to her heart.)

Her small frame walks tautly, her tight jeans are frayed, and her hand holds a cigarette with deliberate might. She is wounded. How in the hell can you believe in any of that crap! I haven't been able to pray since I was so young and they used to force it on me and used the religion to kick me into place to be a nice little girl who never made any trouble, and who I was inside was dying, dying, dying.

Kids get their heads cracked like walnuts by drunken fathers; people on planes get blasted to shreds by terrorists. You're gonna look at this world and then talk about some kind of G-d, and you want to say something about some kind of Jewish G-d who can give you meaning and law in your life that doesn't try to destroy everything you are?

162

Or what if you're gay, and the religious say G-d hates you? Who are they to say so? Then you want to tell me that you can talk to this G-d at this place you call holy because there's this Wall where people pray?! Well, sorry, y'know, but I'll tell you, I haven't prayed since I was a little girl.

Don't anybody dare take away my right to go to that place to see that G-d if I want to do that. I am a Jew, no matter what they think. Jerusalem has seen so much blood. She takes the stone from her jacket and hurls it towards the empty desert at a salmon-rust sunset, and if there is hope in a prayer for this woman's soul, it is there because she does not turn the stone to slice herself nor to make someone else bleed. She screams. She does not know a song and she waits but does not know for what; the possibility of prayer will have to find her.

> May it be Your will, Hashem, my G-d, and G-d of my ancestors, to fill the flaw of the moon that there should be no diminution in it. May the light of the moon be like the light of the sun and like the light of the seven days of Creation, as it was before it was diminished, as it is said: "The two great luminaries" (Genesis 1:16)... Amen.

She says this prayer to bless and greet every new moon, just after Shabbat leaves, with others, while dancing under the moonlight, according to tradition.

Human beings are nothing. G-d is the ultimate reality. She is grateful that she was raised in a home where her brothers and sisters were encouraged to do good for others and to cultivate their talents as they wished, as long as they worked hard, and where each Shabbos day the house was filled with songs, guests, laughing, and the easy contentment that set this day apart.

163

Intellectual pursuits studying literature and philosophy wound back around to the theological underpinnings of all human creations, and as she came to articulate herself more precisely and rigorously, she knew she would study Jewish sources. During her graduate work she became increasingly aware of new systems of thought that challenged her basic beliefs in G-d, and although she never considered these provocative assertions as profound threats to the solidity and elegance of the Jewish models of meaning, which she knew to be her blood and breath, she had to face the mysteries and contradictions in her mind.

Clear-light faith stones gain gravity and the density tumbles in her brain. She comes to Jerusalem to the university with her husband and young children and the persistent energy of her increasingly restless, intuitive intellect, which seeks for itself sophisticated understanding.

Women's roles in Judaism? She feels comfortable in her communal participation. Yet there is this question—is it just to be stopped? She reads feminist theorists whose texts, she acknowledges, speak to a vital yet vague aspect of her being.

Stone crater cracks the crevice beneath her feet and she treads carefully, but she walks, she listens, she prays daily, and she begins to talk with stones pressing against her tongue. Deep inside she feels that this, too, is of G-d and will be reconciled, in its time.

So one by one they came to Jerusalem in this year, carrying or bearing or delighting in the stones they each kept, which kept them, as many stones and as many women as there are letters in the *aleph-bet*—in other words, all possibilities here, hovering.

Yet possibilities only, a stone alone is but a stone alone. Stones become blocks of sculpted prayer when they affix themselves to more than one, and when two become ten during stone-seed planting and watchful watering, growth here, condensation and later expansion and absorption here, stone to song in prayer here, tree of Torah rooted here, and the sunlight and the darkness and the pruning-fire and especially the soil, here, essential parts if the thing will take a name, if indeed a name it should have.

Part Two: Stone-Seed Planting

The International Conference for the Empowerment of Jewish Women was the title of a weeklong gathering of women at a lavish Jerusalem hotel in December 1988. They offered fruits from their works, mirroring for each other and for the audience models of women articulate, committed, and willing to be—indeed, insisting to be—seen.

Did they think of their ancient foremothers ("all the women whose hearts stirred them up in wisdom" who thus "spun goats' hair" [Exodus 35:26]), those desert dwellers who brought their creations for the building of the first *mishkan* in the wild—those whose hearts were moved had brought in wisdom. From some deep place inside themselves they had the gifts, the vision, and the need to give what they knew to make, each shading of color and texture different and all essential, although no one knew who would come or from where exactly in her journey, or what she would bring or what she would become, until it was done.

She thought, *Celebration, relief, ah, I see she can do it, that's what I was thinking, maybe it's true, oh, G-d, so I'm not the only one, how her struggle shows on the lines on her face, the fortitude, what conviction, she really cares, and I am moved by her, she moves me. Maybe I do have work to do. Maybe there is a place in our covenant, after all.*

165

All during this conference week—when stones were rattling over the floors and thrown across the ballroom expanse, were bouncing against the mikes and were thrust into open calloused hands, and, causing a great rumbling thunder of motion that close to rocked this grand hotel into the nearby valley—the moon was preparing to celebrate her dark renewal upon the face of the earth. Rosh Chodesh Kislev, 5749. Rosh Chodesh, head of the new month, Jewish tracking of temporal life through the timeless cycle of the moon's fullness and waning. This observable activity of nature is a clear sign of the Shekhinah.

It is said that women are especially attuned to moon rhythms, that Rosh Chodesh is a very holy time for women, of dancing and singing joyous prayers of gratitude for life, pleas for health, and continued blessing during the month ahead. Rebirth is promised when the moon is only blackness in the sky. Women have the sight to see the fullness in the Nothing. Rosh Chodesh.

At the conference the idea was born.

It has been done elsewhere, yet never so close to the center of the Jewish psyche. We will take this Torah scroll—soul of Jewish existence, written on animal skins—and we will chant at the Western Wall. We will nest here and use our bodies to channel Torah words as we hold the scroll close. There is healing in hearing our own voices give form to the sacred words, sweet sounds of unification. It is unprecedented here. This action has power. She trembles.

So do others. Throughout Jerusalem the women's stones start tugging at their dress linings and eye sockets and hands and purses and packs, the women whose lives, they think, are taking them along this street or that in Rechavia or Talbieh, French Hill or Nachla'ot. As the decision is made and the vision is enacted, and after the

166

first reading of the Torah (by the women) on the Thursday when the portion is usually read (by the men) aloud, some black-coated men shout "Pigs!" to the women holding the scroll at the Wall. The sound takes irrevocable new form. The women go back a week later to celebrate Kislev's start in a soil-splintering, seed-planting, inevitably formative way.

I have developed a mechanism. When someone tells me something dangerous or hurtful, I turn (it) off.

Confrontation has its costs.

"Women holding the Torah are like pigs touching the scroll"?! Come on, who do they think they are? We can't let them get away with that!

One replies, "But do we want to take a Torah into such a hornet's nest? I mean, look—you see what those men did to the women from the conference. Thank G-d most of them are back in the States now, where they won't be molested for doing a reading. But if we go back to the Kotel with the Torah and try to read from it on Rosh Chodesh, aren't we asking for trouble, and do we want this on our heads? Inevitably we will be seen as the evil instigators— you know, Jerusalem is not exactly a cauldron of sophistication, politically. What are we trying to prove? I really want to know, why do it? What would we gain?"

The first answers, "Listen—it is a question of morals and human rights! I can't live with myself knowing I will passively accept someone's attempt to prevent me from performing a religious act that is not against Jewish law, even according to Orthodox rabbis! It's absurd! This is a question of challenging the abuse of power at a place that is, maybe more than any other in the entire world for a Jew, supposedly open to everyone to pray according to her or his own customs. We can't let this slide by!"

Another joins in, "But why not put our energies into some other place where we won't find so much objection? Isn't this self-destructive?"

A fourth's heart opens: "No way! Not if you really care about being able to pray, Jewishly, in the place Jews have directed their prayers towards three times a day, every day, and after meals, for thousands of years. If you care about relating to this history and trying to live with it now—in your life, your present—then it matters! It matters to our children—so maybe they won't grow up in a world where their relationship to their tradition is as ambivalent as ours is right now. Do you just walk out of a relationship when it gets rough? It is about keeping a commitment to your collective past and at the same time staying true to what you know about your life right now and how that relates to your hopes for the future."

She wants to take her husband and three children to a desert island and live in peace. She is lonely, but she looks her friend in the eye and responds, "Don't you care about our world? There is so much beauty in Judaism—it is who we are. There is so much strength in us as women, how can we let others stop our voices from singing? It's so wrong! And don't you want to sing?"

The young one replies, "Sure, I do—but who says the Jewish songs are those of my soul?"

"Have you tried?" says another, drawing her legs up to her chest on the chair.

"No, but not because I haven't wanted to. I never found a teacher or a group where I could do it. All the places felt so alien. I went to women's groups and only there felt validated."

"So maybe we can try learning the prayers together?" asks an older woman, who has taught Jewish subjects for years. She smiles. Tension is released, sending stones scattering across the tile.

"Why not?"

"Maybe."

"Let's do it!"

"Okay."

"Okay!" She raises her voice loudly from among the others sitting in the metal chairs in a large circle in the borrowed space of the yeshiva's *beit midrash,* lent to the women for this planning meeting. "So we will meet at the Dung Gate at 6:45 in the morning. Every woman should take a buddy and hold her hand as you go in to the Kotel past the guards and the *charedim.* We'll stick together once inside. Let's start davening with *Mah Tovu,* through the *Amidah* and then *Hallel,* and then Rebecca, you'll take the Torah out and we'll lay it on the table there, and everyone gather close in and we'll do the reading, the *Alenu*—and that's it!"

Wide-eyed women gathered to bind prayers and moral convictions and a Torah reading in the chilly morning, challenging G-d to make space for Her daughters and defying the human beings who would deny that space. The women become a cluster aware of its voice; new prayer, now song, having come out on this early morning to band lives together, hopeful, confident, with a new chance at a transformed life.

She walks on the tree-lined Jerusalem street that night, thinking, "It's not about the anger of those others, it's about the wresting free of our right to openly build, it's about the belief in 'we' linked to 'Jew' linked to prayer after all." The prayers gather around them, over time, the lilt and cadence of the beautiful voices and faith grow more as the soul-strength comes out. It was a shock to see the Torah scroll almost on the ground next to the Kotel. A *charedi* man with horn-rimmed glasses has run over to the women's side. He spills chairs in his wake, shouting, "Torah here!!! Forbidden!!!" and as he pushes his big body violently into our midst, he lunges with the crazed look of a murderer and careens into the metal table, thrusting it heavenwards. The prayer books go flying down, the Torah scroll too, until two of the women catch it, save it, and birds squawk. Who are the faithful here?

We link arms, shaken, and as a group cover the scroll and walk, humming a *niggun,* and leave that cold space. We will not be rushed, we say softly to each other, keeping our heads up. The Torah is with us and our shock and the shaking and tears as we stand together afterwards in the garden in the back. What shall we do? Can someone actually want to hurt us and see a Torah ripped in order to keep women's hands off it?

> For My thoughts are not your thoughts, neither are your ways My ways, says the Lord. For as the heavens are higher than the earth, so are My ways higher than your ways, and My thoughts than your thoughts. For as the rain comes down, and the snow from heaven, and returns not there, but waters the earth, and makes it bring forth and bud, that it may give seed to the sower, and bread to the eater; so shall My word be that goes out of My mouth; it shall not return to me void, but it shall accomplish that which I please, and it shall prosper in that for which I sent it. (Isaiah 55:8–11)

And who among women or men knows the will of the Lord?

Part Three: Desert Blocks in the Rock Garden

They speak of the ruling in the desert, where they set up camp to hear the word of the Lord. Concerning matters of dispute between the tribes, the officials of the law convene and listen. They hear the

cases of both. *Justice, justice, shall ye pursue.* Here in the Israeli Supreme
Court, under the Tents of Meeting they gather, three black-robed
judges with mahogany gavels looking down on a silver-haired,
white-*kipah*ed, blue-eyed rabbinical administrator of the Kotel, his
assistant, and their (female) lawyer, on the one side. On the other
are twenty-five women, known by this time as Women of the Wall,
and their duo of (male) legal representatives. The gavels boom and
the oral recitations are made while the chief rabbi and the women
watch spears thrown. The women have charged the Court: Should
there be a ruling today regarding why the Court will not keep men
from throwing chairs at praying Jews, and spitting women from
tearing flesh and beating with prayer books the other females on
site? Why will police not intervene as women—who, coming now
regularly for six months every Rosh Chodesh and every Friday
morning—try to pray at the holy center and endure such ambush?

*More time is needed to investigate this matter, they say. The interim procedure
demands that women get protection only if they pray minus Torah, minus prayer
shawl, minus song.*

Endure, endure, spiritual law, thy ways are not man's ways.

Next case—Ethiopian matrimonial proceedings, next to stand!

While under Tent of Meeting, court resumes and judges blow
gavels to herald the opening of the case of Ethiopian Jews whose
rights to marry and be counted as Jews the religious courts throw to
question. Dark-skinned men in white tunics and holding long wood-
en staffs have sat on brown wooden benches next to Wall women during the entirety of the case of the Women of the Wall versus the
Religious Ministry and Rabbi Meir Yehuda Getz of the Kotel.

Justice, justice, writ in stone and proclaimed throughout the land.

Rosh Chodesh, following the court ruling and according to
the decision handed down, have agreed to leave Kotel for Torah

reading and now are used to carrying scroll to garden site near in Jewish quarter after Kotel prayers. Short-term displacement for long-term return. Court/judge said, Try to turn two thousand years of history on its head, what do you expect?

Thirty women walk to the Churva Synagogue, in the Old City center, into the courtyard with its ancient stone altar, and lay the Torah down. They begin to unwrap and bless in joy.

I look up from next to the scroll. I see my friend with her two arms extended. She is trying to block the big stone-arch entrance-way to this sanctuary, as droves of shouting angry men are running fast, surrounding us. One's tremendous nostrils flare; his black eyes spit as he screams, "Dogs! You're no better than dogs!!" I go to my friend to link my hand to hers and with the other press my palm to the cool side of the arch. They will not get through, I think, we must protect this place. I stand firm and stretch wide, and one lifts a bright red hardcover prayer book and slams it down on my wrist. It stings, I cry put the hand back up while it was down one got through now he wants to leave butts his body hard into mine and again and again he hits me hard in the chest he wears jeans and a white knitted *kipah* glasses tefillin still a knob on his head and he lunges again at me shouting and I push back with the might of my self I hate him he pushes me down and down and onto stone floor I spill on top of another woman her leg bleeds I reach out and grab his ankle as he tries to run away I scream "Police!" and police-and-police. And finally, finally one comes slowly over I have the man's sandal it has come off in my hand and as the police detain him I get up from the ground and watch him unwrap the prayer straps from between his two eyes before he is taken to jail.

An hour later, I sit alone in the grey-walled, smoke-filled police station with the officer taking my report. I give him my particulars, and he holds his pen and he does not ask me to begin the story; rather, he begins to give me advice. He says, "Listen. Let me tell you something. I have lived here all my life, I have worked as a police officer for many years. Let me tell you," and he points to the *kipah* he wears, "I am religious. I know what I speak. With those people you cannot talk, you cannot reason. But with you, I can talk. I watch you girls getting beaten and I know this cannot be stopped, because you cannot talk with them. There is no solution there. But with you, I can talk. You are intelligent. So listen. We have enough troubles in this city. Don't cause more anger. You and I both know you are right. There is nothing wrong with what you want to do. Look. If you just don't sing, you won't bother them, and you will help us keep the peace. Don't sing—just don't sing here, please—women never sing here!" Please, be good girls and shut thyselves up and go thyselves back to the caves and darkness whence thee came, that we may all be peaceful once again.

Do not sing, he tells me as I sit next to him with a bruised chest and two arms swollen from the blows from these Jewish brothers. They can hit, they can scream, and the ones to be stopped are those who want to sing, though the prayerbook words want all souls to sing a new song to G-d every day.

It is dark; I see nothing. No one else at all has come here. Where, I don't even know, only that this journey is so alone. It is my reality.

What is prayer? she says.

Absorb us into Your light and transform us through Love. I say, I will, Amen.

(What would he say? Is prayer different for a man than for a woman? Does a man cry out differently than a woman? Does G-d really wear tefillin?[2] Or, is G-d a girl, or does Source exist beyond and in both genders, so is prayer hu—man cry, hu—man song, hu—man longing to be Whole?

I say, prayer. You sing because something like "goodness" fills you or some quiet hint hovers surrounds your conscious experience whispers and you try to reach that, because, why, sometimes you don't even know. There's G-d.

Hebrew prayer. Open prayer book and you chant and you condense collective Jewish soul through your own finitude aligning with Creator's Infinite emanations. You feel your part in the Jewish part of all of creation, you move yourself to that awareness when you commit your thoughts and breath to meeting those words. You link.

Every day, and over time the words work on you. They shape you. They push you through darkness and they wrap you in a silent light that you know ever more intimately. This is your soul's life living, and this collective journey is so alone. Not good or bad alone. Just alone.

She sings. She takes her guitar and plays again and again in a melody she creates as she plays, in Hebrew, words from Psalm 104, "I will sing to Hashem while I live, I will sing praises to my G-d while I endure. May my words be sweet to G-d . . . Bless Hashem, O my soul, *Halleluyah!*"

As she sings, one voice, then two, then ten, then twenty women joining, lifting hands, near the sea in the desert's mi(d)st. She doubts, she doesn't say, she doesn't know, but she considers prayer words and likes to sing with the others in a group. She opens the book after keeping it long closed.

She looks to her friend and their eyes meet and there is a smile that touches each of them deeply. What is prayer? What is drawing close?

What is Torah? Letters of light in the desert come give forms of flesh to soul's infinite cry, *selah*[3] and always, desert-blooms milking the drink in the stone.

They receive the borrowed Torah from a Jerusalem yeshiva the day before Shavuot.[4] She, having been sent to pick it up, now guards it carefully in her Talpiot home, nestling Torah against her hip while at the breast carrying her infant son, on this day before the holiday where Torah milk streams into the smiling mouths of Jewish babes, world over. Where, here, Jewish women will rejoice at the Kotel at dawn.

It is said in rabbinic texts that the women and the men received the Torah differently from G-d on the day when Moses descended from the mystery, alone, in the clouds over Mount Sinai. That the women received the Torah revelation first, in the form of laws nuanced and subtle, intuitive and soft. The men, it is said, heard the Word as a harsh, minutely detailed and rigidly defined system of laws and codes. The commentators etching this contrast in revelatory inclinations base their understanding on a reading of a verse in the Torah itself,[5] in which the people of Israel are named twice, first being called *Beit Yaakov*—the girls, they say—and then, immediately following, *Bnai Yisrael*—the boys. The boys sense that the girls drink differently, thirst differently, need different sustenance from that which they, the men, directly know. The rabbis also proceed to define that difference from their experience alone, Shavuot, the festival celebrating the Torah given to the Jews—*Bnai Yisrael? Beit Yaakov?* She paces the living room, nursing her child and guarding the Torah scroll wrapped in the red-velvet covering.

After these eight months since the conception, this cluster of women, *Shirah Hadashah,* will hear cantillation of Torah words on this Shavuot directly from their own mouths, at the Kotel. A Sacred Undertaking; after a term of praying, reading Torah, battling *charedi* women and men and the Supreme Court of Israel; creating and attending classes together and continually briefing the press; after countless group meetings during which policies, strategies, goals were defined; after having women and men world over join the women's prayers in "solidarity" during Passover, the festival of freedom and birth; after song and dance and tears and voices grown strong and sometimes hard and articulate; hearts grown wider, sometimes cracking; souls stretching, doubting, returning, evolving; after this time laced together by Rosh Chodesh.

Close to the dawn, on this Shavuot morning—she who took the Torah from the yeshiva vomits in her home and lies sick with the knowledge that if she takes the Torah to the Kotel, where the women are now waiting, violence will ensue, the women will be hurt, worse than ever, her body is so weak and sick from this knowing and she vomits again, remembering: how she was called to come alone to the office of *HaRav* of the Kotel that afternoon, she representing the women, he the powers of the rabbinic state. So harsh the lines and facts cold down her back so black the decree—if Torah is taken to Wall, violence is promised and we cannot protect you, this is the warning. Cold, no softness between the lines of law(lessness) such as this, no will towards union heading into this holiday, she gags on curdled cream sliding down her bowels; so when the three women waiting finally at sunrise go to her house to see why her family has not yet come, they find her slumped in a chair, tears on her robe, husband holding baby on his chest and caring for her. She repeats the Rav's words. Her strong body has wilted from the sickness of the violence promised on this day of supernal unification, now when letters in her belly are retching apart. The women hold her and try to comfort. She says she cannot take the Torah to the group.

So the three of them take the Torah, concealed carefully in cloth and blanket and secured in a red duffel bag, and they walk fast through wilderness aware of the danger and shaking with anticipation of receiving Torah, and blows. They proceed past the gas station and lion statues and up the rocky hill into the Old City, breathing hard.

And hide the scroll, as planned, in the Jewish Quarter apartment of a *ba'al teshuvah*⁶ woman who teaches Kabbalah, one now defining herself as "orthodox," who not long before was radical and active in gay rights causes. She protects the Torah, though she will not pray with the women.

After prayers at the Kotel and *Hallel* in the garden, while they sing and many others, critical, look on at this group that has become a spectacle—women leading their own?—one slips away and retrieves the hidden scroll.

What is this that presses against my chest? This that I have chosen to carry? I feel black letters soaring into my heart, physical skin-scroll I hold with my hands against my flesh and I walk on this holy day to the women—G-d what revelation do You manifest? that there should be such pain and physical aggression resisting women who need to hold You close? You and we, both wanting to be held? If it isn't so, why has it gone this far? Why do You allow me to hold You so close and walk, now? Purify, purify, purify, please, our hearts to serve You in truth.

My hands are burning holding Your words—please let no one attack me if he sees me carrying this scroll, I am exposed and vulnerable in the open courtyard in the middle of the Jewish Quarter, please, not too much farther and my heels click so loud against the stone, just get me past those boys with the *peyot*⁷ and screaming so loud, thank You. I'm through, I see our lawyer, he prances back and forth quickly, brow knit deep, he is telling the police to watch, though I don't trust the police they won't help us, G-d please guard our reading, please open my ears I want to be fit to receive Your gift, does it take strength to be soft enough to listen? . . .

I descend the dark-stone, steep steps to the garden and the women are there in a circle, they arc dancing and singing, waiting for the Torah to arrive and I smile wide as I bring It down, thank G-d, we have made it despite the dangers, I am jubilant, it is beautiful this group and as she takes the scroll from my arms and they begin to unwrap Her, I want to cry for joy, here we are, the climax of so much alone and so many wishes and prayers and struggles and studies, women-we-circle round the Torah, we unite, not alone, She bears Herself with us and I hug a woman nearby.

Black-flash absence of the Presence, the one who took the Torah is at home, her body sick, I miss her, the one who kept the Torah at her apartment keeps her body apart, though she agrees in principle with what we do, I miss her, too, the unification not yet whole, but scroll unwinds, we are here, we read and listen to the telling, the purification, the commandments, the shofar, the cloud, the revelation, and while men and boys in black crowd on the ledge surrounding the women, they scream, the women try to ignore them, on this festival-day of union and outpouring of Divine Love.

When suddenly my hand hard stinging it burns, from the heights of the black-world yeshiva they have stoned me it hurts I am terrified chastened does the revelation and reception of Your will have to be filled with terror? Are we so wrong to beckon You like we do? Is it they who are so wrong, so wrong to try and hurt another life, another Jew, to scream obscenities on Your day, I am sick for the hatred between Jews and ache for Your Exiled Body to ReTurn.

178

Too, this beginning is ending. It is Rosh Chodesh Elul[8] and the one who was sick on Shavuot looks to the faces of the others in this garden and smiles as she holds the shofar to her lips. She, and another woman, too, they both blow together and at the same time, we gather in and listen as a third sounds the call, listen, listen piercing the ear and maybe our hearts closing our eyes, holding her hand, listen, stones singing life to the valleys beneath, we are no longer building alone.

SUSAN ARANOFF

The Politics of Women of the Wall

The Politicization of Religion in Israel

ISRAEL, BORN IN 1948 as the Jewish homeland or state, is a democracy whose national identity is rooted in religion and whose ancient heritage has a tradition of theocracy.[1] Israel's population today includes numerous Orthodox Jews who remain unabashedly committed to theocracy. Consequently, balancing democratic versus theocratic tendencies continues to be a major challenge for Israeli governments, a challenge made more daunting by a proportional representation electoral system, which makes extremist, narrowly focused political parties both viable and influential in Israel.

Thus far in its history, Israel has found it impossible to separate religion from politics, synagogue from state.[2] Israel's governments, rather than being neutral referees permitting Jews from all branches of Judaism equal opportunity to exercise their religious rights, have passed legislation that enfranchises Orthodoxy and disenfranchises other streams of Judaism. The primacy given to Orthodoxy in Israel has generated acrimony and divisiveness amongst Israeli Jews. The favored position of Orthodoxy also has strained the relationship between Israel and non-Orthodox diaspora Jews

180

who feel a sense of delegitimization and disempowerment of their branch of Judaism in Israel.

Given Israel's singular mix of democracy and theocracy combined with the heterogeneity of Israel's population, and Israel's role as a spiritual center for a very diverse world Jewry, it seems that controversy over the role of religion in Israeli society was inevitable. The list of issues that have sparked confrontation over religious coercion in Israel is long. Major synagogue and state issues that have grabbed headlines in Israel and the diaspora have included street and business closings on Shabbat; Orthodox rabbis calling on soldiers to disobey their officers if ordered to withdraw from territory; "who is a Jew or a rabbi" and who controls conversion, marriage, and divorce; the seating of non-Orthodox representatives on local religious councils; army exemptions and financial support for tens of thousands of male yeshiva students; thousands of *agunot* unable to remarry under Israeli law administered by Orthodox rabbinical courts; and the denial of freedom of religion at the Kotel.

Of all the issues listed above, the denial of freedom of religion at the Kotel has received the least attention from Israeli citizens and politicians, despite periodic, well-publicized violent attacks by *charedim* on Jewish groups praying at or near the Kotel, and despite the earnest protests that the situation evokes from American Jewry. This essay analyzes the politics of synagogue and state in Israel and explains why the struggle of Women of the Wall, which struck a chord in the American Jewish community, had minimal resonance in the Israeli political system and, consequently, has been delayed for more than thirteen years by ineffectual Israeli Supreme Court decisions and Israeli government stalling tactics.

The Politics of Women of the Wall

The politics of Women of the Wall is multifaceted, for it involves politics in so many arenas—the internal politics of ICWOW, Israeli politics, Israel-diaspora politics, and American Jewish communal politics—each with its own dynamic and all interacting with each other. We begin with an examination of the internal politics of ICWOW in its formative years, followed by analysis of the other facets of the politics of Women of the Wall.

ICWOW'S INTERNAL POLITICS

Numerous political and ideological issues arose during the formative years of ICWOW in early 1989. Who would have the power to recruit new board members, and should recruitment of new board members be regulated so as to maintain some balance in the representation of the various branches of Judaism and of the nonaffiliated? Should we accept board members based solely on their ability to contribute funds to our cause? Should our decision-making process be by majority rule or by marathon rounds of discussions in an exhausting attempt to decide by consensus? What should be done about the unequal sharing of the workload?

The two issues that stand out in my mind as particularly crucial in determining the character of ICWOW are our guidelines for prayer services and our guidelines for media relations during our struggle. The decision to adhere to Orthodox interpretation of Halakhah was made with little debate, but the decision to limit the use of secular media proved to be contentious, as concern for Israel's international image and political standing had to compete with our commitment to women's religious rights—or, to state the issue more broadly, freedom of religion in Israel.

CHOOSING HALAKHIC SERVICES ACCORDING TO ORTHODOXY

From the beginning, ICWOW included women from all streams of Judaism—Orthodox, Conservative, Reform, Reconstructionist, unaffiliated. Nonetheless, ICWOW chose to adhere to Orthodox guidelines. Why?

Part of the answer to this question can be found in the history of women's *tefillah*, or prayer groups. During the 1980s and 1990s, separate services for women developed in the Orthodox movement but not in the Conservative, Reform, or Reconstructionist movements, because women in these three branches already had the option of full participation in egalitarian services. Therefore, it was Orthodox women, the only group of Jewish women still barred from full participation in their synagogue services, who had the incentive for developing models for separate *tefillah* groups. A second reason that the idea for a separate women's service at the Kotel emerged from the ranks of Orthodox women is that many members of the other branches of Judaism had felt alienated from the Kotel for many years because of the *mechitzah*. Non-Orthodox women were often put off by the Orthodox trappings of the Kotel—not just the *mechitzah*, but also the general lack of accommodations for women: no opportunity for organized prayer, no reading tables, a small helter-skelter collection of *siddurim* and *Chumashim* in the women's section. Orthodox women continued to focus on the Kotel as a sacred site where services were similar to those they experienced in their own synagogues. It was daring but natural for Rivka Haut to think of bringing women's Orthodox *tefillah* to the Kotel, because such services had been taking place for years in Orthodox synagogues in New York and numerous other cities.

A third reason for choosing Orthodox services was our awareness that if we did not adopt Orthodox standards, Orthodox
women would not attend our services or, in all likelihood, support
our struggle. Non-Orthodox women who have been involved in
the Kotel struggle have been most generous in allowing Orthodox
practice to prevail,[3] and our services at the Kotel as well as the solidarity services we sponsored elsewhere therefore have been conducted in accordance with Orthodox standards. Despite this, many
Orthodox women, even those who were active in women's *tefillah*
groups and leaders of Orthodox feminism, remained reticent and
ambivalent about our struggle to pray at the Kotel, and Orthodox
rabbis, even those who permitted women's *tefillah* in their synagogues, did not support our right to pray in an identical fashion at
the Kotel.

A fourth factor in our choice of Orthodox halakhic guidelines
was the pervasive sentiment within our group that the conflict that
was increasingly dividing various segments of the Jewish community from one another was tragic and that our group could set an
example of *ahavat chinam*, mutual love and respect for Jews across
the spectrum.

A fifth reason for adhering to Orthodox standards of Halakhah
was legal tactics. By adhering to Orthodox halakhic standards, we
narrowed our petition and strengthened our case. ICWOW was not
petitioning the Orthodox-dominated religious bureaucracy of
Israel for the right to hold Conservative or Reform services. We
were petitioning for the right to hold Orthodox services like those
held in numerous Orthodox synagogues around the world. Thus,
we hoped that we would deprive our opponents, the Orthodox
rabbis and Orthodox political parties of Israel, of the argument
that what we were demanding was a violation of Halakhah.

The narrow religious sectarianism of our opponents would be exposed if and when they obstructed even services like ours, which numerous Orthodox rabbis permitted in their synagogues. It would be apparent that the violent and virulent objections to our services were primarily due to psychological, social, or political reasons, not halakhic ones. The misogyny of the Orthodox factions that opposed us would be revealed for all to see. This in itself would be a step toward liberating Orthodoxy and the Kotel from the misogyny that was being passed off as Halakhah. Indeed, in 1988, Rabbi Meir Yehuda Getz, then the government administrator of the Kotel, declared that what we were doing was not against Halakhah. Furthermore, in his 1994 Supreme Court opinion, Menachem Elon conceded that ICWOW's services were halakhic, although he argued that *minhag hamakom* (prevailing custom—i.e., *charedi* custom) and *charedi* threats of violence barred us from the Kotel.

Thus far, the Supreme Court has allowed our opponents, who rely upon Elon's arguments, to prevail. Even the court's unanimous May 22, 2000, decision, which strongly castigated the government for years of foot-dragging, contained no practical, enforceable implementation and left our opponents in control of the Kotel. In the longer run, the rigid intolerance reflected in violent attacks on our halakhic services at the Kotel may ultimately undermine our opponents' credibility and their influence over religious life and Jewish holy sites in Israel, including the Kotel.

SETTING POLICY FOR MEDIA AND PUBLICITY

In late 1989, ICWOW presented a Torah to our Israeli sisters and filed our lawsuit against the Israeli government officials responsible for barring us from praying with our Torah at the Kotel. Within days of these historic events, differences of opinion began to emerge about ICWOW's policy toward non-Jewish media and public relations activity in non-Jewish arenas. ICWOW's leadership at the time was a small group of five or six, and some of the group had begun advocating contacting non-Jewish media, but there was strong opposition to this, and we convened a meeting in our Jerusalem hotel lobby to resolve the dispute. After some intense discussion, which revolved around the power of secular media and the potential damage that negative publicity could do to Israel, a vote was taken that set a policy of barring ICWOW's contact with the non-Jewish, or general, media and restricting ourselves to contacts with Jewish media only. WOW, however, did not adopt such a policy.

I was a strong opponent of seeking coverage in the general media and presented the following arguments in support of my position. The general media are unfriendly to Israel and would seize the opportunity to run a story that showed Israel in a negative light. Israel certainly needs to improve its treatment of women in the home, in the courts, and at work, but I was uncomfortable with the prospect of *The New York Times* running an article about discrimination against women in Iran or Afghanistan, followed the next day or week by an article about ICWOW and religious discrimination against women at the Kotel.

I was also concerned about the broader impact of negative publicity on Israel in the general media. Unfavorable coverage of Israel in the general media could have had political repercussions for Israel far beyond what ICWOW could imagine. A perception of a weakening of American Jewish support for Israel could weaken Israel's position in the American political system.[4]

Finally, and more specific to the Kotel issue, a highly publicized Jewish challenge to Israel's administration of the Kotel could reignite and add credence to challenges to Israel's sovereignty over Jerusalem. If Israel's administration of the Kotel was being challenged by diaspora Jews, Israel's sovereignty over Jerusalem, which contains the holy sites of other religions, could be called into question. Agitation by ICWOW in the general media could potentially fuel demands for the internationalization of Jerusalem and weaken Israel's negotiating position in any peace process. I felt strongly that even though our cause was just, Israel's policy and negotiation strategy on Jerusalem should not be undermined by media attention generated by diaspora Jews.[5]

I also pointed out a possible boomerang effect that potential supporters who felt strongly, as I did, about these issues might be alienated from ICWOW's cause if we were instigators of negative coverage of Israel in the general media.

When we returned to the United States, differences over publicity and public relations surfaced again in the form of two ICWOW directors' suggestion that a resolution supporting ICWOW be introduced in the New York City Council. Once again, I strongly opposed casting the State of Israel as a villain in a general public forum such as the New York City Council. Concern about shielding Israel's international political position and public image carried the day again, and the City Council resolution proposal was abandoned. Sometime later, the board reaffirmed our "no general media" policy again. We were tying one hand behind our back by shunning the general media and negative publicity for Israel, but concern about damaging Israel took precedence at that time.[6]

Thus, the guidelines of our struggle were forged: We would pursue our religious rights strategically and aggressively within the Israeli political and judicial system and seek allies within the diaspora community, but we would stop short of embarrassing Israel in the general media or foreign political arenas.

ICWOW and Israeli Politics

Although ICWOW's struggle was initiated in Israel's Supreme Court, very quickly ICWOW found itself tangled up in Israeli politics rather than Israeli courts. The 1994 Supreme Court decision was a victory in principle for ICWOW because two out of three justices ruled that we had a right to pray according to our custom at the Kotel, and even the one dissenter, Associate Chief Justice Elon, ruled that our services were halakhic.[7] Practically, however, the decision was a defeat, because in casting the tie-breaking vote in our favor, Chief Justice Shamgar also recommended that ICWOW seek to actualize our rights through Israel's political system, where ICWOW was hard-put to find allies.

ICWOW AND SECULAR ISRAELIS: THE POLITICAL ALLIANCE THAT NEVER MATERIALIZED

Periodically during the State of Israel's history, there have been political clashes and compromises between secular and Orthodox parties and groups. But confrontation between secular and Orthodox Jews in Israel intensified in the 1980s and 1990s.[8] This intensification can, to a large degree, be traced to two factors: first, the increasing influence that Orthodox parties have gained over government policies,[9] and second, the increasing impact that Orthodox parties' uncompromising stands have had on the daily lives of secular Israeli Jews.

Given the heated and growing opposition to religious coercion in Israel during the 1990s, it would seem that ICWOW and WOW should have easily found allies in our struggle against the monopolization of the Kotel,[10] but we did not. Israelis opposed to yeshiva army exemptions, coercive Shabbat regulations, and Orthodox hegemony over conversion should have been natural allies of ICWOW and WOW, but the alliance never materialized. A more careful comparison of the Kotel to the other religious controversies reveals a key difference that explains why the other issues have made it onto Israel's political agenda but freedom of religion at the Kotel has not.

SECULAR ISRAEL VERSUS ORTHODOX ISRAEL: THE ISSUES THAT MATTER

The religious issues that have galvanized secular Israelis have one common trait—they matter to secular Israelis! They matter because the Orthodox parties' influence over those issues is perceived as having created major costs or dislocations for secular Israelis.

Secular Israelis have organized major demonstrations and initiated Supreme Court cases to protest coercive and intrusive Shabbat laws, and compromises have been reached, sometimes favoring the Orthodox, sometimes favoring the secular. In the late 1990s, secular Israeli political parties supported the creation of more liberal conversion institutes in order to meet the demographic challenge of integrating tens of thousands of Soviet immigrants, many of whom are not halakhically Jewish. Forty years of vociferous protests by the Conservative and Reform movements about the delegitimization of their rabbis and their conversions never succeeded in making any inroads into Orthodoxy's total monopoly on conversion. Change came only when it mattered to Israelis.

Israelis have also pressed for change regarding the army exemptions for tens of thousands of yeshiva students, exemptions that secular Israelis resent increasingly because of their perception of the role of the Orthodox in resisting ceding territory in return for promises of peace.[11] Legislation to restructure these exemptions has been passed, and more proposals for change are under review.

These thorny synagogue-and-state issues are far from resolved, but the Israeli government, Knesset, Supreme Court, and citizenry have grappled with them and moved toward compromise and solutions. Secular Israelis were affected by and agitated about these issues, and they demanded that the political system respond to their concerns.

SECULAR ISRAEL VERSUS ORTHODOX ISRAEL: THE KOTEL DOESN'T MATTER

While all of this took place, however, our lawsuit stagnated in the Court and in a never-ending series of government commissions. The political freeze at the Kotel reflects the fact that the impact of Orthodox monopolization of the Kotel on the lives of secular Israelis is virtually nil compared with the impact of the other issues. Secular Israelis find it hard to fathom why ICWOW would invest so much blood, sweat, and tears for the right to pray near some ancient stones placed there by that rather unsavory character Herod. Well-known Labor Party politician and feminist Yael Dayan, when asked to join ICWOW at a service, hesitated, saying that she found praying in a beautiful field with birds in flight overhead a more inspiring setting.[12] Anat Hoffman, a WOW stalwart and the Meretz Party's representative on the Jerusalem City Council, reports that some of her Meretz colleagues think her Kotel involvement is "crazy." Yet a major plank in Meretz's platform is freedom from religious coercion.

Given secular Israelis' indifference to the Kotel versus *charedi* "territoriality," it made no political sense for Labor or Likud, the two major secular parties in Israel during the 1990s, to waste political capital by antagonizing Orthodox parties over the Kotel issue. The main issues that concerned Labor and Likud in the 1990s were the peace process and security. Neither Labor nor Likud was going to alienate potential Orthodox coalition partners and thus risk losing the opportunity to govern and carry out life-and-death security policies. The Meretz Party also did not ally itself with us, despite the fact that its drive for freedom from religion and our drive for freedom of religion are two sides of the same coin.[13] Throughout the entire negotiation process between ICWOW and various Israeli governments, there was a convergence in the interests of the secular and Orthodox factions with regard to freezing the current situation at the Kotel. The secular were indifferent to Orthodox control of the Kotel, and the Orthodox were adamant about maintaining it. In the horse trading of Israeli coalition politics, control of the Kotel was one victory that the secular parties could easily grant to the Orthodox parties.[14]

ORTHODOX ISRAELI WOMEN SEEKING CHANGE: ANOTHER ALLIANCE THAT NEVER MATERIALIZED

Another segment of the Israeli population that might have lent support to ICWOW but did not was the cadre of Orthodox women who have pushed for higher Jewish learning for women, training women as experts in Jewish law in the areas of divorce, *niddah*, and kashrut, seating women on religious councils, and reform in the area of halakhic divorce. For example, Leah Shakdiel, whose struggle to be seated on the Religious Council of Yerucham led to a landmark supportive Israeli Supreme Court decision, has been ambivalent about ICWOW and WOW. Support from these Orthodox women would not have carried the day for ICWOW, but it would have encouraged us and reduced our sense of isolation. Why was that support not forthcoming?

There are many possible reasons for Israeli Orthodox women's reticence about the Kotel. Women's rights at the Kotel and women's *tefillah* groups in general are simply a low priority for Orthodox Israeli women[15] compared to the other "growth areas" where they have invested their energy. Given the low priority they assign to women's *tefillah* groups, Orthodox women may feel it is tactically foolish, at least for now, to endorse ICWOW and inflame the *charedim* and alienate rabbis, politicians, and laypeople who might support their other efforts. Perhaps it is also the pluralist over-tones of ICWOW, the diversity of our board, and the parallel efforts of non-Orthodox movements to pray at the Kotel that have kept these more progressive Israeli Orthodox women away from ICWOW.

Still, the efforts and successes of these Orthodox women may yet help to pave the way for ICWOW in Israel's judicial and political arenas. The Israeli rabbinate resisted the intro-duction of women pleaders, *toanot*, in the rabbinical divorce courts, but the Supreme Court overruled the rabbinate. The Orthodox parties resisted seating Leah Shakdiel on Yerucham's Religious Council, but the Supreme Court overruled them. In 1999, Rabbanit Emunah Henkin, whose institution, Nishmat, had recently graduated its first group of "experts" in *niddah*, floated the idea of religious councils paying for the services of these women. This too may lead to confrontation and litigation. As the Supreme Court and the Israeli public become accus-tomed to seeing the more right-wing elements of Orthodoxy yield ground, ICWOW may have a greater chance of prevailing in court and in the Knesset. Time will tell whether these Orthodox female leaders in Israel and their supporters will eventually align with ICWOW and WOW.

Perhaps the most surprising case of an Orthodox woman not giving strong support to ICWOW is that of Alice Shalvi, who headed the Israel Women's Network (IWN) during the first ten years of ICWOW's struggle. The IWN included women from all streams of Judaism, and Shalvi was internationally respected as an elder stateswoman of Israeli feminism, yet she was often reported to be downplaying the importance of supporting ICWOW's efforts. This lack of support from Shalvi, who was politically to the left of the other Orthodox women just discussed and who in 1998 crossed over to the Masorati movement, seemed incomprehensible, almost a betrayal. However, when I testified at the Sheves Interministerial Committee hearing in 1991, Shalvi was present and made remarks that clarified her position. She began by explaining that she objected to the transformation of the Kotel into an Orthodox synagogue. This personal conviction prevented her from giving unreserved support for ICWOW's cause, which did not challenge Orthodox control of the Kotel. Notwithstanding her personal position, she then called on the Sheves Committee to accommodate ICWOW's services. As with the Orthodox women discussed above, Shalvi's support would not have won the day for ICWOW, but her unexplained reservations concerning the group were a source of distress for its members for many years, and it probably perplexed and discouraged potential ICWOW supporters. More recently, Shalvi has stated openly and explicitly that ICWOW's struggle is not, in her opinion, an issue that should be given high priority.

For a variety of reasons, some explicitly stated and some not, Orthodox Israeli women did not rally to ICWOW's cause. They did not have the same vision that ICWOW did—that challenging gender discrimination at the Kotel was crucial to liberating Judaism from misogyny and to advancing the entire Jewish feminist agenda.

THE MASORATI AND REFORM MOVEMENTS: CONVERGENT AND DIVERGENT STRATEGIES

The only segments of the Israeli population that actively supported ICWOW were the Masorati and Reform movements. The Reform movement lent a Torah for the first Kotel service in 1988. Members of WOW and ICWOW recall that, in addition to Orthodox individuals, both the Masorati and Reform movements made a Torah available for WOW services in 1989 until ICWOW presented the women of Jerusalem with a Torah of its own in December. Also, during that early period, when the Israeli women were bravely and devotedly maintaining services at the Kotel in the face of great hostility and even violence, several supportive men used to hover on the periphery of the Kotel plaza, which gave the women a sense of security should there be an outbreak of violence. There was discussion and consultation about our lawsuit and the possibility of the Masorati and Reform movements joining us as co-petitioners for equal rights at the Kotel.

However, these two non-Orthodox movements were almost as politically embattled in Israel as ICWOW. Representing a relatively small number of Israeli voters, these two movements had long been discriminated against by the Israeli government. What they lacked in numbers in Israel, they made up for in the large numbers of politically active Jews affiliated with these two movements in the United States. Periodically, the issue of "Who is a Jew or who is a rabbi" surfaced in Israel in connection with the Law of Return.[16] Each time this happened, an alarm from American Jewry was able to squelch Israeli Orthodox attempts to modify the Law of Return's definition of who qualifies as a Jew. However, as for securing equal rights for their counterparts in Israel, the Conservative and Reform movements had been stymied by the same political forces that stymied ICWOW.

ICWOW was faced with a decision of whether to explore an open alliance with the Masorati and Reform movements or to accept their help and advice as silent partners. In principle, every member of the ICWOW board objected to the discrimination against the Masorati and Reform movements in Israel and believed in equal legal status for all the streams of Judaism. We all sensed that we might be the "nose of the camel" that would introduce the beginning of freedom of religion for all Jews at the Kotel, but we hesitated to weigh down our lawsuit with broader arguments about religious pluralism in Israel. Our chances of establishing women's *tefillah* at the Kotel seemed better if we stuck with our narrowly drawn lawsuit, which petitioned only for Orthodox group services for women. And our progress, we hoped, might indeed pave the way for improving the status of the Masorati and Reform movements in Israel.

So, after internal discussion, we decided it was tactically unwise to openly ally with these two movements. Informal consultation with members of the Masorati and Reform movements continued throughout the long years of litigation, but we each pursued our agenda independently. Sometimes our strategies converged, but sometimes they diverged. In the late 1990s, for example, when the Masorati movement had become more active in its own litigation seeking freedom of religion at the Kotel, there was a risk that its

newly active pursuit of its rights might be used to delay the resolution of our lawsuit, which was by then ten years old. The Masorati movement thoughtfully signed an affidavit stating that its
petitions and negotiations should in no way impede or delay
ICWOW's claims at the Kotel. On the other hand, ICWOW and
WOW were disappointed when the Masorati representative to the
Ne'eman Commission voted in favor of Robinson's Arch as a solution for ICWOW and WOW, when we were opposed to this proposal. In the summer of 2000, the Masorati movement reached
some sort of agreement with the Barak government allowing egalitarian Masorati services at Robinson's Arch. After about six
months, however, the Masorati movement was reportedly dissatisfied with the way the agreement was being carried out.

The Israeli Supreme Court

Like the U.S. Supreme Court, Israel's Supreme Court has become
the forum in which politically weak groups seek redress when their
basic rights are violated by those who wield greater political
power.[17] In the United States, the courts often led the way in civil
rights and religious freedom long before elected officials passed legislation to more clearly define and ensure these rights. Likewise, at
a time when Israel's Knesset and government were not prepared to
grant women freedom of worship at the Kotel, ICWOW turned
to Israel's Supreme Court for justice.

Israel's Supreme Court functions in a very different political
culture than the U.S. Supreme Court, and it is far less insulated
from political pressure than its American counterpart. Israel, unlike
the United States, has no written constitution that guarantees such
rights as freedom of religion. In the United States, the Supreme

Court may be called upon to decide how best to protect freedom of religion, whereas Israel's Supreme Court must wrestle with the question of whether freedom of religion is part of Israel's political culture at all. The Israeli government's refusal to give comparable recognition and funding to Reform and Conservative rabbis, rites, synagogues, and schools is part of the Israeli government's ongoing establishment of one form of religion, which would be unconstitutional in the United States and which tends to undermine any effort to guarantee free religious exercise.[18]

In addition, in the absence of a written constitution, the status and authority of Israel's Supreme Court is tenuous because any decision made by the Court can be overridden by legislation passed by a simple majority in the Knesset. Thus, if the Israeli Supreme Court were, for example, to establish greater religious freedom at the Kotel, the Knesset could annul the Court's decision. Given the political balance of power with regard to religious issues, the Supreme Court would have risked a humiliating reversal if it had tried to order and effectively implement freedom of religion for women at the Kotel. Such a reversal might undermine the prestige and power of the Court for years to come.[19]

In the course of the protracted litigation of this issue, one question on which ICWOW and WOW have had some pointed debate is the question of how aggressively our attorneys should push for a clear-cut court decision—win or lose, a clear decision. In 1994, for example, ICWOW wanted to appeal the Shamgar decision that shunted our case into Israel's inhospitable political arena. There was resistance from some members of WOW who did not want to appeal. ICWOW prevailed, but it was quite a struggle. The issue of not antagonizing the Court or forcing a decision surfaced again when ICWOW and WOW differed over whether to reject or accept the Court's proposal to put the Kotel on the agenda of the Ne'eman Commission. ICWOW resisted this latest attempt at settlement through the political process, but WOW felt that we should accede to the Court's recommendation to show our goodwill and flexibility yet again.

WOW's women, being at the Kotel month in and month out, were less focused on the Court as the only battlefront. They sensed opportunities for introducing more ritual for women at the Kotel and for educational outreach. WOW sometimes felt that less vigorous litigation in the Court might calm the political atmosphere and allow for creating more ritual "facts on the ground" for women at the Kotel. Indeed, while the Court was studiously avoiding making any decision legitimizing our rights, WOW creatively introduced new and uplifting religious experiences at the Kotel that women had not available to them before, such as *Megillah* readings, bat mitzvah celebrations, and learning sessions. Such activities stretched the boundaries of acceptable practice at the Kotel without evoking any violence or government crackdown. The activities even attracted some smiles and an occasional good word from women at the Kotel who normally would count themselves among our critics. This enhancement of religious services for women at the Kotel was an inspiring accomplishment.

WOW was at times concerned that ICWOW's pushing the Court for a decision would force a negative decision that might result in even tighter restrictions at the Kotel, which might then block WOW's growing activities. ICWOW, on the other hand, felt inclined to force the Supreme Court to decide, perhaps because of our remoteness from the positive energy of WOW's activities and perhaps because of our American conviction that Supreme Court judges will not sacrifice their integrity on the altar of political bargaining. We thought there was a chance that, if forced to decide, the Court would feel compelled to uphold its two-out-of-three-judge decision, which recognized our right to pray at the Kotel according to our custom.

Ultimately, it didn't seem to make any difference how hard we pushed for a decision, for the Court systematically and resolutely avoided making any decision. Fortunately, no new regulations were promulgated that interfered with WOW's various activities at the Kotel. As long as the Court did not force the issue, our opponents seemed content with the fact that the electrifying and spiritually empowering image of women with a Torah scroll and tallit was barred from the women's section.[20] They were either unaware of or willing to tolerate WOW's other religious activities at the Kotel.

ICWOW and the United States: Communal Politics

One of ICWOW's earliest experiences with communal politics in the United States was the 1988–1989 campaign to raise funds for a Torah that ICWOW planned to present to our sisters in Jerusalem. Donations for the Torah and to support ICWOW's struggle poured in from Jews of every stripe, but the strongest support came from the Reform movement. The Association of Reform Zionists of America (ARZA) took on the responsibility of collecting and processing donations from its members. On more than one occasion during this fundraising campaign, I spoke to a prominent Reform movement leader. He asked if we wanted their public endorsement or if it might prove more of a liability than an asset. ICWOW at the time thought it would hurt rather than help. He understood and continued vigorous fundraising efforts for ICWOW.

Jewish communal support for ICWOW took other forms besides fundraising. The American Jewish Congress accepted ICWOW's proposal to present a Torah to the women of Jerusalem as part of an American Jewish Congress mission that included women from across the spectrum of Judaism. During the period when the Mancal Commission was functioning, ICWOW received letters of support from the various institutions of the Reform, Conservative, and Reconstructionist movements. Hadassah, the American Jewish Committee, and US/Israel Women to Women added their voices as well. With this outpouring of support in the form of letter writing to the Mancal Commission, ICWOW was able to testify to the Commission in 1991 that our claim had the support of a large number of American Jews. However, when ICWOW consulted with several of the general communal organizations about joining us as co-petitioners in the second stage of our lawsuit, none would go that far. Fear of alienating donors should their organization become a litigant in a lawsuit against the State of Israel probably held them back.

In contrast to this response from liberal American organizations, Orthodox organizational support for ICWOW was virtually nonexistent during the first ten years of our struggle. Although ICWOW received some financial contributions from Orthodox sources, the financial support from non-Orthodox sources was greater by far. Even American Orthodox feminists kept their distance from ICWOW. The Orthodox Women's Tefillah Network, already in existence when the Kotel struggle began, did not endorse ICWOW. I found that within my own Flatbush Women's Tefillah Group, and in the Riverdale *tefillah* group, feelings about ICWOW were mixed.

No prominent Orthodox female leaders publicly endorsed or joined ICWOW, despite numerous and frequent contacts with

ICWOW and its four Orthodox board members. The Jewish Orthodox Feminist Alliance (JOFA), founded in 1998, ignored the Kotel issue for two years. However, following the May 2000 court decision, there was some movement, and JOFA published a statement congratulating ICWOW, although it stopped short of calling on Orthodox women to support ICWOW and join WOW at the Kotel. No other Orthodox women's organization has expressed any support for ICWOW or WOW. Some Orthodox women seemed concerned about challenging the Israeli government or being involved in a confrontation focused around the Kotel. Another concern voiced by some Orthodox feminists who hung back was that freedom of religion at the Kotel for Orthodox women might strengthen the demand for similar freedom for the non-Orthodox, something these women viewed as undesirable.

Nor did Orthodox rabbis who supported women's *tefillah* in their own synagogues come forward to support ICWOW's lawsuit. Prior to the formation of ICWOW and the initiation of our lawsuit, Rabbi Avraham Weiss did write a letter in May 1989 to Israel's Minister of Religious Affairs, Zevulun Hammer, pointing out that Halakhah permits women to pray with Torah and tallit. He then expressed his support for women's right to pray together anywhere, including the Kotel, as long as they pray as a group that is not a minyan. He called on the government to ensure women's safety while praying at the Kotel. Weiss never lent support to ICWOW and our lawsuit, but his defense of women's halakhic rights to pray with Torah and tallit and to pray as a group at the Kotel is noteworthy.

In sum, ICWOW garnered written endorsements and financial support in the United States from the non-Orthodox streams and from general Jewish communal organizations, which represented a vast and communally active segment of the American Jewish community, but this kind of support could not deter Israeli politicians from engaging in their bad-faith delaying tactics. As long as denying women's rights at the Kotel wasn't costing Israeli politicians any votes or threatening diaspora support for Israel, Israel's political system was unresponsive to ICWOW's petition.

Some Final Thoughts

The vision and implications of women with a Torah and tallit at the Kotel were intolerable to the *charedim*, controversial to other Orthodox Israelis, and irrelevant to secular Israelis. Given this political reality, the Israeli Supreme Court was the one forum in which ICWOW and WOW could hope that right would prevail over political might. Thirteen years of litigation have shown that the Court has not yet decided to decide. The reasons for the Court's evading the issue are complex. The Court may be protecting its own status in the Israeli political system by refusing to issue a decision that will be reversed by the Knesset. Perhaps unconsciously influenced by the patriarchal values of traditional Judaism and Israeli culture, the Court may simply not comprehend the legitimacy and significance of ICWOW's mission. The Court may view itself as protecting Israeli society from a violent and divisive confrontation over a question that is of little importance to the vast majority of Israelis. The Court may be biding its time, refraining from issuing an enforceable Court order until the political balance of power is more receptive to such an order. Even the Court's unanimous May 22, 2000, decision, which strongly criticized the government's bad-faith foot-dragging, only increased the political pressure on the government. The Court, once again, stopped well short of imposing a specific solution by judicial order.

It is difficult to predict the long-term prospects for ICWOW and WOW's struggle because of the many factors that could affect the future of women's religious rights in Israel. Among those factors are shifts in Israel's security and economic situation and therefore in the alignment of political parties in government coalitions; developments within Israeli feminism, particularly Orthodox feminism; the types of resolutions that may emerge on religious issues such as conversion, Shabbat laws, and army service deferrals; changes in Israelis' attitudes toward religion as Israel's sizable Arab population (20 percent) and large non-Jewish Russian community become more politically assertive.

Continued external threats to Israel's security sustains the *charedim's* leverage regarding control of the Kotel in exchange for their support of vital military and diplomatic policies of various government coalitions. Likewise, under such conditions, religious coercion at the Kotel has continued to be of little concern to secular Israeli politicians and voters. Certainly, violence at the Temple Mount has made change at the Kotel very hot to handle and discourages secular Israelis from disturbing the status quo.

If, on the other hand, there should eventually be progress toward peace, the *charedim* and other Orthodox parties may find their political clout reduced as Labor and Likud reorient themselves toward dealing with economic and social issues and paying more attention to the needs of voters who currently support the Orthodox parties. If a portion of these Orthodox voters shifts to Labor and Likud, these Israeli political parties may feel freer to resist the religious coercion that mars Israel's image as a democracy. In the competition for a more fluid Israeli electorate, Labor and Likud may then find themselves competing on issues they ignored before, such as women's rights. Furthermore, if peace blooms, diaspora Jews may feel freer to press for their religious rights at the Kotel. Finally, de-escalation or increased escalation of tension at the Temple Mount may in time bring about a reconsideration of the discrimination against women and non-Orthodox Jews at the Kotel.

Internal social and cultural ferment may also affect the ability of the Orthodox parties to maintain religious coercion in Israel and at the Kotel. As Israel copes with the rights of its Arab population and the personal status of its large non-Jewish Russian population, Israel may be forced to develop more flexible policies on the relationship between synagogue and state and to ponder the meaning of the Jewish State once the Orthodox official monopoly has been eroded. Israeli political leaders may have to rethink their routine capitulation to *charedi* demands that alienate Israeli Jews from Judaism and diaspora Jews from Israel. Orthodox insistence on exclusive control of the Kotel may suddenly seem incompatible with a more diverse and less theocratic State of Israel.

With the easing of Orthodox religious coercion and the growth of multiculturalism in Israel, Israeli Jews may find themselves searching for a form of Judaism that provides a comfortable personal Jewish identity and national Jewish identity for the Jewish State. It would be a fascinating twist in the tortuous history of Judaism's survival if the *charedim*, the Orthodox rabbinate, and the Orthodox political parties were someday to find it desirable to find common ground with the likes of ICWOW and WOW in order to formulate a role for Judaism in Israel that can serve the democratic Jewish State in the future.

LESLIE J. KLEIN

Dominion of Arrogance

Don't pray here
    Torah wrapped and bundled
    Against the cold December day
    We walk in groups to the Wall
Don't pray so we can hear you.
Don't read from our Holy Book
Don't touch our Holy Words
Don't even stand next to us while we pray
You are defiled
You are disturbing us distracting us with your defilement
You are not as Holy as we are
    We will spit on you we will throw garbage on you
    We will wound you with flying books and chairs
    We will bear down upon you with arms linked and feet
        stomping
                Hovering as the cloud over Sarah's tent
                Nourishing as the waters of the moving well
                Searing the soul as surely as
                Hannah's prayer
                This thrumming circle of Torah chant
            They will not prevail
No matter how tightly they seek to close the gates
Arms linked and feet stomping power surge false righteousness
Prayers of women will fly over the heavens, chanting Torah words 'til
    the slender silver thread gives way
And Life's tenuous hold levels all to one in God's brightness pure soul.

PART III

Denominational Views

RABBI HELENE FERRIS

Why? A Reform Rabbi's Answer

IT WAS 6 A.M. on 22 Kislev 5749; Thursday, December 1, 1988. Just a few hours had passed since approximately one hundred women at a conference had concluded a difficult debate as to whether or not we should go to the Kotel. How would it be interpreted by the right-wingers? The left-wingers? The secularists? The government? The public? The media? The *charedim?* The consensus was that we just wanted to participate in a morning Torah service at the Kotel, even though women had never prayed there together before. I am sure there were many different motives for choosing to do what we did. To naive me, it was an ordinary and natural event, for as a Reform Jew, I never had any restrictions on prayer and on honoring the Torah. How awesome to do so at the Kotel!

The *sefer Torah* loaned to me by Hebrew Union College had been in my hotel room throughout the night. My sleep had been fitful, filled with fearful thoughts: Would anyone harm a woman alone in a Jerusalem hotel with the sacred scroll next to her? What would happen as I carried the Torah out of the room to the bus? Would our group be able to reach the Kotel in peace and return in peace?

As I dressed, there was a pounding at the door, and my heart pounded as well. I thought I heard my name mispronounced, but it was only a waiter outside the room next door announcing *serveece, serveece* (room service), not *Fereece, Fereece!*

The group arrived safely at the Kotel with the *sefer Torah*. There were more media people than we had expected, and we politely answered their many questions with one simple statement: We've come here to pray.

In front of the Kotel, about seventy of us gathered, surrounding the Torah, which lay respectfully covered on a small table. We began the morning service, quietly chanting the appropriate prayers. As we lifted the Torah to begin the Torah service, a few older women began to scream: *HaTorah lo l'nashim!* "The Torah is not for women!"

The uneasiness and tension were building. I looked up and saw men peering over the *mechitzah,* raising angry voices, but a bit confused as to what to do. It wasn't until I began to chant the opening words of the Torah portion *Vayeshev* ("Now Jacob was settled in the land where his father had resided, the land of Canaan") that I heard that eerie sound, which haunts me to this day—the sound of the rattling of the fiberglass panels of the *mechitzah* being shaken violently by the black-hatted men leering and screaming in our direction. My heart was pounding. I shall never forget the feeling of utter panic. I completed the chanting, as did the other two women after me. The service was hurried along because of our fear of the gathering yeshiva students, and when it was completed, we surrounded the person carrying the Torah and quickly walked to our bus. We returned in physical safety to the hotel; our souls, however, were wounded, and still have not healed many years later.

Since that very day, I have been deeply involved in the struggle for women to worship as men can, together, with their voices raised to God, embracing Torah, hugged by tallit. I have been on the board of directors of ICWOW from the beginning and have been its treasurer for most of these years. I have made trips to Israel on our behalf, have spoken to various groups about our raison d'etre, and have been part of our fundraising efforts. I have "surfed" on every positive and negative wave in the wake of the numerous court and committee decisions and have read every word of the vast e-mail correspondence that our group generates to keep in touch. From time to time, I must admit, I stop and ask myself: Why am I doing this? Why do I subject myself to this aggravation? I am a busy Reform rabbi with a growing congregation that is extremely active in both Jewish learning and *tikkun olam.* There are many causes that demand my attention. After all, I do not need permission to pray out loud as I wish, almost anywhere I wish, with Torah, *kipah,* and tallit. Ah! Could it be that because I, as a Reform rabbi, know so well how powerful an experience it is to do just what the Women of the Wall are fighting to do that I remain in the struggle with them? Maybe, but there is more to it than that. It is the place of the struggle. Why should I care about the place? Then I realized: Just because the Kotel has been for me such a despised symbol of women's exclusion, that very place now lures me to the cause.

I believe that the exclusion of women from various aspects of the life of our people has had dire consequences, inhibiting the flourishing of our tradition. Confining Jewish women to the home was putting us in a prison without allowing us to develop the spiritual resources we could have brought to our faith. To deny the Jewish people the talent of fifty percent of our resources not only denigrated women and denied women a sense of belonging but also greatly impoverished our people. To deny women access to the study of Torah and the experience of communal prayer kept the insights that we could bring to our tradition from enriching that very tradition. Denying women complete access to the Kotel also denies the Jewish tradition aspects of the spiritual meaning of Jewish survival. Furthermore, placing restrictions on our participation in any aspect of our faith denies each of us as individuals a creative and spiritual dimension of our being.

I believe that the Wall, along with the assembly of the Jewish people who gather in front of it, is a manifestation of the vibrancy of our people. Going to the Wall was always a way of keeping alive periods of history that were dynamic, creative, and spiritually meaningful. It reminded Jews of the First and Second Commonwealth and helped them to maintain the spiritual resources that ultimately led to the Third Commonwealth. Praying at the Wall helped Jews to keep alive the dream of Jewish autonomy.

Today, the Wall not only represents the glory of the past; it also symbolizes the hope for the future, which must be built by all of our people. Any restriction on women at the Wall says to us: You are not really part of the Jewish people. You didn't share the past and you can't share the future.

So my answer to *Why?* is this: I refuse to be excluded from Jewish history. The Wall, symbolizing our national experience, has been a focus of past tragedy and future hope. It is my past and my hope, and I will fight to be part of them! If it were not for the achievement of Jewish prayer and study and continued hope, we would not have been prepared for the rejuvenation of our people in the land of Israel and the establishment of the Jewish State. The Wall is a symbol of the promise of our people, that we will be a light unto the nations, that we are God's witnesses to the world. I will remain part of the light. I will remain a witness for God for the future of Israel, for the future of the world.

BERYL MICHAELS

Encompassing Diversity

THE MOST POWERFUL EXPERIENCE of the International Women's Conference was the prayer service that was held at the Western Wall. It was 7:30 A.M. on Thursday morning when approximately seventy women arrived at the Kotel carrying a *sefer Torah* in our arms, along with a card table and prayer books. We came to the Wall, where we set up our table, carefully placed our *sefer Torah* on it, and participated as Rabbi Deborah Brin from Canada conducted a halakhically correct morning service. Women were, for the first time in memory, performing the obligation of *tefillah* (prayer) and reading from the Torah for themselves (rather than having to listen from their side of the *mechitzah* as the men read). It was truly an all-encompassing moment as women from the secular to the Orthodox came together, demonstrating the strength that comes from hearing each other, from the determination to be whole, and from the desire to find the path that would allow all of us the dignity of real communal prayer.

Much of the beauty as well as the dissension came from our diversity as Jews. Rabbi Helene Ferris, in celebrating this aspect of our conference, said, "Our diversity began at Mount Sinai, and our diversity must endure if Israel is to endure." I cannot translate or transmit the passion, the concern, and the love for Judaism that was evident at this conference. There was universal determination that women will not be written out of Jewish history.

213

The privilege of this experience will always be with me. We went to the Wall to pray as our mothers had not done before us. We left, singing and dancing with our Torah in our arms, joyful that we had indeed begun to take our rightful place in our people's history, to reach back through the millennia of our heritage and to go forward with new traditions.

RABBI DEBORAH J. BRIN

Against the Wall

We had a halakhic prayer service at the Wall.
Women from all sectors of the Jewish community
were there. We said prayers and read the Torah. It
was done as a religious and spiritual experience.

—PRESS RELEASE (JERUSALEM, DECEMBER 1, 1988)

THE FIRST INTERNATIONAL JEWISH FEMINIST CONFERENCE was highly
charged with the intensity, passion, tension, and urgency that only
a room full of six hundred Jewish feminists from all over the world
could create. Each one came to the gathering in Jerusalem with her
own understanding of what it means to be a woman, a Jew, and a
feminist. The variety of our experiences was astonishing, and it
seemed practically impossible for us to understand one another
across the barriers and chasms of culture, language, class, country
of origin, country of domicile, sexuality, marital status, education,
life experiences, profession, age, and relationship to Jewish tradition
and law. I have a vivid memory of Norma Baumel Joseph, an
Orthodox feminist from Montreal, passionately declaring during
one of the plenary sessions, "Just because you can label me doesn't
mean that you know me."

There were huge gatherings for plenary speeches, panels, and
presentations. There were workshops, caucuses, networking in the

215

halls, and a constant buzz and hum of activity. In the middle of all of this, Rivka Haut quietly spoke with individual women about holding a prayer service at the Wall—a Thursday morning service that would follow tradition and include a Torah reading. I was one of the women whom she approached to help plan and lead the service.

I resisted the idea at first. I think that my first reaction was to reject it out of hand. I had long ago decided never to daven in a place with a *mechitzah,* and the Wall has a tall one. I think that what finally won me over was a deep-felt sense that Rivka and I compassionately understood one another. She needed to have a diversity of Jewish feminists praying together, as women, strictly according to Halakhah. Despite the perception, this is not a contradiction in terms. We wanted to show that there are no halakhic prohibitions on women praying together as a group as long as the group is not constituted as a minyan. Rivka was specifically asking me to lend my support to her and her endeavor. Who could say no to this righteous, gentle, and extremely passionate feminist?

Announcements were made about the service at the Wall and sign-up sheets circulated. All the next day, women stopped me to ascertain whether I had any clue that what we were doing was dangerous. Had we arranged for police protection? In case we found ourselves in jail, did we know of an attorney who would assist us? Enough pressure to call it all off had been applied by the conference organizers and others, especially Israeli women, that we agreed to have a meeting with all of the women who planned to go to the Wall with us and decide if we were really going to do it.

At the meeting, it was agreed that the decisions reached that evening would be by consensus and that they would be binding on all who went to the Wall the next day.

We bring the Torah to the Kotel (Dec. 1, 1988). From left: Daphna Israeli, Phyllis Chesler, Francine Klagsbrun (carrying the Torah), Rivka Haut.

Above: A male worshiper stands on a chair to curse us (Dec. 1, 1988).

Left: Rivka Haut and Phyllis Chesler with the Torah at the Kotel (Dec. 1, 1988).

A *charedi* woman attempts to snatch a sacred book from a WOW member (Spring 1989).

Security guards drag WOW worshipers away from the Kotel (Spring 1989).

WOW members refuse to leave the Kotel and are dragged away by security guards. Seated woman in the center is WOW leader Bonna Haberman (Spring 1989).

Barbara Wachs, *z"l*, tells *charedi* woman "I only want to pray" (Rosh Chodesh Sivan, June 1989).

Charedi woman and male Israeli security guard confront WOW at prayer. Barbara Wachs is in white hat (Rosh Chodesh Sivan, June 1989).

ICWOW tries to pray with newly donated Torah (Nov. 1989). From left: Susan Aranoff, Norma Baumel Joseph, Rivka Haut, Susan Alter, Rabbi Helene Ferris.

WOW and ICWOW pray joyfully together (Nov. 1989). Ruth Laibson is in center.

Rabbi Shlomo Carlebach, *z"l*, joins our Torah dedication ceremony (Nov. 1989).

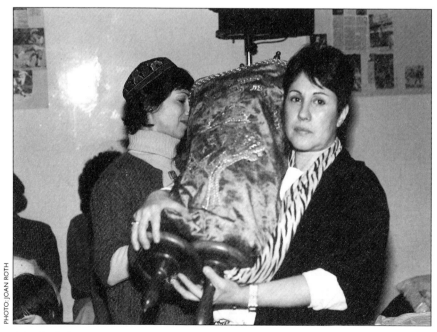

Torah dedication ceremony (Nov. 1989). From left: Shulamit Magnus, Phyllis Chesler holding the Torah.

ICWOW at prayer overlooking the Kotel plaza (Nov. 1989). Left to right: Rivka Haut, Phyllis Chesler, Susan Alter, Susan Aranoff, Ruth Laibson, and unidentified woman.

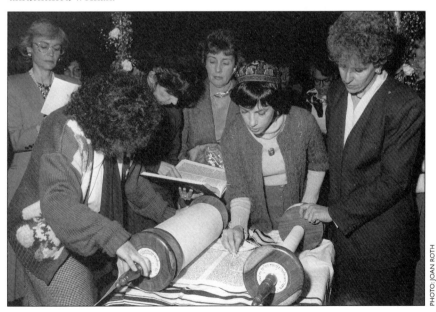

Torah dedication (Nov. 1989). From left to right: Rivka Haut, Norma Baumel Joseph, Susan Alter, Shulamit Magnus reads from the Torah, Susan Aranoff. Ann Lewis looks on.

A male worshiper throws a chair at us.

Left: ICWOW prays at a site that overlooks the Kotel (Nov. 1989). From left: Rivka Haut, Phyllis Chesler, Rabbi Helene Ferris, Susan Aranoff.

PHOTO: JOAN ROTH

PHOTO: JOAN ROTH

ICWOW with the newly dedicated Torah (Nov. 1989). Third from left: Shulamit Magnus, Phyllis Chesler, Norma Baumel Joseph, Rivka Haut (holding the Torah), Susan Alter, Harriet Kurlander, Faigie Fein, Susan Aranoff.

Sunny Korda celebrates her bat mitzvah with WOW (June 1990). Korda holds the Torah, Bonna Haberman holds a *siddur.*

WOW celebrates Purim with a *Megillah* reading at the Kotel. Far left, standing, WOW member Haviva Ner-David; Anat Hoffman seated second from left; Jessica Bonn reading from the *Megillah.*

Israeli soldier reads from the Torah (June 2000). Behind her is Knesset member Galia Galon. WOW member Danielle Bernstein looks on.

ICWOW Board meeting in Brooklyn, New York at Phyllis Chesler's home (June 2000). From left seated: Lilly Rivlin, Susan Aranoff, Bonna Haberman. Standing from left: Susan Alter, Rivka Haut, Miriam Benson, Rabbi Gail Labovitz, Phyllis Chesler, Vanessa Ochs. Not shown: Rabbis Helene Ferris and Marion Shulevitz.

WOW member Betsy Kallus carries the Torah (July 2000).

In the Israeli Supreme Court (Nov. 2000). From left, WOW members Anat Hoffman and Danielle Bernstein.

ICWOW meeting with Frances Raday in the Manhattan home of Merle Hoffman (July 2001). Seated from left: Phyllis Chesler and Rabbi Gail Labovitz. Standing from left: Rabbi Marion Shulevitz, Susan Alter, Susan Aranoff, Frances Raday, Rivka Haut.

ICWOW conducts a women's prayer service on an El Al flight to Israel.

The women seated in the front row are (from left to right): Rahel Jaskow, Danielle Bernstein, and Anat Hoffman. Standing (from left to right) are: a journalist, Beatrice Safran, Rolinda Schonwald, Chaia Beckerman, Betsy Kallus.

A woman praying with WOW.

There were several complex issues that needed to be decided: Would we go to the Wall at all? If we went, would we bring a Torah and read from it? Since we had reason to fear violence if we went with the Torah, how would we protect it and ourselves? It was going to be halakhic davening, but what did that mean about wearing pants or *kipot* or *tallesim?* We knew that the press was aware that we were planning on going to the Wall because of the announcement of an emergency meeting about it during that evening's plenary session on "Women, War, and Peace." How were we going to maintain a dignified spiritual experience with the press corps in our faces?

Remarkably, we did achieve consensus, and in the process we created a plan, a shared identity, and a goal that united us. We ended the meeting with decisions and agreements about what we would do and how we would conduct ourselves. We would go to the Wall with the Torah. We would have sentries on the outside of the circle keeping a lookout, and Norma Joseph would watch for a signal from them that would indicate if we needed to close ranks around the Torah and leave as quickly as possible. We could wear whatever we wanted, based on our own customs. If questioned by the press, we would simply say, "I came to pray; we came to pray."

That night, after the meeting (*Oy*, was I drained!), Rivka, Norma, and I met to plan the service itself. Even though it was to be a halakhic service, there were a few key issues that needed to be worked through with respect, creativity, and compassion before our work was done for the night. Of course, I remember the issues that were most important to me. Inside the halakhic framework, a group of women praying together does not count as a minyan. Therefore, I was not to lead any of the prayers that require a minyan in order to be recited. I didn't feel that strongly about omitting the *Barkhu,* but Kaddish was a different story. My father, may his memory be a blessing, had died six months before. I was not going to lead a prayer service at the Wall without saying Kaddish for him. Rivka gently explained that all of our needs could be met if I simply would announce that the service was over and then invite the others to join me as I said Kaddish.

With this and other accommodations to each other's requirements, needs, and sensitivities accomplished, the service was planned and we were ready. I am amazed at how powerful the listening and singleness of purpose had to be in order for so many of us to be heard and our needs honored in the davening. Anxious, fearful, excited, and exhausted, we went to our rooms and our beds hoping for sleep and wondering what the morrow would bring.

Tense with anxiety and excitement, worried about the potential for violence, we boarded the buses. We arrived at the Dung Gate at 7:30 A.M. The press corps and the soldiers were all waiting for us.

We came to pray. We set up as quickly as possible, Geela Rayzel Raphael (an incoming student at the Reconstructionist Rabbinical College) led us in *Pesukei d'Zimra* (the first section of prayer) while others set up a portable table and set the Torah down. We prayed together for a while before the disturbance began. The ruckus started with a religious woman on our side of the wall shouting at us and pounding on the shoulders of the women on the outside edge of the circle. We stayed focused and would not let her disrupt our prayers or our Torah reading. Her shouts of distress attracted the attention of the camera crews, who tried to get into our side of the fence. Then some religious men began to catch on to what we were doing and started yelling at us. It was like davening in a war zone. Despite our fear, despite the men who shouted at us with rage-filled voices and faces, we managed to stay focused, read from the Torah, and pray.

218

Our tradition teaches that women's voices should not be heard in a synagogue because they are a distraction to men who are trying to pray. Yet the deliberate attempt of these men's voices to interrupt our service only drove us to deeper concentration.

My back was to the Wall that all of the others were facing. Often terrified in crowds, I suppressed the urge to flee by concentrating on the prayers as well as the sensory data important to our safety. I saw the raging men on my right, the soldiers deep behind the circle of women, and every gesture from our posted sentries. The gathering of women before me pressed against me like a weight. I was aware of the Wall behind me, inanimate, ancient, and solid. Each moment formed the shape of the next moment, and I reiterated so often that it seemed like a chant: "Stay with me, stay focused."

The signal from Norma was barely a nod, but with my heightened awareness, I knew she was indicating that it was time for us to leave. I announced that the service was officially finished, and then I invited those who wanted to join me in a *shehecheyanu* and the mourner's Kaddish. When the Kaddish was over, the group burst into *Oseh Shalom* (a prayer that speaks of God as the creator of peace) and quickly moved away from the Wall. I was the last to leave the Wall. I had been standing with my back against it, holding my place as the prayer leader, surrounded by women who were tightly packed together. I followed along behind, feeling attentive as a sheepdog, making sure that everyone kept moving and was safe. As I walked away from the Wall, I remember thinking, "Now I really am a rabbi." (I had graduated from RRC in June 1985.)

Looking back at myself through the lens of who I have become and what I have experienced since then, I can see the impact that "going to the Wall" had on me and my rabbinate. I think about how naive I was about public events, media coverage, and photographic records of historic moments. After the event itself, we found ourselves trying to manage the media—which was far too late, but we did the best that we could. I recall long and passionate conversations with Phyllis Chesler in which she taught me a lot about the importance of networking and how to get publicity for your radical actions.

In retrospect, I realize that one of the sparks that flamed in me at the Wall in 1988 was how to listen to what people need, bridge the gaps, and create the space in which Jewish expression can take place. At the Wall that day, I was able to hold the focus of a disparate group of women and create a spiritual space in which each could craft her own meaning and experience. I have learned how to channel the energy, focus the excitement, and move a group through the deep structures of a ritual, liturgical, or educational experience.

That group at the Wall was for me a onetime gathering. Now, as the associate chaplain at Grinnell College, I work with a more stable group. As I deepen my understanding of the community I serve, an intuitive, emotional negotiation around comfort levels for "doing Jewish" takes place within the framework of tradition, custom, and law. This is an integral part of who I am and how I function as a rabbi. As I get to know others, I can weave them into the community through their interests, passions, and talents.

It is very unusual to have such an extraordinary experience at the beginning of one's career. Momentarily thrust into the international limelight, I was unprepared to stay in the middle of it all. It brings to mind a theatre director who said to me, "If you start with a scream, where do you go from there?" Where I went was back to my congregation in Toronto. In 1992, I moved to Albuquerque, New Mexico, where I worked with elders, helped to start a *chevra kadisha* (Jewish burial society), and worked as a hospice chaplain. In 1997, I returned to the Midwest, where I was raised, to take my current position as associate chaplain at Grinnell College in Grinnell, Iowa. Despite the isolation, I love being the spiritual leader of this tiny academic shtetl. I am proud to be an agent of change within Judaism and the wider world and to take my place as a teacher and transmitter of our history and sacred traditions.

ALIZA METZNER

My Father's Tallit

TRAVELING AS A GROUP of women with Rabbi Judy Shanks, we found it easy to feel comfortable. We carried with us the comfort and freedom of prayer and expression that we feel as Reform Jewish women in the United States and at Temple Isaiah in Orinda, California. Trying to pray in Israel, we did not always feel comfortable or accepted. At times, we felt scared, out of place, and even threatened. How ironic that we were on a pilgrimage, an *aliyah* to discover and declare our Judaism, yet we could not always openly pray as we wished. In places like Safed, we literally had to find a place to hide. At the Western Wall, the Kotel—the most awe-inspiring place in Israel—we were literally forbidden by law from praying out loud or as a group.

Women on the Temple Isaiah Women's Trip to Israel met with the Women at the Wall and prayed at the Kotel. The devotion of these women and the beauty of their voices overwhelmed us. Although they stood as far back from the Wall as possible and covered their mouths as they prayed, the intertwining melodies, the fervor of their prayer, and their devotion to Judaism could not be stifled. Their voices rose up, escaping their lips, and circled above us, just as the doves circled overhead. On "the wings of prayer" their voices rose, ours joined with theirs, and we felt an intense spiritual energy as we were collectively united with each other, our foremothers, all those who have come before us, and all those who will come after us in Judaism. We felt the awe and comfort of being close to God, but what we did was illegal. We could have been arrested.

I carried with me a tallit and a dream of my deceased father. My father had wished to take our entire family to Israel, to feel our connection, discover our heritage, and visit relatives. This did not happen in his lifetime. To honor and remember my father, I wanted to wear his tallit as I said Kaddish for him at the Kotel. I wanted to do this with the women on the Women's Trip, as I needed the support in prayer and emotion that a minyan brings. I was to discover that I could neither wear my father's tallit nor say Kaddish out loud. I was to discover that no event, whether a holiday or personal, no birth, no baby naming, no bat mitzvah, no wedding, no prayer, not even Kaddish, may be uttered out loud at the Kotel by women as a group. Where was the freedom of access and prayer for women?

SHULAMIT MAGNUS

A Wall That Matters and Others That Don't: A Meta-Denominational View

THIS ISSUE, FOR ME, going to the Wall as we do, goes to the heart of matters and so tends to put other things into secondary relief. This is a highly emotional issue. Denominational affiliation for me, to put it mildly, is not. Let me try to explain why to me, the Kotel matters so much and other dividers do not. They are walls from which I distance myself and that I even reject.

Going to the Wall came as a suggestion during the First International Conference of Jewish Feminists in Jerusalem in 1988. It was not a formal part of that meeting's agenda. It just happened when Rivka Haut posed the idea of a women's service, with Torah reading, and then circulated it among the women gathered at the conference, myself included.

The conference took place in December. I had been in Israel since August for a sabbatical year. It had been my practice, since Israel got the Kotel back in 1967, to go to Jerusalem, to the Kotel, first thing after landing. I had first been to Israel the year before the Six Day War, and one of many searing memories of that trip was of Jerusalem divided by wall and barbed wire, and my inability to go to the Kotel. I remember my sister and me walking around,

224

looking for places—Mount Zion, the YMCA tower—from which we could see into the Old City, hoping to catch a glimpse of the Wall (obviously, we had no idea of the Old City's layout), and feeling the anger, pain, and injustice of having the desire for spiritual fulfillment denied by walls of hate, spite, and cruelty.

Then, miraculously, we got it back. I remember listening furtively to a transistor radio during class (normally, I was a very obedient student), the wire for the earphone threaded up my sleeve into my ear, and hearing, astonished, that Israel had captured Old Jerusalem and its soldiers had taken the Wall. I ran out of class, just tore out, to call my sister, passing an Israeli-born teacher on the way and calling out, *Kavashnu et Yerushalayim!* "We captured Jerusalem!" Not *they,* but *we.*

The Kotel is a place of millennial Jewish yearning—of prayers, hopes, and pain; of longing for redemption, for union with the Divine Spirit, for an end to dispersion and to powerlessness. It is a place of collective memory, sanctified by century upon century of prayers and supplications. The Wall just looms there, its massive stone upon stone, rough hewn, worn smooth by centuries of fingertips and tears and kisses.

Normally, I would go there the day after my arrival in Israel, excitement building as the bus wound higher into the Jerusalem hills, as the air changed to mountainous and the familiar landscape emerged. Once in the city, I would walk as much of it as I could, wanting to savor every minute of just getting there, thinking in amazement: This is what generations of Jews wanted to do and could not, and here I am, a free Jew, in a Jewish state, the sun shining, people bustling, stores and buses, children scampering about, normal—and I walk to the Kotel. I felt redemption. I didn't theorize it. I experienced it and rejoiced, and I wanted that overflowing gratitude to find its place of expression.

This year in Jerusalem was different. When I landed, I had the familiar urge, but the emotional energy that normally fueled it was missing. The Kotel had been turned into an ultra-Orthodox shul with segregated sections and silenced women. I think what really did it was the time I was there and a bar mitzvah happened, and I saw the mother of the boy straining from a chair on the women's side, attempting to see and hear what was going on, on tiptoes and with craned neck. It was a sad, forlorn sight. To see degradation at a place of ultimate spiritual connection was too painful a contradiction and perversion. To have to choose between fullness as a Jew and self-respect as a woman, to have to bifurcate that which is whole and interwoven, felt like an act of inner violence. I did not feel peace and gratitude at the Kotel. I felt anger, and it was too painful to feel anger there of all places. So I did not go, except once, when my mother came, and I took her out of respect for her desire. Not going also felt awful, of course, given how I yearned to go. There was no good resolution.

Rivka's suggestion shone like a laser beam through months of depressive cloudiness on this issue. Yes, it would be the Kotel as the authorities had construed it, but it would be entirely different to go there with a group of women and to read Torah. The experience would be redeemed and made whole.

It was even more appealing a prospect precisely because it came from Rivka; it was not an organizational event, it would just be whoever chose to go. It would just be us, for us. More delicious still, Rivka had made it clear that she was Orthodox and that the service would have to be halakhic—that is, that there would be prayers we would not say because they require a minyan, and, in accordance with the traditional rabbinic definition, we would not constitute ourselves as one.

226

The conference was taking place in the midst of the (first) infamous "Who is a Jew" controversy and an orgy of mutual hatred and vilification stirred up by that campaign—which, as has been noted, was not about who is a Jew but who is a rabbi. It was a play for religious domination, using Israel to delegitimize whole sections of (non-Orthodox) Jewry. Rivka made her appeal for meta-denominational cooperation quite consciously. If women who ordinarily would never constrain themselves in this way would do so now out of understanding and love for our Orthodox sisters, we would perform a powerful act of *tikkun*, healing, and have an experience none of us would otherwise have: women's group prayer at the Wall, an expression of Jewish and women's solidarity. Sickened by the spectacle of *sinat chinam*, wanton hate, that was assaulting us daily, disgusted with the fanatical factionalism that pervades Jewish life, the obsession with power and domination, this to me loomed as a supreme opportunity for *ahavat chinam*—"wanton love"—and as a way I could go back to the Kotel, as I yearned to, feeling whole.

I was as uncomfortable with the constraints as anyone. Mine had been a long, difficult odyssey on the issue of rabbinic law, and many women and I had arrived solidly in a feminism that refused to compromise or inhibit our Judaism. Turning womanness into disability was a self-injury I would not inflict. I would no longer, as I had for five years, participate in a women's prayer group I myself had founded that omitted anything because we were women.

This was different. I would not frustrate the desire of other women to go to the Wall for prayer on grounds of ideological purity. That was "their" fractious game, and I would not play it. Second, the Kotel was still the Kotel—to all of us. It was time to focus on what we shared, not what divided us. Going to the Kotel as an individual had become untenable for me, but going in a group of women made it possible to overcome the degradation and have a religious experience unimpeded by rage.

A religious experience it certainly was. I had not prayed with such feeling in at least twenty years, since the Wall was liberated in 1967. It was fervent and joyous. I shivered in the chill of the early morning air and in the emotion of what we were doing—women, beautiful voices ringing out; deft, skilled handling of the Torah; affirmation, celebration.

I had declined to lead prayers because of the constraints and all they symbolized, but I readily accepted part of the Torah reading. I had always loved the Torah reading even when I could participate only passively, by listening, and I had grown to love it more once I began to chant Torah myself. The portion was about Joseph. My part contained the words "I have dreamt a dream." I never dreamed that such a dream could be dreamt, much less realized.

It was realized because the women decided that it was more important to listen and truly hear one another than to "win." It was not being right that mattered, but being whole. To be whole meant, paradoxically, to compromise, to give up parts—important parts—of our positions. Difficult as that was, it was preferable to the hollow satisfaction of frustrating and hurting one another in the cause of truth. That is what carried us to the Wall that day.

What some of us compromised was obvious, but the Orthodox women compromised merely by praying in "mixed" and "heretical" company; by doing what some had been doing in small, quiet gatherings—reading Torah—in public, at Judaism's holiest site; by proclaiming that they were feminists, that they knew the rabbinic rules, including what was halakhically acceptable (like this service), and were asking no one's (read: no man's) permission.

For days afterwards, I tread ground lightly, as if I were hovering above it, a smile on my face, feeling so privileged, so full of love and gratitude, feeling generous toward strangers and an inexpressible peacefulness. That Shabbat, in shul, I *benched Gomel*—that is, said a blessing traditionally recited when one escapes danger—not because of the violence that threatened that day (and later came into full expression), but because that prayer thanks God for having "granted me all manner of goodness," which is exactly how it felt.

What happened next was shocking, appalling violence, cynical manipulation by state authorities, and incredible ugliness. The politicization of all this, and the attempt to characterize us by the standards of those who were opposing and attacking us, was an astounding exercise in psychological projection and distortion that would be comic were it not so serious.

It was serious not only because of what this group of women was being denied but also because of what that denial signified for the rule of law and the possibilities of religion in the State of Israel, both of which were being corrupted, with dangerous consequences for civil society and for the soul of Israel. From being a national symbol par excellence, one so capable of unifying sentiment that it was made a prime strategic goal for military commanders in 1967, the Wall had been co-opted and made into the arch-symbol of intolerance and mindless hatred. I shall never forget the morning when one ultra-Orthodox fanatic, having charged into the women's section, actually attempted to overturn the table on which the women had placed the *sefer Torah.* He would have thrown it to the ground—an unthinkable sacrilege (was the Torah no longer the Torah because women had it?)—had not Bonna Haberman caught it upon her hugely pregnant belly.

Denominationalism does not have to degenerate into such depravity. I am enough of a student of American Jewish society, and of Jewish history in general, to appreciate the crucial importance of options, varieties, and choices. If anything, I am a very eclectic Jew. I cannot fit comfortably in any one movement, but I have learned from all of them, which is possible, of course, because they each have distinct positions, traditions, and ideologies. I only wish that the movements would acknowledge learning from each other instead of stoking their differences and being obsessed with relative power. If only there were a denominationalism that consciously saw itself as part of a larger pluralism, a denominationalism of *elu v'elu*—"these and these are [both] the words of the living God." In other words, "This is what I believe and practice, I do so passionately, and I know there are other sets of beliefs and practices, held by sincere, honest Jews, who disagree utterly with me. What is our common ground, and how can we honor one another?" I am grateful that there are enough varieties of belief and practice that most people can find a religious and communal home somewhere. I do not deny the need for different movements in Judaism.

With regard to the Kotel and the struggle for women's right to pray there in a group with Torah, tallit, and tefillin, I think that denominationalism is irrelevant and destructive. I have welcomed and worked to solicit any and all support for our cause but have resisted, along with everyone else in the ICWOW, any effort to have us subsumed under a denominational or organizational umbrella that some periodically attempted to hoist over us.

It has been essential for us to remain unaligned so that we could maintain control of our agenda. Several groups would have been happy to harness the symbolism of this issue, expressing at times a distressing kind of jealousy over the media attention we were getting compared to those pushing other feminist Jewish issues. We resisted the attempt to hierarchicalize issues (being told that abuses of religious divorce law, wifebeating, or economic discrimination against women were "more important" than the Kotel). We did so although many of us are also active in those other struggles (my own mother was an *agunah,* unable to obtain a religious divorce).

We did so because this one had a particular resonance that could not be lost: women's claim to religious majority in Judaism. As I took to putting it when I spoke to Israeli officials or public groups, women are Jews—not just daughters of Jews, wives of Jews, and mothers of Jews, but Jews. ("But of course," said the then Minister of Religious Affairs when I said this to him. "Oh, really?" I countered. "Where else in the world would a group of Jews be physically attacked at prayer and the State of Israel not vehemently protest, whereas here, the state itself is condoning and rationalizing the violence and condemning and restraining us? Why, except that we are not seen as Jews with as much right to pray at this place with each other as the thugs assaulting us?")

Once we had ceased bringing a Torah or prayer garments, or even making ourselves heard outside the tight circle of our group, the violence nevertheless continued and even worsened. We were being attacked not so much for what we were doing as for who we were: women claiming Judaism, women who do not "know their place," women who consider all of Judaism their "place." The issue was our religious autonomy, our religious majority, taking ownership not just in secular pursuits but also in the religious sphere. That was what was so intolerable about the sight of us with a Torah scroll, against which there is no halakhic prohibition. We were presuming on the male prerogative of Judaism.

Once I realized that, I knew it was not a question of explanation *(hasbarah)* in the way we first attempted it—bringing along rabbinic texts and having designated women go over to people who were screaming at us, or doing worse, to explain that there was no sacrilege involved. They were yelling at us and assaulting us in visceral recognition of the challenge we represented to the male face of Judaism. There was no way we could defuse that, because that was precisely what we were doing.

Paradoxically, it was by remaining halakhic that this reality was unveiled. Rabbinic law was not the issue, since we abided by it. Something else also was going on. As Phyllis Chesler said to me on the phone one Rosh Chodesh (I always called her and/or Rivka to report on what had gone on at that month's davening, in stupefaction over what we were encountering), "That is patriarchy you are facing."

We did not begin this to challenge patriarchy but simply to do something good and holy; nor were we halakhic out of strategic considerations, but out of love for one another. We learned, as have generations of women before us, that patriarchy needs to control spiritual and religious energy precisely because it is so primal, so fundamental.

At the very least we were a threat to the social order, particularly in Israel, in which women either have rejected Judaism as an archaic form of oppression—leaving it unchallenged to the Orthodox male establishment, as the latter prefers it—or, if they are religious, have been socialized to believe that women's route to holiness is vicarious, through enabling men to study, pray, and run communities. They have been taught to see themselves as handmaidens of holiness.

If women, however, are Jews, then they must find their own route to Torah, and that means an end to the benefits to men of free female labor whose merit is redeemed only in heaven. By breaking the bonds of women's "rightful place" in Judaism, we threatened to incite a slave rebellion. No wonder the "masters" (the most common Hebrew term for *husband* literally means "master") declared war on us.

So this issue is radical—it goes to the root. We were not going to let it get submerged or subsumed or engage in a battle of whose cause is first. The only way we could highlight what was at stake here was by eschewing any organizational affiliation, however much we welcome support. To put it otherwise: this cause is good for Jewish women—not this or that kind, just women.

The question of the Women of the Wall gripped diaspora Jewry, but the women who actually go to the Wall—month after month, year after year, in rain, wind, and heat—are Israeli. The denominational and organizational divisions that mark American Jewish life are distant considerations in this context, if considerations at all. On the other hand, diaspora women, especially North Americans from across the denominational spectrum, have been critically engaged in this struggle, raising the phenomenal amounts of money required by the seemingly endless legal process. It would make little sense for the Israeli women to affiliate in a way that would marginalize or alienate their sisters abroad.

We represent *Klal Yisrael,* the community of Israel, in a way no other Jewish group does. We are the only religiously diverse group I know of in the Jewish world that joins together for a religious cause. Over the years, our diversity—of opinion and sheer personality (we are an opinionated, contentious bunch)—has been at times difficult to navigate, but we have been exposed to varieties of belief and points of view that each of us would never have entertained otherwise. Where else do you have Reform, Conservative, and Reconstructionist rabbis, Orthodox Talmud scholars, radical feminists, and none-of-the-aboves, from three continents, debating religious practice under the assumption that we were going to have to come up with a scenario we all could accept? I cannot express how precious this aspect of the frequently maddening crusade has been. No organizational clarity and support would have been worth what we have learned from each other—principally, respect, not just in theory but in reality.

Ironically, that which could have sunk us from the outset—gender-segregated services, when all but the Orthodox minority among us pray in mixed egalitarian settings—ended up being a bridge between the Orthodox and the most radical of the feminists. Women's prayer services can be immensely powerful experiences; I highly recommend them to anyone who has not been in one. The all-female face and sound of Judaism is an astoundingly affirming experience (once you've experienced it, you can appreciate what men have always enjoyed and taken for granted, and begin to grasp the extent of your own marginalization in this religion). Furthermore, in all too many "egalitarian" settings, men still dominate, with women as passive or even more passive than in traditional services. Judaism is still male-identified. For women and girls, women's prayer services are a safe space to take on and "wear" this practice—literally, with tallit; to try new roles, and to have the inestimable encouragement of seeing their gender as the norm in active partic-ipation and leadership. There is nothing quite like witnessing an older woman getting an *aliyah* for the first time, encouraged by the experience and support of other women doing this; or celebrating a girl's bat mitzvah among the women whose ranks she now joins, even if she will also have a celebration in a mixed setting. A women's service is a place where women are self-sufficient religiously, and that is rare and incredibly potent. For many of us who had never experienced, or would even have rejected the idea of, a women's service, this cause was the venue for these lessons, which happened only because we were so diverse and so respectful of each others' needs. That happened only because we were us, and we preserved our autonomy.

So this is about a Wall, and about walls: one that matters, and others that must be overlooked for the sake of that fragile but precious compromise that is so difficult and so holy.

SANDY STARKMAN

A Moving Experience

I HAD THE PRIVILEGE of participating at the Women of the Wall in 1994, Rosh Chodesh Elul.

I expected a large crowd, but I think there were only twenty of us. We stood in the corner, away from the wall and at the back of the women's section. We started to daven *Shachrit* quietly, with only a whisper from each of us. One woman came from the front of the women's section to tell us that we were bothering her and the other women, and that the men will hear us, too. How could we "Americans" do this? She appeared to be about twenty-five, born and maybe raised in metropolitan New York. Tamar Asher then finished davening the *Shachrit*.

We were told that the service was "Orthodox"; we didn't recite the *Barkhu* or Kaddish. Whatever required a minyan of ten men was excluded.

It was a very moving experience for me—first, from the standpoint of being with a group of women at the Kotel who were not Orthodox, as I am not. I have actually been the *shaliach* (prayer leader) in my shul's Rosh Chodesh *Maariv* service on several occasions. Second, frankly, there was a bit of terror, after the woman started harassing us. I don't think we were bothering her by the level of our voices any more than any other person davening, except what we were doing was apparently so abhorrent to her. She did to us exactly what she accused us of doing to her. It seems to me that the Torah teaches not to do to others what is unpleasant to you or what others did to you that is unpleasant.

Anat Hoffman conducted *Hallel* and the Torah service. I was thrilled to be given the first *aliyah* in honor of my fourteenth wedding anniversary. (I'm also a *bat kohen*, but in my own shul I cannot be called for that *aliyah*.) I actually know the Rosh Chodesh reading and was so touched by those few minutes. I wish my husband had been there to celebrate with me.

Miriam Glazer of the University of Judaism, and Merle Feld, poet and playwright, participated, along with Betsy Platkin Teutsch and some of her friends from Philadelphia and the Reconstructionist Rabbinical College.

It made me sad that knowledgeable women who are interested in davening are being harassed by other Jews. The Kotel shouldn't be a place for only a certain type of Jew. We need to work together, to agree to disagree in a respectful way, and eliminate the *sinat chinam*.

HARRIET PASS FREIDENREICH

Impressions

AS A COMMITTED EGALITARIAN CONSERVATIVE JEW, I have always felt uncomfortable visiting the Western Wall, let alone praying there. How could my prayers have meaning at a place where women are so clearly subordinate and not permitted to pray aloud? Indeed, on some of my visits to Israel between 1967 and 1987, I tried to avoid the Kotel entirely, even when I was in Jerusalem for Tisha B'Av.

On my most recent visit, however, during Hanukkah in 1997, I had one of the most meaningful and memorable experiences of my life while davening with the members of Women of the Wall on Rosh Chodesh Tevet. It was not hard to identify the group that gathered toward the back of the women's section that morning. While the men were shouting and making a great deal of noise in their section, we offered our prayers fervently but with much restraint and quiet dignity. I was deeply moved by the woman leading *Shachrit*, who had such a lovely voice and a baby on her back. Even the *charedi* women who argued with us and complained that we were disturbing their prayers could not destroy the devotion with which we were davening.

For me, however, the most special moments occurred while we were singing *Hallel* after we had retreated to the Archaeological Gardens above the Wall. Wrapped in our *tallitot*, for the first time, we opened up our voices in wholehearted prayers of joy and praise. Never before had any prayer sounded so beautiful to me! It is a memory I will always cherish. The *charedi* men who peered at us through the openings in the walls obviously did not approve of what we were doing, but they did not interrupt us, as they evidently did not feel that we were invading their sacred turf while davening in the remains of a medieval church.

Two sisters from Texas celebrated becoming bat mitzvah that morning by reading Torah and giving a thoughtful *d'var Torah* on the meaning of Rosh Chodesh. I noted that their male relatives were merely observers at this service, rather than true participants—a reversal of the gender norm for bar mitzvah ceremonies at the Wall. Those young girls made their family proud that day, and I was happy to be able to share their *simchah* with them, although for me it would have been even more symbolic if they had been Israelis rather than American Jews.

I do not normally give *tzedakah* at the Kotel, but this time I knew that I had found exactly the right place to donate the money a member of my congregation in Yardley, Pennsylvania, had given me before I left for Israel: the legal defense fund of WOW. Here was a cause that I deeply believe in, and I know my convictions are shared by many other Jews, both American and Israeli, even if they do not contribute to WOW themselves.

That experience during Hanukkah in 1997 gave me hope that maybe someday in the not-too-distant future women will be able to pray at the Kotel as loudly and as openly as they choose, whether separately with other women or together with men. Only then will I feel truly comfortable as a Jewish woman at the Wall—or as a Jew in Israel.

LILLY RIVLIN

Meditation and Conflict:
A Journey on Paper

I AM IN AN ASHRAM IN INDIA in the midst of a Vipasana meditation. Per instructions, I am watching my breath go in and out. We are told that it is the mind that gets us into trouble. To be fully conscious of the breath means that you are on the way to enlightenment, but the road is full of obstacles called thoughts. Hence, says the instructor, if there are thoughts, just let them pass by. I watch my thoughts. What a mess; a panoply of flotsam and jetsam go by. Alas, I get involved in one thought: I have to resign from the board of Women of the Wall.

It is December 1998. I had just flown from Israel to India. When I got on the plane at Ben-Gurion Airport, I felt about to explode from the conflicting voices around me, mostly manifesting in the deep fissures between the secular and the Orthodox. Hatred between Jews was palpable. It was everywhere. All I wanted was peace and quiet, and I thought I could find it in India. Instead, what do I get? Internal conflict.

"I go all the way to India to meditate, and here I am on the way to nirvana, and this is what comes up! Women of the Wall?" A rush of thoughts.

"Must be quite deep in you to come up at this point."

"Yeah, it's deep. It's central. It's yin-yang. It's I-Thou. It's a core issue."

240

I don't believe in an external, intervening God, and I certainly don't believe in a halakhic Judaism that brings people to this painful moment in time of Jews hating Jews for the way they worship, of Jewish men preventing Jewish women from praying aloud at the Wall, wearing a tallit and carrying a Torah.

I do a side riff on God and His masculine associations. The same thing always happens to me in the synagogue: every time God's masculinity comes up, those interfering thoughts begin making their noise. Why He? Who is He? Usually when I start singing the liturgy, they stop. I try to push these thoughts out of my mind. Now my mother joins the waning voices: *Gey klap.* Go hit your head against the wall. Could she have meant *the* Wall? I imagine myself hitting my head against the Kotel. It hurts.

An incident with my former lover pops into my thoughts. We are driving in the streets of Jerusalem at night. He is an assimilated Jew returning to his roots. He wants to go visit the Kotel. We drive past the Valley of Siloam, Gei Ben Hinom, up the steep road where a Jerusalem sculptor was killed years ago when he rode his motorcycle on a Friday night, oblivious of the Shabbat steel chain that blocked the road. We park at the top of the hill that leads down to the Dung Gate. I can't bring myself to go with him. I am too angry. It is during one of the many periods when WOW's case is being batted around between the Supreme Court and one of several commissions that will "study" the situation. It is at the time when one of the options offered WOW by the Commission is to pray in the Arab section. My lover is disappointed in me; after all, I am his guide back to the Jewish people. Sulking, he exits the car and disappears into the night, making his own way to the Wall. He doesn't understand why I am so angry.

The mind is associative. I am seven years old. It is pre-state Jerusalem. It must be Shabbat, because I wear a large bow in my hair and I am holding my father's hand as we walk down the narrow corridor of stairs leading down to the Kotel. Anytime my father takes me with him, it is a celebration. He is usually working and has no time for me. The Kotel itself is fronted by a narrow passage sandwiched by stone dwellings. It is not the Kotel of today with its wide esplanade of enormous space and dignity. Old men and women sit or stand in prayer. There is no *mechitzah*. My father, a joker, looks around furtively and pulls a piece of paper from a crack in the wall where devotees have stuffed their dreams and wishes. He reads it aloud, perhaps to me; my memory, which is white and gray, lacks details. The note is from a woman beseeching God for a child. I am shocked that my father has intervened between God and a stranger whose privacy is violated. He laughs salaciously, and I am scarred for life.

Other associations with the Kotel crowd my mind. In 1967, immediately after the Six Day War, I rushed to the Wall like everyone else. It was a Jerusalem morning abundant with light. I stood there filled with emotions. We, the Jewish people, were back at the Kotel again. Not long after, I was on top of Mount Scopus, in charge of English-speaking volunteers who had flocked to Israel after the war. One of the volunteers caught my attention, a nice kid with drugged-out blue eyes, a sailor hat, and the hippie accessories of a tinkling bell hanging on a leather thong and a peace band around his ankle. Later, I would write a short story about seeing him again that autumn, on the first Simchat Torah of the Jews, for many years, at the Wall, this time high not on drugs but on the emotion of thousands of years dancing through him.[1]

I remember a full-moon night at the Kotel. A few of us had decided to watch the sunrise. We arrived at the Kotel about 3:00 A.M. We were imbued with the miracle of a unified Jerusalem, and I was still drawn to the magic of the ancient stones of the Kotel. We were young and hopeful. A few men prayed at the Wall. Like a lover in slow motion moving toward her beloved, I approached the Wall. The weeds embedded in the cracks of the wall reminded me of the hairs on the chin of my Bubbe Mina, my great-grandmother who lived to 103. I couldn't bring myself to enter on the right side of the *mechitzah;* instead I slowly, almost stealthily, approached the wall on the left side, the men's section.

I am about to enter when suddenly I feel a tap on my head. Startled, I realize I am in Buddha hall, just tapped by the Vipasana instructor reminding me to be conscious of the incoming and the outgoing of my breath. I resolve to tell Phyllis Chesler, who brought me on to the board of Women of the Wall, of my decision. When I arrive back in New York I call her.

"Chesler," I say, "I have to resign from the board. I think it's absurd to pray to a wall. It's idol worship. I don't want to be a hypocrite."

Chesler, a radical feminist, has become an ardent student of Torah in the last few years. She finds satisfaction in Torah study and is devoted to the WOW cause. She is patient. She listens. "Rivlin, think about it a few more days, and then we'll talk about it. Maybe meditate on the decision."

Chesler—as I call her (this form of addressing her appeals to my *Damon Runyan* aspect; it seems tough, almost masculine, and it suits our relationship)—and I go back several decades. We have shared many feminist events, struggles, and quarrels. As a Jewish feminist, I have been fortunate to be part of a group of women

243

who decided more than twenty-seven years ago that we were not going to be left out of the tent, like Miriam. I was part of a feminist seder together with Esther Broner, Naomi Nimrod, Phyllis Chesler, Letty Cottin Pogrebin, Bea Kreloft, Edith Issac Rose, and Michelle Landsberg. We developed a tradition that has been adopted and adapted by thousands and thousands of Jewish women today. We delved into the books and customs of our people, joining women such as Judith Plaskow and Aviva Cantor Zuckoff in their individual exploration and reinterpretation of the canons. We are a fortunate generation because we reached for the Promised Land and got there to the extent that we carved out a respectable place for ourselves. We refused to be exiled to the wilderness.

In 1988, together with other Jewish women, I was a member of the American Jewish Congress's organizing committee, chaired by the inimitable and unforgettable Bella Abzug, that put together the first International Jewish Women's conference in Jerusalem. Jewish women of all denominations, from all over the globe, gathered in Jerusalem. It was a heady event. The sheer energy of hundreds of Jewish women coming together in Jerusalem under the feminist banner was explosive. Many of the participants had never before been exposed to core issues of feminism. Women were shaken, several were traumatized, others were confirmed, all were moved—some to action. Bella Abzug led us in a demonstration on the issue of "who is a Jew." Meanwhile, another group had organized itself: a multidenominational group of women that included ICWOW founders Rivka Haut and Phyllis Chesler walked to the Kotel carrying a Torah. They prayed in a non-minyan group in the women's section of the Kotel next to a *mechitzah*. In retrospect, it was a historical moment. As Phyllis Chesler wrote elsewhere, Orthodox women made a brave religious alliance with non-Orthodox women, facing criticism of their association with "*Reformiot*," "feminists," and "Godless politicals."

I was not part of that first group. I was back at the conference site, together with Letty Cottin Pogrebin and Bella Abzug, ironing out some administrative issues related to the running of the conference. Still, even had I not been so occupied, I doubt that I would have joined the women praying at the Wall. It was not my issue. Afterwards, though, due to my friendship with Phyllis, I kept abreast of WOW's struggle. I attended a fundraiser at Letty's home and made a small contribution. I did some fundraising and publicity work for them as a paid professional. In 1995, Phyllis asked me if I wanted to join the board. By then I had concluded that WOW's legal struggle in the Supreme Court of Israel was the nose of the camel, that WOW's struggle was at the core of the feminist struggle to be in the tent and not in the wilderness. Until pluralism was acceptable to the Jewish people, I could not rest easy, for there would be no room for me, for women like me, or, as has become evident in the last few years, for Jewish men and women of other than the Orthodox denominations. I meditate.

When you consciously breathe in and out, eventually you come to the very center of your being. There are two gaps between the breaths: one after inhaling and immediately before exhaling, and another after the exhalation and immediately before the inhalation. Between the incoming breath and the outgoing breath is your center. Sometimes in that space I have experienced the cosmic center. Perhaps it is what some experience in prayer. It a feeling of exaltation, of well-being, a sense of being at one with the universe. The blood courses through the body, unobstructed, and I feel part of the cosmos. "The moment one recognizes that all is one, love arises on its own accord," says the guru. I become aware of why I want to resign. I am angry. I have not been able to see that love among *Klal Yisrael* toward the Other, even toward the other gender. Does Jewish religion exclude the spiritual, I ask myself? Are we, the Jewish people, so traumatized by our past that we have forgotten the soul, the spirit, love? What does it all have to do with the Wall?

Meditation, I conclude, will not furnish me with an answer to this question. I am losing my focus; free association has its creative aspect, but my Jewish passion for reason prevails. What does it all mean? A wall. The Wall. The Wailing Wall. The Western Wall. *HaKotel?* Why do the women of WOW want to be there? Why are so many forces combining to resist them being there? What is going on? In frustration, I turn to my books.

True, it is not an ordinary wall. A remnant of the western supporting wall of the Temple Mount that remained intact since the destruction of the Second Temple, it is, according to *Everyman's Judaica,* "the most hallowed spot in Jewish religious and national consciousness and tradition." How did it become such an awesome site? For centuries it stood forlorn and unattended; where did all this attention come from? It is not even mentioned in my treasured leatherbound *The Modern Traveler—A Popular Description, Palestine: or, The Holy Land* (London: 1824), a compendium of various European travelers, including Chateaubriand, Dr. Clarke, Mr. Buckingham Maundrell, Pococke, and Dr. Richardson. Richardson, according to the editor, "has been found the most minute and faithful" eyewitness, "in particular, his account of the Mosque of Omar which the Doctor had the singular good fortune to be four times permitted to visit; a favor never before extended to a Frank."

Dr. Richardson's account of his visits to the Sakhara (Mosque of Omar) and al-Aksa is fascinating in its details, but the omission of any mention of the Wailing Wall relates to my present preoccupation. Why is there no reference to "the most hallowed spot" for the Jews by these erstwhile travelers?

A description of the condition of the Jews in Jerusalem refers to two synagogues and includes an arresting portrayal of the "Jewesses in Jerusalem," which I include for the benefit of my readers.

> The Jewesses in Jerusalem speak in a decided and firm tone, unlike the hesitating and timid voice of the Arab and Turkish females; and claim the European privilege of differing from their husbands, and maintaining their own opinions. I never saw any of them with veils; and was informed that it is the general practice of the Jewesses in Jerusalem to go with their faces uncovered; they are the only females there who do so. They seem particularly liable to eruptive diseases; and the want of children is as great a heartbreak to them now as it was in the days of Sarah.

I cannot imagine my independent female ancestors not praying at the Wall if it was such a hallowed spot for our people. I persevere. In Father Barnabas Meistermann's *Guide to the Holy Land* (London: 1907), there is only a slight reference to the Wailing Wall.

> At about 108 yards from the B-ab es Sils'ele'h, on the west, we come to a final portal of an Arab palace of the thirteenth or fourteenth century, on the right. The left-hand comer is taken up by a little Arab library. There we turn into a street on our left, and by many roundabout ways we arrive at the Wall where the Jews assemble to pray and to lament, especially on the eve of the Sabbath and of feasts, from three o'clock in the evening.

From *Histoire de l'Art*, "la Judee," 168:

> Hadrian had forbidden the Jews to enter the city. But
> under Constantine they were allowed to weep on the
> sacred rock once a year, as the Pilgrim of Bordeaux, St.
> Gregory Nazianzen (Senn. xii.) and St. Jerome (Ep. Ad
> Hedibiam) inform us. In the twelfth century, accord-
> ing to Benjamin of Tudela, and probably after the
> arrival of the Arabs in the seventh century, the interi-
> or of the wall, 40 yards long, was left to the Jews as a
> place of prayers and tears.

Father Barnabas Meistermann describes the "Wailing Place":

> This wall is a beautiful sample of Jewish architecture.
> The primitive construction is still intact to a height
> of 42 feet above the actual ground. The eight or ten
> last layers are of a later period. The same wall, with
> its splendid embossed blocks, goes down to a depth
> of 84 or 90 feet into the ground.

How could Richardson and other European Christian travelers
have ignored this forty-two-foot-high wall? Perhaps it was surrounded by rubble when they came upon the site. Perhaps the Turk-
ish rulers kept the travelers away from the site. Perhaps the Jews, too
occupied with survival, were not flocking to the Wall.

Even the late poet Dennis Silk, in his book *Retrievements: A
Jerusalem Anthology*, published in the halcyon days after the Six Day
War, did not mention the Kotel. The work, a collection of numerous eyewitness accounts by ancient, medieval, and modern travelers to Jerusalem, omits the Wall. How can this be? I ask myself.

On the other hand, I do remember from my childhood recurrent
images of pious Jews praying at the Wall—on fabric, on wood, in
photographs, and in etchings. Is the Wall, then, alive and well as an

image, but missing from the pages of literature? In *Gates to the New City* (New York: Avon, 1983), editor Howard Schwartz traces the evolution of the Shekhinah from the personification of God's presence in the world to the kabbalistic period, in which the Shekhinah becomes the personification of the feminine presence of God, and then, finally, in the *Zohar* (2:203a), to the Shekhinah's independent existence. It is as an independent spirit, says Schwartz, that the Shekhinah appears in literary tradition, usually associated with the Wall.

I remembered a hot, shadowless day of shimmering white light, the kind of day when all lines, edges, and silhouettes become wavering brushed strokes. I stood in front of the Kotel and watched a white dove take off, and I knew it was the Shekhinah announcing my dear aunt's death.

In between the cracks of the Kotel grows the hyssop plant. Stand before the Kotel silently and be embraced by its fragrance, especially on a hot summer night after midnight. As it grows, it widens in the cracks, while it blends modestly into its surroundings, like wild oregano. It is the main ingredient of *za'atar*, a Mediterranean spice. The hyssop, it is said, is the opposite of the mighty cypress tree. Associated with humility, hyssop is the lowliest of plants.

The Kotel has become a religious and national symbol. I no longer can find the Shekhinah at the Wall. I cannot go to the Wall; I am too angry. Perhaps that is why I have the utmost respect, love, and gratitude to the faithful women of WOW who go there each Rosh Chodesh, and on Simchat Torah, Purim, and other *chagim* (holidays), come rain or shine, to pray in the women's section.

Last year I saw *Man of the Wall,* a film by Hertz Frank, a Latvian Jewish filmmaker who immigrated to Israel five years ago. The Kotel has been featured in scenes of films, in newsreels, and in documentaries, but it has never had an entire film devoted to it. A poetic documentary on the meaning of the Western Wall today, the film is a collage of images and sounds. We see men praying, all kinds of men: *charedim*, knitted *kipot*, Ashkenazim, Sephardim. Men. There is a twenty-second pan to the women, and that's it—no more. It is the men's wall. No big deal, it's not a conscious ideological point; it just is a fact of life. We see the business of the wall in the late hours of the night: An Orthodox clerk, whose livelihood it is to put the *pinkasim* (notes) into the cracks of the Kotel, carries his busting-at-the-seams briefcase. He stuffs the *pinkasim* into the cracks, and perhaps he says a prayer; mission accomplished, he departs. Next scene: At dawn, Arab workers in front of the Kotel sweep away the *pinkasim*, most of which have already fallen from the cracks. The central character, a former Haifa actor—a look-alike of Tevyah as played by Topol, charismatic with loving eyes, a ruddy healthy complexion, dressed all in white in the style of Rabbi Shlomo Carlebach—dozes nearby. At some point we learn that he has left his wife; but no matter, now he has become a true believer. Most of his waking and sleeping hours are spent at the Wall. He is a lover of the Wall. In watching him I had an inkling of the ecstasy and the joy of a true believer. I immediately thought of the women of WOW. Perhaps among them there are women who experience such ecstasy and joy in the presence of the Kotel.

As for me, I will always be an observer of this phenomenon, but the writing of this piece has been a meditation on the meaning of the Kotel. More than ever I appreciate my sisters in ICWOW and WOW in their determination to pray at the Kotel. Women have been silenced for thousands of years. All over the world women are silenced. Each one of us has had the experience of being silenced. Ironically, the denial of WOW's two demands—the right to be able to pray aloud and the right to carry a Torah—are both aspects of the silencing-women tradition, of women not being heard (or listened to) and not being seen (or being invisible). I write a prayer: "Oh, hear my voice, oh, see me carry the Torah." For me, WOW's struggle is a political one, which has become inextricably tied up in the Orthodox-secular conflict, which, paradoxically, prevents both the secular and the Orthodox from having a spiritual experience at the Kotel. If the Shekhinah is to be found at the Kotel, it will only be in the Messianic Era, when Jews of both genders and all denominations can find their souls at the Wall. I continue to meditate. I no longer think of resigning. I will not abandon this struggle. It is mine as well as theirs. Women's spirit, like the Shekhinah, has been in exile and wants to be home. Besides, I'm in good company: such a diverse group of religious women—feisty, spirited, quirky, profound, impetuous, dogged, and all sincere; otherwise they could not be representing this point of view in the public space. In between the breaths, I am in total peace. Sometimes I visualize my sisters praying aloud and carrying the Torah to the Kotel.

GAVRIELLE LEVINE

Chodesh Tov

I TURNED MY HEAD and saw a few women standing together, speaking quietly at the entrance of the women's section. I casually walked toward them and cautiously asked if they intended to pray together. A woman arrived carrying a large, lumpy duffel bag. It became clear that in order to minimize confrontation, the Torah that we would read from this morning was transported incognito. Our numbers grew. Midway through *Shachrit,* I saw that we were now at least fifty women praying together. Women who had been praying individually at the Wall walked back to us—to berate us, to tell us we were sinning and we were wrong to be praying as a group. At the conclusion of *Shachrit,* Bonna Haberman suggested that we wish each other and women not in our group a *chodesh tov* ("good month"). I was astounded. These women who had been so antagonistic—who would want to offer them kind wishes? I was frozen, but others, including Bonna, walked up toward the Wall and approached the women.

We walked as a group, a parade of women away from the Western Wall plaza, past the security area, up several long flights of stairs, following the duffel bag. By now our numbers had grown. What a variety of women: Israelis, Americans, "regulars," tourists, students; Orthodox, Conservative, Reform, and Reconstructionist Jewish women praying together; religious women who replaced their hats with *kipot;* many wore *tallitot.* The Torah was placed on a table and rolled to the reading for Rosh Chodesh.

After wishing each other a *chodesh tov,* we left our courtyard—ready to continue the day, just like any other morning.

RABBI SUSAN GROSSMAN

The Tears of My Soul

I LOOKED OUT THE WINDOW as our plane approached Ben-Gurion Airport, as one of dozens of Conservative Rabbis who had come on pilgrimage to *Ha-aretz*, the Promised Land, to join our colleagues for the Rabbinical Assembly Convention in Jerusalem in the winter of 1998. I carried with me a plain plastic bag filled with more than two hundred *kvitlach* (handwritten notes to God). During the weeks leading up to my trip, my congregants had pressed these small pieces of paper into my hand when I passed them in the hallway or after a meeting. They piled up in my mailbox and on my desk. Each *kvitel* was laboriously folded into a small bundle. Each contained prayers, fears, and dreams that my congregants hungered to believe would find a way past the gates guarding the Heavenly Throne if only delivered to a protective niche in the Kotel, the Western Wall.

The Kotel: lodestone of Zionist aspirations and religious fervor, the wall of massive Jerusalem stones that supported the western side of the Temple Mount and within it the Holy of Holies.

I grew up knowing it as the Wailing Wall, the wall where generations of Jews went to bewail our fate as an oppressed and abused people. With the establishment of the modern State of Israel and the unification of Jerusalem under Jewish sovereignty, this wall is now referred to by its geographic designation, the Western Wall, or simply as the Kotel, "the Wall," as if there is only one wall of importance in the world, as if Jews no longer need to weep.

254

Having boarded the bus that would carry us all to Jerusalem, I thought of the *kvitlach* I carried as *shaliach*, a ritual messenger, to the Holy Land. "As soon as I drop off my luggage at the hotel, I need to go to the Kotel," I told my colleagues seated around me on the bus. It was decided. Four of us would split a cab and go together, four female colleagues as it turned out: three congregational rabbis and a hospital chaplain.

I live in the West, but my heart yearns for the East. Walking through the army checkpoint into the plaza before the Kotel, my eyes soaked up the colors of the holy city of Jerusalem like a sponge absorbs water: the pale blue of the sky, the green of army khakis, the red of good-luck threads women offered for the price of a donation, the black of coats covering the *charedim*, the platinum gold of the Wall itself, the maroon covers of the small prayer books piled high on a table in the middle of the women's section.

We walked up to the table and each picked up a prayer book. It was time for *Minchah*, the afternoon prayer. Then we stopped and looked at each other hesitantly.

We were four Conservative rabbis from America, thrilled to be standing before the Western Wall, which had drawn us like iron to a magnet all the way from our respective homes in Washington, Maryland, New Jersey, and New York. With all our souls we wanted to lift our voices and sing our praises to God for the ability to witness the miracle of the first glimmerings of redemption, for the fact that we had made the trip safely, for the well-being of our families and our congregants. Each of us had a long story she could tell about how she finally found her way as a woman and as a modern Jew to rabbinical school and ordination. Most of us hadn't been to Israel since our ordination and yearned for the uplifting privilege to stand before the Kotel as the dedicated servants of God and

God's people Israel, spiritual heirs to the long line of rabbis who had stood here before us, in good times and in bad. We stood together as rabbis who wanted to fulfill our *chiyuv,* our obligation to pray three times a day, here at the Kotel, at the heart of Judaism, rather than back at the hotel, which could be any hotel anywhere else in the world. We stood as women who realized that if we lifted our voices out loud, we would be breaking the law governing the Kotel and we could be arrested, or cause a scene, or possibly even be hurt. We looked into each other's eyes and nodded sadly as we each took our prayer book and made our way separately to find a place by the wall. One colleague later told me she had never felt so angry. Another said she had never felt so empty, as if the Wall could hold no meaning for her any longer since there was no real place for her here. The third spoke of the irony of coming to Israel only to be undermined as rabbis and discriminated against as Jews.

I carried my bag of *kvitlach* to the Wall and searched and stretched until I had found a niche for each one. Only then, relieved of my task as *shaliach,* could I attend to my own soul's needs.

Having found a place by the Wall near the center of the women's section, I leaned my head against it and closed my eyes as I davened *Minchah.* The cool stone on my forehead felt like my mother's hand when she would cradle my face to comfort me when I wept. If my soul could have shed tears at that moment, a river would have flowed out of me and down those Kotel stones to the foot of the plaza. A flood of tears would have swept away the *mechitzah,* the partition separating the women's section from the men's section, from which I could hear the faint murmurings of the minyan I was denied.

We found our way back, to each other, quiet now, less ebullient. There should be three sections in front of the Kotel, we decided (as if we could decide such things): a men's section, a women's section, and a mixed section.

A few days later, during our convention, a group of male and female colleagues prayed *Minchah* together at the southern wall. A tour from an Orthodox girls' yeshiva waited patiently for us to complete our prayers. Standing on the stairs leading onto the Temple Mount, in the very footsteps of the pilgrims who had last climbed those stairs almost two millennia ago, I was tremendously moved. Yet, my solitary *Minchah* at the Kotel several days before seemed to weigh down my words as I stood praying as one of many Conservative rabbis before Hulda's Gate.

One does not leave *kvitlach* at the southern wall. Excavated, it presents an open and welcoming expanse to all who seek to come close to its ancient stones. Only at the Western Wall does one leave *kvitlach.* Like those bits of paper, reduced in size, all air squeezed out of them to precariously fit with the others already there, Judaism at the Kotel also seems reduced in size and squeezed so tightly that the winds of change and growth, compassion and acceptance, mutual respect and *ahavat Yisrael*—love of the people of Israel—do not reach its courtyard.

No matter how pressed and squeezed those *kvitlach* may be, we believe that God releases the words of the *kvitlach* even as God releases the bound. That is why I can return to the Kotel with my own *kvitel* in hand. It contains a prayer that all Israel learn to honor the distinctive gifts that each Jew, regardless of gender or movement affiliation, brings to the service of God in this world. *B'mheira b'yameinu,* may it occur speedily in our lifetime. And let us say amen.

MARION KRUG

Beyond My Wildest Dreams

TWICE IN MY LIFE I have felt the palpable presence of God. The first time was in 1967 at a vigil outside the White House. Israel had been attacked and the American Jewish community reacted strongly and forcefully. Hundreds of Jews from all over the country had converged on Washington in a demonstration of solidarity with Israel. Suddenly, as we were standing there, a hush fell upon the crowd and a whisper flew from group to group: "The war is over." At that moment, we were *am echad b'lev echad*, one people with one heart, and we all felt the Divine Presence. It was a moment that will stay with me the rest of my life.

The second time I was so privileged was in 1988, when a group of women held their first prayer service at the Kotel, the Western Wall. When I was on a train, without food, without water, and without heat, going to an unknown destination in Poland, I never thought that I would live to see Israel. Now here I was, praying at the Wall with other women and together with Jews of every denomination. To daven at the Kotel, I thought, was about as close to heaven as I could get, and when I was asked whether I would do a section of the Torah reading, I could hardly contain myself. To be offered such an opportunity was beyond my wildest dreams.

Much has been written about what took place that day. What no one seemed to focus on in the aftermath was the effect that this service had on its participants. As soon as we returned to the conference, I could sense a different atmosphere. It wasn't that we all suddenly dropped our agendas in favor of the common good, but there was a different tone to our discourse, one that indicated that we were willing to listen to one another with open minds and hearts.

In the years since 1988, the Women of the Wall have been fighting an uphill battle for an acceptance that may never come. It certainly is a battle worth fighting. I would do the same thing in a heartbeat, knowing what I know now about politics, religion, and the politics of religion. Anything that has the power to unite such diverse personalities is good for the Jews, and what better place to achieve unity than at the one remnant of the site that is the heritage of all of our people?

To this day, I have a special feeling for those with whom I stood in prayer at the Kotel. Many of them have views diametrically opposed to mine, but each of them is concerned in her own way about the survival of Judaism and the Jewish people, and all of them are my sisters. Although our paths may not be in perfect alignment, we walk together to the utmost boundaries, and when our paths diverge, we respect our differences.

PART IV

Halakhic Theory
and Ritual Objects

RIVKA HAUT

Orthodox Women's Spirituality

This essay is dedicated to the memory of my
beloved husband, Rabbi Yitzchak Haut. Oh,
Sweetie, are you gazing through the window?

> Lo, One stands behind our Kotel,
> Gazing through the window
> peeking through the lattice (Song of Songs 2:9)
> gazing through the window—in the merit of the
>   forefathers
> peeking through the lattice—in the merit of the
>   foremothers.[1]

THE STORY IS TOLD that for many years the Kotel was hidden, intentionally buried under mounds of garbage in order to conceal its existence. Only after the intervention of a Muslim ruler was it revealed, never to be buried again.[2] The Kotel, representing the longing of the Jewish people for renewal of the Temple, is a tangible symbol of the glory that once was and that we long to return to. The Midrash teaches that since the destruction of the Second Temple, the presence of the Shekhinah has never left the Western Wall.[3] Therefore, it serves as a current substitute for the Temple as the locus of Jewish prayer.

Similarly, Jewish women's spiritually has, for years, existed as an underground well, its waters sweet and pure, but rarely surfacing. Today, as the entire Kotel is uncovered from the debris of centuries, revealing even its earliest layers, down to its bedrock, so too is women's spirituality bursting forth from centuries of public silence. Jewish women's religious involvement has begun to match that of Jewish men. This is true for every stream of Judaism today.

In the twentieth century we have witnessed the acceptance of women as rabbis and cantors and the creation of liturgy that includes women. Even in the Orthodox world, the sector of Judaism that has most strongly insisted that women not participate in public religious life (*kol kevudah bat melekh pnimah*—the glory of the King's daughter is within), women's spirituality is currently experiencing a widespread revitalization.

In this essay, I concentrate on women's spirituality within the Orthodox world, focusing on women's prayer groups and how they are transforming synagogue life. I also explain how Women of the Wall arose directly from them.

From our beginnings as a people, Jewish women have shared in our religious life. On the shores of the Reed Sea, Miriam, sister and counterpart of Moses, led the women in song, a separate song, a counterpoint to Moses' Song of the Sea, with additions: music and dance. The Bible records the deeds of some women, such as Deborah and Hannah, the songs they sang and the prayers they prayed.[4] The rabbis credited Hannah with having a major impact on the prayer life of the Jewish people.[5] In ancient Israel, in the Temple, women were always present, bringing sacrifices and attending public events.[6] After the destruction, when the synagogue replaced the Temple as the site for public worship, women joined men in the synagogue, and their presence sometimes even influenced

Halakhah.[7] However, men retained control; they alone were the active participants in synagogue services.

In some communities, women may have conducted their own services. There is evidence that in medieval Worms there was a separate room for women's prayers.[8] In other parts of the world, remnants of separate prayer rooms for women may be found.[9] In Europe, before the Second World War, Jewish women, variously called *fierzogeren, forelainers,* or *zogerken,* helped other women to pray.[10] They stood in front of the *ezrat nashim* (women's section of the synagogue) and prayed aloud, translating the prayers into the vernacular (Yiddish, Judeo-Italian) so that uneducated and illiterate women who did not understand Hebrew could pray along with the congregation. Many families today (including my own) proudly relate that their ancestors, their great-grandmothers and grandmothers, functioned in this role.

Also in Eastern Europe, prayers, called *techinahs,* were written specifically for women and incorporated in *siddurim* for women, which also were called *techinahs.*[11] Many women today still pray from *techinahs.*[12]

Fierzogeren and *techinahs* were tolerated by the rabbis. They involved a language considered inferior to the Hebrew of the learned. They involved women and the uneducated. They did not challenge the social order, nor did they rebel against rabbinic authority. However, their very existence illustrates the widespread, longtime belief that women's prayers are important and desirable to God.

In the twentieth century, a radical change in the position of women occurred in the form of a flowering of Jewish women's education. In the past, each generation had a few outstanding women who managed to overcome formidable barriers and become educated, but the majority of women remained ignorant. In pre-war Europe, Sara Schnirer convinced the rabbinical authorities that, in order to stem the tide of assimilation, women must receive Jewish education.[13] A slow but steady growth in women's education ensued, and now, at the dawn of the twenty-first century, the gates of Jewish classical learning are wide open to women.

The breakthrough in education means that today women have access to classical learning that in the past was available only to men. This revolution has brought about many changes, resulting in religious authority no longer being the sole domain of men but now being open to the influences and participation of women. Yeshivas, even Kollels[14] for women are thriving. These schools have had a major impact on Orthodoxy as a whole. Women are graduating with degrees enabling them to be authorities in halakhic issues such as family purity.[15] In rabbinical courts in Israel, women are serving as *toanot*.[16]

In the non-Orthodox world, the revolution in learning has led to female rabbis and cantors. In Orthodoxy, it has paved the way for the creation and growth of women's prayer groups.

The rise in women's education occurred in a bloodless way. Rabbis unhesitatingly supported it. For example, the late Rabbi Joseph B. Soloveitchik, acknowledged leader of modern Orthodoxy, taught the first Talmud class for women at Yeshiva University. However, despite the tremendous changes in education for women, two other areas remain the same. Women are still victimized in religious divorce, with very little progress, despite years of activism on the part of Orthodox feminists.[17] In the synagogue, despite the increase in learning, women still remain marginalized.

Throughout the centuries, women attended synagogue but had no active role in services. Halakhah imposes more stringent prayer obligations on men than on women.[18] This disparity in obligation means that women are not obligated in public prayer, may not be counted with men in a minyan, may not lead men in prayer, may not read Torah for men. Only those whose halakhic obligations are equally stringent (or more so) may discharge these obligations for each other. In all Orthodox congregations, a *mechitzah* separates the sexes and prevents mingling.[19] Women do not read Torah in order to discharge the congregation's obligation to read Torah three times a week, which was initiated by Ezra the Scribe.[20] Women are not given *aliyot*, which, while not strictly forbidden, is yet not practiced because of the "honor of the congregation."[21] (However, see below.) Women are welcome in the synagogue as attendees, congregants, contributors, and helpers at *kiddush*, but in most Orthodox synagogues, they are kept at a distance from any physical contact with Torah scrolls.

Late in the twentieth century, the undercurrent of women's spirituality, deeply hidden in the Orthodox world, running silent and deep, emerged as a strong, flowing stream of living waters.

In the 1970s, a revolution affecting the prayer life of Orthodox women began. Simultaneously, in various parts of the world, women began gathering together to form women-only prayer groups, small congregations of women who prayed together, read Torah, studied, and celebrated life-cycle events. Eventually known as women's *tefillah* groups (WTGs), they sprang up in different communities, each thinking they were unique, not knowing that other groups of women were engaging in the same thing. Soon they became aware of other such groups and began to work together.

The rise of WTGs is directly related to the increased educational opportunities for women. Once women had direct access to talmudic and rabbinic texts, without male intervention, many halakhic facts emerged. One most important revelation was the fact that women may handle, touch, lift, and read from a Torah scroll.[22] Despite centuries of *bubbe meises* (folklore), of mistaken information that women's bodies were too unclean to have direct contact with a *sefer Torah*, women now learned that Halakhah actually-ly permits women, at all times of the month, to have physical contact with a Torah scroll. The door to women's *tefillah* groups was open.

I was a founder of one of the first halakhic women's *tefillah* groups. In my neighborhood of Flatbush, Brooklyn, New York, a few women had been gathering together in my home for Shabbat afternoon Talmud study. We constantly discussed our dissatisfaction with the many synagogues in our area, where we sat behind high *mechitzot*, found it difficult to hear the service, and felt passive as pray-ers. We served no synagogue function, our presence mattered not at all to the service, and we were totally denied physical access to Torah scrolls. I had been searching for a place where I, together with my two daughters, could feel comfortable and pray well, to no avail. The other women had been embarking on similar search-es. We realized that what we wanted, what we needed, was simply not available, and that we had to create such a prayer environment for ourselves and our daughters. We decided to begin praying together in a small group, and to read Torah as well. A group of five women began to study how to *leyn* (to chant the Torah with cantil-lation). We were taught by more-than-willing men—our husbands, fathers, brothers, sons, and even a local cantor who volunteered to teach us. As word spread through our neighborhood, the group of five grew, and after months of study we began to meet once a month, on Shabbat mornings, to conduct prayer services.

We were careful to adhere strictly to Halakhah, and so we did not constitute ourselves as a minyan. This means that we omitted all prayers for which a minyan is necessary. Our prayers were limited to the liturgy recited by an individual, male or female, who prays alone. We saw ourselves not as a congregation, *tzibur,* in the technical halakhic sense, but as a group of individuals who came together to pray. We read the Torah portion of the week from a scroll, and chanted the appropriate *haftarah,* but not in order to discharge the communal obligation, as women are not so obligated. Our reading was technically for educational purposes, so that we might learn Torah, and we chose to follow the synagogue order of readings. We made other technical changes as well, in order to satisfy strict halakhic requirements.[23]

By establishing women-only prayer groups, we were not seeking to become egalitarian. Indeed, we separated from men and created our own space because we did not believe that true egalitarianism is possible within Orthodoxy, as Halakhah does not view women as being equally obligated with men in the performance of some mitzvot.[24] Nor did we necessarily wish that it were so. We merely sought to establish that the prayers of women are as equally important and desirable before God as are the prayers of men, to teach our daughters to conduct our own dignified services in which we were the active participants, and to experience beautiful and uplifting prayer.

To our surprise and delight, we soon discovered that other groups of women were doing the same thing and that a few rabbis were supporting these efforts.

This was my entry into the world of halakhic women's prayer groups. It has led me down a path that has enriched the religious lives of my mother—may her rest be eternal—my daughters, and now my granddaughters. For a few blessed years I was privileged to have four generations of my family participate in *tefillah* groups. My European-born mother came from a most Orthodox family and led a traditional life from birth to death. She was an intrepid shul goer, never missing a Shabbat or holiday service for all of her eighty-two years, with the exception of a few months when she was housebound after breaking a leg. She taught me to pray daily. Some of my earliest memories are of my mother not permitting me to go out and play until I recited my morning prayers. My mother joyously joined the Flatbush Women's Tefillah Group as though she had waited for it all her life. For a number of years, the group met in the basement of her home. She enjoyed telling me that her grandmother, for whom I am named, would have loved the group, as she too was a devoted shul goer who attended services daily and even had the key to the women's section.

I have since seen many elderly Orthodox women who, upon encountering prayer groups for the first time in their lives, instantly shed all their years of physical separation from Torah scrolls, take their places at the *bimah*, and with tears in their eyes and trembling hands, kiss the Torah and recite the blessings as they receive *aliyot.*

My daughters participated in the Flatbush Tefillah Group as teenagers. Now they are married women, mothers themselves, and live in Riverdale, New York, where they attend the Riverdale Women's Tefillah Group. My grandson, Ariel, when a baby, often came with me to the Flatbush group. My granddaughters, Ayelet and Esther Eleanna, each had their *simchat bat* in *tefillah* groups, and they regularly attend together with their mothers. My family is representative of the experience of many middle-aged Orthodox women today. The prayer communities we created a mere twenty-five years ago, revolutionary as they were, have now become the tradition of our granddaughters. The previously underground source of women's spirituality now runs as a mighty river, visible to all, and many drink from its pure waters.

Once begun, *tefillah* groups proliferated rapidly. They served as magnets for educated women who were searching for more active participation in group prayer. However, they were also met with fierce opposition from the rabbinical world. In the early 1980s, every major Orthodox rabbinic journal published articles severely critical of *tefillah* groups. Rabbis denounced them from their pulpits and produced halakhic proclamations declaring them prohibited. Some rabbis went so far as to attack the women personally, accusing us of impure motivations, arrogance, impiety, and even of not being "normal."[25]

Many women experienced personal pain because of their attendance at *tefillah* groups. In the Orthodox world, defying rabbinic authority is no small thing. I was warned by people in my community, some of whom I had considered friends, that I was damaging my children's futures by remaining involved. Who would want to marry them? I was asked. Nevertheless, my husband, an Orthodox rabbi, actively supported my involvement. He endured the insults and jeers of his peers and steadfastly stood by me and our daughters. He taught our daughter Tamara to *leyn* and chant *haftarah*, and she became the first woman in my family history to read Torah. We women needed men to teach us synagogue skills that we lacked, and many men generously and eagerly offered their help.

Despite the formidable obstacles of rabbinic disapproval and our own lack of synagogue skills, the women persisted. Knowledge that our actions were within halakhic guidelines fueled the determination to continue. Having once tasted the deep satisfaction of praying together, reading from a Torah scroll, we would not return to our formerly passive state in the synagogue.

In order to strengthen the groups, to share information and unite against the rabbinic assault against *tefillah* groups, the Women's Tefillah Network (WTN), possibly the first organization formed by Orthodox women for a purely religious purpose, was founded. One of the earliest meetings took place in my home on a Sunday afternoon. It has since grown into an international organization that has an active e-mail list, enabling women and men from all over the world who are interested in issues involving women and halakhic prayer to dialogue and share information.

The efforts of the WTN have succeeded beyond our original dreams. *Tefillah* groups have become a standard feature of modern Orthodoxy. From Australia to Sweden to Israel, there is hardly a sizable Jewish community that does not have a women's *tefillah* group. Many of the groups have been able to emerge from private homes, living rooms, and basements and now meet in synagogue rooms and *batei midrash* (study halls), with the blessings of rabbis and congregations.

Tefillah groups have been developing in two directions at once. One has been to create women-only environments in which women can pray and study together, celebrate bat mitzvahs, engagements, and baby namings. New liturgy has been written.[26] The first efforts towards creating a *siddur* for women have begun.[27] Praying together in women-only groups is viewed by many not merely as a concession made necessary by halakhic limitations, but as something desirable in itself, sometimes even to be preferred to mixed-gender groups.

At the same time, *tefillah* groups have pushed for greater synagogue participation for women, when halakhically permissible. The influence that WTGs have had on the Orthodox synagogue itself is great. Many synagogues no longer restrict physical access to Torah scrolls to men; the Torah is carried through the women's section so that the woman may touch it and kiss it. In a few synagogues, the Torah is actually handed over the *mechitzah* and given to women to carry themselves through the women's section. One or two congregations even honor women with *aliyot*. Mindful of the talmudic statement that it is only the "honor of the congregation" that prevents giving women *aliyot*, these congregations have decided that, to the contrary, their honor is greater when women also receive *aliyot*. In some shuls, women open the ark and even lead Friday night *tefillah*.

It is out of this background that WOW emerged.

In 1988, I was invited to attend an American Jewish Congress feminist conference in Israel to talk about WTGs. This was at the height of the "who is a Jew" controversy, when Jews of different denominations fought bitterly with each other. The conference included Jewish women of all denominations. The Shabbat before I left for Israel, I thought about organizing a women's prayer group at the Kotel. In 1986, I had attended a conference in Israel where I helped organize a women's service each morning in the hotel. This time it seemed right to pray together at the Kotel rather than the hotel. After all, the Kotel is a prayer magnet for so many, our holiest site, finally in Jewish hands. I thought more about this on the plane, and during the conference's opening session, I whispered to my friend and comrade in Orthodox feminism, Norma Baumel Joseph, to ask whether she thought that having a WTG at the Kotel was a good idea. The smile on her face was all the affirmation I needed.

Norma and I set about organizing a women's service at the Kotel.

We were determined to include women from every denomination. Our *tefillah* had to be halakhic, so that Orthodox women like ourselves could participate, but we wanted to have the active involvement of women from across the Jewish spectrum, as befitted a service at the Kotel, the place of prayer for all Jews.

Organizing the first service was extremely difficult. We had to overcome the many hesitations of non-Orthodox women, as we were asking them to join in a halakhic *tefillah*, involving many changes from their usual practice. We would not constitute ourselves as a minyan, which posed a major obstacle for some. Ultimately, we managed to convince many that a united service, in which all women could participate, had to be halakhic and was the only and best way to act, as we would thereby set an example for the entire Jewish world that we could stand as sisters and together pray to God. The gracious acceptance of these ground rules was and remains, in my opinion, the greatest accomplishment of WOW.

On Thursday morning, December 1, 1988, more than seventy women joined together and conducted a halakhic women's service, with Torah reading, at the Kotel. We did not know—how could we?—that we were beginning a new chapter in the history of Jewish women and prayer, yet we felt the momentous nature of our act. It was an extraordinary experience for me, combining both private and public prayer at that sacred site. I palpably felt the presence of the Shekhinah there at that place at that moment. Truly, the Shekhinah never left the Kotel and was waiting for us, Her daughters, to return.

Since our first prayer service at the Kotel, there has been a women's group prayer presence there at least once a month. This volume is the story of the courageous and pious women of WOW, and of the International Committee of WOW (ICWOW). These

274

two groups have had a major impact on my life.

Soon after returning from Israel after the first service, I was invited to the Reconstructionist Rabbinical College in Philadelphia to talk about WOW. I gladly went, expecting a warm welcome, but instead I was greeted with antagonism and scorn. How can Orthodox women, an oppressed minority, victimized by patriarchy and yet choosing to remain within its confines, be considered feminists? they challenged. Orthodox women, who are unable to become rabbis, who are not counted in a minyan, who endure the inequities of halakhic marriage and divorce, now insist that other women adhere to their prayer limitations. Why should WOW operate under Orthodox rules? The fact that WOW actually developed as a direct result of Orthodox women's prayer practices seemed to elude them.

I was shocked at the expressed hostility toward Orthodoxy and its women. Orthodox feminists such as I choose not to stray from our communities. We value the excellent yeshiva system, the family-centered values and community, the commitment to lives of Torah and mitzvot, which are all the hallmark of Orthodoxy. Isn't feminism about women's right to make their own choices? Why wasn't the choice of Orthodox women to remain within our communities, to try to right its wrongs while enjoying its many benefits, afforded the same respect as other women's choices? As I was leaving, one of the female professors quietly apologized to me and tried to explain, saying that the students had preconceived attitudes about Orthodox women. I left feeling that I had been the target of intense bigotry.

The dilemma of Orthodox feminism was made clear to me then. Here we women were, committed to an Orthodox interpretation of Halakhah, fighting for our rights, choosing to remain within our Orthodoxy community while attempting to make it more hospitable to our aspirations, and at the same time having to fight against being perceived as weak, downtrodden victims who passively accept misogyny and choose to remain within its confines. We were misunderstood among feminists who refused to recognize our unique brand of Torah feminism, and we were also viewed with suspicion and disdain within our Orthodox communities.

Our painful isolation among feminists was brought to a head when Judith Plaskow published a letter in *Tikkun*, expressing the view that Orthodox women cannot be feminists. She too was critical of WOW's having chosen to adhere to Halakhah. ICWOW, by then already formed and made up of different types of feminists, reached out to dialogue with her. Knowing that women like Phyllis Chesler, whom she considered a "true" feminist, were among us, she met with us and, as a result of the discussion, attained an understanding of what we were about. For a while, she even joined our board.

Now, thirteen years later, it is clear that WOW has had a major impact on the way other feminists view Orthodox feminists. The three conferences of the Jewish Orthodox Feminist Alliance (JOFA)[28] have brought together Jewish feminists of every denomination, who are invited as guests, Plaskow among them. Most Jewish feminists now accept Orthodox feminism as a legitimate feminist option. The hostile reception I received at the Reconstructionist college is unlikely to be repeated today.

In the summer of 2000, I was invited to a Coalition for Advancement in Jewish Education (CAJE) conference as a scholar-in-residence for Shabbat. Wandering into what was listed as a "women's Friday night service," I saw that musical instruments were being used, which is halakhically prohibited on Shabbat. I was upset that this service excluded halakhically committed Conservative and Orthodox women, and I made my distress known. Other women were also upset, and on Shabbat day, a small group of us decided to organize a women's *Minchah* service, with the blessing of CAJE's organizers. Although we were of different denominations, there was an immediate understanding that our service would be a halakhic, non-minyan one. The non-Orthodox women, whom I expected to have to convince of this, as I had to do in the past,[29] were, to my surprise and delight, themselves adamant that this be the case. I thanked everyone who prayed with us for joining our "WOW-style service."

Clearly, WOW has set a standard, enabling women to pray together across denominational lines. We women have, together, walked a different path than our men, who generally are unable to pray together and separate into different prayer groups at conferences. We have managed to transcend serious denominational differences and approach God, who is God of us all, together. Members of a religion racked by factionalism, we have succeeded in this, and it is possibly our greatest accomplishment.

As WOW has affected Jewish women of every denomination, it has also had an important impact on WTGs and on Orthodox rabbis. Soon after WOW began, I noticed that a number of rabbis who had previously been opposed to WTGs began to be supportive. More WTGs arose, and the number of rabbis who were willing to be halakhic advisors increased. I believe that this occurred because, when WTGs were the "new girls on the block," they were targeted by rabbis who feared any change. Now that WOW looms large, many rabbis realized that they could actually now accept WTGs, for there was something *more* extreme to oppose! And oppose they did.

I remember appearing at a panel discussion with two rabbis who permitted WTGs in their synagogues but who were opposed to WOW. Not there at the Kotel, they cried, anywhere else but there! Although they could cite no halakhic reasons for this dichotomy—approval of WTGs and disapproval of WOW—they uttered sentiments such as "WOW provokes violence" and "WOW disturbs other worshipers at the Kotel," in essence implying that WTGs should remain private, hidden behind closed doors, not out in the open air for all to see. This attitude still prevails. While WTGs have won increased Orthodox rabbinic support,[30] WOW as yet lacks outspoken rabbinic support, despite the fact that WOW is simply a WTG that meets at the Kotel and regularly and intentionally incorporates women from all across the Jewish spectrum.[31]

There is also ambivalence about WOW on the part of some women who are themselves members of *tefillah* groups. At first, in 1989, I felt open hostility on the part of some WTG supporters who feared that the emergence of WOW would cause a resurgence of the severe criticism that erupted against women's *tefillah* in the early 1980s. Many women simply felt that we had "gone too far." Even my own mother, a staunch supporter of *tefillah* groups, had difficulty accepting WOW. She never actually said so, but I sensed her doubts and silent reservations. Yet she proudly displayed a large newspaper photo of me with other women carrying a Torah to the Kotel on her kitchen wall.

In 1989, some *tefillah* group activists accused me of having hurt the cause of WTGs, a charge that caused me much anguish. I had to defend my actions and my commitment to WOW time and time again. I was told that by becoming involved in this struggle, I was jeopardizing my work with *agunot*, a charge that has proven to be false. I firmly believe that when women may freely and openly pray together at the Kotel, reading from Torah scrolls, that image will have a positive effect that will ripple through the religious world, helping to raise the image of women in their own eyes as well as in the eyes of men. I hope that this will ultimately lead to a general improvement in the lives of Orthodox women, both in spiritual matters and in family dynamics.

It now seems clear that WOW has not caused any real harm to WTGs. While still subjected to periodic abuse,[32] on the whole they have thrived and are flourishing. Many new groups have arisen, many young girls celebrate becoming bat mitzvah in them, many babies have been named in them, many brides have had *aufrufs* (prewedding rituals) in them. They are an integral part of the modern Orthodox scene, and even though some WTG members still oppose WOW, many more have become supporters.

The 2000 legal victory in the Israeli Supreme Court that acknowledged our rights empowered some Orthodox women to offer support. JOFA, whose chairwoman, Blu Greenberg, participated in the first *tefillah* and has prayed with WOW many times since, sponsored an ad in Jewish newspapers congratulating WOW. The Women's Tefillah Network newsletter, which lists halakhic WTGs in every issue, includes WOW among all the rest. A few groups have actively supported WOW,[33] but most have no official position. Many of the women who join in WOW's prayers are active members of WTGs. Among the women who join WOW when visiting Israel, it is often the Orthodox women, accustomed to praying in women-only groups, who are the most comfortable, as this is their usual and by now traditional prayer environment.

WOW dares to pray together as a women's congregation, in full view of the Jewish world. Sitting "at the door of the tent of meeting" as the *tzovot* (assembly of women) in the Torah are said to have done, WOW's primary message is that the prayers of women are as acceptable and desirable to the God of Israel as the prayers of men. Moreover, WOW's mission proclaims that women may have the same physical access to holy objects, Torah scrolls and tefillin, that men have. It is precisely this that causes the extreme reactions on the part of some fanatics. For so many centuries, women and Torah scrolls have been physically separated, not for halakhic reasons but because of underlying fear and disgust at women's bodies. WOW shows the fallacy of this reasoning, and therein lies its perceived danger.

WOW was from its outset, and remains, a *tefillah* group whose practice is halakhic. Yet it is unique; it is on the cutting edge. Unlike most WTGs, WOW has no single rabbinic advisor. Unlike Orthodox *tefillah* groups, composed mostly of Orthodox women, WOW has a different agenda. It transcends any particular denomination to promote all inclusive *ahavat Yisrael* (love of Israel). WOW includes Orthodox, Conservative, Reform, and Reconstructionist, female rabbis, secular women—all are welcome. Most *tefillah* groups have the same members and some guests. WOW has a core group that determines policy, but it also includes students spending a year in Israel as well as visitors to the Kotel who happen to join a particular *tefillah.* Beyond the rabbinic and communal disapproval that many *tefillah* groups routinely deal with,[34] WOW faces physical violence and constant lawsuits. Unlike *tefillah* groups, which meet behind closed doors, WOW meets outdoors, exposed to noise, cameras, and stares of tourists. Facing danger together has forged the core group into a tightly knit sisterhood.

WOW is the only WTG to have come under direct physical attack. WOW's services have sometimes been conducted as if in a war zone, and concentration in these situations has been difficult.

WOW is often filmed when praying; the camera is an intrusion and must be ignored in order to allow focus, *kavanah,* in prayer. Because of the location, in addition to the usual jeers and verbal attacks of *charedi* men, they must also endure the antagonism of other women.

The sometimes vocal but more often silent antagonism from other women has proven to be a most difficult challenge. While no longer fearing physical attacks (kicking, spitting, snatching away of prayer books) that have occurred in the past, the members of WOW try to establish communication with *charedi* women who share the same space. It is painful that WOW's very presence upsets some pious women who are not accustomed to seeing women pray together in groups. WOW would like to change these attitudes but is unsure how to best accomplish this. It has made many attempts to meet with its female opponents, to discuss and explain and, most of all, to assure them that WOW's prayers are halakhic, traditional, and not an affront to the sanctity of the holy site, which they all strive to protect.

There are many variations in practice among the various WTGs. As with any congregation, each has its uniqueness. So does WOW. Much discussion has ensued about issues such as which blessings should be recited before and after the Torah reading. There is a difference in approach between rabbinic advisors of WTGs as to whether blessings are permitted at all, and if so, which ones. The technical aspects involve weighing various halakhic options and approaches. Most assume that women may not constitute themselves as a minyan and therefore must omit prayers for which a minyan of men is necessary. Exactly which prayers are they? This is not unanimously agreed upon.

For example, there is controversy swirling around *Barkhu,* the opening phrase of the blessing before reading from the Torah.

Most WTGs do not permit its recitation, accepting rabbinic rulings that declare it to be permitted only in a minyan. However, many women who join WOW and are honored with an *aliyah* are accustomed to reciting *Barkhu.* At first, WOW prohibited this practice, then for a time permitted women whose custom it is to recite it. They had solid precedent, as a well-known Orthodox Israeli synagogue, Yedidyah, permits its WTG to recite *Barkhu.*[35] Therefore, some members of WOW thought that if there is halakhic precedent, why not permit it?

This issue came up at the height of one of WOW's major crises. In the immediate aftermath of the 2000 Supreme Court decision, there were many important issues with which to deal. Misleading and incorrect publicity was appearing in the press; the women were asked to speak to reporters, to appear on radio and TV, and within our own ranks there was major disagreement about exactly how to interpret the Court's decision. In the midst of all the discussion about immediate strategy, one of the women suddenly raised the issue of *Barkhu.* I could hardly believe my eyes when I read on our board's e-mail that this was being raised at that time, amid the swirl of publicity and decision making. Then I was once again absolutely convinced that the women of WOW were truly pious, truly spiritual, that their most important goal was to conduct proper religious services.

The sudden and surprising inquiry about *Barkhu* was followed by serious discussion, and the board members all had a chance to weigh in on it. It came down to this: Should WOW be concerned about not offending or surprising Orthodox women, veterans of WTGs, who join WOW when visiting Israel and are startled to hear *Barkhu* recited? Or, should WOW, since it is multidenominational, allow recitation of *Barkhu,* as there are Orthodox rabbis who permit women to recite it? Should WOW follow the most stringent view, or should it be flexible and accept certain practices as long as there is Orthodox halakhic support and precedent, even though such are the opinions of a minority?

This critical issue is far from settled. The entire question of women and minyan is not as clear as many think. There are a few halakhic authorities who permit women to constitute a minyan, as long as they pray in a women-only group. The late Rabbi Shlomo Goren, *z"l*, in his capacity as chief rabbi of Israel, wrote a halakhic decision about WTGs in which he permitted women to recite all prayers recited in a minyan, including *Barkhu*, Kaddish, and *Kedushah*. The opinion was written on his official stationery. Although he later tried to reinterpret his written decision, stating, in the first WOW lawsuit, that he was unaware that he was responding to a practical question and meant his decision to be "theoretical," it is clear that he knew that the question involved a particular group of American women in Baltimore. Moreover, he never changed his original decision in writing.[36] There are other Orthodox rabbis who permit ten women to constitute a minyan. Very few have spoken openly about this; more have privately expressed this view while asking that they not be quoted.

For now, WOW is not constituted as a minyan. In 1988, I permitted Kaddish to be recited at the first *tefillah,* after carefully announcing that the service had officially concluded and that those who wish to form a minyan to recite Kaddish might do so at that point. This procedure has sometimes been followed by WOW and sometimes not. Clearly, these halakhic issues are complex, easy solutions are not possible, and WOW's decisions in determining precise halakhic practice are fluid at this point.

As for me, my own opinions have slowly changed. When I first became active in *tefillah* groups, I completely opposed any deviation from the halakhic parameters that were set for us by our rabbis. I opposed forming ourselves as a minyan; I believed that we should adhere to the most stringent view. I no longer feel that way. After my parents' deaths, I recited Kaddish each morning in my neighborhood synagogue,[37] where at times I had to sit in the coat closet and often was unable to hear the daily service. I was distressed at being unable to recite Kaddish in my WTG, the same group that my mother—may she rest in peace—loved to attend and for a while hosted in her home. I began studying the rabbinic sources dealing with women and minyan.[38]

My local WTG embarked on a search for Orthodox rabbinical support permitting the recitation of Kaddish in a women's congregation. They spoke with some rabbis who were willing to say in private that they believed it to be permissible, but who refused to state their views publicly and asked not to be quoted. Ultimately, the group decided not to permit it.

Perhaps in the future some WTGs will constitute themselves as minyans. WOW's future path in these technical halakhic matters is unclear. On the one hand, WOW's mission is to create a comfortable prayer environment for every Jewish woman. The members of WTGs around the world should be able to join WOW when they visit Israel. For this to continue, WOW must retain the strictest construction of Halakhah. On the other hand, WOW should try to accommodate the needs of non-Orthodox women whenever possible, which means permitting all practices that are possible and permissible within Halakhah, as long as there is Orthodox precedent for them. This dilemma is as yet unresolved.

WOW perseveres, a small group facing enormous challenges. It is a halakhic group that welcomes women from every stream of

Judaism. It is a group that remains halakhic while determining whether that means accepting the stricter views of the majority of rabbis or the more lenient minority views. It is a group whose energies have been diverted from Torah study, education, and probing halakhic sources and precedents to litigating in court, raising monies for legal expenses, and dealing with physical violence, verbal violence, and silent expressions of disapproval.[39]

Despite these formidable obstacles, WOW has achieved much. It has shown the Jewish world an example of courage and of deep devotion to prayer and sisterhood. It has been a major factor in enabling the spirituality and piety of Jewish women, present but hidden throughout centuries of synagogue life, to emerge as a strong, visible, and undeniable part of mainstream Judaism.

I am immensely grateful to God that I had the privilege of organizing the first women's *tefillah* at the Kotel. I have worked hard as a board member, contributing what I can, mostly to the halakhic discussions and decisions. In 1990, I traveled to Israel with Susan Alter for the purpose of helping our attorney Arnold Shpaer deal with the halakhic issues involved in our lawsuit, as he had insisted that he needed help and refused to complete our brief until we came. As a result of that first lawsuit, we won the Court's acknowledgment that our practices do not violate or challenge the rule of Halakhah at the Kotel. I have translated some of the legal material into English in order to assist board members who cannot read complicated Hebrew legal briefs. In February 2000, I participated in a "tour" of the Kotel area with the Supreme Court judges who were deciding our case. Ultimately, and to our great surprise, the judges decided in our favor.

While in Israel, my husband and I went on another tour, that of the tunnels underneath the Kotel. This guided walk allowed us to

stand before the huge stones that make up the earliest level of the
Kotel, the stones that stand on bedrock. At a certain spot, the group
was told that that particular location is opposite the exact area
where the altar once stood. As we approached this narrow area, we
noticed some *siddurim* placed there for those who wish to pray in
that holy place. Our small group filed slowly past, and some of us
stopped briefly to pray. On one side of me stood a Hasidic man;
another Orthodox man stood on my other side. The three of us
prayed silently, standing abreast. It was for me a stunning, absolutely pure moment of prayer. When we emerged from the tunnel, I
realized that there we were, underground, *mechitzah*-less, closely
standing side by side as men and women together, and nobody
seemed to notice or care. How different than the situation above,
in the revealed area of the Kotel!

WOW is never far from my thoughts. Each month I fear for the
women, lest they suffer violence from their fellow Jews, and lately
when they bravely gather at the Kotel despite intermittent attacks
from militant Arab youths who have sometimes rained down stones
on Jews worshiping at the Kotel.

In the summer of 2000, one of my daughters took her little
daughter with her to pray together with WOW. Ayelet, my
granddaughter, then four years old, was offered the honor of
helping to dress the Torah scroll. She told me about it later that
day, in a transatlantic phone call. My joy was great. As she spoke,
I had a vision of my late mother, with her mother and grandmother—may they rest in peace—and myself, my daughter
Sheryl and her daughter Ayelet, my daughter Tamara and her
daughter Esther Eleanna, each of us being embraced by the arms
of those who preceded us, while embracing those who follow
us, joining each other in prayer.

I believe that my great-grandmother would approve of my religious life, although it is, in some ways, different from her own. I am sure that I will similarly approve of my granddaughters' religious lives, which probably will also differ from mine.

For "Lo, it is the merit of the foremothers, peeking through the lattice," through the barriers that separate those no longer alive from those yet living, peeking to see if their legacy remains unbroken.

We are, each of us, links in the long and strong chain of Jewish women's halakhic prayer journeys, our links to the God of Israel.

NORMA BAUMEL JOSEPH

Shema B'Kolah:
On Listening to Women's
Voices in Prayer[1]

JERUSALEM, 1988. It began for me with a laugh during morning
prayers. Rivka leaned over and suggested that we go to the Kotel
on Thursday to daven, and I just laughed. It was laughter filled
with unexpected joy and a great deal of incredulity. Would we
really have our usual women's prayer service at the Kotel? As the
days passed and the plans developed, these sentiments recombined
with anxiety. Could we really do it? Would they try to stop us?
Would we manage to pull it all together? What would happen to us
in the process?

The ensuing developments over the next thirteen years involved
civil courts, Jewish legal investigation, international cooperation,
individual fortitude, and incredible persistence. Much has happened
for two linked groups of women: Israeli Women of the Wall and
the International Committee for Women of the Wall. In 1989,
both groups joined in an interminable legal action during which, for
the first time in history, the religious rights of Jewish women were
argued in a court of law. It was potentially momentous, yet in sub-
stantive ways nothing has happened: the Israeli courts and government committees have continuously avoided any operational

288

decision or closure. By not rendering a decision, the state has effectively silenced both groups of women.

In this essay I wish to address that silencing; not the court process itself, but the conceptual application of Judaic norms concerning silence and the voice of women, especially in prayer. The laws prohibiting a man from listening to the voice of a woman singing are consequential only in the Orthodox community today. A woman's voice, like her hair, is considered to be sexually enticing. Men might be distracted and tempted to listen to her. Essentially, because of fear of sexual indiscretions and men's inability to control themselves, women are silenced. Thus, in talmudic rhetoric, the voice of a woman is declared sexually arousing and hence to be avoided. Yet in the earlier biblical period, women were definitely not silenced; both their voices and their prayers were readily accepted by God and the community of Israel. In particular, *Shema B'Kolah*, the command to Abraham from God that he should listen to Sarah's voice, poignantly frames this issue. I do not consider it coincidental that our experience connects with Sarah's, with her voice and laughter, and with Hannah's archetypal offer of silent, whispering prayer. Ironically, it is precisely in the realm of synagogue participation and prayer that this restriction of voice renders women silenced, hence religiously invisible.

Prayer envelops and involves the contemporary experience of women's muteness and invisibility in the Jewish world. This is particularly true given the increasing prominence of synagogues in modern Jewish life, especially outside Israel. Many of the historical traditions and realities of women's prayer have been misunderstood and misrepresented. If some women today wish to pray at the Kotel with Torah, tallit, and voice, the questions are raised automatically: Why now? Why this way? Why change?

Praying at the Kotel has become a way of publicly proclaiming inclusion in Jewish history and religious practice. Even before 1967, prayer at the Kotel was desirable but contentious: rioting and political debates surround its history. However, it was then a non-Jewish government that tried to restrict Jews. Now, ironically, it is a Jewish government that is silencing female Jews. That government is attempting to turn the Kotel—traditionally a place of individual prayer—into a synagogue, where, according to Orthodox standards only, women cannot join the communal standard of prayer. Women's group prayer at the Kotel raises questions of law and custom. It asks whether prayer there is public or private, individual or communal. It insists on clarifying women's place in communal prayer.

Legal treatises about the permissibility of women's prayer groups, such as the one by Aryeh and Dov Frimer, or the question of women's prayer at the Kotel with Torah and tallit in Justice Menachem Elon's 1994 decision, have concluded that there is no decisive legal prohibition. The confusing element of custom has not been thoroughly defined or confined. Yet the one remaining legal issue of women's voice appears to be the least disputed. As we will see in this essay, there are halakhic and moral grounds for allowing women to pray at the Kotel in full voice. At the outset, it must be clarified that the *kol ishah* issue is not really at the heart of the Kotel debate. It is not even fully articulated in the legal case presented by both sides. Practically speaking, it is not possible to hear the women from the men's side of the partition. Even at our first service there, we remained as far away from the men's section as possible. We did not want to disturb or distract; to be disturbed or distracted. We only wanted to pray. Our voices were not raised in rebellion but in invocation. Why should the voices of women be so threatening?

Paradoxically, the only real halakhic problem, that of voice, is the least contentious one. Conceivably, the offensive issue is the sight of women in prayer shawls holding the Torah scroll. Perhaps the women look too much like men, and that is where the threat lies. However, their voices are always the voices of women. In fact, there have been times when the women have been able to chant the *Megillah* there and no one has complained. Nonetheless, the whole Kotel case is about silencing women, and that is the question to be examined here.

Historical Presence

Despite rumor to the contrary, historical texts indicate that women did go to synagogue regularly.[2] Tractate *Sofrim* (18:4) mentions that women were great synagogue goers and that it was a duty to translate the biblical and prophetic portion of the week for them. Pious women did not merely attend on the Sabbath but were regulars at least on Mondays and Thursdays.[3] The synagogue structures of the European medieval period clearly indicate that women attended services.[4] Earlier texts also indicate women's presence and activity during prayer.[5] They prayed separately in the designated women's section. Some women, such as thirteenth-century Urania and Richenza, were eulogized as synagogue singers.[6] Often unable to participate or even hear the main service, they relied on knowledgeable elders, wise women, *zogerin*, to direct them in some format of prayer—separate prayer. Sometimes working at their own pace and level of understanding, often substituting Yiddish prayers known as *techinahs*, following their own female leaders, these women prayed publicly and communally.[7]

Long before the nineteenth-century debate between Reform and Orthodox Jews concerning the use of a language other than Hebrew during a prayer service, it was deemed permissible to translate the Torah reading for women. Following the statement in *Sofrim*, the medieval Rabbis approved Yiddish translations for women's prayers. Of significance is the implied and accepted notion that women would be praying on their own, publicly, and, though informally, still in a group. Certain modifications were allowed so that women could pray, participate, and understand. The question remains as to format and halakhic requirements.

Women's Responsibility

The laws of prayer for women might appear to be clear and rabbinic. According to the Talmud (*Berakhot* 20b), women are exempt from reciting the *Shema* but obligated in *tefillah*. There are many permutations and combinations of this basic mishnaic statement in rabbinic law, but the bottom line is that women are obligated to pray every day. According to some interpretations, primarily following Maimonides, the basic mandate is biblical and any prayer or petition will do. For others, such as Rabbi Israel Meir HaCohen (Hafez Hayyim), author of the *Mishnah Berurah* (*OC* 106:4), the consensus is that women must recite the basic standing silent *Amidah* in the morning and afternoon. Detailed extensive lists of additional obligatory prayers and times for women fill many books and are even available on the Internet.[8]

These debates translate into a series of distinctive rules and complicated prayer formats. The issues surrounding women's obligation to pray include prayer with a fixed content, at a fixed time, communal or individual practice, delegation, source, context, and intent. Despite the complexity of the issues involved and the disagreement between different commentators and decisors, there is general agreement that women are obligated in daily prayer.

Moreover, although they are exempted from the *Shema*, the *Shulchan Arukh* further elaborates that women should definitely say the *Shema*, though not necessarily at a specific time (*OC* 70:1). This requirement is based on the rabbinic concept that the *Shema* is a declaration of faith, of acceptance of God's dominion, which is equally indispensable for women and their spiritual existence. It is noteworthy that having begun with a seemingly clear and simple rabbinic text, later authorities had to restate the obligation to prayer and reinterpret the exemption of the *Shema*.

The impact of such legal provisions is a separate story, not for inclusion here.[9] Suffice it to say that women in traditional communities did pray. It seems strange that in the twentieth and twenty-first centuries, many religious women do not pray because they think that prayer laws do not pertain to them.[10] Of course, the exemption and hence frequent absence of women from public timely prayer is embedded in the entire tradition. Even the *Magen Avraham*, Rabbi Avraham Gumbiner (seventeenth century), commented on women's inattention to this commandment.

Given this rabbinic concern and the acknowledged importance of prayer, it is interesting to record the current increase in women's praxis as well as the rabbinic reactions to the variant patterns. Contemporary discussions focus on the location and format of women's public experience of prayer.

Tefillah B'Tzibur: Communal Prayer

Certainly, this generation has approached the challenge of women and prayer differently than did premodern communities. Instead of nonperformance, absence, illiteracy, or use of translation, modern-day daughters have been taught the language and the skills necessary for prayer. Women raised in this manner know how to pray and do so. Significantly, every yeshiva for girls requires that the girls daven in school, blurring the border between public and private, communal and individual.

In the 1970s, some women, mostly Orthodox, decided to look into other forms of communal prayer. In several communities, women, in conjunction with their rabbis, established prayer groups in order to maximize their personal prayer experience.[11] The focal point was Rosh Chodesh, traditionally known as a woman's holiday.[12] Women's services at the Kotel derived from this initiative. The backlash has been vigorous and unexpected.[13] The debate surrounding the halakhic status of such expressions has neither reached consensus nor eliminated the growing phenomenon.[14] Women continue to gather in small groups to participate in a halakhically recognized combined form of public, personal, and communal prayer. They know beyond a shadow of a doubt that they can touch, read from, and dance with a Torah. They act out of a sincere commitment, requesting that the permissible be permitted them. They reclaim some of the traditions of the medieval women with their *zogerin* and share with the yeshiva girls a skilled and informed all-woman's prayer experience.

Communal prayer in this context has several connotations. Literally, it refers to the act of prayer performed by a group of equivalent individuals who acknowledge their shared or joint praxis. Halakhically, it refers to the presence of a ritual quorum of ten. Politically, it refers to a representation of the community. According to Orthodox sources, that specifically excludes women, whereas Conservative usage includes adult women in the count of ten.

The question of how to refer to groups of women who pray together disturbs the Orthodox community. They are individuals praying together, but do they form a community? Socially, they do; halakhically, they do not. Some authorities say that women form a *kahal*, a congregation, and others use the term *tzibur*, a collective.[15]

Added to this semantic deliberation is the following uncertainty: Is their prayer public or private? In one revealing linguistic twist, Moshe Meiselman explains that for women, private prayer is an exalted opportunity and attainment. However, he also states that "the Talmud regards communal prayer as superior to individual prayer and hence more readily acceptable."[16] Are women considered spiritually inferior that they require a lesser vehicle for religious worship?

More disturbing, perhaps, is the question of women's inclusion in the normative congregational prayer service. For example, questions about the recital of the Kaddish prayer by women raise the issue of whether the woman's section is part of the synagogue halakhically. Some claim that women cannot say Kaddish from behind the *mechitzah* because the women's section is not properly part of the synagogue. How, then, are women incorporated into the praying community? To what degree is their presence during communal prayer permitted, required, exempted?

Words take on suggestive and consequential meanings in these contexts.

Shema: Listen

What does it mean to listen, to hear? Why does the basic credo of Jewish liturgy begin with that command *Shema?* This charge, or fundamental pledge of allegiance, was considered so vital that, although abstractly exempt, women were nonetheless bound to pro-claim it. "Hear, O Israel"; know this, listen and understand!

Dictionary meanings for that word include *hear, listen, attend, pay heed, learn, infer, deduce, understand, obey.* Each one of those words offers different and subtle insight to the challenge of women's prayers. Multiple metaphors and models become precedents and should be applied.

Shema B'Kolah: Abraham and Sarah

In its most basic form, this statement—"In all that Sarah says unto you, listen to her voice" (Genesis 21:12)—God admonishes Abra-ham, who is unwilling to follow the counsel of his wife, Sarah. The-ologically, the Bible presents a scenario of a man being told by God to obey a woman in a situation of familial strategy that has consequences for the future of their joint mission.[17] Why must God intercede? Equally intriguing is Rebecca's use of that phrase, com-manding obedience from her son Jacob in deceiving Isaac (Genesis 27:8, 13). Is this, too, the will of God?

What does this all mean in the language of rabbinic inter-preters? What do we learn from these stories, and how can they be applied? Enter the world of text and pretext, of exegesis and eise-gesis. Can we legitimately interpolate the various renderings of *Shema* from the dictionary—listen, heed advice, obey, understand? Listen and learn!

Hearing Advice

On an elementary level, the text indicates that to listen is to weigh this advice seriously. Clearly, Abraham had heard Sarah. The command "Hear, O Israel" cannot be simply physical, an oral or aural mode. The text of the story indicates a serious consideration: take her advice! It most likely is not meant in the sense of absolute obedience,[18] but in the sense of giving weight to her words. Many take the phrase to indicate acceptance. *Shema Yisrael* in that sense commands that Israel accept God's commanding presence.[19] So, too, Abraham is instructed to accept Sarah's counsel. Conceivably, it conveys the sense that he is to count her words carefully, for they are of equal import with his own. God has chosen to inform Abraham that he is not the only decisor.

Understand

The declaration of faith that is encapsulated in *Shema Yisrael* demands apprehension and comprehension. Understand, Abraham, what Sarah's claim is, what her worry is, what motivates her. Understand her perspective.

Feminist Jews, especially those involved in women's separate prayer services, might wish to apply this command to rabbinic opponents:

> Understand what our plea and our problem is. Stop misreading us. We wish to participate! Not to rebel or remove ourselves from community. We wish to give voice to our spiritual/religious commitment. Our presence at the Kotel is an act of religious enhancement; a means to further participation and expression of faith. It is an acceptance of the yoke of heaven.

Feminists understand the ritual act of participating distinctly. To participate is to be fully involved, to challenge oneself and act out one's commitment. In this sense, prayer involves verbal communication as

297

well as action and the use of the artifacts of liturgy. Holding and reading from the Torah is not merely symbolic; it is a real, transformative act of commitment to that Torah. The biblical command to wear *tzitzit* (fringes), translated into the practice of using a tallit (prayer shawl) for prayer services, can be extended to women as another voluntary act of involvement and commitment.[20] Women's sincere attempts to increase their participation in ritual Judaism command at least an attempt at understanding.

The standard for participation has changed in the modern period. In the biblical, ancient, and medieval periods, men and women were rooted in the collective. Although individuals were not without individuality, individualism as a mode of being was nonexistent. Nevertheless, in the biblical period, women and men were able to celebrate their personal experiences publicly through sacrifices. After the destruction of the Temple, Jews in general had fewer personalized rituals, but membership in the community was still self-evident. In the modern period, that sense of rootedness and belonging was subverted and replaced with a powerful emphasis on public religion and individual display. Participation in this context means active ritual responsibility and agency.

Motives

In generating an interpretive approach to these texts and issues, the formidable question of motives takes primary position. Intent and motive play a considerable role in Jewish law concerning ritual matters.[21] Often, a legal decision will hinge on the motives of the person involved and not just the permissibility of the act itself. Murder is forbidden, but self-defense is compulsory. If a wedding is performed in a synagogue in order to replicate the Christian practice of a church wedding, then the act is forbidden. Obviously, today with so many rabbis participating in weddings in synagogues, the ceremony definitely is considered kosher. There are many examples of this distinction in all legal systems.

Discussions of women's motives in ritual participation often refer to the talmudic phrase *nashim somchot reshut,* "women may, but are not obligated to, lay hands" (*Chagigah* 16b; *Rosh Hashanah* 33a; *Eruvin* 96a). The talmudic references are specifically about permitting women to place their hands on the Temple sacrifices but are understood as typifying the definitive debate about women assuming optional rituals. They also speak to an ancient acceptance of women's motives and spiritual needs.

The problem arises when determining that motive. Who decides, and how? Who knows whether my motives in wearing a prayer shawl are arrogant or pious? If the former, then the act is forbidden; if the latter, then it is praiseworthy. Thus, understanding the motives of women involved becomes part of the legal decision-making process.

Various contemporary decisions concerning women's ritual participation hinge on just such a determination. In the responsa (Jewish legal decisions) of Rabbi Moses Feinstein, there are some interesting examples, the most notable being *Hanashim Hasha'ananot* (*Iggerot Moshe, OC* 4:49).[22] In that text, Rabbi Feinstein articulates his position concerning women and ritual participation. He posits that since some women today are influenced by external movements, they want to practice differently. They are angry and think they can change the law. Although he notes that they are *shomrei Torah,* faithful to the Torah, he calls them heretics nonetheless. Because they want to change practice, he thinks that the root of their desire stems from a denial of the eternal nature of the Torah. Their motives render the requested acts forbidden.

Remarkably, in the very same paragraph, he notes that women may, of course, opt to perform rituals, such as shofar and *lulav*, from which they are officially exempted.

> To be sure, permission is given to every woman to per-
> form mitzvot (ritual obligations) that the Torah did
> not command her. They are even considered to have a
> duty and a reward in the performance of these obli-
> gations. In fact, according to the judgment of the
> *Tosafists* they are entitled (authorized) to make the
> appropriate blessing. As is our custom women observe
> the commandments of shofar and *lulav* and even make
> the appropriate blessings. Accordingly [lit., given this],
> even *tzitzit*.[23]

These acts are encouraged because Rabbi Feinstein has no doubt that the motives stem from a keen desire to fulfill God's law. Women who are conscientious about these extra practices are deemed righteous. Only those who are influenced by the women's movement are called rebellious. He further clarifies this point in issuing his decision:

> However, since (in our case) it is not for this purpose,
> rather the desire comes out of a rebellion against God
> and his Torah, it cannot be an act of mitzvah at all.
> On the contrary, it is a forbidden act, forbidden as a
> heresy that she expects a change in the laws of the
> Torah.[24]

In fact, in an unpublished but widely circulated letter written in his name by his grandson on the issue of women's prayer groups, he says:

> However, as a matter of theory alone, it is possible to
> state that were there a group of religiously observant

women whose considerations were solely for the sake of heaven and without any contesting of God's Torah or Jewish custom, why would it be appropriate to prevent them from praying together? They could also read from the Torah scroll, but they should be careful not to do so in such a way as to cause error that this constitutes the congregational reading.[25]

This text does not endorse women's prayer groups, but it does reveal the theoretical validity of the act. Between the righteous and the rebellious, the distinguishing factor is motive. And nowhere do we hear the voice of the women involved.

Similarly, in a case involving a request to change from a balcony to a kosher *mechitzah*, Rabbi Feinstein forbids the switch (*Iggerot Moshe*, OH 2:43). He proclaims that the women's complaint that it is difficult to climb the stairs is merely a subterfuge for their real purpose: they wish to sit together with men, as in the Conservative movement. He does add that the structural change would be permitted for spatial reasons. The decision is made based on an attributed motive.[26]

Contrasting the above decisions with two of Rabbi Yechiel Yaacov Weinberg (twentieth century) underscores the divergence in rabbinic perspectives. Rabbi Weinberg understood that women's desire to participate publicly in Jewish ritual could constitute a religiously permitted act. In two critical decisions, that of the permissibility of a bat mitzvah ceremony (*Sridei Aish* 3:93) and the renowned case in France of women singing Sabbath songs with men (*Sridei Aish* 2:8), he is attentive to motive as a favorable and crucial factor. A girl's feelings of dignity, pride, and self-worth motivate the need for a bat mitzvah celebration. In fact, he insists on some kind of a celebration—but not in the synagogue. As well, women in

France and Ashkenaz would "feel insulted and discriminated against if we were to forbid them from participating in the delight of Sabbath by singing Sabbath songs."[27] Clearly, the decisions themselves do not rest entirely on motive. In fact, both Rabbi Feinstein's and Rabbi Weinberg's final decisions about the bat mitzvah ceremony are, intriguingly, quite similar.[28] The distinguishing component, however, is the positive play that Rabbi Weinberg gives to women's motives and reasons for inclusion. According to his understanding, those wishing to institute these practices are working for the sake of heaven. In this format, women are not silenced, even though their voices have still not been heard.

*K*ol Ishah: **The Voice of a Woman**

The quintessential declaration at the heart of this issue is the talmudic reading of a statement in the Song of Songs (2:14), "Sweet is your voice, comely your appearance." The Talmud interprets, *kol b'ishah ervah*—the voice of a woman is nakedness, licentious, provocative, sexual incitement, forbidden. The various translations foreshadow the labyrinthine rabbinic clarification and application of this principle.[29] There are three principal talmudic texts:

> *Berakhot* 24a: Shmuel said: Woman's voice constitutes an erotic stimulus, as it says, "Sweet is your voice, comely your appearance." (Song of Songs 2:14)

> *Kiddushin* 70b: Shmuel said: "One may not greet a woman." May one send her a greeting through her husband? No, because Shmuel really said, "One may not greet a woman at all."

Sotah 48a: Rabbi Yosef said: "If men sing and women respond, that is unchaste. If women sing and men respond, it is as destructive as fire to flax."[30]

The chasm between the biblical approbation of women's prayerful songs ("Miriam responded: Sing to God" [Exodus 15:21]; "Deborah sang" [Judges 5:1]; "Hannah prayed" [1 Samuel 2:1]) and the talmudic disdain is more than a matter of chronology. It bespeaks a cultural shift of major proportions and is evident in Shmuel's facile subversion of the Song's praise of women into a striking condemnation.[31]

Ironically, for many who accept Shmuel's dictum banning a women's voice, the text of the Song itself is never to be taken literally. Relying on Rashi's interpretive model, they read the Song as a metaphor for the relationship between the people of Israel and God. The ArtScroll edition of the Song, in fact, translates the complete text as metaphor exclusively. Nevertheless, they accept the talmudic ban on women's voices that is predicated on the literal rather than figurative reading of that biblical text.

That first talmudic text appears in the context of determining the appropriate format for the recitation of the *Shema.* Thus, for many it necessitates a prohibition for a man to recite the prayer when a woman's voice is heard. There are variant ramifications: a woman's voice is forbidden only when the *Shema* is being recited, or it is forbidden always—even when the *Shema* is not being recited. It is forbidden if the woman is the man's wife, only if she is his wife, only if she is a temptation, or only if she is forbidden to him. It relates to the sound of an individuated voice, and is applicable in the synagogue, only in the synagogue, or never in the synagogue. For some the proscription applies to men; for others it applies to women. Who is charged with this restrictive responsibility? For some it is a matter of custom and familiarity, while for others it correlates with a man's intention to derive "forbidden" pleasure. For a few it engages a moral lesson rather than an absolute law.[32]

The second text is used by Rabbi Judah to chastise Rabbi Nachman for attempting to send a message to Yalta (Rabbi Nachman's wife) using Rabbi Judah as an intermediary (*Kiddushim* 70a). Greetings from men to women become suspect even when a husband is involved. In this context, the prohibition devolves onto the issue of social interaction, familiarity, and affection. It is relational rather than liturgical. Banning a woman's voice inevitably restricts women and limits male conversations. It also reifies rabbinic mistrust, not of women but of men, and their skepticism about male control of their own sexuality. Unable to control their own thoughts, they silence women.

There are other anecdotal stories in the Talmud that demonstrate this stricture against discourse. The most famous is that of Beruriah, who chastises Rabbi Yossi of the Galilee for asking her a wordy question: "Galilean fool! Have not our sages said: Do not converse much with women?" (*Eruvin* 53b).[33] She is probably mockingly referring to the statement by Yossi ben Yochanan in the *Mishnah Avot* (Chapter 1): "Do not converse much with a woman." This sentiment is further accounted for in a talmudic warning that too much conversation with a woman will lead to wrongful intercourse (*Nedarim* 20b). No longer focused either on the voice of a woman only or on the statement of Samuel, these stories combine to restrict and insinuate. The result is a culturally familiar and purposeful separation of the sexes.

The final pericope comes the closest to the current halakhic standard but is not necessarily cited as the prooftext in confining the ban on women's voices to singing. There are numerous explanations of the stipulated distinction allowing for a preferred and minimal standard. The implication is that under ideal conditions, men and women will not sing responsively together. The worst case scenario would have men listening and responding to female vocalists. The context here is neither prayer nor common conversation, but unambiguously a festive gathering. This statement was used by the early Rabbis to prohibit female entertainers, vocalists, and musicians. In the medieval period there are numerous examples of female entertainers, especially at weddings.[34] Interestingly, the text cited in *Sotah* does not rely on Samuel's dictum, nor is it bound to a woman's voice.

The above sources emerge to substantiate the sexual nature and potential allure of a woman's voice. The question remains: Is it the voice that is sexually stimulating and indecent, or is it the woman who is the forbidden element? At any rate, listening to women is a distraction to prayer, to purity, to maleness. The bans are developed to forestall any illicit relationship or improper thought that arises from this aural interaction.

Strikingly, the contemporary practice developed by the later sages applied the prohibition to singing and not to conversation.[35] For the majority of *poskim*, halakhic decisors, it is forbidden to listen to a woman—any woman anywhere—sing, but it is perfectly permissible to listen to her speech and to have a conversation. The consequences of this shift are enormous and obvious. Modern Orthodoxy is almost unimaginable otherwise. Men and women interact in all phases of contemporary life—the marketplace, the school, and the synagogue—and women's voices in these spheres is indispensable. In fact, Rabbi Feinstein allowed women to teach men of all ages, and men to listen to a talk from a woman, even in a synagogue. The nonsinging voice of a woman is not an issue. His concern with the law that prohibits singing is to define the age category, limiting it to "women" over twelve (*Iggerot Moshe, OH* 1:26).

One of the most historic decisions is that of Rabbi Weinberg, who permits the boys and girls in the youth groups of Germany and France to sing together. He relies on numerous arguments and on the previous leaders of the community. His decision renegotiates the social function and motivational factors. Women's motives to participate in a religious service are not debased. Cultural factors are included in rating the pertinence of the act. Rabbinic courage is called upon as he recalls the reinterpretation of a statement in Psalms (119:126): *Et la'asot la'Shem*. "It is time to work for God, as they have violated Your law." Used carefully by rabbinic decisors, it has facilitated change as a directive meaning: it is time to break the law of God in order to preserve the law of God.[36]

The current controversies revolve around the assorted occasions concerning listening to a female vocalist. Not only is a mixed choir forbidden, but also many prohibit men from attending concerts and even listening to a woman on radio or on tape. These conclusions, however, must be aligned with some historical precedents. Not only did several women sing prophetic songs, but also women were official mourners (Jeremiah 9:16; 2 Chronicles 35:25; *Moed Katan* 3:9). The medieval record is even stronger. "The surprise is that women were not silent. They sang throughout the Middle Ages, when they were permitted and when they were not, and the sources bear witness to their voices."[37]

Wailing—using one's voice as an act of mourning—might be said to preclude any improper lustful thoughts. Yet if context eliminates lust, what about women's voices in prayer? In the past, women did sing prayers with and for women. What about women uttering prayers when men can hear? In an internal citation in the *Sedei Chemed*, Rabbi Chayim Medini (nineteenth-century Jerusalem) notes an earlier source who concludes that if women are not singing love songs, and men do not intend to derive pleasure, women may be heard reciting praises to God and wailing at funerals.[38] Thus, context and content combine in some situations to permit listening to the voice of a woman. The complex cases of both *Megillah* reading and Kaddish recital by women surely apply here but require separate attention.[39] Remarkably, the discussion to forbid or permit either act seldom revolves on the factor of *kol ishah*.

Notably, Rabbi Ovadiah Yosef determines that a woman may recite the *Gomel* prayer of thanksgiving.[40] He is not the only one to do so, but his argument is noteworthy. He specifies that the woman must say the full blessing from behind the partition, in the presence of a minyan and the Torah, and *b'kol*—in full voice! Not only must the men listen, but also they must respond. In a striking footnote he elaborates on the permissive factors: time—the prayer is over too fast for lewd thoughts to develop; place—there is no suspicion of lewd thoughts in the synagogue, where God's presence dwells; method—recitation is not singing; precedent—in banning women from the theoretically permissible *aliyah*, the Talmud (*Megillah* 23a) advances only one reason, *kavod hatzibur*, honor of the community. Rabbi Ovadiah Yosef argues that if women were prohibited from reciting prayers in the synagogue, the Talmud would have relied on that for this prohibition. The absence of such an argument leads him to allow men to hear women's voices in a prayer in synagogue.[41] The implications of such reasoning are vast. One final contrast: for Rabbi Yosef the synagogue is protected from distracting lewd thoughts, while for Rabbi Feinstein the marketplace is neutralized.

Contemporary responsa have redefined the category and characteristics of *kol ishah*. The topography of this legal map is open for investigation and implementation.

This inquiry into the silencing of women could not be complete without interfacing rabbinic law with biblical story. Miriam leads the women through song and dance to praise God—truly, an embodied prayer. Commentators concerned with *kol ishah* violations infer that the women separated for this celebration. So a separate women's service could be deemed permissible rather than rebellious in deserting the male congregation. Deborah lifted her voice in song, proud and strong. Again, comments concerned with *kol ishah* note that her voice was linked to Barak's. Accordingly, mixed singing has its biblical precedent.

The critical paradigm for the voice of women in prayer is, of course, Hannah. Initially, the story destroys notions of the seclusion of women and attests to their presence in and easy access to holy public places. The present dichotomy between public and private prayer is likewise challenged. Certainly, the talmudic dictum that we learn prayer from Hannah presents an image of and precedent for women at prayer; of women's creative contribution to the prayer of men; and of the possibility that prayer might address a woman's particular needs.[42] The story emphasizes the acceptance of a woman—of her location, of her motives, of her actions, and of her words. It also portrays a male dignitary who acknowledges his error in misreading her. Both God and Eli listen to her voice.

A final irony: given the powerful biblical representation of women at prayer, the total absence of any women in the traditional prayer book is astounding and humiliating. Women are rarely named, quoted, and acknowledged in the prayer book.[43] The biblical presence does not warrant this liturgical absence!

Shema B'Kolah, the command to listen to the voice of a woman, resonates in these texts as it does today. Women's experiences and expressions can be reflected in the communal context, but silencing women obliterates understanding and partnership. Women's prayer groups did not arise from rebellion—quite the opposite. Like the women who chose to accept the responsibility of shofar or *lulav,* these women chose to further their ritual practice and deepen their understanding of prayer. Their actions, like those of their biblical foremothers, are for the sake of heaven.

Shema Kolynu. Listen to our voices. Have compassion. Accept our prayers. God listens to our voices. Do not turn us away empty handed.[44]

VANESSA L. OCHS

Women and Ritual Artifacts

AS ONE WHO STUDIES RELIGION from the perspective of material culture (meaning artifacts—or more prosaically, things), I became the director of ICWOW who inevitably gravitated toward reflecting upon some of the objects of contention at the Wall (including the Wall itself). I became responsible for cultivating and chronicling some of the new things that have come into being in the Women of the Wall's brief history. From this vantage point, I offer these thoughts on things old and new at the Wall—assuming, as I do, that things, like people and texts, are teachers.

A Story of Things

The story of the Women of the Wall is a story of things. It is a dramatic story of things desired and things denied, things that sanctify and things that desecrate, things that bring one closer to God and things that make God distant, things that create community and things that destroy it, things that can be holy vessels or lethal weapons, things that recall history and things that rewrite it. The story of the Women of the Wall is the story of things whose valence changes depending on who is using them, how and where they are used, and who has jurisdiction over how they may be used. It is, in particular, the story of things that can become holy,

310

despised, or dangerous when women decide to make, own, sell, give, use, embrace, inhabit, touch, or wear them.

This story of things depends, as all stories do, upon who does the telling. For example, if I wear a tallit at the Wall, I will tell a story of being wrapped in God's presence and by the presence of the four matriarchs, whose names are inscribed on my particular tallit in threads woven at each of its corners. If I wear a tallit at the Wall and an ultra-Orthodox man tells the story, he might tell a story of being provoked to violence, a story of heroism, in which he saves the tallit and Judaism from being desecrated by women by hurling chairs at them.

If I wear a tallit and the police do the telling, they might tell a story of just doing their job, for if a woman wears a tallit at the Wall and they notice her, they arrest her, and if she resists, they drag her away.

If I wear a tallit and the politicians do the telling, they might tell a story of bargaining points, a story that would change depending on what was at stake at that moment. Should they wish to score points with the ultra-Orthodox, they might lobby to keep my tallit-wearing illegal; if they wish to woo or placate Jews of the liberal movements, they might lobby to legalize my tallit-wearing. Should they have nothing to win or lose, they will delay and dawdle, assigning the issue to a governmental committee for endless deliberation.

The Rules

The government of Israel currently shapes any telling of the story of things at the Wall through a group of rules that govern gender behavior in the use of Jewish ritual objects at the Wall. Although an Israeli Supreme Court ruling on May 22, 2000, declared that women's halakhic rights at the Kotel are legitimate and must be facilitated by the Israeli government within six months, the government was granted an appeal. Thus, the rules of the last thirteen years still stand. Many religious rules can be broken without punishment in the state of Israel—no one goes to jail for driving to the beach on Shabbat or gets fined for eating meat and milk together—but these laws concerning women at the Wall are *civic rules* that can currently result in arrest, a fine, and possibly a jail sentence.

RULES FOR WOMEN

1. Women may pray aloud together in groups elsewhere in Israel, and women may pray alone and aloud at the Wall, provided they wear modest clothes. Jewish women may not, according to civil law, pray aloud together at the Wall.

2. A woman may wear whatever she chooses on her head throughout Israel: a *kipah,* a shawl, a wig, a cowboy hat, or a tourist's cap. A woman may wear whatever she likes on her head at the Wall. Over her shoulders at the Wall, a woman may wear a poncho, a fur coat, a Batman cape, or a nun's habit. A woman may not, according to civil law, wear a tallit at the Wall.

3. A woman may read from *Megillat Esther* on Purim or the Book of Lamentations on Tisha B'Av anywhere in Israel. As no law specifies that women may *not* read from *Megillat Esther* on Purim at the Wall or the Book of Lamentations on Tisha B'Av at the Wall, they do so. A woman may also read from the Torah scroll itself elsewhere in Israel, but a woman may not, according to civil law, read from the Torah scroll at the Wall.

RULES FOR MEN

Men are not forbidden from praying in groups, praying aloud, wearing prayer shawls, and reading from the Torah scroll at the

Wall. No laws specify that men may not throw stones and chairs at women who pray at the Wall. When men have thrown stones and chairs, our experience in the last thirteen years suggests that the Israeli government prefers to look the other way, as if it were assumed that the men were provoked; that is, the women who "made" them do it are to blame.

The Wall Itself

The Wall itself is a complicated artifact. Made of natural stones shaped and structured in antiquity, the Wall has been considered by Jews to be holy by virtue of its once having been an outer, western wall of the Temple. The holiness of the Wall, then, is holiness one step removed, holiness by association, holiness by the proximity created by memory. One might well ask: How far away from the Wall could one get and still access the mystique of its holiness? Does it matter if you can't touch it? Does it matter if you can't see it?

This question of the boundaries of a thing's holiness was recently tested by the Israeli government in a case that has a certain superficial likeness to the case of WOW. (A significant difference is that women's prayer at the Wall, as it is carried out by the Women of the Wall in accordance with Orthodox guidelines, was determined to be halakhically permissible, according to Justice Menachem Elon of the Israeli Supreme Court; egalitarian prayer has not been subject to such analysis.) In October 1999, the Israeli Conservative movement (called Masorati) was on the verge of accepting an Israeli government proposal that they hold their egalitarian (i.e., mixed-gender) prayer services not at the Wall itself but at Robinson's Arch at the southern end of the Wall. (Previous attempts by liberal egalitarian groups to pray at the Wall were met by the violence of the ultra-Orthodox.) Rabbi Ehud Bandel, president of the Masorati movement, was reported to have said, "It's the same wall, the same stones, the same holiness" (*The Jewish Week*, October 22, 1999). Even though this alternative area was clearly not "the" Wall from the perspectives of memory, geography, or even popular sentiment, it still possessed "enough" holiness through its contiguity to the Wall to make worship there *feel* meaningful. Physical distance from the Wall itself did not make this alternative site less holy for this rabbi.

There were, as always, other political issues at stake here. My own interpretation is that the Masorati movement decided that it could demonstrate its goodwill in negotiating and a readiness to "play ball" with the government by accepting the *less* desirable prayer space (and less experientially holy) in exchange for generous concessions from the Israeli government concerning the Masorati movement's more pressing issues at that time, such as the right of liberal rabbis to be able to participate in conversions and weddings in Israel. The Masorati movement would not give up forever their claim to pray *at* the Wall but would consider waiting until a more auspicious time, when there were not other issues at stake. Thus, even though Bandel might have optimally preferred a police-protected, nonviolent prayer space at the Wall itself, he could protect the dignity of his movement in saying that if they were to accept the proposed alternative, they were not being hoodwinked, for the alternative site was holy enough in its own way.

At this same time, some leaders of the Reform movement were *not* swayed by such reasoning and would *not* consider abandoning the Kotel as the site for their egalitarian prayer, calling it a "central national shrine of the Jewish people." Indeed, since the establishment of the State of Israel and the collective construction of contemporary Israeli national sentiment through celebratory, initiation, and commemorative rituals, the Wall is considered by many, even secular Israelis, to be *the* national shrine of Israel, with Masada as its only competition. I do not believe that this has come about only because the Wall represents the idealized piety of the ancient Temple cult, the remembered splendor of the annual pilgrimage extravaganzas, or Jewish tenaciousness despite centuries of loss and destruction. Rather, I believe that the Wall also represents for many the celebration of rightful ownership reclaimed and the blessing of having the power to protect one's sacred space.

Expressing his refusal to accept a site other than the Wall for egalitarian prayer, Rabbi Ammiel Hirsch of the Reform movement reportedly claimed, "Robinson's Arch in *not* the shrine of the Jewish people called the Kotel . . . Robinson's Arch cannot replace the Western Wall." Interestingly enough, some Israeli Masorati leaders may have inadvertently expressed similar sentiments (that the Arch might be *less* holy than the Wall) by insisting that their acceptance of the Arch as a prayer site was contingent upon the government taking specific upgrading steps. These include making the site accessible, as there is now an archaeological dig in front of the Arch, and providing essential accessories for prayer: a Torah, an ark, prayer books, and benches. A third contingency, one that the government may be at a loss as to how to ensure, is allure: the alternative prayer space must be able to have a drawing effect. Rabbi Jerome Epstein, a Conservative leader in the United States, is reported to have said that the "area around Robinson's Arch is just as appropriate as any other area of the wall [for prayer]. If it brings us together. . . ." (*The Jewish Week*, October 22, 1999).

Thus, one might well ask the following: If the Robinson's Arch site could not be made accessible by the government, and if it could not act as a sufficiently powerful magnet to bring people together for prayer, would it still be considered a "holy enough" Jewish site? To answer this question, one need only ask, "If the Wall itself were not accessible, and if there were no prayer implements at the Wall, and if people could not gather there for prayer, would it still be a Jewish holy site?" Indeed, between 1948 and 1967, this was precisely the situation at the Wall, and despite all this, the holiness of the Wall was not compromised. In fact, periods of the Wall's inaccessibility to Jews have possibly increased its holiness in the religious imagination. One could even suggest that in post-1967 Israel—where the Wall has been transformed into a giant outdoor Orthodox synagogue, where tour groups hold mass bar mitzvahs and parades of tourists from foreign countries snap group photos, and where *charedim* have thrown rocks and feces at women or at women and men who were worshiping there together—the Wall is being desecrated.

In May 2000, the Conservative movement formally accepted the proposal to pray at Robinson's Arch. It is their hope that this will be an interim solution. The Reform movement has not yet accepted this alternate site.

The Wall I Know

Because this is the story of the Wall I am telling, I offer some parts of the story that hold particular relevance for me. Before 1967, the Wall was a place that Jews could neither see nor touch; its being forbidden heightened one's longing for it. There was also the break-your-heart irony: since 1948, the Jews at last had a homeland, but the holiest place of all in the holiest city was off-limits to Jews. This was like knowing of Jews who were alive but endangered in a far-off land, beyond being rescued. What did it mean for a Jew to be denied a place at this pre-1967 Wall? In the community's mind, I imagine, it meant being denied presence at the place where Jewish history, memory, God, and the Jewish people convened; it meant absence at the place where, according to some, God was most intensely present and readily attentive. It meant that you could go home, but not be fully there.

I had been taught that the rocks of the Wall had a human heart. Or, to translate the lyrics of Naomi Shemer's anthem "Jerusalem of Gold" literally, they were rocks with the *heart of a man.* The literal translation is not far off the mark, as the first photographic images emerging of Jews standing at the newly regained Wall in June 1967 were of men: soldiers, rabbis, even soldier-rabbis. The props they held were not only men's props, but the various symbols traditionally associated with Israeli Jewish males: shofars, yarmulkes, tefillin, *tallitot,* and guns. I, fourteen years old during the Six Day War, recall being so jubilantly tearful and so relieved and happy to finally be on a Jewish "winning team" that got its rightful property back that I hardly even noticed that the new victorious Jews singing God's praise and thanking God for victory at the Wall were all male. Maybe it was not just the exuberant emotion that made me suddenly gender-blind, for if you had asked me then to imagine "a Jew," the picture that would have come to mind immediately was not myself or my mother but rather my grandfather or one of my uncles; or perhaps a generic Hasidic man or Moses holding the Ten Commandments.

By 1968, the site had been transformed from ancient ruins forbidden to Jews to a Jewish pilgrimage shrine. My father, who visited later that year, brought back a photograph of himself praying at the Wall. It was not included in the family album but was framed and displayed near my mother's Sabbath candles, like a pebble that had been brought back from the grave of a *tzaddik.*

There was more. The Wall previously had been a gender-neutral space (and there are photographs taken before 1948 of men and women praying at the Wall, unsegregated by gender). Now, for the first time in Jewish history, it was configured like an outdoor Orthodox synagogue, with chairs and prayer equipment for men who prayed in groups together on the much larger area to the left of the *mechitzah,* and with fewer chairs and fewer prayer books for women who prayed alone on the smaller right side.

I saw the Wall for myself when I stood before it a year later. In my teenage eagerness to have "a religious experience" at the Wall, one that could compete with the heavy, moving sacred moments my friends boasted about, I failed to notice how the valence of the Wall had shifted by the presence of this *mechitzah,* unequally placed, separating men and women. Had I had noticed, I might have only remarked that the site seemed more familiarly Jewish now, less an archaeological ruin and more reminiscent of my grandparent's *shtibel,* a place I once found cozy and dear, if not a little creepy for a child, with its darkness and the droning of men praying, each at his own pace and to his own tune. How would I have reacted if someone had pointed out to me that the Wall, a space of all Jews, had been physically transformed into the space of one particular denomination of Jews that separated men and women and excluded women from participating actively in communal prayer? I'd have felt miffed, perhaps, but likely would have brushed it aside. For I, like so many Americans and Israelis of the time, had been wired to equate Orthodox practice of Judaism with "being really Jewish"—that is, doing Judaism the right way, the way it was meant to be, the way it was always done since antiquity.

318

The Wall of 1967 is no longer the one I see. Fast-forwarding thirty-five years, feminism has transformed the Jewish landscape. In the same period of time, Jews of liberal denominations worldwide have come to feel more self-confident, claiming their different expressions of Judaism to be legitimate, not inauthentic or watered down. If we look at the material changes alone, we can immediately see the differences in synagogue worship and sacred study. The seats of honor on the *bimah,* held by the rabbi, cantor, and president of the synagogue, are now filled by women, who can and do hold all three roles, as well as by men. The classes in the rabbinical seminaries of the non-Orthodox movements are also filled with women as well as men, and dormitories have been built to accommodate female seminarians. The symbols of Jewish belonging, commitment, and leadership are no longer "for men only" props. Many women now wear *kipot* and *tallitot,* and some wear tefillin. Many women know how to read the Torah scroll and know how to execute the complicated choreography of taking the Torah from the ark, parading it, unwrapping it, scrolling it to the right place, blessing it, reading from it, lifting it, dressing it, parading it once again, and returning it to the ark. Even in those Orthodox synagogues where women pray together in women's *tefillah* groups from time to time, women are now playing the role of "the Jew" formerly played by men alone, and they are playing it in "full costume" with prayer shawls and various versions of head coverings. In Orthodox settings such as Drisha, the women's Torah study school in New York City, women are donating Torahs for women to use in their worship so they do not have to wait for the men to finish using "their" Torah so it can be borrowed.

Early on, as the landscape was beginning to transform, it looked so peculiar to me. I felt as if I were at a Purim costume ball where the women, instead of dressing up as Queen Esther, had come as modern versions of Mordechai the Jew. But the eye accommodates quickly, more quickly perhaps than the rational mind. Soon, for me—in that blink of an eye that took a decade—a woman wearing a *kipah* and tallit, holding and reading the Torah, looked "natural." In fact, when I leave for synagogue now, my daughter and I run down our checklist: "Did you take the keys, lock the door, remember your tallit, *kipah,* and prepare your Torah reading?"

Given the sensibilities of this moment, it is not surprising that when the First International Conference of Jewish Women took place in Jerusalem, ritual, notable for the material objects put into service, was strategized and carried out.

The Ballet of Objects at the Wall

In this ballet of objects, here is the basic choreography: Given that the Wall has been experienced by many as the holiest site for *all* Jews (regardless of denomination, county of origin, age, skin color, gender, and level of observance), it made sacred sense for Jewish women gathering from all over the world to bring a Torah scroll, the most sacred object for all Jews, to the Wall, where it would be read as part of a women's morning prayer service. Such a plan could be envisioned only by a group of women who finally knew what to do with a Torah, beyond kissing it as it paraded by. Many, but not all, women of all the denominations had learned the laws and customs pertaining to the Torah scroll, ranging from how to acquire one, how to store it, when and how to take it out from the ark, how to place it on the lectern, how to be the one who calls people from the congregation up for *aliyot* and offers blessings on their behalf, how to move from right to left after one's *aliyah,* how to scroll the Torah to the correct section, how to prepare to chant from the Torah, when to pause to offer blessings on behalf of the sick and those who have survived dangers, how to lift the Torah up, dress it, and so forth. In many other religions, such complex choreographies are left to the ritual experts, not to laypeople.

Any slip in this elaborate communal choreography would constitute a disgrace, a shame. For the Torah is heavy, but not just in weight. Drop it, and the entire community must fast in atonement. When a woman lifts the Torah scroll over her head slightly, unrolled for the congregation to see it, I have seen frantic men surround her, holding their arms up high, ready to break the Torah's potential fall. I have seen people hold their breath when a woman holds up the Torah. How curious! I have seen women holding very heavy children and balancing babies in one arm and umbrella strollers and diaper bags in another as they have boarded buses or trains, but I have rarely seen helping arms extended, and I have never heard breath being held.

For the first Torah reading at the Wall, WOW borrowed a Torah from Hebrew Union College. That Torah, brought by women to the Wall, was used as the Torah is used by Jews; it was read and treated in the prescribed manner.

Ancient Jewish Categories of Holy Objects

To better understand the Wall and the other objects used by WOW for worship, fundraising, and public information, let us first consider one traditional system of categorizing Jewish objects, in which the objects range from the most holy to the forbidden. Ethnographer Samuel Heilman describes in his study "Jews and Judaica: Who Owns and Buys What?"[1] that according to ancient classification, there are four categories of Jewish objects in the "holy range":

1. *Klei kodesh:* Holy objects. These objects are "sancta of the highest order," because they have the name of God written on them one or more times. They are considered sacred whether in use or not. Extensive rules govern how they are to be made, stored, used, handled, repaired, and disposed of (through burial). This is generally the case: the more holy an object or site is, the more rules there are that govern every aspect of it. Examples of *klei kodesh* are a Torah scroll or a mezuzah parchment. Although it may surprise some, *klei kodesh* do not become impure or less sacred if they are touched by someone who can be designated as being impure by Jewish law (e.g., a menstruating woman). Folkways (*minhagim*) have, in this instance, trumped Jewish law, and there have been Jewish communities that banned menstruating women from the synagogue, assuming that their state of *tumah* (ritual impurity) could be communicated to the Torah scroll. What docs make *klei kodesh* invalid or unacceptable for use is some flaw in the object itself, such as a torn Torah scroll or a mezuzah parchment with a letter smudged out or miswritten. If these flaws are addressed and repaired by experts working according to rigid rules, the *klei kodesh* can be restored to their former status. It is the correctly written name of God on the appropriate surface that makes an object most holy.

2. *Tashmishei kedushah:* Accoutrements of holy objects. These objects are accoutrements associated with the *klei kodesh;* they enclose or activate them. Examples are the cover for a Torah scroll and the case that holds the mezuzah parchment. While in principle the *tashmishei kedushah* are considered to be more sacred when they are actually in use, in practice they are treated as "constantly holy." Just like the *klei kodesh,* they have an "inherent sanctity" and thus must be treated with special care and be handled in precise ways. Thus, for instance, when a cover is

removed from the Torah scroll being read, it is carefully set aside; and when it is time to "dress" the Torah once again, the "person who dresses the Torah" is considered to be receiving an honor. He or she is called up by name and can receive a special blessing.

3. *Tashmishei mitzvah:* Ritual implements. These objects do not have sanctity in themselves. They acquire sanctity when they are being used, as required, to fulfill a mitzvah, a commanded act. Unlike the *klei kodesh* and the *tashmishei kedushah,* they do not have to be handled with special care, because they do not contain or enclose God's name. They can even be thrown out, especially after they have already been used for their purpose. Examples of *tashmishei mitzvah* would be an *etrog* and a *lulav,* which both can be discarded after Sukkot. Heilman calls this class of objects "liminal," "para-sacred," "parasitic sharers in a charisma not altogether their own." Nonetheless, in practice, people tend to associate *tashmishei mitzvah* with *tashmishei kedushah,* and therefore choose to handle them with care—for instance, one might choose to carry one's tallit in a special protective bag or take care not to throw one's yarmulke on the floor. In some cases, *tashmishei mitzvah* are treated in Jewish law precisely like *tashmishei kedushah.* For instance, in the Talmud, we learn that a cup used to fulfill the commandment of saying a blessing over wine for the Grace after Meals must be treated in specific ways: "It must be rinsed and washed, it must be undiluted and full, it requires crowning and wrapping, it must be taken up with both hands and placed in the right hand, it must be raised a handbreadth from the ground, and one who says the blessing must fix one's eyes on it. Some add that one must send it around to members of the household (*Berakhot* 51a)."

4. *Reshut:* Optional ritual implements. These "quasi-sacred objects" have no inherent sanctity, as they are not required by law in order

to fulfill a mitzvah. Rather, they are optional: permitted, but not necessary or even mentioned in legal texts. Examples include a dreidl, a box to hold coins for charity, and a cutting board for challah. Yet in practice, these objects enhance or embellish the performance of Jewish ritual. They participate in *hiddur mitzvah,* literally meaning "the glorification of the commandment." They have what can be described as a "sacred feel." In fact, in Heilman's estimation, the more ornamented or artistic the *reshut* object is, the more sacred it can seem. Consider the beautiful, professionally crafted seder plate purchased at a Jewish museum, or the tallit bag that is individually designed and needlepointed. Heilman finds objects in this category of particular note.

> Although objects of Judaica have undoubtedly been affected by the changing context of Jewish life, the greater change by far has occurred in the domain of the . . . "quasi-sacred." This is because so much of this material is associated with custom and changing tradition and because these are affected more easily by the impact of acculturation. . . . It is safe to say that many of the objects which today are to be included among Judaica would not have been so catalogued at another time and it is not inconceivable that others will yet enter in the future while other objects will fall into disuse and become curios of a bygone era.

The Objects of the Wall

Before suggesting an alternative mode of categorization, I offer some description of the small "family" of objects that have found their way into the brief history of the Women of the Wall. They include: note cards, a women's Torah, T-shirts, pins, a Torah duffel, a coverlet, two types of tambourines, a *tallit katan,* and a *tallit gadol.*

WOMEN OF THE WALL NOTE CARDS

Several photographs taken by Barbara Gingold of WOW's initial prayers at the Wall were printed in Jerusalem and sold for fundraising until the supply ran out. The photograph, entitled "Women of the Wall, no. 1," is of Rabbi Geela Rayzel Raphael and Rivka Haut praying together at the Kotel next to the Torah. There is a third woman in the background, and it is interesting to note that the three women exhibit some of the range of women's prayer attire that can be seen in both pluralist and denominational settings. Raphael is wearing a prayer shawl made of an ornate nontraditional tallit fabric and no head covering; Haut wears a lace scarf draped over her head and no prayer shawl; the third woman is wearing a traditional prayer shawl and the Bucharan yarmulke favored by both men and women in the Jewish Renewal movement. The cards served to spread the image of women praying at the Wall when the issue was no longer covered in the secular and Jewish presses, creating a new icon of contemporary Jewish women's piety, one that contrasted with the inherited images of Jewish women praying behind the curtains of a synagogue balcony or, even more familiar, the Jewish woman praying alone before her Sabbath candles.

WOMEN'S TORAH

ICWOW was eventually able to purchase a Torah specifically for WOW so it would not have to borrow one. ICWOW leaders made a special expedition to Jerusalem with that Torah, speaking movingly of the historically significant trip as "women bringing the Torah to the Women of the Wall." Over time, the Women of the

Wall would decide how their Torah could be safely transported from the various places where it was temporarily stored to the Wall (where it could not be read during prayer services) to the site at the Archaeological Gardens (where it could be read). An army duffel was used.

FROM "HOLY DUFFEL" TO THE COVERLET

The possibility of a more elegant carrier for the WOW Torah came about when an ICWOW supporter, Sandy Lepelstadt, who originally offered to provide WOW with a *yad* (a pointer used for reading the Torah), was asked if she might instead underwrite the creation of an alternative gift that would bring dignity, beauty, and honor to WOW's Torah reading. Artist Rabbi Jinny Roth Isserow, who had designed the ICWOW T-shirt (see below) was willing to create what she called a "duffel-bag *aron.*" She designed a prototype for what ICWOW affectionately and jokingly began to refer to in their internal e-mail correspondence as "Holy Duffel."

However, WOW feared that an elegant carrier might bring unwanted attention to the Torah they brought to the Wall, potentially endangering both the Torah and the women accompanying it. The plain duffel, inelegant and prosaic, did the job. Responding, Rabbi Roth Isserow designed and fabricated a coverlet with an applique of women of all ages to place on the table upon which the Torah would be read by WOW when it was brought to the safety of the Archaeological Gardens. WOW received the coverlet as a gesture of solidarity, a sign of the presence and support of the international community of supporters.

WOMEN OF THE WALL PINS, T-SHIRTS, AND *TALLITOT*

Leah Gordon of Pasadena, California, designed and created pins that were sold briefly at the Wall when Rosh Chodesh services were held to support WOW. Although these pins did not catch on, they did serve briefly as a way for WOW supporters to express pride, commitment, and solidarity.

These days there is no cause, no institution, no class reunion that does not have its own fundraising and identity-building T-shirt, and ICWOW was to be no exception. Rabbi Jinny Roth Isserow produced a magnificent T-shirt depicting women praying and dancing with the Torah at the Kotel. Printed on white T-shirts, the image is of a Wall of pink stones with tufts of greenery before which tiny women, holding a Torah, dance. These shirts were initially sold at the Wall at WOW Rosh Chodesh davening and were later made available to supporters abroad through the mail. The handling and shipping activities connected with these T-shirts could be construed as tedious work, but we could also see them as *avodah*, sacred work and worship, not unlike the minute sacred tasks carried out by priests in the ancient Temple.

The tallit came about in discussions between Jerusalem Councilwoman and WOW activist Anat Hoffman and Bezalel-trained artists Yair and Yael Emanuel of Jerusalem. The *tallitot* are decorated with flowers of Israel and the names of the matriarchs.

A *tallit katan* created by a WOW activist, who herself wears one, was sold in Israel. It has not caught on in the United States, as most Jewish women who wear a *tallit gadol* do not wear a *tallit katan.*

A portion of the earnings of all these creations (negotiated with each artist) has been donated to ICWOW and WOW to cover legal and administrative fees.

WOMEN OF THE WALL TAMBOURINES

In 1992, Philadelphia Judaica artist Betsy Platkin Teutsch created a tambourine to honor and support WOW and ICWOW. Nearly a thousand tambourines have been sold, raising thousands of dollars that have gone toward defraying legal costs. In 1999, Teutsch created a second tambourine, and it has been sold to help WOW and other Jewish feminist causes. Both tambourines have been used to accompany the singing and dancing at feminist seders and Jewish women's retreats and conferences; they have been given as gifts at baby-naming and bat mitzvah ceremonies; they have been included as ritual objects in Passover seders and *havdalah* ceremonies and have been used as healing amulets (even hung on intravenous poles!). Many are displayed in the homes or offices of Jewish feminists; when hung on the wall or displayed on a shelf or table, these tambourines seem to say, "The spiritual freedom of Jewish women is a cause in which I believe." Teutsch has been told that the tambourines have had the power to "shape a life moment." How they will eventually be used in liturgy and as "objects de Judaica" remains to be discovered.

At this moment, the tambourines have only partially found their way into the WOW davenings at the Wall. According to a February 3, 1998, e-mail to WOW and ICWOW directors from WOW activist Chaia Beckerman of Jerusalem:

> Tambourines—I brought one to Rosh Chodesh Shevat, and was dying to take it out during Hallel, but we davened at the Kotel, where I fear the *repercussions of percussion*. Only one was sold. The cost is prohibitive for many in the Israeli group, and so far no visitors have stepped forward. The main thing—I still have plenty of tambourines to dance together with Miriam in this week's *parshah*. *Az yashir* . . . Israel (and all) women: we must inspire one another to sing! *Az nashir* (and then we shall sing).

The image on the first tambourine, called "Thanks for the Chair," is of a women's service at the Wall. On the women's side of the *mechitzah* are nine adult Jewish women and two small girls; they are in the midst of the Torah service. The women are dressed in a variety of sacred garments, expressive of the range of Jewish women who are now attiring themselves for prayer. A tenth adult woman flies over the top of the *mechitzah* to "make the minyan." She is Miriam the prophetess, with a tambourine in her hand. She is not the Hollywood image of an ingenue with long, dark hair and the perfect features of "a Semitic beauty" who looks as if she were about to appear in an Israeli dance festival. Rather, she is a grown woman, perhaps in her forties of fifties, her hair covered in a kerchief, and her eyes, big and dark, match the eyes of all the other women.

The second tambourine, entitled "Women at the Sea," illustrates a multigenerational group of Jewish women who look like a blend of the biblical Miriam and Israelite women and a group of Jewish women at a contemporary Jewish Renewal retreat. Depicting the women's victory dance after crossing the sea, it demonstrates that contemporary Jewish women identify with Miriam, who was empowered to use her voice, her instrument, and her dancing body as expressions of faith. Teutsch noted that the new tambourine "needs less explanation, since the context is accessible and familiar to people" (personal conversation, May 30, 1999).

Interestingly, at about the same time, Lubavitch women were also selling tambourines and creating out of them an old-new Jewish women's ritual object during the months prior to the 1994 death of the Lubavitcher Rebbe. Many Lubavitch women I encountered believed that their rebbe would not die but rather would arise as the messiah. They made the analogy between the optimistic

Miriam and her timbrels and the modern Lubavitch women who would demonstrate their optimism and faith by having their own tambourines ready for the coming of the messiah. Just before the rebbe's death, at his funeral, and in the weeks of mourning, Lubavitch women were distributing plain tambourines and were decorating them with puff paints and ribbons. Some were hung on walls and others were carried everywhere, in baby-bags, backpacks, and in the carrying pouches of strollers. Today, decorated tambourines are still available for purchase in the shops in Crown Heights. They feature images of the Old City of Jerusalem, a cameo-like photograph of the late Lubavitcher Rebbe, and the words, in Hebrew, "Welcome, King Messiah."

All these tambourines, thematically linked to the prophetess Miriam, have been and continue to be conduits through which new Jewish women's rituals are constructed, tried out, formally introduced, popularized, developed, and transmitted. These objects reflect the process by which "contemporary Jewish women have struggled to retrieve a usable past."² The tambourines symbolically belong to Miriam, or to the part of Miriam that resonates within each celebrant. Judaism evolves by reconstructing cultural reality in ways otherwise overlooked.

Although the tambourine clearly is a musical instrument, its musical capacity is rarely developed among Jewish women, who use it more as a prop in identifying themselves as Miriam's heirs. Like Miriam, whose narrative and actions are always linked to the community of Israelites, the tambourine has its origins in the living Jewish community. Being created for use in homes or in women's gatherings, the tambourine is free from constraints that might have been imposed were it intended for synagogue use.

Reflecting upon the Objects: Applying the Ancient Categories to the Wall and Other Objects of Women of the Wall

Within Heilman's system of classification, what category does the Wall fit into? Clearly, it is not among the *klei kodesh*, as God's name is not written upon it. Speaking poetically, however, one might say that Jews who have prayed and cried at the Wall through the years have "inscribed" God's name on the Wall through their words and their tears. (In fact, in the nineteenth century, visitors to the Wall would literally inscribe their own names on the Wall, a practice that was ended.)

It also could be argued that as people write tiny messages to God called *kvitlach* and place them in the crevices of the Wall (or even send faxed or e-mailed prayers to the Wall), the Wall might be included among the *tashmishei kedushah*, as it holds slips of paper that *might* have God's name written on them, and hence it encloses *klei kodesh.* This seems unlikely, as *kvitlach* are not treated as sacred objects—no one rises in their presence, anyone can write them in anyway whatsoever, they are left out in the rain, and when they fall from the Wall, they are swept away unceremoniously by workers.

Is the Wall, like the *tashmishei mitzvah,* an object that acquires sanctity when it is being used to fulfill a mitzvah? Although one may fulfill the mitzvah of saying the mandatory prayer services or reading the Torah or rejoicing in a bar mitzvah at the Wall, could one really say that a place that serves as a backdrop for a mitzvah is "being used to fulfill" the mitzvah? If that were so, that would mean that a catering hall or hotel ballroom, when used as a setting for fulfilling the mitzvah of marriage, acquired sanctity, at least temporarily. Some would accept this; others would not.

Should the Wall be included among the *reshut* objects? We have already seen that within this system the Wall neither possesses inherent sanctity nor is it required by law in order to fulfill a mitzvah. One could argue that the Wall fits among the *reshut* objects, as it enhances or embellishes the performance of any Jewish ritual that takes place in its presence. If the Wall is a *reshut* object—and I believe that Heilman is correct when he says that *reshut* objects are "most associated with custom and changing tradition"—then we might conclude that the Wall, its meanings, and its traditions and rules for use will be deeply influenced by acculturation, the ways of behaving and observing as a Jew that reflect the influences of time, place, and culture. This would suggest that the Wall has been and currently is among the Jewish ritual objects most highly shaped and altered by human experiences.

Ultimately, although the ancient categories might satisfactorily explain the dreidl or the tallit bag, I am not convinced that they work sufficiently to make systematic sense of the Wall, an icon that seems to contain the whole range of Jewish memory. The ancient categories may fall short for us when we consider not only the Wall but also any of the other objects that have become part of Women of the Wall's worship.

One object used by WOW, the Torah itself, can be categorized among the *klei kodesh*. The coverlet, upon which the Torah scroll is placed, can be categorized among *tashmishei kedushah*. The other objects are more difficult to categorize along traditional lines, as they merge characteristics of *tashmishei mitzvah* and *reshut*. Their sacredness in the context of WOW extends beyond these narrow boundaries.

In summary, I propose that we consider that all the objects used by WOW and ICWOW link the women who use them to four traditional Jewish ritual practices concerning charity, communication, transmission, and symbolic identification.

1. *Charity.* The object creates opportunities for the purchaser to give *tzedakah* (charity).

2. *Communication* (or, publicizing the miracle). The objects allow those who encounter, use, wear, or display them to engage others in conversation about the issue of the right of women to pray at the Wall. The term *pirsumei ha-nes* is most familiar in the context of Hanukkah, when Jews are obliged to light their menorahs in a place where they can be seen by those who pass by in order to publicize the miracle of the holiday. (Originally, the lights were lit outside the house; now, they are usually lit in a window.) In the context of Hanukkah, the message publicized is that it is not enough for those who recall God's gracious miracles to recall them and retell them in the privacy of their homes. One needs to spread the story for others to learn or remember, and one needs to identify oneself as belonging to those for whom this memory of the miracle is central. In the context of Women of the Wall, when one wears a WOW T-shirt or displays a WOW tambourine, one is inevitably saying to others, "This means that I am a supporter of WOW." It obliges the supporter to tell the story of the tenacity of WOW (which seems more miraculous as the years go by without our cry being heard) and to imagine together what a miracle would be celebrated on the day when Jewish women of the world can gather freely to pray together at the Wall. Most dramatically, one who stands with WOW at the Wall announces that through the placement of her body, she approaches God.

3. *Education.* Jews are obliged to teach the key sacred stories to their children, speaking about them at home and wherever they go. She who wears a WOW T-shirt, wears a WOW tallit, or uses or displays a WOW tambourine is inevitably bound to find more ways to tell the story of the denial of spiritual rights to Jewish women,

to her own family, and to those she encounters in her life. By the object, she is reminded that the story bears repetition, lest listeners assume that it is an inconsequential issue or that it has been happily resolved or sadly abandoned. The obligation to tell the story to one's children (or one's students) recognizes that it is possible that the work of WOW may not be accomplished in the lifetime of the founders, and that the vision and the strategy must be passed on to the next generation. This, in fact, is already being done, as we see our daughters and students praying at the Wall with WOW, first with us, and then, when they grow older, on their own, and as the next generation takes on supportive responsibilities.

4. *Transmission.* At the Passover seder, one recites, "In every generation, one is obligated to see oneself as having personally gone out from Egypt." To that end, one physically touches or eats the Passover symbols of shankbone, matzo, and bitter herbs in order to have the visceral experience of imagining oneself as an Israelite who was rescued from slavery and rejoiced in freedom. Like the Passover symbols, the new ritual objects of WOW, when worn or displayed, make one feel as if she personally prayed at the Wall, survived the hail of metal chairs, and braced herself to focus her concentration to keep on praying. Thus, the bearer of the objects needn't feel bad for not literally being in Jerusalem with the Women of the Wall this month (or at all), just as one who offers prayers and not sacrifices at the Holy Temple still has the experience of being in God's presence.

PHYLLIS CHESLER

Toward a Psychology of Liberation: Feminism and Religion—a Conclusion

WHEN I VISIT ISRAEL, I usually go straight to the Kotel. My former husband, an Israeli, treated this as a diaspora aberration, but he always solicitously waited for me while I prayed. In 1977, when I was pregnant, my physician called and told me that I would have a son. In *With Child: A Diary of Motherhood,* I write, "It's late Friday afternoon. A holy quiet has begun in the city. I go to the Kotel and press my stomach against it. Idly, perversely, I think to go to the men's side, claiming my rightful presence there. I contain a male child. They'd probably stone me to death. 'Hear, O Israel, I am One. Mother and Child. Male and Female. Past and Future.'"[1]

For years, the Israel I visited was the feminist Israel. This time too (1988), Israeli feminists met my plane and drove me to Haifa, where I toured the shelter for battered women and rape crisis centers—services that I'd only envisioned when I first visited Haifa in the early 1970s. I remember having coffee with then Knesset member and ardent secularist Marcia Freedman, and joking, wistfully, about whether in the future a plaque would be mounted to note where such shelters—which did not yet exist—once stood. In 1975, MK Freedman and other Israeli feminists wanted to "demonstrate" at the Kotel. (I remember lettering a placard in Hebrew that read: "If the rabbis want the Kotel, then let them leave the Knesset.") Martin Buber's granddaughter and an ex-Berrigan nun who had recently converted to Judaism were among those who planned to join us; a group of feminists was coming from the Negev. We called this off. Religious Jewish women were not ready to claim sacred ground.

In November 1988, I lectured at the Haifa Women's Center to a standing-room-only crowd of Israeli activist leaders. When I talked about a feminist government in exile, Nabila Espanioly, a Palestinian feminist, announced, to general laughter, that now she understood that her struggle was for a feminist as well as a Palestinian state. "And," she said, "I'll probably see a Palestinian state long before we'll ever have a feminist state."

I was in Israel to attend the First International Jewish Feminist Conference in Jerusalem, which had been coordinated by the American Jewish Congress and the Israel Women's Network. On their behalf, at our first meeting as a conference, the late Bella Abzug, *z"l*, ordered us to turn out the next morning to demonstrate against the Orthodox rabbinate and the State of Israel on the issue of "who is a Jew." I stood up, protested, and asked in what way this issue was a feminist one, and might we not first achieve an understanding of the issue more democratically before we allowed ourselves to be led like sheep to The Headline.

"You," she bellowed, "sit down."[2]

A few hours after participating in a plenary session on women and religion, I heard that women were meeting to plan a prayer service at the Kotel. The room was packed, the mood both electrified and somber. Once it became clear that the American Jewish Congress had already sent out a press release, I got everyone to agree that we would not talk to the media but would, instead, only say, "We have come to pray." As women started to leave, one woman remained seated, wringing her hands. "Don't go," she implored. "Why do you have to go? We can pray right here in the hotel." These were the words of one of Israel's leading Orthodox feminists. I was shocked. "But you must come with us," I said. Her fearful face remained agonized. Sadly, she did not join us.

One by one, I sought out my North American feminist colleagues. "Please come with us," I said, "this is important." Disgust, scorn, and impatience crossed their faces. Most would not join us. Years later, many changed their minds, but no one ever acknowledged to me privately that she'd misjudged the importance of this Orthodox-inspired grassroots feminist moment.

I returned to my room at 2:00 A.M. I was hot, I was cold, I was hungry, I was nauseous. Why am I doing this? I'd averaged about two hours of sleep each night since I'd left New York seven days earlier. Clearly, it was beyond me to go; I'd pushed myself too hard. I canceled my wake-up call. Nevertheless, I was dressed and ready long before the agreed-upon meeting time of 6:50 A.M. I had a tape recorder running in my handbag. I wanted the police to have a record in case we were attacked.

A small group of us tightly "guarded" a gaunt, ecstatic Francine Klagsbrun as she carried the Torah. When we reached the Kotel, the women swiftly donned their *tallesim* (angel's wings, capes of sheltering glory), their prim head scarves and exotic skullcaps—and they became Jews. We stood before the Wall, under the morning sky, and began the Thursday morning service.

Without knowing it, this is what I'd longed for all through my Orthodox, Borough Park childhood. This was my missing link, a dream come alive—my dream, "*halom halamti*," "I dreamed a dream," words that we in fact read in *Vayeshev*, the Torah portion of that week.[3] I was lost in time, in a reverie. "Would you do us the honor of uncovering the Torah for us?" Rivka Haut asked me. It was a transformative honor. It wedded me fatefully, faithfully, to this struggle. Years later, I asked her, "Why me?" Her answer: "You had such an otherworldly expression on your face."

We had stepped onto holy ground, experienced a moment in time in which we constituted a sacred congregation; we'd had a glimpse of what might be possible if women dared to claim their religious inheritance without patriarchal approval or support. The power has lasted. For example, whenever I meet another first-time davener, we both smile, from deep within, and embrace. Words barely matter. We greet each other not as the strangers we truly are, but as participants in holiness. On that day, praying in an all-female group felt right, miraculous. This feeling carried us that day, and forever after, high above the roar of ugly sound that rose, higher and higher, louder and louder against us. It was the sound of a riot, a lynch mob, Khomeini's men in tefillin and *tallesim,* our psychologically and theologically challenged brothers. We hastily concluded our service and reboarded the waiting buses.

Jubilation was ours. Rabbi Deborah Brin, who had led the davening, asked, "How do you say 'Right on!' in Hebrew?" We cheered, clapped, wept, laughed, talked, and exchanged names. I passed around a sign-up sheet. By midafternoon, I suggested to Rabbis Brin and Helene Ferris that we return to the Kotel for the evening service.

Clearly, I was out of my mind, high.

"Rivka," I said, "we've just crossed a psychological sound-barrier. This is a major event in history." She simply said, "Do you really think so?" Oh, I did; I still do. "Crossing over" is so Jewish a venture: from a pagan worldview to a monotheistic one, from this world to the next one, from daily life to sacred time. *Ivrim* (Hebrews) literally means those who "cross over": Avraham's rivers, miraculously parted Red Sea waters, the Jordan River into The Land.

In my view, the act of women praying with a Torah at the Kotel has the power to psychologically transform the way Jewish women see themselves and each other. When this becomes an everyday sight, Jewish women and men will have undergone another sea-crossing. The consequences will be subtle, continuous, enormous, and ever-reverberating.

Alas, many otherwise enlightened people underestimate the psychological importance of organized religion and religious symbols. As a liberation psychologist, I'd been writing about female role models, and about God's female face, since the early 1970s. As long as we psychologically continue to envision God (or Jews) as tall white men with long white beards, the goals of gender equality will never be realized. Thus, I believe that our struggle will have a profound psychological impact on Jewish women's self-esteem and respect for each other in every area.

I had theorized about this for years. Putting such theories into action had eluded me—until now. And what a grand, symbolic action it was. I had, therefore, expected broad feminist support for this struggle. I was naive. What we experienced instead, at least initially, was profound apathy and some hostility from both secular and religiously active feminists who had left either organized Judaism or Orthodox Judaism. Many had sound reasons, which nevertheless did not make their lack of support less painful. It took me a while to understand that our struggle had no "natural" constituency. That existed only in the future. In our lifetime, it might remain entirely mystical in nature.

In the diaspora, feminist Reform, Reconstructionist, and Conservative Jews were, understandably, ambivalent about supporting a women-only, non-minyan prayer group. As Jews, and as feminists, they had fought very hard for egalitarian mixed-gender minyans, new God-language, and women's right to be ordained as rabbis. In 1990, feminist theologian Judith Plaskow published a piece in *Tikkun* magazine in which she argued that what we were doing sacrificed egalitarian principles to Orthodox principles, and that we would never "win by playing things safe." Although she viewed our struggle as "sacred," she also thought it was "only one very small step in the larger transformation of Judaism." We disagreed with her in the pages of *Tikkun*. To her feminist credit, Plaskow met with us, withdrew her own response to our letter, signed a joint statement instead, and agreed to join our board. Other commitments made it difficult for her to stay.[4]

Like Plaskow, most religiously active feminists in North America are staunch egalitarian integrationists. They are used to praying in mixed-gender minyans. They do not want to compromise this principle or desert their denominational affiliation. They could not understand why, as a group, we were willing to give up saying certain prayers that require a minyan (e.g., *Barkhu* and Kaddish), in order to pray together at the Kotel.[5]

I live in Park Slope, Brooklyn, which is multiracial, multiethnic. It is populated by old leftist, antiracist, and feminist activists; young, out lesbians and homosexuals; families with young children; trendy cafes and bookstores; lawyers, social workers, therapists, teachers, poets, rabbis, a shelter for battered women; and the odd citizen who actually supports whatever government is in power. My Conservative egalitarian shul reflects our population.

Most feminist egalitarians tend to be gender-neutral and there-fore liberals—which is no crime; some of my best friends are lib-erals. However, gender-neutrality and integration are not always in women's best interests. For example, girls and young women often do better in girl- and women-only schools; gender-neutral legisla-tion sometimes has been used against battered women and custo-dially and economically embattled mothers. (Of course, what preceded gender-neutral legislation was also used against women.) However, since men remain the gender-neutral standard for what is considered "human," many employers still do not provide coverage for birth control for women. Some employee health plans cover abortion and some don't, but most do cover Viagra. Of course, gender-neutral legislation has also benefited both women and men; the want ads as well as many jobs are no longer segregated by gen-der, and students of both sexes are increasingly entitled to the same educational and athletic opportunities.

Orthodox women, including feminists, are not always egalitari-an, gender-neutral integrationists. Politically speaking, some are radical, others liberal, still others quite conservative. Many Ortho-dox women tend to be essentialists who believe that men and women are different; some may even believe that women are supe-rior or inferior as a result. My experiences of anti-Semitism among non-Jewish and Jewish feminists in the early 1970s and at the Unit-ed Nations (where I worked at the end of that decade) drove me to spend some time with "out" Jews. Only Orthodox Jews were "out." I spent some time in Crown Heights. My Shabbos hostess was a Lubavitcher Hasidic woman. She once took me aside and said, "Let the men have their titles and their public displays of importance. They are not as strong as women. Men need this encouragement. We give birth to life. Our every act is holy. We are

341

always close to God, not just when we pray." I told her, "Perhaps you're right, but you sound just like a radical lesbian separatist."

Patriarchal Judaism and painful Jewish family dynamics have sent so many Jews "out" to practice Jewish ethics on behalf of other tribes, often with no understanding that they are practicing *religious* Jewish ethics. Thus, praying in a women-only group so that Jewish women of all denominations would be able to pray together may not have been seen as a radical enough feminist effort. Ironically, many feminist, egalitarian, and progressive Jews are quite comfortable working for the material or educational needs of women, including those of other tribes, religions, classes, or races. To date, they have not valued the potential importance of working for the religious and spiritual needs of all Jewish women, including Orthodox women.

The denominational wars continue to rage among religious Jews; secular and antireligious Jews are not attracted by the commotion. Even if I, personally, have other prayer options, because Orthodox women have pioneered women-only prayer groups, it is a feminist act to join them—if only at the Kotel. Women of the Wall wish to remain "connected" to *Klal Yisrael;* we'd rather be whole than right; we do not want to win on principle but lose each other in so doing.[6]

During this struggle, I learned that the most important feminist support we had was not necessarily "out there," but "in here"; it was the support that the handful of us gave each other by doing the work and refusing to give up. How could we? We believe that women are Jews, created "in God's image"; that our souls yearn for freedom, without which we cannot serve God; and that, painfully, the pharaoh we face is Jewish and sometimes even feminist.

Almost immediately after our first prayer service, I invited Rivka Haut to accompany me to *Tikkun* magazine's first national conference in December 1988. She was reluctant. "Are you sure that these people will be interested in this?" "Yes," I insisted, "trust me, it will be all right." I was so wrong. Michael Lerner graciously allowed me to speak at the opening plenary; Arthur Waskow, in full, flowing beard, kept beaming as I spoke. The feminists who had signed up for my workshop, however, were disgusted. Within five minutes, one woman angrily protested, "I did not come here to discuss the psychology of prayer or religion." A second woman said, "I don't believe in God. If I did, it would be in a goddess and not necessarily a Jewish one. Patriarchal religion oppresses women, it does not liberate us."

It would take years before I was able to master this dialogue, years before feminist Jews would understand that the right to practice one's religion is as important as the right to live without being religiously coerced, and that women are entitled to spiritual as well as physical and economic autonomy and integrity.

Within months of that first prayer service, female worshipers at the Kotel were met with violence. We founded ICWOW, turned each of our home offices and kitchen tables into "WOW Central," were on the phone to Jerusalem, organized and publicized our Solidarity Services for WOW under siege, struggled to have ICWOW become a nonprofit organization, and initiated a grassroots campaign to purchase a Torah and donate it to WOW. We celebrated its dedication under the Jerusalem stars. I wanted to hire our own private security detail because our lives had been threatened. No one harmed us, but threatened with the loss of its kashrut license, the Laromme hotel refused us the room we had booked. We found a nearby schoolhouse and celebrated and read from the Torah there. In 1989, Women of the Wall became name-plaintiffs in the Israeli supreme court. ICWOW joined within a year. I continued to recruit new women to our board, write press releases, talk to the Jewish media, and attend board meetings. I also became our fundraiser.

WOW has been the recipient of great passion and admiration and of great hostility and opposition. Often we have functioned like a Rorschach test. Those who are afraid of and angry at misogynist Orthodoxy see us as too Orthodox and project their anger onto us; those who are angry at secular and anti-Orthodox Jews see us as too radically feminist and likewise project their anger onto us. We have absorbed a great deal of neglect, opposition, misunderstanding, excitement, love, and deep appreciation. ICWOW has slipped through these polarized restrictions into the interstices to become a stubborn, active force in history, defying expectations, representing no one except ourselves.

We must be doing something right to excite so much passion among so many.

Israeli feminist support was, initially, nonexistent. In the mid-1970s, I remember listening to a heated conversation among some secular feminist sabras in Jerusalem. The feminist criticism of the Israeli government and Orthodox rabbinate was so intense, so extreme, that, tongue-in-cheek, I suggested that they apply to Saudi Arabia for political asylum. Now, the hard-heartedness of some of my longtime secular Israeli feminist comrades was even worse. "Phyllis, have you taken leave of your senses? What are you doing with these God-besotted fundamentalists?" Eventually, after many years, some Israeli feminist secularists "got it"—that is, they realized that the right to practice one's religion is as important as the right not to do so. Some ardently secular Israeli feminists began to treat this struggle with puzzled but grudging respect. For example, Shulamit Aloni, who was well known as Israel's antireligious Knesset member, offered to help us quietly.[7]

Initially, the Israel Women's Network (IWN) tried to join the lawsuit. Unfortunately, the Court refused them standing. From that moment on, Dr. Alice Shalvi, IWN's tireless, eloquent, and accomplished director, repeatedly told North American feminist and progressive philanthropists that our lawsuit and struggle were entirely "marginal" to Israeli women; that the majority of WOW's members were recent immigrants from English-speaking countries and therefore did not speak for "real" Israeli women. Although Shalvi did testify on our behalf before one of two Knesset commissions, her persistent criticism and refusal to support us was keenly felt.

For years, another leading Israeli feminist, Leah Shakdiel, who herself had won an important legal victory, did not support us.[8] However, for a variety of reasons, Shakdiel, a hero to Orthodox feminists for her struggle to be admitted to the Religious Council of her city, distressed many of them by publicly and privately criticizing WOW as a group and especially some of the ritual practices of some of its young Orthodox members.

One might argue that ICWOW's kind of activism is revolutionary in that it brings Jewish women of every denomination together and gives Orthodox women access to public group prayer as only Orthodox men and non-Orthodox Jews currently enjoy it. ICWOW may also represent a new kind of religious pluralism, another visionary and pro-Orthodox way of approaching God—one equal to that of equality feminism.

However, both secular and religious non-Orthodox feminist Jews mistrust the feminism of Orthodox women because Orthodox women are psychologically *conceived of,* from afar, as women who accept and seek to justify women's second-class citizenship in the synagogue. Non-Orthodox feminists ask, What does it mean to be committed to women-only prayer in the women-only section next to a *mechitzah* at the Kotel? Will ICWOW set feminist progress back? Are we playing into the hands of our misogynist opponents?

Many Orthodox women—including those who are judges, physicians, stockbrokers, and professors—do have different and more burdensome family obligations than their male counterparts. (This is true for most other groups, too.) In general, Orthodox girls and women are not given the same amount of time to study as boys and men are given, nor are they intellectually and religiously mentored, as boys and men are, to inherit positions of religious authority. Most Orthodox women do not oppose this; however, the Orthodox feminists do. Amazingly, paradoxically, a potentially transformative revolution in religious learning among Orthodox girls and women is also underway.

After countless conversations (and countless media misperceptions of us), I came to understand that most people, including feminists, tend to judge ICWOW mainly in denominational but not in feminist terms. Few consider the possibility that compassionate identification with the spiritual needs of all Jewish women is as much a feminist priority as constituting an egalitarian minyan is.

Many people continue to resist understanding that we are the *only* multidenominational and pluralist prayer group among Jews, that male Jews of different denominations do not pray together—anywhere, not even at the Kotel. This is WOW's great feminist achievement. It is an achievement made possible by the persistence and hard work of only a handful of grassroots "kitchen table" feminists and by our conscious decision to make sacrifices and take risks in order that women of every Jewish denomination will, in the future, be able pray together in the *ezrat nashim* at the Kotel.

Early in 1989, I called upon Jonathan Jacoby, then at the New Israel Fund (NIF), for help. He did not hesitate. He immediately led me to Lynda Bronfman and Linda Levinson, who together funded our entire legal bill for the first phase of the lawsuit. The American Jewish Congress, the New Israel Fund, the Reform movement, Kol Ishah, and US/Israel Women to Women also helped us in a variety of ways; they continue to do so, both here and in Israel. We have enjoyed no other organizational support, although many organizations and individuals have written letters on our behalf to various Knesset commissions.[9]

No one in Hollywood or on Wall Street ever emerged to fund "the real Yentl," as I put it in letter after letter beginning in 1989. Diaspora Jewish leaders have not financially supported us in a major way, but the people have. Our supporters are mainly religious people who have been influenced by feminism and who are acting in its name. Our supporters are not secular antireligious feminists— even though without their years of pioneering work, this struggle would probably never have taken place. Our grassroots support is enormous. Year after year, hundreds, perhaps thousands, of individuals, both men and women, have written significant, modest checks to ICWOW for WOW and have purchased WOW tambourines, *tallesim*, T-shirts, and greeting cards. A handful of small, woman-led family foundations have modestly funded us once, sometimes twice.[10]

I have fought as hard as the next feminist for my principles, but I have rarely committed myself to a long, arduous struggle merely because it was in my narrow "self-interest" to do so. (I personally will not be praying at the Kotel in the *ezrat nashim* every day; I neither pray with others every day nor do I live in Jerusalem.) One's capacity to transcend self-interest, even at one's own peril, always at one's own peril, renders one "dangerous," for such a person cannot always be contained by appealing to her or his self-interest.

Traditionally, women-only groups have been lesser places, less valued.[11] But— dare I say it? Women-only prayer groups are different from mixed-gender prayer groups and are worthy in and of themselves. Women-only praying together constitutes a powerful force, a unique vibration—not "better," not "worse," only "equal" and "different."

For example, last year I celebrated Simchat Torah in my egalitarian Conservative shul. We had several Torah scrolls out; a women-only group gathered at one. Two women were "in charge." Woman after woman came up for an *aliyah.* The first woman wept because it was her first *aliyah.* The second woman needed help in reciting the blessings. Quietly, lovingly, we helped her. There was no competition, shame, or terror here, only encouragement and collective pride. The moment two men came over and joined us— two perfectly nice men, by the way—the mood changed. Suddenly we all became a shade more uptight. Perhaps we felt that the men were watching and judging us; perhaps we wanted to be the gender in charge of everything and felt we'd lost our adult or psychological authority when men joined us. Perhaps one of the many ways of approaching God runs along gender lines. For example, I have noted that women hold the Torah like a beloved infant; men almost never do. Thus, mystically speaking, as women only, engaged in group prayer, we may radiate one hue and not another, constitute one vibration and not another.

Yet, imagine my situation. My liberal, progressive, left-leaning, secular feminist comrades were criticizing me for associating with fundamentalist (and presumably reactionary) women, and I was being viewed with ongoing suspiciousness by those very "fundamentalist" (and fabulously feminist) women. I must admit that my

Orthodox sisters both thrilled and terrified me. Their learning thrilled me, but I was terrified of their disapproval. In the 1940s and 1950s, I had rebelled against a rigid, joyless Borough Park Orthodoxy, one in which girls did not become bat mitzvah or become rabbis and cantors. My mother had suffered and become embittered by my brazen disobedience, which included embracing Zionism and much, much else. Would my new Orthodox comrades also reject me for being "different"? The fact that I now lived with a woman was not the problem. ("It's not against Halakhah to do so" was the immediate ruling on that issue.) Far more important were my friendships with prominent American feminist "goddess worshipers."

In November 1989, after we dedicated the Torah to the women of Jerusalem but before we signed on as name-plaintiffs in the Israeli Supreme Court, I was most unpleasantly grilled in a Jerusalem hotel room about whether or not I was a "goddess worshiper." I now understand that perhaps in some ways I was, but at the time the gravity of the question was lost on me. Of course, since then, I have both changed and clarified my views. Today, I might say that imagining God as a "He" or a "She" is, in a sense, "idol worship"—the idols, Rachel's *terafim,* are hidden not in our saddlebags but in our minds. In 1989, I refused to answer this question. I maintained that this is a private matter of faith and conscience, but because I'd worked so hard for us that first year, being so mistrusted unnerved me and broke my heart. I wrote a very beautiful, mournful, letter of resignation, but the letter was not accepted and we continued working together as before.

Participating in this struggle has deepened and transformed me in radical ways. Some might even say that I was merely returning to my roots. This is not exactly true. As I've noted, when I was a child, girls had no future in terms of learning; the women I knew did not pray together in a group or in a way that uplifted their spirits. Men remained the final and only religious authorities. Having prayed at the Kotel in 1988 allowed me to move toward something that I must have wanted all my life. Beginning in 1989, I began to study Torah informally, mainly with Rivka Haut and other Orthodox or previously Orthodox women. I have recently published my first *d'var Torah;* I hope to publish others soon. My modest learning fills me with joy and comforts me.

My new Orthodox sisters were, surprisingly, far more "righteously aggressive" in some ways than most of the liberal secular feminists whom I knew. For example, in 1989, WOW was being physically and verbally assaulted at the Kotel; the police refused to protect us or to arrest the perpetrators of violence. Each month, I spent hours on the phone with Jerusalem WOW members who were being attacked for trying to pray. What could I or ICWOW do? We learned that the Minister of Religious Affairs, Zvulun Hammer, was delivering a speech in Lawrence, Long Island, at an Orthodox synagogue. Name-plaintiff and New York City Council member Susan Alter is married to Gilbert Klapperman, who was the shul's rabbi at one time. Susan Alter, Susan Aranoff, Rivka Haut, and I descended en masse upon Lawrence. The moment Minister Hammer closed his mouth, my sisters were upon him. Their hands shot up; they were speaking, first one, then the other. The minister abruptly ended the public discussion, but he was not to escape. They were fierce, all over the man, all talking at once. We followed Minister Hammer into a side room, where we four women surrounded him. Everyone spoke at once, all in too-rapid Hebrew. "How dare you . . . you had better . . . we will go public . . . we demand protection for the Women of the Wall." Caught up, swept away, I, mainly in English, said that we would hold him personally responsible if a single hair on a single woman's head was harmed. I also felt a little sorry for him—he looked terrified. We were probably his worst nightmare. However, my Orthodox sisters knew that Orthodox rabbis and ministers could be corrupt, hypocritical, and dangerous to women, and they behaved accordingly.

I hadn't seen anything this confrontationally feminist since the late 1960s and very early 1970s. In a sense, theirs was a greater, not a lesser, bravery. These Orthodox women were not "exempt" from public scorn because Susan Alter's husband was the shul's former rabbi; on the contrary, they were exposing themselves and their families to potentially serious ostracism because of their beliefs.

At least ten variables characterize ICWOW's struggle for Jewish women's religious rights. Our struggle has been waged by (a) secularly and (b) religiously educated women who (c) live in a feminist era, (d) are influenced by feminist ideas, (e) are themselves religious or engaged in the feminist creation or refinement of Jewish ritual, (f) are committed to practicing, not just preaching, both feminist and religious principles, (g) were in the right place at the right time, and (h) were, from 1994 on, able to remain connected through e-mail technology. I also believe that this particular struggle has required (i) a model of feminism as service to others rather than a model of feminism as service to oneself and (j) the opportunity to "put one's body where one's ideas are." This was once the motto of European existentialist intellectuals; it also defines our struggle. It is crucial to fight for territory. In this case, the territory is both real and highly symbolic.

Questions remain. From a feminist and psychological point of view, is women's participation in traditional Jewish practice (either in women-only prayer groups or in gender-integrated groups) reactionary, revolutionary, or both? Is women-only space "settling for too little" when it allows women of all denominations to pray together? Can feminists engage in prolonged legal and political battles without fortifying themselves in a collective spiritual way? What unique approaches can religious feminist thought bring to bear against the mistreatment of women? In what ways does it help to conceive of violence against women, as well as women's inequality, as a sin against God? Does thinking like this empower feminist struggle?

The members of ICWOW often disagree with each other. I have come to think that we each represent a different hot-blooded "tribe," and that women have yet to work out our sibling, biblical rivalries. Over the years, ICWOW's boards came to understand that our differences did not matter as much as our common vision. We are proof that feminists can work together even when we disagree and are politically and theologically "different" from one another—as long as we respect and value one another for those very differences and remember to acknowledge each woman's accomplishments on our behalf. Women, feminists included, have such a long history of acrimonious dealings with one another that a little civility, generosity, and appreciation goes a long way. Women are inspired and encouraged by it, dispirited in its absence.

Despite the enormous inequality of the work load (we have, among us, a handful of "doers," a handful of "opinion granters," and a handful of "disappearing-reappearing" board members), we remain connected. Over the years, many of us have threatened to resign, not once but many times; some have dropped out for a while. Women drift in and out and assume different levels of responsibility; some are not heard from for months, even years, then suddenly they're back, adding their voice to the discussion. No one, not even I, dares say that so-and-so is no longer "one of us." No one gets removed from our e-mail group list unless she asks to be. Even those who remain quiet still read our discussions. Whoever can help, does so.[12]

I have been blessed with a capacity to work on a book for many years, in profound isolation, without the slightest encouragement, and to participate in a struggle like this for many years, with little support and against formidable opponents. No matter how heavy a work-burden this struggle has imposed upon me, no matter how much suffering bearing this burden has meant, I could never resign from this struggle or resign myself to losing it.

In a sense, the way our group has been publicly treated is the way that women, one by one, have been treated behind closed doors. Our public struggle is bringing this into the light. As feminists, we hold the perpetrators of such violence accountable. We challenge the traditional perception that women are unfit to stand on sacred ground, and we base this challenge on our love for and understanding of our tradition.

What do I think my own contribution has been? In addition to sometimes working almost full-time and around the clock on our behalf since 1989, subsidizing the struggle with my own funds and office resources, recruiting some of the "best and brightest" for our boards, perhaps my presence has served as a "bridge" between the denominationally identified women: it has allowed each woman to "see" how feminist all of us really are. Perhaps my former secular worldliness allowed the secularists who in time did come to support us to understand that this was indeed a radical feminist struggle for women's human rights.

I've learned a great deal. I've learned that it takes enormous patience to put one's principles into practice and that doing so is a process, that nothing important happens quickly. I've also learned that when a woman demands to be treated as a human being, even

353

if she defines her humanity as (only) a "separate but equal" place at her Father's table, she will be viewed as a revolutionary and treated accordingly: badly.

On March 6, 1996, while Israel reeled from four terrorist bomb attacks in Jerusalem and Tel Aviv, WOW went to the Kotel to read the story of how Esther saved the Jews of Persia. They dedicated their reading to Sara Duker, the young Jewish American woman who was killed in one of the Palestinian suicide bombings and who had been planning to join WOW at the Kotel for this Purim reading. No woman said, "Oh, it's the wrong time; there are more important things to worry about." No one wavered, hesitated, had the slightest doubt about the importance of what they were doing or worried about what others might think. For women, this is the first and most important (psychological) battle we have to win: not caring about what others may think, not seeking approval or popularity, being willing to risk discomfort and even danger for the sake of feminist principle. This kind of psychological self-sufficiency might serve as a model for all disenfranchised "others" who also wish to claim sacred ground.

On August 11, 2000, *The New York Times* printed a photo of three armed Israeli female soldiers reading from the Book of Lamentations on Tisha B'Av at the Kotel. It is very powerful. This image has psychological "legs"; it will travel like wildfire through our collective imaginations. In my view, women cannot succeed in politics or the professions until they are—and are seen as—capable of both defending the people and of talking to God on the people's behalf. Armed female soldiers at prayer are an entirely new sight. It evokes no previous memories. These three young women are, I think, three visitors (angels perhaps) from the future. I salute them.

CHAIA BECKERMAN, BETSY KALLUS,
AND RAHEL JASKOW

Epilogue: Rosh Chodesh Adar 5762 (2002)

ON WEDNESDAY MORNING, February 12, 2002, Rosh Chodesh Adar, Women of the Wall read from a Torah scroll at the Kotel. There were no riots, no thrown chairs or stones, no arrests. Indeed, hardly anyone noticed. A few women yelled at WOW, but nothing else happened. Rahel Jaskow and Betsy Kallus led the service; Haviva Ner-David and Aliza Berger *leyned* from the Torah.

It has taken WOW thirteen years to once again conduct a full prayer service at the Kotel. Whatever happens from now on, we know we will persist until the day comes when Jewish women will be as free as Jewish men to pray to God together at the Kotel.

Chaia Beckerman

It was a rainy, windy morning, but the turnout was surprisingly good. We have some real stalwart faithfuls here this year. We prayed *Shachrit* under umbrellas, during which time the weather cleared a bit, and Haviva suggested that since so few other women were at the Kotel and our singing the *tefillah* was attracting no attention whatsoever, we just read where we were, using the literature stand that appeared some months back, a kind of Plexiglass small table surface with compartments at the side for various pamphlets and brochures and an overhead surface bigger than the rest to keep rain off. We took a poll among the five *vatikot* (regulars) present (Anat, Haviva, Betsy, Rahel, and I), and we decided to go ahead. There was one abstention plus a lot of trepidation on my part.

During *Hallel,* a few women rolled the Torah to the right place, which worked well as a test to see if there would be any response. There was none—not surprisingly, since we had the table surrounded and it was visible only if one was passing right by, which few women were. It may even be that some of our own women, focused on their *tefillah,* didn't see what was happening and realized what we were planning only when we explained quickly after *Hallel.* (One woman to whom I spoke while the rolling was happening apparently left; she voiced concern that what we were doing was too provocative.) We made it clear to all that this had not been planned in advance, but rather, we saw an unexpected opportunity, and if the police asked us to stop, we would have to do so. In case of trouble, participants were to take their cues from the old-timers.

Betsy led the Torah service, giving the *aliyot* to the regulars, which is highly irregular for us. (Usually we ascertain who is celebrating a special occasion, has never had an *aliyah,* or has never been to Israel before, and we hand out the *aliyot* accordingly, but today we were not anxious to stretch out the proceedings!) Each of us added a fervent *shehecheyanu* after the concluding blessing. Anat and I clutched each other afterward, incredulous. Betsy's collective *Mi Sheberakh* for the event was replete with Adar and Purim references, and everyone chimed in with *layehudim hayta orah v'simcha v'sasson v'yikar* ("The Jews had light and gladness, joy and honor").

We had pulled it off. Had Na'ama Shiloni not brought a lot of heavy plastic with which we covered both table and Torah, we couldn't have done it in such weather.

We have been coordinating our prayer services with the police for many months. They usually stand back in the plaza. This time, we stood so they wouldn't see what we were doing. The police were cool at first but eventually upset that we were there so long, past the time when the police protection usually ends because we have gone upstairs. Unfortunately, the president of Jerusalem Emunah was at the Kotel and saw us and railed against us; I hope she vented enough to feel that she has no need to do anything further.

This certainly is not the first time we have seen how little the way events play out has to do with our endless plans and discussions. I think of the positions that I, for one, have advanced at countless meetings over the course of years: civil disobedience takes extensive groundwork, outreach, buildup, assigning of roles; we're not prepared for it yet. At the point we decide not to wait any longer, we should begin with the step of wearing *tallitot* at the Kotel—far less inflammatory than reading Torah. (How wrong I was; *tallitot* would have been far more obvious today than our encircled Torah!) And yet the moment came and we seized it, and while one can argue that we were better prepared to do so because of discussing hypothetical scenarios, the fact is that taking advantage of a rainy day was not one of them. Some women, hearing that it has been thirteen years since we opened the Torah at the Kotel, commented that this was a bat mitzvah celebration. Quite apt, and then again, so different from elaborate visions discussed in the spring and summer of 2000, of women coming from near and far to mark our twelve-year-anniversary visions, now overtaken by geopolitical events.

It was exciting and moving. *Shehecheyanu v'kiyimanu v'higiyanu la'zman hazeh!* What a privilege to say this after an *aliyah* at the Kotel! *Kol hakavod* to all who came and participated. Danielle and other regulars were sorely missed. *Yasher koach* to all those who have supported us over the years.

Betsy Kallus

This was an historic occasion. It was pouring. A typical rainy Rosh Chodesh of this sort usually would mean that we would have fewer than ten people. Today, thanks to the hard work of Na'amah Shiloni and the volunteers, we had close to twenty, including visitor Rabbi Melanie Aron from Las Gatos, California. We were also quite strong in the local department with Chaia, Anat, Haviva, Rahel, me, and a few others. Rahel led *Shachrit.* Near the end of *Shachrit,* we made the decision to stay at the Kotel, given the fact that it was pouring and there was no response to our presence on either side. Interestingly, during the middle of *Shachrit,* we heard loud shouting on the men's side. It turns out that the feelings of some group of daveners had been offended by another group of daveners. I guess we are not the only ones who get yelled at! Anyway, we decided to stay there. During *Hallel,* we quickly rolled the Torah to the right place in *Parshat Pinchas.* I led the Torah service. When it came time to march the Torah around, someone said not to march around, so as not to draw attention to us. I gave *aliyot* to the veteran members of the group, including Anat, Rahel, Chaia, and myself. Each of us added a fervent *shehecheyanu* after our concluding blessing. I gave all of us a collective *Mi Sheberakh* for the event. We wrapped up the Torah, and during this part I did march with the Torah because if we had not attracted attention by this time, when would we?

Rahel concluded *Musaf* quickly, given the police pressure to move on.

As the Torah service ended, the head of Emunah Jerusalem, who is also a member of the city council, came over and began to berate us. Peggy Cidor, WOW's coordinator, quickly deflected her by asking her to be interviewed on the camera by the Beit Berl students who had come to film us, as they were working on a project about us. Since she is a politician, I hope that she was satisfied with this attention.

Chodesh tov and *yasher koach* to all of us.

Rahel Jaskow

It was raining, and grateful as I was for that, still I dreaded an hour-long davening in the rain, since the women's section is completely open to the elements (unlike the men's section, which has lots of indoor space). We completed *Shachrit* and *Hallel,* which we usually do at the Kotel before going upstairs to the Jewish Quarter for the Torah service and *Musaf.* I was leading, and two friends of mine took turns holding an umbrella over me.

I was pretty scared this morning, along with everybody else, when we made our decision. In fact, I joked, "Can I abstain?" But I voted in favor just the same. This morning's experience reminded me of something I once read in a book about a women's food taboo in Hawaiian culture. One day, a group of women decided to defy the taboo. They ate together in the darkness, terrified that they might die instantly and clutching each other for support. Once they proved to themselves that they could eat those foods safely, they returned to their men and told them that the taboo was off. Sometimes I think this last bit probably took more guts than the actual deed itself!

Once the decision to complete our service at the Kotel was made, the atmosphere seemed to change. I sang *Hallel* with all the concentration I had, and everyone was right there with me. Somewhere deep down I felt that everything would be all right, but I still wasn't completely sure. More than thirteen years before, an angry mob had thrown chairs at women's heads the last time women had dared to read from a *sefer Torah* here. Had thirteen years of seeing us every month praying, but without a Torah, changed anything? I fervently hoped so. During *Hallel,* one woman came and scolded us for singing aloud. My job was to keep singing no matter what, and that's what I did. I think someone else might have tried to talk to her.

The rain tapered off just in time for the Torah service, and we dried the structure and got it ready. We held the Torah service with great excitement, but we kept our feelings low-key so as not to attract too much attention. Our trepidation was palpable, but as the reading progressed smoothly, so did our joy. Even the police officer assigned to guard us was impressed by the level of emotion. I got the last *aliyah* and thought, "Surely somewhere we have ancestors who would have given all they possessed for a moment like this." For the first time, I realized fully how special it is to be able to pray there. Each woman who received an *aliyah* said *shehecheyanu.* At the end, I led *Etz Chaim Hi* in full voice, thinking, "This is it, we've done it, and nothing's happened." We read Torah at the Kotel in full view of anyone who cared to watch, and no one threw anything. We're safe and sound and free. We can sing to God out loud here, and nothing will happen to us. I was almost floating.

Some women saw what we were doing and came to scold us. One said, "You're committing a transgression. May God have mercy on you." And I, high as a kite by that time, said softly, "He already has."

One of us was wearing a tallit that day: me. The crimson wool cape I made for WOW has a hood, armholes, four corners, and *tzitzit* (with *tekhelet*). This is one of the reasons I made it—so that it would be a kosher tallit but less noticeable, less "in your face" than the kind we're more used to. With capes like this, at least in colder weather, women can fulfill the mitzvah of tallit at the Kotel without attracting unwanted attention. I've worn it for *tefillot* there several times already and hardly anyone noticed, just a few sister daveners who stood close to me and noticed me holding the *tzitzit* during davening. One WOW member even asked me once if I hide the *tzitzit* somehow when davening is over. I don't. They're always hanging down in plain sight, which shows me that people see what they expect to see, members and opponents alike.

I should tell you that the davening felt special to me even before we made the decision to read Torah "downstairs." I sensed, and I think others did too, that today was different somehow. It wasn't just the rain of blessing for which we've waited and prayed for so long. There was something else in the air. I don't know what it was, but I feel that there were others with us whom we couldn't see. I like to believe that Rabbi Irwin Haut was there with us, smiling upon what we were doing and, I hope, *shepping nachas.*

For me, today's *Hallel,* indeed most of the *tefillah* after we decided to hold the Torah reading at the Kotel, was an experience of *gilu b'radah,* "rejoicing with trembling." I relish the excitement and exaltation of today's davening, and I also look forward to the time when a women's Torah service at the Kotel will elicit as much reaction as the Torah service in any local minyan. But I hope that when that day comes, we'll still be able to keep the excitement and exaltation going.

A Chronology of
Women of the Wall

NOVEMBER–DECEMBER 1988

The first International Jewish Feminist Conference was held in Jerusalem. Seventy Jewish women gathered for a prayer service and Torah reading at the Kotel. The service was disrupted by curses and threats from some ultra-Orthodox men and women at the site.

JANUARY–FEBRUARY 1989

A group of Jerusalem women continued regular prayer services at the Kotel. Violent attacks from ultra-Orthodox opponents ensued. The police refused to provide protection.

MARCH–APRIL 1989

Four women, represented by the firm of Kadesh and Ganor, submitted a petition to the Israeli Supreme Court asking for an order to allow women to pray together with Torah and tallit and to protect them from the continuing violence. The International Committee for Women of the Wall (ICWOW) held a series of solidarity services all over North America.

MAY–JUNE 1989

The Supreme Court heard the case of Women of the Wall for the first time. The State was given six months to respond to WOW's petition. The Court issued a temporary injunction ordering women not to pray at the Kotel with Torah and tallit. Women continued to

pray at the Kotel without Torah or tallit. Ultra-Orthodox opponents now demanded that women not pray aloud, because *kol b'ishah
ervah* ("the voice of a woman is nakedness").

JULY–AUGUST 1989

After further violence and harassment by female security guards
hired by the Administrator of the Kotel, WOW returned to the
Court to request a speedier response from the state and protection
of its right to pray out loud. Both requests were denied.

DECEMBER 1989

ICWOW purchased and donated a Torah scroll to the Israeli
WOW and traveled to Israel for a dedication ceremony. The ceremony was not held at the Laromme Hotel as planned because the
Jerusalem Rabbinate threatened to revoke the hotel's kashrut license
if the ceremony was held on its premises. ICWOW's attempt to
pray with this Torah, as it had done the previous year, became the
basis for ICWOW joining the lawsuit in the Supreme Court. On
December 31, a new regulation was passed by the Ministry of Religious Affairs and the Ministry of Justice to "prohibit any religious
ceremony at a holy place that is not in accordance with the custom
of the holy site and which offends the sensitivities of the worshipers at the place." The penalty for violating this regulation was
six months in jail and/or a fine.

APRIL 1990

The state filed its response, a 150-page compendium of halakhic
opinions concerning women's rights to pray out loud as a group,
wear *tallitot,* and touch or read from the Torah scroll.

JUNE 1990

ICWOW, represented by Arnold Shpaer and Peter Gabel, filed an independent lawsuit with the Israeli Supreme Court.

AUGUST 1990

To demonstrate the interest of Israeli Jewish women beyond those directly involved in WOW, and to give WOW's lawsuit greater legal and political clout, the Israel Women's Network (IWN) submitted a motion to the Court asking to be allowed to join the lawsuit as a co-petitioner. The court refused. WOW and ICWOW were on their own.

FEBRUARY 1991

The Supreme Court heard oral arguments on the case. Solidarity services were held in Stockholm, Sweden, and in cities across North America.

While the legal case continued to meet with governmental stonewalling and delay, WOW chose to pursue a strategy of "creating facts on the ground," increasing and regularizing its presence at the Kotel. Despite the enormous restrictions and constant risk of danger, WOW continued to pray quietly at the Kotel without a Torah, celebrate bat mitzvahs and *aufrufs*, conduct learning sessions, and read the *Megillah*. Full Torah readings were held "in exile" at the Archaeological Gardens. On occasion, the services were calm; at other times, the women were subjected to hate and violence at the hands of other Jews.

The state's brief relied upon a variety of rabbinic opinions. Some were directed against women's prayer groups in general; some were specifically directed against WOW. Some were taken from general halakhic literature about women's issues. The following is a selection of these views contained in the state's brief against us:

"This is an offense to all the righteous women of all the generations and an offense to the women who come daily to pray and an offense to the Torah of Israel."

—RABBI MORDECHAI ELIAHU, SEPHARDIC CHIEF RABBI

"Since [the Plaintiff's] coming intensifies controversy, it is definitely more appropriate for [them] not to come at all to the Kotel than to come and instigate fights and confrontations. . . . This is definitely the work of Satan . . . to increase arguments and to arouse criticism of Israel."

—RABBI AVRAHAM SHAPIRA, ASHKENAZI CHIEF RABBI

"When women create their own congregations the Shekhinah is not present and their prayers are not heard. . . . Instead of *kedushah* we have *kedeshah* [prostitution]. Never have we heard, never have we seen anything as strange as this since the time of Moses our Rabbi until today. Not even the Reform Jews would have conceived of such a thing. The women have created this by drawing upon an unclean source called 'women's lib,' whose purpose is to overturn the words of the living God. These women who rush to create their own groups and who form minyans . . . [also] do everything to bar conception from taking place. God should save us from this. From this [their use of birth control], we see that their motivation is not for the sake of heaven and [that they] run after that which is forbidden. . . . They neglect their husbands and their children rather than helping their husbands, which was why they were created."

—RABBI MENASHE KLEIN

"Women's nature is more suited to raising children and therefore God did not obligate them to study Torah and to keep timebound mitzvot . . . and no fighting [about this] will change [it]. Women who are stubborn and who wish to fight and to make changes are considered heretics who do not have a share in the world to come. . . . Tefillin need careful attention and a clean body."

—RABBI MOSHE FEINSTEIN

"Although according to Halakhah, women may be permitted to wear *tzitzit,* it is considered arrogant for a woman to do so. Even though women are halakhically permitted to touch, hold, and even read from a Torah, any gathering of women for the purpose of reading it in the framework of a women's minyan is a gathering whose basis is the desire to equate the status of women to that of men in the world of Jewish law. . . . In some places where it is customary to have women's minyans, their intention is to make it seem that women are as important as men and may be part of a minyan. One who intentionally and willingly lies in matters of Torah and falsifies the laws of Torah is considered a heretic. Women are desecrating the holy places."

—PROF. ELIAHU SCHOCHETMAN

"The women who constitute themselves as a minyan [are] just like Korach and his group. . . . Their main motivation is to create something new for its own sake, to get newspaper publicity, glory, to be known as leaders and sometimes just to rebel against tradition . . . and their chief motivation is truly to uproot everything [all of Judaism]. . . . It is our obligation to teach the learned and educated women to fix their souls as our rabbis in yeshiva taught, 'Teach yourselves to be normal.'"

—RABBI HERSHEL SCHACHTER

"I did not stop the women [with a Torah] from entering the Kotel plaza [for the first time] and I even calmed the furious people by explaining to them that there is nothing halakhically, legally prohibited except for the fact that this is against custom and not accepted. I thought in my innocence that this was a one time event and [would] pass and vanish from the world."

—RABBI MEIR YEHUDA GETZ,
ADMINISTRATOR OF THE KOTEL

JANUARY 1994

The Supreme Court issued a decision on ICWOW and WOW in which one judge (Justice Shlomo Levine) supported women's rights to group prayer at the Kotel, one judge (Justice Menachem Elon) denied these rights, and the third, Justice Meir Shamgar, recommended that the government set up a commission to resolve the matter in the political arena.

FEBRUARY 1994

ICWOW and WOW requested permission to appeal the Court's decision. The request was denied. The Court stated that "the doors of the court are open" if the Commission does not provide a proper remedy.

MAY 1994

A government commission, henceforth referred to as the Mancal Commission, was appointed to propose a solution to the issue of women's prayer at the Wall. No women were appointed to it. ICWOW undertook a massive campaign to recruit individuals and organizations to lobby the Commission.

NOVEMBER 1994

The Commission failed to meet its first deadline. The government granted it a six-month extension.

FEBRUARY 1995

ICWOW and WOW were finally granted permission to testify before the Commission. Six Israeli women and one representative from the United States testified.

MAY 17, 1995

The Mancal Commission, which had already received a six-month extension of its original deadline, failed to meet its deadline. WOW and ICWOW filed suit demanding that (1) the Commission be ordered to meet its mandate immediately; (2) the Court issue an injunction against the government, prohibiting any further deadline extensions for the Commission; (3) a temporary injunction be issued allowing women wearing *tallitot* to pray aloud at the Kotel with a Torah scroll; and (4) the state provide police protection for WOW. Judge Dalia Dorner rejected the request for an injunction preventing the government commission from being granted further extensions. A hearing on the rest of the lawsuit was set for eleven months later—April 14, 1996.

JULY 1995

Despite complete inaction, the Commission was granted another six-month extension until November 17, 1995.

NOVEMBER 1995

In response to Prime Minister Yitzhak Rabin's assassination, WOW and ICWOW reaffirmed their commitment to oppose the rationalization of all forms of terror. After complete failure to fulfill its mandate, the Commission allowed its November 17 deadline to pass with no report issued.

MARCH 7, 1996: PURIM

On Shushan Purim, WOW held a study session and reading of *Megillat Esther* at the Kotel. The study session was dedicated to the memory of Sarah Duker, an American student killed in the first no. 18 bus bombing in Jerusalem; Duker, before her untimely death, had expressed her plans to attend the session. WOW leader Chaia Beckerman recorded, "We had almost twenty women by the time we started and at least thirty by the time we got to the *Megillah*. . . . The first *Megillah* reader was Michal Shiff-Matter, who teaches cantorial students at Hebrew Union College. She has a voice you can't rein in. She was dressed up as a *charedi* man, so if we were going to have any problems, we would have had them right away. The guard did come over when we began, but one of the women bribed him with cookies. We were shushing Michal some at the start when her gorgeous voice really sailed, but the wonderful thing about starting with her was that once we saw that we were okay with her reading, we knew we could sing out. One *charedi* woman had joined us by the end of that chapter. There was a real sense of triumph and wonder at our success as the reading progressed. We were attracting a fair amount of attention from women and from tourists in back of the Wall, but the men's section was oblivious. Church bells were ringing by the time I was reading chapter 4, so I was chanting in full voice to be heard. It was an incredible feeling to sing without restraint at the Kotel! Everything followed spontaneously: WOW leader Rahel Jaskow and then other women joined in a *shehecheyanu* as someone pointed out that this was probably the first time women had ever done this at the Wall."

APRIL 1996

WOW and ICWOW returned to Court for a hearing of the May 1995 petition. The petition was strongly supported by affidavits from the Reform and Conservative movements in Israel, stating that these movements did not want their own demands concerning the Kotel to be used as a further delaying tactic by the government. Despite WOW's objections, the government requested and was granted a one-month delay. On April 2, the Mancal Commission finally issued its report, proposing that the Women of the Wall be moved to the southeastern corner of the Old City wall, a site outside the Old City itself in Arab East Jerusalem, where anyone already has the right to hold prayer services. The location is not a safe one for Jews. On April 21, the government appointed a new ministerial commission to decide if and how to implement the Mancal Commission's report. ICWOW immediately initiated a letter-writing campaign to the new ministerial commission.

MAY 1996

WOW and ICWOW's delayed April hearing (for the suit filed in May 1995) came before the Court once again. The government was again granted a delay, this time until July 29, 1996.

MAY 23–24, 1996: SHAVUOT

WOW organized a *Tikkun Leyl Shavuot* (all-night study session) at the home of WOW leader Anat Hoffman and a dawn service at the Kotel for the holiday of Shavuot. According to WOW leader Betsy Kallus, "We went with our Torah scroll wrapped in a tallit, which we carried into the plaza behind the Kotel area. We moved deeply into the women's section as close as we could physically get to the women's side of the Wall. We ended up standing by the long stone wall that extends almost to the women's water fountain. Tamar Asher led *Pesukei d'Zimra* with singing, and Deena Aranoff led a beautiful *Shachrit* and *Hallel.* At *Barkhu,* she began a fabulous melody of Reb Shlomo [Carlebach], *z"l,* which had us singing loudly and joyously. There was some response from the *charediot,* but mostly either they ignored us or joined in with the singing. Several non-*charediot* who were in the area joined us in our prayer group. We also read the Book of Ruth. Several young *charedi* girls tried to stop us by saying it was forbidden for women to read *Megillat Ruth;* by and large, their mothers shushed them so they could hear the *Megillah.*

"We took the Torah scroll up to the Archaeological Gardens, where we read Torah and said *Musaf.* Once we were isolated and away from the Kotel, we were vulnerable to the threats of passersby, who included a number of yeshiva students. One group came in with about seven or eight teenage boys. They spat on the floor in front of us, insulted us and threw a bag of *bamba* [Israeli junk food] into the open Torah scroll. We pointedly ignored them and continued reading. An older Sephardic man came in with his son when we were at the blessings for the sick. He stood, listened for a couple of minutes, wished us a *chag sameach* (joyous holiday) and left."

JUNE 1996

Israeli elections gave newly expanded influence to the ultra-Orthodox parties. WOW and ICWOW vowed to persist in the struggle for women's equality and religious freedom. Praying aloud with Torah and tallit in the women's section at the Kotel remained a crime punishable by imprisonment and/or fine.

JULY 24, 1996: TISHA B'AV

WOW and ICWOW leader Bonna Haberman wrote, "I just returned from the reading of *Eichah*. . . . There must have been forty women who participated, with a large group of soldiers perched on the earthy raised area adjacent to the women's section who listened attentively. Our reading drew much interest and participation. We sat well inside and read with full voice, and chanted *kinot* afterwards. . . . Many wept. It felt like a homecoming; very bittersweet. We definitely felt part of our people."

OCTOBER 1996

The Israeli Supreme Court ordered the Ministry of Religious Affairs to pay WOW and ICWOW five thousand shekels toward legal costs for their "interminable delays" and for the disrespectful "recommendation" that WOW pray at the southeastern comer of the Old City, a site entirely outside the Old City and outside the Jewish Quarter.

NOVEMBER 12, 1996: ROSH CHODESH KISLEV

WOW leader Betsy Kallus writes, "We arrived at the Kotel with about eighty women. I began leading the morning service and had barely gotten started when we heard shouts and screams coming from the men's side. There were approximately twenty to thirty men standing on chairs leaning over the *mechitzah*, shouting at us. One of them threw a *shtender*, a small wooden podium used by *cohanim* during the prayer for peace, at us. Another threw a chair. I learned from my husband, who was wrapped in his tefillin and tallit standing amidst these men, that when he and a friend tried to calm the other men down, they called him a goy, a Nazi, a Reform Jew, and any number of other epithets. We saw a number of the ultra-Orthodox women trying to quiet the men. The screaming continued, and two police officers—a man and a woman—came up to us and told us that we should leave immediately. When we said that they should get rid of the people attacking us, not us, we were told that the police did not have the capacity to protect us from them and therefore we should move away. We were pushed to an area about one hundred feet away, at the far end of the Kotel. We regrouped there, surrounded by a phalanx of police and journalists. Once again, we began to daven and sing out loud. Several ultra-Orthodox men tried to interrupt us, but the police pushed them away. Rahel Jaskow led us in singing *Hallel* in full voice, which concluded with singing and dancing to one of Reb Shlomo Carlebach's *niggunim.* A small but not insignificant victory for us."

JANUARY 1997

Rabbi Emanuel Rackman, chancellor of Bar-Ilan University, issued a statement of unequivocal public support for WOW's right to pray in its fashion.

MARCH 4, 1997

The Israeli Supreme Court ordered the state to "show just cause within ninety days why WOW's lawsuit against the government should not succeed." One day later, a Shas-sponsored bill passed a preliminary vote in the Knesset. The bill would turn the Kotel from a national site into an ultra-Orthodox synagogue. This bill reflected the fear among our ultra-Orthodox opponents that WOW would win a victory in the Supreme Court and represented an attempt to override that possibility. WOW had been informed that the chairperson of the Knesset Interior Committee, Druse MK

Sallach Tarif, will not allow the Shas bill to proceed. However, Shas could still dislodge the bill from the Interior Committee by bringing enough political pressure.

MARCH 10, 1997: ROSH CHODESH ADAR II

According to Betsy Kallus, "Rosh Chodesh Adar II was great. We had about fifty or sixty women, mostly regulars. I led *Shachrit,* and Rahel Jaskow led her usual exquisite *Hallel,* which we sang at the Kotel in moderately hushed voices. One man observed that at the moment we started to sing *Hallel,* the sun came up fully and the birds started singing. . . . Barbara Sutnick's oldest daughter *leyned.* A younger daughter will be called to the Torah on Rosh Chodesh Tammuz!"

MARCH 25, 1997: PURIM

Betsy Kallus writes, "The *Megillah* reading was wonderful, funny, and expressive. . . . The atmosphere was relaxed, I think because of it being Purim, no one was paying much attention to us or to what we were doing. We started off with about fifty women. Curious tourists, *charediot,* other Israeli visitors, all stopped to listen and smile. The most common response was *kol hakavod* ('all honor to you')."

JUNE 1997

The government commission issued its report: "Decision 14 of the Ministers' Committee on Jerusalem: Prayer Arrangements at the Western Wall Plaza in Relation to the High Court of Justice Case of 'Women of the Wall.'" The report recommended maintenance of the status quo, under which women's group prayer at the Kotel was illegal. One week later, the state filed its response with the

374

Supreme Court and attached the decision of the government commission. Both documents represented a clear acknowledgment that the state was unwilling to protect the legal and halakhic rights of Jewish women at the Kotel.

JUNE 11, 1997: SHAVUOT

WOW leader Haviva Ner-David joined an egalitarian Conservative minyan for Shavuot morning davening at the Kotel. In her account of the event, she emphasizes the importance of seeing WOW within the context of the broader struggle for religious pluralism in Israel. She writes, "I was at the Kotel early this morning, and we joined the egalitarian minyan that was davening near the entrance to the Kotel plaza. By the middle of the Torah reading, we were surrounded by hundreds of *charedi* men, who proceeded to push and shove us, kicking and spitting and screaming: 'Nazis, *goyim*, because of you the Shoah happened!' They were throwing liquids and other things at us out of the windows of their yeshiva. Thank God no one was really hurt, but the police, of course, made us leave. There were crying children. They were even screaming these awful things at the children. . . . Being there this morning made me feel intensely that our fight is the same as the fight of Reform and Conservative Jews on this issue. These *charedim* don't care if we are not technically a minyan or that we have halakhic backing from some Orthodox rabbis. They see liberal Orthodox Jews as just as 'other' as Conservative and Reform. And women reading Torah with or without men is desecrating the Torah in their eyes. It was when they saw women reading from the Torah that they really went wild. I don't label myself Conservative or Reform, but I feel a need to join this group to lend support. I hope that next year more people will do the same."

AUGUST 11, 1997: TISHA B'AV

Betsy Kallus and Chaia Beckerman report, "The reading of *Megillat Eichah* went wonderfully, unlike the Conservative egalitarian minyan that was broken up by the police. Once the ultra-Orthodox started screaming, the police began their litany of 'We can't protect you, you'll have to leave now.' WOW gathered in the middle of the women's section and davened *Maariv.* Betsy led services and then we sat down on the ground and began reading. A group of policemen stood at the back of the women's section, looking at us as if they were expecting trouble. Chaia thanked them but asked them to move back, telling them we were an observant group that regularly came on Tisha B'Av and never had trouble. They agreed to move back. Marga Hirsch led us in chanting a dirge to Jerusalem afterward and we sang beautiful minor-key melodies. We could have sung at any volume. Many women joined us after we started, even *charedi* women. There were other groups around us. There was also a group of *charedi* women and their daughters listening to one of their number read *Eichah* in Yiddish. A wonderful event, quite noneventful. *Kein yerbu* ('May there be many more')."

SEPTEMBER 1997

Shortly before the date of WOW's court hearing, Nili Arad, the lawyer representing the government, made several proposals, including establishing another Ne'eman Commission (along the lines of the Ne'eman Commission then working on issues of conversion), and/or allotting WOW a place to pray at Robinson's Arch, adjacent to the Kotel.

SEPTEMBER 24, 1997

Supreme Court hearing. Pushed by the judges, WOW and ICWOW reluctantly agreed to participate in Ne'eman Commission meetings to find a solution at the Kotel. After eight or more years of intolerable delay, after ineffectual commissions and attempts to foist other locations on us (including one proposal of a site outside the Old City altogether!), WOW and ICWOW opposed these proposals. The Commission was rejected as a stalling tactic. Although Robinson's Arch is next to the Kotel plaza and is a continuation of the Wall, the area in front of it constitutes a large archaeological site and is unsuitable as a prayer site. Access to the Wall is limited, and the state has given no indication that it intends to develop the site to make it suitable for our purposes. (In fact, the government suggested that it plans to develop the site for tourists.)

WOW and ICWOW's lawyer, Frances Raday, argued eloquently: "I find it intolerable to support the idea of compromise or delay on the issue of religious patriarchy versus women's right to equality." However, it soon became clear that the judges believed that the women were being recalcitrant and intolerant for not considering these proposals. WOW and its legal counsel determined that there was no choice but to accept the new commission. Justice Eliahu Matza urged WOW, "You can lay down your conditions for the structure and terms of reference of the Commission. You can make sure that it will only discuss the way to implement prayer arrangements in the *ezrat nashim* (women's section) of the Kotel or in a special prayer area at Robinson's Arch."

WOW agreed to present minimal terms for participating in the Commission within two weeks. The judges stated that WOW would have a hand in dictating the terms and makeup of the commission and that members of WOW would sit on the Commission. The Court indicated that WOW would be welcome to return to the Court should WOW and the government be unable to agree to terms or the Commission fail to meet its mandate. To WOW's dismay, the Commission did not begin its work until spring. While WOW was to have a key role in determining the other members and setting terms for how long the commission had to complete its work, its influence was minimal. Nonetheless, it was the first time WOW members had even been part of bodies discussing the issue.

NOVEMBER 30, 1997: ROSH CHODESH KISLEV

According to WOW leader Jessie Bonn, "WOW received the Torah table cover *(parokhet)* created by Rabbi Jinny Roth Isserow that was commissioned and presented by Sandy Lepelstat. Many thanks and solemn sentiments of sisterhood were inspired by the special *parokhet*. The dancing, floating, pulsating women of all ages and shades depicted on the *parokhet* inspire, lend honor to the Torah, and protect it from the cold drafts emanating from the stone table of our exile. Caressing the many-textured fabric and examining the figures has become a favorite Rosh Chodesh treat."

DECEMBER 1997

According to WOW leader Danielle Bernstein, "Since last winter three members of WOW have been meeting about once a month with a group of *charedi* and Conservative women. The meetings were initiated by a *charedi* woman living in the Old City who was disturbed by the violence at the Kotel. We began, not knowing exactly what to expect. Slowly, we clarified our different positions. The personal connections woven in the meetings brought with them acceptance. The last meeting took place before Shavuot, with a clear agenda: to address what could be done to prevent violence on Shavuot. The dialogue was very interesting and fruitful. One of the Conservative representatives shared her plan to organize an egalitarian minyan. It was suggested that we make use again of the *p'sak halakhah* issued last year by the *badatz* of the *charedi* community condemning violence. It was decided to ask the rabbis who signed the *p'sak* if they still stand behind their declaration. There will be a new printing of the leaflet and each of us will distribute and post it wherever we can. That's what actually happened! On Shavuot, when the Conservative minyan was verbally harassed, there were *charedi* people showing the *p'sak* to all. This, and the help of the police, enabled the Conservative minyan to pray as it wished. We will keep meeting: these discussions have proven not only interesting on a personal level, but also effective."

MARCH 1, 1998

Anat Hoffman, member of the Jerusalem Municipality and a WOW activist, addressed a well-attended brunch meeting in New York City co-sponsored by ICWOW and US/Israel Women to Women. Hoffman's update of WOW's activities included an analysis of Jewish women's status in Israel. The question period was lively. Such gatherings are a way for WOW to do outreach and give women who are interested in the cause an opportunity to have firsthand knowledge and contact with WOW's activists.

MARCH 14, 1998: PURIM

Following WOW's custom, women read the Scroll of Esther aloud, and for the first time in WOW's nine-year history, women also sang and danced together.

MARCH 29, 1998

Meeting of the Ne'eman Commission. Several key members are absent.

APRIL 27, 1998: ROSH CHODESH IYAR

According to Betsy Kallus, "We had a group of about fifty women, including a sweet group of teenage girls from a New Jersey Solomon Schechter high school. We sang strongly and, remarkably, there was no disruption of our davening or requests by *charedi* women to shush when we sang. When we went up to the Archaeological Gardens, one of the students read Torah. I felt we had crossed some line at the Kotel. We had sung out loud, gathered in a significant group without disruption. We need to make facts on the ground work in our favor, one issue at a time."

MAY 1998

Meeting of the Ne'eman Commission. Present at the meeting were Rabbi Prof. Nahum Rabinowitz (Birkat Moshe Yeshiva), Oded Weiner (coordinator of Holy Sites), Rabbi Hillel Kohn (legal advisor to Ministry of Religious Affairs), Ilana Keller (legal advisor to Minister of Internal Security), Ariel Weiss (friend of Ne'eman), Reuven Hammer, Gideon Meir (legal advisor for Israel-Diaspora Relations), Bobby Brown (legal advisor to prime minister on Israel-Diaspora Relations, spokeswoman for Ministry of Treasury), Rabbi Uri Regev (Israel Religious Action Center), Anat Hoffman (WOW), Jessica Bonn (WOW), Chaia Beckerman (WOW), Betsy Kallus (WOW), Prof. Dov Frimer (committee member), Itzik Fried (assistant to Minister of Treasury), Yair Wolf (assistant to Yigal Bibi of Ministry of Religious Affairs), Shimon Malka (spokesman, Ministry of Religious Affairs), Yehoshua Yishai (responsible for budgets, Ministry of Religious Affairs), Asher Ohana (executive director of Office of Religious Matters), and Chairman Yakov Ne'eman.

Ne'eman asked the representatives of the Ministry of Religious

Affairs for its possible solutions to the problem. Oded Weiner, claiming he was not authorized to offer solutions, provided the status of four previous solutions:

1. *The Kotel Katan,* a site in east Jerusalem, was disqualified for national reasons.
2. The southeast corner was rejected by WOW.
3. The area near the Hulda Gate was rejected by WOW.
4. The southern wall was rejected by the Antiquities Authority.

The only remaining option was the area by the security gates separating the plaza from the Dung Gate, under the steps leading up to the Archaeological Gardens. This is currently a parking area and would have to be approved by the police and the rabbinate. Ne'eman suggested that the feasibility of this sight be investigated by all parties as well as the construction of some structure that would protect women there. Hoffman stated that WOW could consider this and other options only if the information was complete. WOW determined that if it were to accept any space other than the women's section of the Kotel, written assurance would be given that WOW could still continue praying in the women's section according to current custom. Ne'eman suggested that a date for a tour of the field be set before Shavuot.

MAY 26, 1998: ROSH CHODESH SIVAN

According to Betsy Kallus, "Jessie Bonn led *Pesukei d'Zimra* to warm us up for *Hallel,* followed by Andrea Cohen Keiner's beautiful *Shachrit* and *Hallel.* Like last month, the singing was extremely spirited, loud, and strong. We were not harassed at all. One *charedi* woman came up and praised the davening. The Torah reading was lovely: one of the visitors read two of the *aliyot,* and another woman offered a brief *d'var Torah.* Andrea offered to teach any woman who wanted to know how to put on tefillin up in the Archaeological Gardens.

MAY 31, 1998: SHAVUOT

Betsy Kallus reports, "As usual, the Kotel was packed with people. We moved well inside the women's area close to the low wall that rises up to the ramp leading to *Har HaBayit* (the Temple Mount). When we began to daven, we were surrounded on all sides by mostly *charedi* women. Initially, women tried to shush us; however, that ceased pretty quickly. Some of our members sat on the hillside next to us where they sang and clapped while the davening proceeded. When we began reading the Book of Ruth, other women joined us, including *charedi* women. After *Megillat Ruth*, we walked to the Jewish Quarter to finish our davening. As we moved up the stairs to the Jewish Quarter, we could see and hear the near-riot that was going on, in reaction to the egalitarian minyan's attempt to pray at the Kotel. Against the far wall near the exit to the parking lot, police barricades were set up and large numbers of police were preventing *charedim* from attacking the minyan. Significantly, the minyan succeeded in completing its davening with police protection.

After services, we went to Susie Schneider's (of the WOW–*Charedi* women–Conservative dialogue group) for kiddush. Susie received us warmly and was eager to hear what happened. One of the important outcomes of the dialogue group, which had been meeting since December 1997, was that Susie printed up for Shavuot (with our consent and cooperation) posters and flyers that were distributed throughout the Old City and *charedi* neighborhoods, calling on people to refrain from violence on Shavuot. During the near-riot, a large number of *charedim* were holding these posters. Every time one of the posters was knocked down, another one reappeared. I learned after the fact that Common Denominator, an Aish HaTorah group, had sponsored the dialogue project and had recruited people to hold the signs. I believe that the fact that there was so little violence was due in large measure to these signs and posters. I don't know if this would have happened if we had not had the dialogue group. In my opinion, the dialogue group has been one of the most important and productive activities of the past year.

JULY 1998
The members of the Ne'eman Commission tour the Kotel area.

SUMMER 1998
WOW leaders decided to set up a "tallit table" in Zion Square as a way of doing more active and direct outreach to Israelis. The following accounts describe the experience of staffing the table for the first time.

According to Betsy Kallus, "At our last meeting of WOW, we decided that we wanted to do more aggressive outreach to Israelis. With Anat Hoffman's help, we got permission from the municipality to set up a folding table with literature about WOW, a sign-up sheet, and of course, our beautiful *tallitot*. As women passed by, we invited them to don a tallit and say the *berakhah* (blessing). Of course, many women said that it was forbidden, or that they were not religious enough; one Ethiopian woman said that she would have done it, but she was in *niddah* at the time. During the hour and a half that we were there, many women put on *tallitot*, some for the first time. Women asked for sources on *tallitot*, asked to attend WOW prayer sessions, and requested that we send them photographs of them wearing the tallit (we had a photographer with us). There were approximately an equal number of religious and secular women who put on the tallit.

Later, a group of *charedi* young men came over and started asking questions. One of them came over to the table where Bonna, Haviva, and I were standing, and started shouting, 'Forbidden, forbidden!' He then lifted the table and threw it and all of the contents, including *tallitot, siddur,* and various papers, into the air. The table landed on the ground, narrowly missing Haviva's son's head. One of the legs of the table broke. Anat and Bonna went racing after the attacker, who was caught and arrested by the police."

According to WOW leader Jessie Bonn, "Despite the sour ending of our pilot project, we should all take heart from the surprisingly positive response to our table. Never before had I realized how desperately important it is for WOW to start talking directly to the people, not through the press but through our confident, spiritually soaring and plain *menschlich* presence. This is the most efficient way to desensitize, desensationalize. But more than that, women will begin to try it themselves, experience it on their bodies, in their *neshameahs. Yishar kokhenu* to all the daughters, women of Israel who opened their hearts today to tallit."

SEPTEMBER 1998

The Ne'eman Commission issued its report, concluding that WOW should pray in the Robinson's Arch area immediately south of the Kotel, currently an archaeological site. WOW had no vote, nor was any serious attention given to WOW's compromise proposal of a time-sharing arrangement at the Kotel proper.

FEBRUARY 16, 1999

The state submitted an affidavit by Jerusalem Chief of Police Yair Yitzhaki, arguing that it was WOW who provoked the violence.

The next day the Supreme Court held a two-hour hearing on the petition of WOW and ICWOW to pray as a group at the Western Wall, with Torah and tallit. The following is an account of the hearing by our lawyer, Frances Raday.

"The hearing was on the merits of the case. The bench consisted of Justices Eliahu Maza, Dorit Beinish, and Tova Strasburg-Cohen. The state was represented by Advocate Uzi Fogelman, who is the head of the Bagatz Department in the State Attorney's office. In our statement we referred to the Conservative movement's recent prayers at the Kotel, as that was a fact not mentioned in previous documents. Fogelman filed a new affidavit, signed by Yitzhaki regarding those events. He was also present at the Court hearing.

His affidavit and answers to the judges were not detrimental to our case. In fact, he was maneuvered to say that the issue is not one of police inability to control the crowds, nor is it an issue of lack of manpower. He reiterated the police's anticipation of disturbances should WOW be permitted to pray at the Kotel, but was tackled by the judges, at our behest, as to the police's steps to prevent this and penalize the offenders rather than simply expelling and silencing WOW. All in all, the judges were attentive to our arguments. They allowed us free range to relate to the issues of democracy and the slippery slope of conceding to violent fanatics the power of denying others the opportunity to exercise their human rights. In particular, they listened carefully and appeared to accept my argument that the right of WOW was a right rooted in a specific place—the Kotel—and hence not transferable to Robinson's Arch or anywhere else. The very positive atmosphere in the Court hearing does not, of course, guarantee us a positive decision. We are now awaiting the decision, which I assume will not be given any time soon."

MARCH 18, 1999: ROSH CHODESH NISAN

The following *d'var Torah* was offered by Shira Bernstein, daughter of WOW member Danielle Bernstein, on the occasion of her bat mitzvah at the Kotel on Rosh Chodesh Nisan. WOW member Chaia Beckerman wrote of the event, "We all felt a bit of the *naches* (pride) that Danielle deservedly felt *b'gadol* (in great measure)."

"Today is Rosh Chodesh Nisan, the beginning of the month of our redemption, on which we read the song *(shirah)* that *Bnei Yisrael* sang at the crossing of the Sea. In the Book of Exodus, *Shirat Hayam*, the song sung by Moshe and *Bnei Yisrael*, is fully recorded over nineteen verses. The two following verses mention the song as it was sung by Miriam and the women. 'And Miriam the prophetess, the sister of Aaron, took the timbrel in her hand and all the women went after her with timbrels and dances. And Miriam answered them: Sing to G-d.' That's it. The song is unfinished. There is a midrash that asks why the Torah stops Miriam's song after only one verse. The midrash answers: In future generations, women will complete Miriam's song. Like the song of *Bnei Yisrael*, the 'song' to be sung by a bar mitzvah is fully recorded and planned in our tradition. He will be called up to the Torah, will read *maftir* and the *haftarah*, and will say a *d'var Torah*. On the other hand, the 'song' to be sung by the bat mitzvah is open, unfinished; she is free to choose how to mark the event, and it is a great responsibility for her to find what will really be meaningful.

The way I chose to continue Miriam's song is to lead *Shachrit* this morning. This is meaningful for me because it expresses relations between both woman and woman and between woman and G-d. When the *chazan* or *chazanit* leads the prayers, he or she is creating a connection between the people praying together and is carrying the hearts of the congregation toward heaven.

Tradition places greater importance on congregational prayer than on the prayer of the individual. On the day of my bat mitzvah I have become a part of the congregation, and my blessings may now carry others' blessings as well. Halakhah, Jewish law, traditionally maintains that women praying together are to be considered as individuals and not as a congregation. In my experience, praying together with other women as a group is a distinctive religious experience, different from individual prayer."

MAY 16, 1999: ROSH CHODESH SIVAN

According to Haviva Ner-David, "I had a positive interchange with a woman at the Kotel this morning. She looked moderately *charedi* (ultra-Orthodox). She asked in Hebrew why we weren't davening up at the Kotel, and I answered, 'Because they say it bothers them.' She said, 'Yes, of course it would bother them, you are praying out loud.' She said, 'Why do you pray out loud?' I said, 'That is the way we are accustomed to praying. We find it helps us to pray.' She said, 'Yes, it is very pleasant. Are you *Reformim*?' I answered no. She said, 'Do you pray mixed with men?' I answered no. 'We pray as a group of women.' She said, 'I never heard of such a thing. It's very nice. Shalom to you. We should have peace in Israel.'"

JUNE 15, 1999: ROSH CHODESH TAMMUZ

Haviva Ner-David writes, "This morning at the Kotel was very special. A friend of mine who converted yesterday came this morning for her first *aliyah*. It was very moving and celebratory. During *Hallel*, the men on the other side of the *mechitzah* started to yell at us and throw things, but the police actually did their job and protected us. They told the men to stop throwing things and yelling, and one police officer actually climbed over the *mechitzah* to calm them down. There is a definite difference in the way the police are reacting to us now. Our theory is that it is related to the new government."

According to Chaia Beckerman, "When we were singing *Hallel*, we got enough reaction (turned heads, a lot of shushing) on the women's side that the men's side took note (either that or a woman alerted them). A group of young *charedim* started shouting and a chair came sailing over the *mechitzah*. The police materialized and were right on top of the situation. When the harassment continued and it looked as if there would be more violence, one policeman ran over and hurled himself over the *mechitzah* to contain the guys. Anat took the names of the police in order to commend them.

Also this morning, a beggar who has been around before in the Archaeological Gardens and has to be discouraged from panhandling during the Torah service waited around for the end and in the process took *gelilah* (the honor of binding the Torah) and said a *she-hecheyanu*. She kept marveling at how our service was the same as anyone's, and what was all this *sinat hinam* (senseless hatred) for? And where were we on Shabbat, because she wanted to come join us.

JANUARY 2000

Judges Matza, Strasburg-Cohen, and Beinish toured the Kotel plaza. They proposed alternate sites. Present were WOW and ICWOW representatives and lawyers and those of the government; representatives of the government legal advisor, the police, the Antiquities Authority, and councils responsible for development of the holy sites and East Jerusalem development.

MAY 22, 2000

A three-judge panel of the Israeli Supreme Court (Justices Matza, Beinish, and Strasburg-Cohen) handed down a unanimous opinion in WOW's favor. The opinion was written by Justice Matza, with Justices Beinish and Strasburg-Cohen concurring. In a lengthy opinion, Judge Matza explicitly recognized our rights but transferred the matter to the government yet again, charging it to find a solution at the Kotel within six months. He awarded WOW twenty thousand shekels for legal costs.

In response, the Shas and Degel Hatorah religious parties introduced bills in the Knesset aimed at overriding the Court's ruling. One of these bills would make women's worship at the Western Wall with Torah and *tallitot* (prayer shawls) an offense punishable by seven years' imprisonment.

Nevertheless, this opinion eloquently and explicitly declares that Women of the Wall have the right to pray out loud, as a group, in the women's section of the Kotel with a *sefer Torah* and wearing *tallitot.* These were the grounds of WOW's original stage-I lawsuit from 1990, as well as the grounds of WOW's 1995 stage-II lawsuit. However, Justice Matza and the May 2000 Court stopped short of awarding an actual remedy. Rather, the Court gave the government yet another six months to implement the decision. Justice Matza essentially reiterated the mandate given by Justice Shamgar in the January 1994 decision in the stage-I lawsuit: "We order the government to find a solution for Women of the Wall at the Kotel while taking into consideration the sensitivities of the other worshipers at the site." The government reaction resisting even this limited Supreme Court victory for Women of the Wall was quick and comprehensive.

JUNE–DECEMBER 2000

On June 4, 2000, WOW held a victory celebration that was very well attended. A young soldier in uniform *leyned* from the Torah under WOW auspices. Various Knesset MKs, including Galia

Golan of Meretz, joined WOW in prayer. ICWOW had its annual meeting in New York City in order to be together, either to celebrate or to assist WOW if trouble broke out.

The state filed a request for an appeal on the May 22 decision.

Legislative: Ultra-Orthodox parties fought back immediately by sponsoring a bill in the Knesset that would make women's worship at the Wall with a *sefer Torah* and *tallitot* an offense punishable by seven years in prison (currently the penalty is six months in prison and/or a heavy fine). A second bill would codify ultra-Orthodox control of the Kotel by statute (this control is currently codified in regulations and in the caselaw; see the decision in the lawsuit, stage 1, *Piskei Din* 48, II, 265–358, 1994). On December 13, 2000, the two bills above were combined into one that would jail women for three years for wearing *tallitot* or reading out loud from a Torah at the Kotel. This legislation passed its reading in the Interior Committee.

Executive: Prime Minister Ehud Barak's government refused to follow the Supreme Court's directive to find a solution for women to pray as a group at the Wall within six months of the May ruling. Rather, the government substituted a motion to the Supreme Court, requesting that it cease enforcement of the May decision (meaning, to remove the six-month deadline for the government to find a solution for Women of the Wall at the Kotel), which declared WOW's rights to pray according to the grounds of WOW's lawsuit, and requesting that it review WOW's case again with a panel of nine judges.

Judicial: WOW immediately submitted papers in opposition to the government's motion for the order to cease enforcement and for the additional review. Despite WOW's opposition, those requests were granted by Justice Aharon Barak on November 19, 2000. The Court did explicitly criticize the government for ignoring those very requests. The expanded nine-judge panel consisted of Justices Barak,

Levine, Or, Matza, Heshin, Strasburg-Cohen, Tirkel, Beinish, and England. The judges scheduled a tour of the site on June 28, 2001.

NOVEMBER–DECEMBER 2001

On December 4, proposed bill no. 1924 was voted on in the Knesset. The bill is an amendment to the Holy Sites Law of 1967 and reads as follows: "1. The prayer area at the Western Wall plaza shall be divided into a men's section and women's section by a divider, and prayers by men and women in a mixed group shall not be permitted there. 2. No religious ceremony shall be held in the women's section near the Western Wall that includes taking out a Torah scroll and reading from it, blowing the shofar, or wearing *tallitot* or tefillin. 3. Violators shall be imprisoned for seven years." WOW and ICWOW orchestrated a letter-writing campaign to the prime minister, the justice minister, and the speaker of the Knesset.

FEBRUARY 12, 2002: ROSH CHODESH ADAR

WOW conducted a full prayer service, with Torah reading, at the Kotel.

JULY 25, 2002

Chief Judge Aharon Barak summoned WOW into the Supreme Court and once again, despite all our past rejections of this alternative site, offered us Robinson's Arch. This time, he will ask the government to make some physical improvements to the site at some point in the future. WOW demanded, yet again, that the May 2000 unanimous decision in our favor be implemented.

Notes

Introduction

1 We asked for one hour for each Rosh Chodesh (new month), with the exception of the month of Tishrei, when Rosh Chodesh is Rosh Hashanah.

2 The First Temple was destroyed in 586 B.C.E. by the Babylonians.

3 These stones belong to the Second Temple era. The Second Temple was destroyed in 70 C.E. by the Romans. Some of the upper-level stones were added later.

4 Holy sites and objects seem to be inherently dangerous. The Torah (Leviticus 10:2) teaches that the sons of Aaron, the high priest, were struck dead in the holy place of the desert Tabernacle after bringing "strange fire." Some commentators consider them to have been among the holiest of the Israelites and believe that they were killed because, as Leviticus 10:3 states, God is sanctified by those closest to God. It is unclear what "strange fire" means.

Later in Israel's history, when the people were in the land, men who touched the holy ark itself were killed by God. See 2 Samuel 6:3–8. David was displeased with God for this.

Thus we learn that great care must be taken when dealing with holy places and holy objects, as they themselves contain the potential to cause harm. All who come into contact with them must approach with caution and respect.

5 Only the ashes of a red heifer, a *parah adumah*, can accomplish this. To date, no red heifer has been found, although some do seek one.

6 According to tradition, both Temples stood on the same site, the Second having been rebuilt over the ruins of the First. There are different views on this. According to one view, the area of the mosques themselves is not off limits, and those who maintain that they do know the area where the Temples stood believe that they may, therefore, walk on the Mount without violating Jewish law.

7   Remnants may exist underneath the Mount, but access to them has been denied. Throughout 2001, Israeli archaeologists complained that the Waqf, the Islamic religious council that controls the site, is deliberately destroying ancient, irreplaceable artifacts from both Temples and throwing them in huge garbage heaps. Some archaeologists have sifted through some of the rubble and claim to have found artifacts from Temple times. They accuse the Waqf of deliberately trying to erase evidence of the Jewish past in that area. Indeed, Arab propaganda against Israel asserts that the Jews have no history on the Mount.

8   In an interesting article in *The Jewish Press* ("There's Lots of Law," August 3, 2001), Herbert B. Sunshine, an attorney who appeared before the Israeli Supreme Court in two cases involving Jewish prayer on the Temple Mount, stated that he asked the Court the following:

> If Arabs can pray on the Temple Mount, and if Christians can pray on the Temple Mount, would the restriction of Jewish prayer not constitute discrimination, and *would such restriction then not be a reward for violence?* ... If the fear of violence shapes the law, then violence is the law.

He also asked the Court, If Jews were to forbid Muslim prayer on the Mount, would the Court permit it? Sunshine says that one of the judges responded: *"But Jews are not violent, so the question is not appropriate."*

9   In July 2001, Representative Eric Cantor, a Republican from Virginia, introduced a bill to Congress that would require the cessation of all American funding to the Palestinian Authority until there are no more excavations underway on the Temple Mount. The bill, called the Temple Mount Preservation Act of 2001, has twenty-five sponsors.

10 Orthodox women's prayer groups do not constitute themselves as minyans, which, according to most but not all Orthodox rabbis, require ten men. The group at the Kotel adheres to this limitation and is not constituted as a minyan. See Grossman and Haut, *Daughters of the King.*

11 Her partner, Johnny Misheiker, has been a tremendous asset as well.

12 This area is not in sight of the Kotel. The ramp leading up to the Temple Mount divides it from the Kotel. It is not easily reached.

13 Some Conservative Jews are quite happy with this arrangement, but others are dissatisfied with it for a variety of reasons.

14 This disagreement on how to proceed probably occurred because ICWOW's major contribution to the cause is fund raising and legal strategizing, which enables us to feel most connected, whereas WOW operates "on the ground."

15 This is an incomplete list.

16 One group tried to submit an amicus brief but did not finish it in time. The Israel Women's Network tried to join the lawsuit, but the court did not allow it to do so.

17 The Reform movement has been especially supportive and also sensitive to our desire not to be affiliated with any religious movement. Its leaders have given us advice and have agreed with our decision to accept no alternative site.

Drama in Jerusalem

1 Rosh Chodesh is the beginning of the new Hebrew month, marked by the appearance of the new moon. According to a midrash in *Pirkei de Rabbi Eliezer,* Chapter 45, Rosh Chodesh was given to women because they did not contribute gold to the building of the golden calf. Because the months follow the lunar cycle, they also reflect the female physiological cycle of renewal—another reason for the association of Rosh Chodesh with women.

2 Rivka Haut sent us a detailed report of the New York City meeting.

3 The *Barkhu* portion of the Torah blessing is considered to be one of the *devarim shebekedusha,* holy utterances, prohibited to women by most Orthodox authorities.

Tzitzit and Tefillin at the Kotel

1 In Hebrew the word for women is *nashim.* Since *—im* is generally a masculine plural ending and *—ot* is generally the feminine plural ending, *nashim* is an exception to the linguistic rule. We chose to use *nashot,* similar to the way some American feminists have chosen to use *womyn* (for *woman*) and *wimmin* (for *women*). It is a profemale assertion that seeks to remove linguistic maleness from the female of the species, who has always been characterized as a "derivative" of the male.

The Fight against Being Silenced

1 The *Book of Abudraham,* Third Chapter of Mitzvot, written in the thirteenth century by Maharam of Rothenburg. Professor Shmuel Shiloh explains that the approach of the author is still partially prevalent today.

Stone Song

1 *Tanya* is an eighteenth-century Hasidic text written by Rabbi Schneur Zalman of Liadi. It utilizes many sources of Jewish mystical and philosophical thought as it explores and illuminates mystical concepts in Judaism.

2 This is a metaphor of God used by the Rabbis of the Talmud.

3 *Selah*, when spelled differently, means either "stone" or "always" in Hebrew.

4 Shavuot is the festival celebrating the giving of the gift of the Torah to the Israelites at Mount Sinai, from G-d.

5 See *Mechilta* on *Parshat Yitro.*

6 *Ba'al teshuvah*, "owner of the return," refers to someone who has returned to his or her Jewishness, becoming religiously observant.

7 *Peyot* are sidelocks worn by Jewish men and boys over the age of three.

8 Elul is the month preceding the High Holy Days. Every morning except Shabbat during this month the shofar—the ram's horn—is blown, in order to stir the hearts of those who hear to reflection and corrective action.

The Politics of Women of the Wall

1 Like all the democracies of the world, Israel is a work in progress. It is beyond the scope of this essay to discuss the very complex questions concerning the status of non-Jewish minorities, particularly Arabs, in Israel.

2 Democracies around the world have dealt with church-state relations in a variety of ways. In England, for example, the Anglican Church is the official Church of England. France budgets funds to support religious schools and institutions. Even in the United States, with its doctrine of separation of church and state, the issue is far from settled. Witness the national Christmas tree, federal holidays on Christmas and New Year, and the controversies that continue to swirl around abortion, prayer in schools, and displaying the Ten Commandments.

3 I have often heard people say that in a mixed Jewish group, Orthodox prayer custom should automatically prevail because non-Orthodox Jews can pray by Orthodox standards without violating their religious values, whereas the converse is not true. For many Conservative Jews, participation in an Orthodox prayer service, in which women don't count in a minyan, or in an Orthodox women's prayer service, in which Kaddish cannot be said, may violate deeply held religious values about the respect due to every member of the Jewish community, women and men alike.

4 Israel at the time was receiving and still receives billions of dollars of economic and military aid from the United States.

5 Israel's reputation and record for protecting religious rights at religious sites is always a potential flashpoint in negotiations over Jerusalem and other holy places.

6 ICWOW's internal debate over media and public relations reflects a problem that many diaspora Jewish organizations experience in finding a balance between

maximalist advocacy of a just cause and Israel's best interests versus the fear of weakening Israel in some way. At one point in ICWOW's deliberations, I called several other Jewish organizations to consult with them about ICWOW's public relations policy.

7 On another level, Elon's opinion was highly problematic, for while he wrote that our services were halakhic, he also treated the Kotel as an Orthodox synagogue where *memuneh haKotel* (the rabbi-administrator appointed to oversee the Kotel) would function as a *mara d'atra*, the rabbi in situ with halakhic authority over services at the Kotel. In the diaspora there are many Orthodox rabbis who allow women's *tefillah* in their synagogues, but there are many who don't, and the authority of the latter to bar these services from their synagogues is considered absolute regardless of the more lenient rulings of other Orthodox rabbis.

8 Meimad must be mentioned as an Orthodox party that opposes religious coercion and supports greater separation of synagogue and state.

9 Over the years, as the dominance of David Ben-Gurion's Labor Party eroded, both Labor and Likud became increasingly reliant on the Orthodox parties to form a governing coalition. In the role of kingmaker, the Orthodox parties became more politically assertive and powerful.

10 I use the broad term *Orthodox* rather than the narrower term *charedi* because although the political parties that joined the lawsuit against us were the *charedi* parties Shas and Degel HaTorah, the other veteran Orthodox party, the National Religious Party (NRP), has also played a role in stymieing ICWOW. For example, the Israeli Ministry of Religious Affairs, one of the defendants against whom ICWOW filed its lawsuit, has been in the hands of the National Religious Party for most of the years of the lawsuit. Likewise, the Chief Rabbinate of Israel, which is also a defendant in our lawsuit, is not a *charedi* institution.

11 This is true despite the fact that neither Herut nor Likud are religious parties and despite the fact that Ovadiah Yosef, an eminent Sephardic rabbi, has long endorsed territorial concessions in return for peace. In politics, perception is treated as reality. The spokespersons representing citizens of Judea and Samaria are almost exclusively Orthodox, and this has cast this issue in a secular versus Orthodox light.

12 Dayan did eventually consider coming to a WOW prayer service around November (Hanukkah) 1996, but she was dissuaded from attending because of fear that her presence might provoke greater *charedi* violence.

13 Initially, I attributed Meretz's indifference to an inability to project itself into our religious commitment to the Kotel. As the 1990s wore on, however,

Meretz's reticence regarding the Kotel took on the same pragmatic character as that of Likud and Labor. Meretz, in an attempt to broaden its political appeal, made efforts to combat its militantly antireligious image and have a rapprochement with key Orthodox leaders. This shift in Meretz's political tactics meant that it was even more unlikely to espouse ICWOW's cause.

14 So far even Meimad, an Orthodox party with a commitment to freedom from religious coercion and a member of Barak's 1999 government, has not taken a stand on the Kotel.

15 Kehillat Yedidyah in Baka, Jerusalem, which early in ICWOW's history housed our Torah, has had women's *tefillah* for many years. From time to time, small Orthodox women's *tefillah* groups have sprung up in Israel, usually with a core of North American women, but these groups have sprouted and then disappeared. In September 2000, Hana Kehat, a key leader behind the 1998 founding of the Orthodox Women's Forum in Israel, contacted WOW asking to borrow its Torah for Simchat Torah because Kehat's rabbi in Elazar (Gush Etzion) had refused her request. Perhaps this is the beginning of change with regard to the women's *tefillah* movement in Israel.

16 The Law of Return grants automatic citizenship to every Jew who settles in Israel. Periodically, there have been politically explosive debates in Israel, with the passionate involvement of diaspora Jews, over the definition of who qualifies under this law for automatic citizenship.

17 The politically weak Reform and Masorati movements in Israel have petitioned the Israeli Supreme Court on numerous issues. Women have sought redress in court for discrimination in the workplace and in the rabbinical divorce tribunals.

18 In 1999, Meretz's Yossi Sarid, Minister of Education in the Barak government, announced that schools under the auspices of non-Orthodox streams would receive a fair share of government funding. This represents a move toward more equal treatment for all streams, but it is still a political decision, which is quite different from a right to equality that is regarded as inviolable no matter which party holds political power.

19 Beginning in the 1990s, Israeli Supreme Court judges have been subject to scathing political attacks from right-wing religious factions and have even been threatened with violence; some travel with bodyguards.

20 The regulation barring Torah, tallit, and audible prayer in the women's section was promulgated in 1990, shortly after our lawsuit was first filed.

Meditation and Conflict: A Journey on Paper

1   L. Rivlin, "The Wall Is Not for Climbing," *Jewish Frontier* (Spring 1969).

Orthodox Women's Spirituality

1   *Shir Hashirim Rabbah* (2:9); see also *Shemot Rabbah* (11:2), where the point is made: "Just as there is a distinction between window and lattice, so too is there a distinction between the merit of the forefathers and the merit of the foremothers."

2   *Encyclopedia Judaica*, Vol. 16, p. 467. See also David Rosoff, *Where Heaven Touches Earth* (Jerusalem: Guardian Press, 1998). Moses Hagiz (1672–1744) seems to be the source of the story. For centuries, the exact location of the Kotel was unknown. The thirteenth-century scholar Nachmanides did not mention it in his account of the site of the ancient Temples. According to Rosoff, the digging up of the Kotel occurred in the time of Omar al Khallab (638 C.E.). The Muslim ruler noticed women from around Jerusalem coming to a certain spot to dump their garbage. He inquired of them why they did this, and they said they were ordered to do so by a previous ruler, in order to bury the Jewish holy place that was there. According to this account, the ruler had the mound of garbage dug up, and the Kotel was revealed.

3   For example, see *Midrash Socher Tov* (11:3): "Rav Acha said: The Shekhinah will never leave the *Kotel Maaravi*." The Midrash may refer to the wall of the Temple itself and not the Kotel. However, as the Temple with all its walls has been totally destroyed, we interpret the saying to mean the Kotel.

4   Judges 4 and 5; 1 Samuel 1 and 2.

5   See *Berakhot* 31: "Rav Himnuna said: We can learn so many major *halakhot* [involving prayer] from the verses dealing with Hannah."

6   See Grossman and Haut, *Daughters of the King*, "Women and the Jerusalem Temple," pp. 15–37. Many public events took place in the women's courtyard (where men and non-Jews were also permitted), such as the annual Yom Kippur Torah reading.

7   When discussing the number of people called to the Torah on various holidays, the Talmud, at *Megillah* 22b, takes into account that on Rosh Chodesh *aliyot* are added, as there is no issue of *bitul melachah*, keeping people away from their work, as they would not be working that day. The Tosafot, s.v. *she'ein bahem bittul melachah*, point out that it is not customary for men to refrain from work on Rosh Chodesh, but it is for women. As women do not work on that day, their attendance in the synagogue, to hear the added *aliyah*, would not be affected. This is therefore an instance in which women's presence in the synagogue is assumed, and even affects halakhic decisions.

8 Grossman and Haut, p. 144.

9 In 1998 my husband—*alav hashalom* (may he rest in peace)—and I visited the one remaining synagogue in Rhodes. The woman who was the guardian of the synagogue told me that the building attached to the main synagogue, which is now a small museum, was, hundreds of years ago, the "women's synagogue." She believed that women prayed in that separate building until renovations were done that brought the women into the main building.

10 Grossman and Haut, pp. 59–71.

11 *Techinahs* were written by both women and men. See Weissler, *Voices of the Matriarchs.*

12 See, for example, Zakutinsky, *Techinas: A Voice from the Heart.*

13 See Menachem M. Brayer, *The Jewish Woman in Rabbinic Literature* (Hoboken, N.J.: KTAV, 1986) pp. 171–174. Schnirer maintained that education for women is a necessary protection from assimilation. She did not present it as a value in itself. She probably never dreamed that she was opening the door to higher studies for women, particularly talmudic study.

14 A Kollel is an advanced school for adult women equivalent to those for men—for example, Nishmat, Pardes, and Midreshet Lindenbaum in Israel. In New York, Drisha offers a wide range of advanced studies.

15 Nishmat, in Israel, has begun awarding degrees to women who are experts in the laws of family purity. In the United States a few women have begun studying toward this degree.

16 *Toanot* are rabbinical court pleaders who argue cases for female clients involved in matrimonial disputes in Israeli rabbinical courts. These female experts in Halakhah as well as Israeli civil law provide a woman's voice in a previously all-male system.

17 I have been involved with *agunah* activism for more than twenty years. For a brief discussion of this issue, see my article "The *Agunah* and Divorce," in *Life-cycles*, edited by Rabbi Debra Orenstein, pp. 188–200. Also see Rabbi Irwin H. Haut, *Divorce in Jewish Law and Life.*

18 Men are obligated to pray three times a day, at specific times. They are encouraged to pray with a minyan. Ten men constitute a minyan, which is required for the recitation of certain prayers. According to most interpretations of Orthodoxy (not all), a minyan is made up of men only, and only they may lead prayers and receive Torah honors.

19 For a fuller discussion of *mechitzah*, see Grossman and Haut, pp. 117–134.

20 This is stated in *Baba Kama* 82a, in order that the congregation not go three days without hearing words of Torah.

21 *Megillah* 23a.

22 Maimonides, *Hilkhat Sefer Torah* 10:8. See also Weiss, *Women at Prayer,* pp. 85–98.

23 One of our departures from regular synagogue practice was to have the prayer leader refrain from reciting the *Shemoneh Esreih* until the group finished its individual recitations, and then to recite her individual *Shemoneh Esreih* aloud. Another is for those receiving *aliyot* to defer reciting *Birkat haTorah*, found in the beginning prayers, until they are called for their *aliyot.*

24 Examples are positive timebound mitzvot such as wearing *tzitzit* and donning tefillin.

25 Rabbi Hershel Schachter, "Go Out in the Footsteps of the Sheep" (in Hebrew), *Beit Yitzhak,* Vol. 17 (1984–1985), pp. 118–134. For a fuller discussion of rabbinic opposition and a listing of related articles, see Grossman and Haut, pp. 145–148, and n. 1.

26 A prayer for *agunot* has wide circulation. Also, special *Mi Sheberakhs* have been written for various occasions, such as engagements.

27 At the third Jewish Orthodox Feminist Alliance conference, in 1999, a group met to discuss creating a *siddur* for women. These early efforts have so far produced only discussions but hopefully will lead to practical results in the future.

28 The Jewish Orthodox Feminist Alliance is chaired by Blu Greenberg, who joined WOW at our first *tefillah.*

29 A number of times prior to the founding of WOW, I was involved in attempting to organize joint prayer services for women of different denominations. Once, at a UJA daylong session, we women prayed silently, individually, joining together only for the opening and closing morning prayers, because we were unable to agree on a joint prayer format.

30 There are many WTGs across the world that now have Orthodox rabbinic support. Many of the largest synagogues permit the groups to meet in their buildings. The e-mail listserv of the Women's Tefillah Network has posted lists of supportive rabbis, and their number is growing.

31 There are some well-known Orthodox rabbis who have expressed support, but they are few—for example, Rabbi Emanuel Rackman of New York, and Rabbi Rene Sirat of France.

32 A few years ago, the *Va'ad Harabbanim* (rabbinical board) of Queens, New York, reopened the dispute by issuing a public ban on WTGs, in response to a bat mitzvah that was held in a WTG in a Queens synagogue. This action infuriated many women, who expressed their outrage by joining WTGs, and the entire flap actually helped the WTG movement.

33 The Riverdale *tefillah* group celebrated its bat mitzvah year with a trip to Israel and prayed together with WOW.

34 In Flatbush, Brooklyn, New York, after almost twenty years, the group still

has no home in any Orthodox synagogue in the community, despite years of trying.

35 David Rosen, an Orthodox Israeli rabbi, has permitted the women of Yedidyah's telfillah group to recite *Barkhu*.

36 Goren cited the Tosafot at *Rosh Hashanah* 33a, s.v. *ha-Rabbi Yehudah*. They permit women to recite blessings over rituals that they are exempt from performing but may perform if they so desire. Reciting these blessings is not considered taking God's name in vain and is permitted. Ashkenazi authorities follow this ruling and thereby allow women to recite blessings over *lulav* and *etrog*, for example. Goren extended this ruling to include women in WTGs, permitting them to recite blessings recited in the presence of a minyan, as long as men were not present.

37 This synagogue's daily services are conducted in a small *beit midrash*, not in the regular large space used for Shabbat services. However, a few synagogues, such as the Hebrew Institute of Riverdale, welcome women who attend daily services, whether to recite Kaddish or simply to pray with a congregation, and provide ample and comfortable space for them. In 2001–2002, my daughters recited Kaddish daily for their father at the Hebrew Institute and felt totally accepted there.

38 For example, Rabbi Meir of Rothenberg (the Maharam), cited in *Sefer Abudarham* (Jerusalem: Usha, 1962), p. 130, ruled that in a "city of *kohanim*," honoring a *kohen* for the third *aliyah* might impugn the lineage of the first and second *kohanim* called, implying that they are not really *kohanim*, and so, to avoid this, a woman is called for the third *aliyah*.

Also, see Rabbi David bar Shmuel HaKochavi of Ishtaylah, *Sefer haBatim* (Hebrew), edited by Rabbi Moshe Hershler (Jerusalem: Tzephunot Kadmonim, 1983), p. 236, where he permits women to read from the Torah when services are held at home rather than in a synagogue, since, he states, a group is considered a *"tzibur"* only in a synagogue, not in a home.

39 In addition, during the Arab riots in 2001, WOW also had to endure the danger of rocks being thrown by Arab fanatics, who were on the Temple Mount itself, on Jews praying at the Kotel.

Shema B'Kolah: On Listening to Women's Voices in Prayer

1 Early versions of this essay were presented at the Women's Tefillah Network Conference in 1988 and again in 1989 at the Hebrew University in Israel.

2 See various articles in Grossman and Haut, *Daughters of the King*, especially Grossman, "Women and the Jerusalem Temple," pp. 15–38, and Safrai, "Women and

the Ancient Synagogue," pp. 39–49. Text references include: *Berakhot* 17a; *Sotah* 22a; Leviticus 9:9; *Sofrim* 18:4. See also Solomon Schechter, "Women in Temple and Synagogue," *Studies in Judaism*, Vol. 1, pp. 313–325.

3 Susan Sered's *Women as Ritual Experts*, pp. 112–114, describes elderly retired women who do not know how to pray but go to synagogue regularly as an expression of piety.

4 Medieval European synagogues definitely had a separate women's section, frequently called the *weibershul*. This area, sometimes a room or annex, was so separate that some women, called *zogerin*, would lead the others in prayer. The communities in Worms and Frankfurt built separate buildings for the women. *Encyclopedia Judaica*, s.v. *mechitzah*, Vol. 11, p. 1235; and ibid., p. 192 and p. 226.

The *Be'er Hetev*, in his commentary on the laws of reading the *Megillah*, notes that some young women went to the women's synagogue, *beit haknesset nashim* (*Shulchan Arukh*, OH 689).

There are numerous sources confirming women's presence in the medieval synagogue: Israel Abrahams, *Jewish Life in the Middle Ages* (Philadelphia: Jewish Publication Society, 1981); Emily Taitz, "*Kol Ishah*—The Voice of Woman: Where Was It Heard in Medieval Europe," *Conservative Judaism*, Vol. 38, no. 3 (Spring 1986), pp. 46–61; and Howard Tzvi Adelman, "Italian Jewish Women at Prayer," in *Judaism in Practice: From the Middle Ages to the Early Modern Period*, edited by Lawrence Fine (Princeton: Princeton University Press, 2001), pp. 52–60. For a comprehensive annotated bibliography, see Cheryl Tallan, *Medieval Jewish Women in History, Literature and Art: A Bibliography* (Hadassah International Research Institute on Jewish Women at Brandeis University [HIRIJW] Working Paper, 2000).

5 See Brooten, *Women Leaders in the Ancient Synagogue.*

6 Taitz (n. 4), p. 54.

7 See Weissler, *Voices of the Matriarchs.*

8 Doniel Neustadt, "Selected *Halachos* relating to Parshas Vaeira," Wednesday, January 13, 1999 (www.torah.org/advanced/weekly-halacha). "Issues in Practical Halacha," Issue Number 18—Lag B'Omer 5755 (compiled and published by Kollel Menachem-Lubavitch, Melbourne, Australia, and available on www.havienu.org/html/living.html or through Naftoli Biber at bibern@tmxmelb.mhs.oz.au).

9 For an excellent presentation, see Menachem Kasdan, "Are Women Obligated to Pray?" *The Journal of Halacha and Contemporary Society*, Vol. 1, no. 2 (1981), pp. 86–106. See also Irwin Haut, "Are Women Obligated to Pray?" in Grossman and Haut, pp. 89–102.

10 Hence the numerous articles and books recently trying to confirm that women are obligated to pray and that historically they did so. An interesting series of

articles in Judaism highlights the various readings and consequences of the level of women's obligation. See Judith Hauptman, "Women and Prayer: An Attempt to Dispel Some Fallacies," *Judaism* Vol. 42 (1993), pp. 94–103. Also see Michael Broyde, Joel B. Wolowelsky, and Judith Hauptman, "Further on Women as Prayer Leaders and Their Role in Communal Prayer: An Exchange," *Judaism*, Vol. 43 (1993), pp. 387–413.

11 There are numerous descriptions and discussions of women's prayer groups. See Grossman and Haut, *Daughters of the King*, and Weiss, *Women at Prayer.*

12 Arlene Agus, "This Month Is for You," in *The Jewish Woman*, edited by E. Koltun (New York: Schocken Books, 1975), pp. 84–93; Sue Berrin (Ed.), *Celebrating the New Moon: A Rosh Chodesh Anthology* (Northvale, N.J.: Jason Aronson, 1996).

13 Moshe Meiselman, *Jewish Woman in Jewish Law* (New York: KTAV, 1978); Abba Bronspiegel, *"Minyanim Meyuhadim le-Nashim,"* *Hadarom*, Vol. 54 (Spring 1985), pp. 51–53; Hershel Schachter, *"Ze'i Lach be-Ikvei ha-Zon,"* *Beit Yizhak*, Vol. 17 (1985), pp. 118–134. These authors condemn the women's prayer groups referring to them as minyans, which is the designation for a prayer quorum which these groups have not claimed.

14 The most comprehensive presentation of the halakhic material is in Aryeh Frimer and Dov Frimer, "Women's Prayer Services: Theory and Practice," *Tradition*, Vol. 32, no. 2 (1998), pp. 5–118. Their basic conclusion is that there are no compelling halakhic grounds prohibiting women's prayer groups.

15 The *Mishnah Berurah* uses it in describing women's obligation to recite the *Gomel* prayer (*OH* 219:3). On the other hand, Rabbi David b. Samuel HaKochavi wrote that one of the *gedolim* (great ones) wrote that if ten women pray at home, they can read from the Torah, because the word *tzibur* applies only to prayer in the synagogue. See *Beit Tefillah*, edited by Rabbi Moshe Hershler (Jerusalem: Tzephunot Kadmonim, 1983), p. 236.

16 Moshe Meiselman, *Jewish Woman in Jewish Law* (New York: KTAV, 1978), p. 134.

17 Rabbi J. B. Soloveitchik pointedly presented the shared mission of Abraham and Sarah, signified in their mutual name changes. See *Shiurei Harav*, edited by Joseph Epstein (New York: Yeshiva University, *Hamevaser*, 1974), pp. 51–53.

18 Rabbi Naftali Tsvi Yehuda Berlin (the *Netziv*), in his commentary on this sequence, differentiated between *Shema el*, found elsewhere in the Bible, and *Shema b'*, imputing to the former a sense of obedience rather than to the latter. The story lines themselves do not necessarily fall into that format. As with so much, I am indebted to my husband, Rabbi Howard Joseph, for this information.

19 See the development of this concept in Norman Lamm, *The Shema: Spirituality and Law in Judaism* (Philadelphia: Jewish Publication Society, 1998), pp. 16–18.

20 For a reasoned presentation of the legal issues involved in use of both fringes and phylacteries, see, in Halpern and Safrai, *Jewish Legal Writings by Women*, Aviva Cayam, "Fringe Benefits: Women and *Tsitsit*," pp. 119–142, and Aliza Berger, "Wrapped Attention: May Women Wear Tefillin?" pp. 75–118.

21 There is continuing debate on the place of motive in performance of mitzvot. There are many references to this topic in the Talmud indicating both its importance and complexity as well as a difference of opinions: *Pesachim* 114b; *Berakhot* 13, 33b; *Eruvin* 95; *Rosh Hashanah* 28; *Sukkah* 42; *Nazir* 23a.

22 For a full description and analysis, see my essay "Those (Over)Confident Women: Heretical Insiders in Rabbi Moshe Feinstein's Responsa," in Halpern and Safrai, *Jewish Legal Writings by Women*, Vol. 2 (forthcoming).

23 *Iggerot Moshe, OH* 4:49 (my translation).

24 Ibid.

25 Translation of letter to Rabbi Fund from Rabbi Mordecai Tendler, 4 Sivan 5743.

26 His decision in this case is prompted by the fact that this is the community of Mount Clemens that tried to remove the *mechitzah* previously. See Baruch Litvin (Ed.), *The Sanctity of the Synagogue* (New York: Litvin, 1962), and my "Halakhic Decisions and Political Consequences," in Grossman and Haut, *Daughters of the King*.

27 *Sridei Aish* 2:18 (my translation).

28 See my essay "Ritual, Law, and Praxis: An American Response/a to Bat Mitsva Celebrations," *Modern Judaism*, Vol. 22, pp. 234–260.

29 There are a number of divergent but excellent articles describing the sources and analyzing the results: Saul Berman, "*Kol 'Isha*," in *Rabbi Joseph Lookstein Memorial Volume*, edited by Leo Landman (New York: KTAV, 1980), pp. 45–66; Elyakim Getsel Ellinson, *Ha'Ishah Ve'Hamitsvot*, Vol. 2, chapter 2, sections 24–29 (1981, translated 1992); Ben Cherney, "*Kol Isha*," *Journal of Halacha and Contemporary Society*, Vol. 10 (Fall 1985), pp. 57–75; Emily Taitz, "*Kol Ishah*—The Voice of Woman: Where Was It Heard in Medieval Europe?" *Conservative Judaism*, Vol. 38, no. 3 (Spring 1986), pp. 46–61; Howard Eilberg-Schwartz, "The Nakedness of a Woman's Voice, the Pleasure of a Man's Mouth," in *Off with Her Head: The Denial of Women's Identity in Myth, Religion, and Culture*, edited by Howard Eilberg-Schwartz and Wendy Doniger (Berkeley: University of California Press, 1995), pp. 165–184; Yehudah Henkin, "*Kol Ishah* Reviewed," in *Equality Lost: Essays in Torah Commentary, Halacha, and Jewish Thought* (Jerusalem: Urim Publications, 1999); Mia Diamond Padwa, "For Your Voice Is Sweet . . . An Overview of *Kol Isha*," *JOFA Journal*, Vol. 2, no. 1 (Winter 2000), pp. 4–5.

30 For consistency, all three translations are taken from Getsel Ellinson, *Women*

and the Mitzvot: The Modest Way, Vol. 2, translated by Raphael Blumberg (Jerusalem: World Zionist Organization, 1992).

31 In an alternative reading, the Jerusalem Talmud links Samuel's statement to a different and specifically pejorative text of Jeremiah 3:9: *tractate Challah* 2:1. See Cherney (n. 29), p. 57, and Ellinson (n. 30), p. 98, n. 160.

32 See Berman's (n. 29) presentation of the Ritva's position, p. 53.

33 Translated in Ellinson (n. 30), p. 118.

34 Taitz (n. 29), pp. 47–52.

35 The most persuasive articulation of this position is Rabbi Abraham Gumbiner, *Magen Avraham* to *Shulchan Arukh, OH* 75:6: "The singing voice of a married woman is always forbidden to be heard, but her speaking voice is permitted." That is the decision as found in the *Beit Yosef, OH* 75, and *Aruch Hashulchan, OH* 75:8.

36 Rabbi Weinberg relies on the *Mordecai* (*Berakhot* 80).

37 Taitz (n. 29), p. 47.

38 *S'dei Hemed, Ma'arechet* 100, 42, translated in Ellinson (n. 30), p. 107. Rabbi Weinberg refers to this decision, too.

39 Rochelle Millen, "Kaddish," in Halpern and Safrai, *Jewish Legal Writings by Women.* See responsa *Divrei Yisrael, OH* 35, on *regilut* and Kaddish by women in a minyan; Cherney (n. 29), p. 61, n. 17.

40 *Berakhot* 54b. For women's obligation to recite this prayer, see *Knesset Hagedolah, Mishnah Berurah,* and *Kaf Hachayim* at *OC* 219. Rabbi Ovadia Yosef, *Yehaveh Da'at,* section 15, p. 75.

41 This is markedly different from the reasoning of those like Rabbi Aharon Ha-Kohen, author of *Kol Bo,* who forbids women reading the *Megillah* for men because of *kol ishah.* One could counter that the *Megillah* is sung but the talmudic *aliyah* was the recitation of the Torah portion, which was also sung.

42 *Berakhot* 31a, b.

43 Interestingly, many Sephardic prayer books mention biblical women. The holiday prayer book of the Spanish and Portuguese congregations includes Hannah's name and prayer and references to Miriam. The Lebanese prayer book (Brooklyn: 1993) contains some names of biblical women and Hannah's prayer in the daily prayer section.

44 This is a restatement of one section in the daily *Amidah.*

Women and Ritual Artifacts

1 In *Persistence and Flexibility: Anthropological Perspectives on the American Jewish Experience,* edited by Walter P. Zenner (Albany: State University of New York Press,

1988). See also: Grant McCracken, *Culture and Consumption* (Bloomington and Indianapolis: Indiana University Press, 1998); Joan Newlon Radner (Ed.), *Feminist Messages: Coding in Woman's Folk Culture* (Urbana: University of Illinois Press, 1993).

2 Jack Werthheimer (Ed.), *The Uses of Tradition* (New York: Jewish Theological Seminary, 1992).

Toward a Psychology of Liberation: Feminism and Religion—a Conclusion

1 Phyllis Chesler, *With Child: A Diary of Motherhood* (New York: Lippincott & Crowell, 1979); new edition, with an introduction by Ariel Chesler (New York: Four Walls Eight Windows, 1998).

2 Those who planned and convened this first conference did not anticipate or organize our historic prayer service at the Kotel. Nevertheless, their work provided us with the opportunity to do so. Letty Cottin Pogrebin and Lilly Rivlin worked very hard with the paid staff of the Women's Division of the American Jewish Congress on this conference. In addition, American Jewish Congress organized buses for us to and from the Kotel, and also alerted the world media about our prayer service before it took place. In November of 1989, the American Jewish Congress joined us on our mission to donate a Torah to the women of Jerusalem. They did not subsidize our trip. Despite our pleading, the American Jewish Congress refused to assist us in our legal struggle in any way. I finally persuaded then president Henry Siegman to at least submit an amicus brief on our behalf; he agreed to do so, but literally within an hour, his legal counsel forced him to rescind his offer.

In 2000, the Israel Women's Network (IWN) and the American Jewish Congress organized a second, smaller conference of Jewish women. Rivka Haut was asked to speak about Orthodox feminism. Initially, IWN did not invite Israeli WOW to attend or to present at this conference. We prevailed upon them and, at the last minute, invitations to the Jerusalem-based WOW were issued. American Jewish Congress wanted to pray with WOW at the Kotel. They asked IWN to arrange this. When it became clear that IWN had not, American Jewish Congress turned to Rivka Haut, an invitee, to organize it for them long distance, from Brooklyn! At the last moment, Rivka did so. To the Congress's credit, once it became clear that the service would have to take place without any media (the Supreme Court judges were touring the various sites at that very time), the Congress complied.

3 *Parshat Vayeshev.* This is the first portion of the Joseph trilogy in Genesis. Joseph's father, Jacob, favors his son Joseph over all his sons; this favoritism unfortu-

nately endangers Joseph, as does Joseph's capacity to dream and to interpret his dreams. Joseph's enormous talent, his penchant to "tale-bear" against his older brothers, as well as the paternal gifts he receives, give rise to envy, anger, and a sense of unfairness among his brethren. Finally, Joseph's brothers throw him into a pit. The *parshah* continues with Joseph's being taken to Egypt, sold into slavery, and subsequently imprisoned there.

37:5: *Vayachalom Yosef chalom vayaged l'echav; vayoseefu ode sino oto.* "And Joseph dreamed a dream, and he told it to his brothers; and they increased their hatred of him."

37:9: *Vayachalom ode chalom achair, vayisaper oto l'echav; vayomer hinaih chalamti chalom ode, v'hinaih hashemesh v'hayareach, v'achad asar kochavim mishtachavim lee.* "And he dreamed another, different dream, and he told it to his brothers; and he said: 'Behold, again I have dreamed a dream, and behold the sun and the moon, and eleven stars were bowing to me.'"

4 Judith Plaskow, "Up Against the Wall," *Tikkun* Vol. 5, no. 4 (1990); letter written by ICWOW and joint letter by Plaskow and ICWOW, *Tikkun* Vol. 5, no. 5 (1990).

5 *Barkhu*, literally "let us bless," is a call to the congregation to bless God. The congregation immediately responds, "Blessed is Hashem, the blessed One, for all eternity." This responsive prayer serves as a brief introduction to a forthcoming blessing or set of blessings. *Barkhu* is recited in the morning and evening right before the blessings on the reading of the *Shema* are recited. *Barkhu* is also recited by the one called up to the Torah as an introduction to the blessing over the Torah. Both Kaddish and *Barkhu* traditionally call for a religious quorum.

6 Shulamit Magnus made this point in an interview I did with her that I then published as part of my first piece about us, "The Walls Came Tumbling Down," *On the Issues*, Vol. 9 (Spring 1989).

7 Shulamit Aloni founded Meretz, Israel's Civil Rights Party. Aloni is someone who had been exceedingly kind to me and my infant son in 1980, both in Copenhagen (where I'd been working for the United Nations and had invited her to debate Laila Khaled) and in Israel.

8 Nehama Leibowitz, *z"l*, the revered Orthodox Torah scholar, declined our invitation to deliver a *d'var Torah* upon the occasion of our Torah dedication.

9 Only a handful of Jewish feminist philanthropists funded the present anthology. Dr. Shulamit Reinharz at the Hadassah Center for the Study of Jewish Women, located at Brandeis University, gave us a generous grant toward this work. Ironically, some Jewish feminist philanthropists did fund a film about WOW whose director chose not to deal with our lawsuit and who did not interview some

of our major leaders, such as Bonna Haberman, Miriam Benson, and Shulamit Magnus—all of whom worshiped under siege that first year and all of whom have bravely soldiered on, both in Israel and in North America, since then. Nevertheless, many of us loved the idea that a film had been made about us and believed that enthusiasm for a film might translate into support for our cause. As of this writing, there are a number of other documentary films underway about us.

10 If only one or two philanthropic leaders had funded an office and one staff person for a two-year period, both in New York and in Jerusalem, by now we probably would have membership chapters around the world, a lobbyist in Israel, a lawyer on retainer, a private security detail, a woman's *siddur*, perhaps a woman's yeshiva near the Kotel, and the ability to offer ongoing educational programs about our struggle. As philanthropists know, it takes money to raise money. Without such seed money, we remain rooted to our kitchen tables. Not being properly funded does not mean that we have been "victimized"; clearly, we have both endured and prevailed. However, as a strictly "kitchen table" operation, we have not been able to train our replacements, plan for the future, prepare and distribute liturgical materials, or properly document our struggle for the historical record. Of course, many other worthy Jewish projects have endured similar frustrations.

11 Many women are still more comfortable in women-only settings, partly because women are not yet welcome in male-only places, and partly because, like men, many women are sexists and separatists.

12 For example, ICWOW board member Shula Gehlfuss was active in the early years of the struggle. I remember walking with her to the Kotel in 1989 to daven on an Erev Shabbat. Years later, she became less active. However, she had saved, in a big, legal accordion file, every letter written on our behalf to the Hollander Knesset Commission. She sent it to me; it is rich in human-interest material.

Suggested Reading

Adelman, Penina V. (1986). *Miriam's Well: Rituals for Jewish Women around the Year.* Fresh Meadows, N.Y.: Biblio Press.

Adler, Rachel. (1971). "The Jew Who Wasn't There: Halacha and the Jewish Woman." *Davka* (Summer).

————. (1988). "The Virgin in the Brothel and Other Anomalies: Character and Context in the Legend of Beruriah." *Tikkun,* 3 (6).

————. (1998). *Engendering Judaism: An Inclusive Theology and Ethics.* Philadelphia: Jewish Publication Society.

Anisfeld, Sharon Cohen; Mohr, Tara; and Spector, Catherine. (Eds.). (2003). *The Women's Passover Companion: Women's Reflections on the Festival of Freedom.* Woodstock, Vt.: Jewish Lights.

————. (2003). *The Women's Seder Sourcebook: Rituals and Readings for Use at the Seder.* Woodstock, Vt.: Jewish Lights.

Antonelli, Judith S. (1995). *In the Image of God: A Feminist Commentary on the Torah.* Northvale, N.J.: Jason Aronson.

Bal, Mieke. (1987). *Lethal Love: Feminist Literary Readings of Biblical Love Stories.* Bloomington, Ind.: Indiana University Press.

Baskin, Judith. (1994). *Gender and Jewish Studies.* New York: Biblio Press.

Baskin, Judith R. (Ed.). (1991). *Jewish Women in Historical Perspective.* Detroit: Wayne State University Press.

————. (1994). *Women of the Word: Jewish Women and Jewish Writing.* Detroit: Wayne State University Press.

Baum, Charlotte; Hyman, Paula; and Michel, Sonya. (Eds.). (1975). *The Jewish Woman in America.* New York: Dial Press.

Beck, Evelyn Torton. (Ed.). (1989). *Nice Jewish Girls: A Lesbian Anthology.* Boston: Beacon Press.

Ben-Zvi, Rachel Yanait. (1989). *Before Golda: Manya Schochat—A Biography.* Translated by Sandra Shurin. New York: Biblio Press.

Benson, Miriam, and Harverd, Dorit. (Eds.). (1998). *The Status of Women in Israel.* Jerusalem: Israel Women's Network.

Berkovits, Eliezer. (1990). *Jewish Women in Time and Torah.* Hoboken, N.J.: KTAV.

Biale, Rachel. (1984). *Women and Jewish Law.* New York: Schocken Books.

Brooten, Bernadette J. (1982). *Women Leaders in the Ancient Synagogue.* Chico, Calif.: Scholars Press.

Cantor, Aviva. (1995). *Jewish Women, Jewish Men: The Legacy of Patriarchy in Jewish Life.* San Francisco: HarperSanFrancisco.

Cantor, Aviva, et al. (1982). *The Jewish Woman, 1900–1980 Bibliography* (2nd ed.). Fresh Meadows, N.Y.: Biblio Press.

Cardin, Nina Beth. (1995). *Out of the Depths I Call to You: A Book of Prayers for the Married Jewish Woman.* Northvale, N.J.: Jason Aronson.

———. (2000). *The Tapestry of Jewish Time: A Spiritual Guide to Holidays and Life-Cycle Events.* Springfield, N.J.: Behrman House.

Dennis, Trevor. (1994). *Sarah Laughed: Women's Voices in the Old Testament.* Nashville: Abingdon Press.

Ellinson, Rabbi Elyakim Getsel. (1986). *Ha-Ishah ve-ha-Mitzvot.* 3 vols. Jerusalem: World Zionist Organization.

Falk, Marcia Lee. (1996). *The Book of Blessings: New Jewish Prayers for Daily Life, the Sabbath, and the New Moon Festival.* San Francisco: HarperSanFrancisco.

Fiorenza, Elizabeth Schüssler. (1992). *But She Said: Feminist Practices of Biblical Interpretation.* Boston: Beacon Press.

Frankel, Ellen. (1998). *The Five Books of Miriam: A Woman's Commentary on the Torah.* San Francisco: HarperSanFrancisco.

Frymer-Kensky, Tikva. (1992). *In the Wake of the Goddess: Women, Culture and the Biblical Transformation of Pagan Myth.* New York: Free Press.

———. (2002). *Reading the Women of the Bible.* New York: Schocken Books.

Geffen, Rela M. (Ed.). (1993). *Celebration and Renewal: Rites of Passage in Judaism.* Philadelphia: Jewish Publication Society.

Goldstein, Elyse. (Ed.). (2000). *The Women's Torah Commentary: New Insights from Women Rabbis on the 54 Weekly Torah Portions.* Woodstock, Vt.: Jewish Lights.

Graetz, Naomi. (1998). *Silence Is Deadly: Judaism Confronts Wifebeating.* Northvale, N.J.: Jason Aronson.

Greenberg, Blu. (1981). *On Women and Judaism: A View from Tradition.* Philadelphia: Jewish Publication Society.

Grossman, Susan, and Haut, Rivka. (Eds.). (1992). *Daughters of the King: Women and the Synagogue.* Philadelphia: Jewish Publication Society.

Halpern, Micah, and Safrai, Chana. (Eds.). (1998). *Jewish Legal Writings by Women.* Jerusalem: Urim Publications.

Hauptman, Judith. (1974). "Images of Women in the Talmud." In *Religion and Sexism*, edited by R. Ruether (pp. 196–210). New York: Simon & Schuster.

————. (1998). *Rereading the Rabbis: A Woman's Voice.* Boulder, Colo.: Westview Press.

Haut, Irwin H. (1983). *Divorce in Jewish Law and Life.* New York: Sepeher-Hermon Press.

Haut, Rivka. (1985). "From Women: Piety not Rebellion." *Sh'ma: A Journal of Jewish Responsibility, 15* (294), 110–112.

Hazleton, Lesley. (1977). *Israeli Women: The Reality behind the Myths.* New York: Simon & Schuster.

Henry, Sondra, and Taitz, Emily. (1990). *Written Out of History: Jewish Foremothers.* New York: Biblio Press.

Heschel, Susannah. (Ed.). (1983). *On Being a Jewish Feminist: A Reader.* New York: Schocken Books.

Howland, Courtney W. (Ed.). (1999). *Religious Fundamentalisms and the Human Rights of Women.* New York: St. Martin's Press.

Kantrowitz, Melanie Kaye, and Klepfisz, Irena. (1986). *The Tribe of Dina: A Jewish Women's Anthology.* Montpelier, Vt.: Sinister Wisdom Books.

Kates, Judith A., and Reimer, Gail Twersky. (1994). *Reading Ruth: Contemporary Women Reclaim a Sacred Story.* New York: Ballantine Books.

Kirsh, Jonathan. (1997). *The Harlot by the Side of the Road: Forbidden Tales of the Bible.* New York: Ballantine Books.

Koltun, Elizabeth (Ed.). (1976). *The Jewish Woman: New Perspectives.* New York: Schocken Books.

Lacks, Roslyn. (1980). *Women and Judaism: Myth, History, and Struggle.* Garden City, N.Y.: Doubleday.

Laska, Vera. (Ed.). (1983). *Women in the Resistance and in the Holocaust: The Voices of Eyewitnesses.* Westport, Conn.: Greenwood Press.

Leitner, Isabella. (1978). *Fragments of Isabella: A Memoir of Auschwitz.* New York: Dell.

Lowenthal, Martin. (Trans.). (1977). *Memoirs of Gluckel of Hameln.* New York: Schocken Books.

Nadell, Pamela S. (1998). *Women Who Would Be Rabbis: A History of Women's Ordination 1889–1985.* Boston: Beacon Press.

Ochs, Vanessa L. (1990). *Words on Fire: One Woman's Journey into the Sacred.* New York: Harcourt, Brace, Jovanovich.

Orenstein, Debra. (Ed.). (1994). *Lifecycles, Volume 1: Jewish Women in Life Passages and Personal Milestones.* Woodstock, Vt.: Jewish Lights.

Orenstein, Debra, and Litman, Rachel. (Eds.). (1997). *Lifecycles, Volume 2: Jewish Women on Biblical Themes in Contemporary Life.* Woodstock, Vt.: Jewish Lights.

Ostriker, Alicia Suskin. (1994). *The Nakedness of the Fathers: Biblical Visions and Revisions.* New Brunswick, N.J.: Rutgers University Press.

Pardes, Ilana. (1993). *Countertraditions in the Bible: A Feminist Approach.* Cambridge, Mass.: Harvard University Press.

Plaskow, Judith. (1990). *Standing Again at Sinai: Judaism from a Feminist Perspective.* San Francisco: Harper & Row.

Pogrebin, Letty Cottin. (1991). *Deborah, Golda, and Me: Being Female and Jewish in America.* New York: Crown.

Riskin, Shlomo. (1989). *Women and Jewish Divorce.* Hoboken, N.J.: KTAV.

Schneider, Susan Weidman. (1984). *Jewish and Female.* New York: Simon & Schuster.

Sered, Susan Starr. (1986). "Rachel's Tomb and the Milk Grotto of the Virgin Mary." *Journal of Feminist Studies in Religion, 2* (2), 7–22.

———. (1989). "Rachel's Tomb: Societal Liminality and the Revitalization of a Shrine." *Religion, 19,* 27–40.

———. (1992). *Women as Ritual Experts.* New York: Oxford University Press.

———. (2000). *What Makes Women Sick: Maternity, Modesty, and Militarism in Israeli Society.* Waltham, Mass.: Brandeis University Press.

Shazar, Rachel Katznelson. (Ed.). (1975). *The Plough Woman: Memoirs of the Pioneer Women of Palestine.* New York: Herzl Press.

Shepherd, Naomi. (1993). *A Price below Rubies: Jewish Women as Rebels and Radicals.* Cambridge, Mass.: Harvard University Press.

Sheridan, Sybil. (Ed.). (1994). *Hear Our Voice: Women in the British Rabbinate.* Columbia: University of South Carolina Press.

Trible, Phyllis. (1984). *Texts of Terror: Literary-Feminist Readings of Biblical Narratives.* Philadelphia: Fortress Press.

Umansky, Ellen M., and Ashton, Dianne. (Eds.). (1992). *Four Centuries of Jewish Women's Spirituality: A Sourcebook.* Boston: Beacon Press.

Wegner, Judith Romney. (1988). *Chattel or Person: The Status of Women in the Mishnah.* New York: Oxford University Press.

Weiner, Kayla, and Moon, Arianna. (Eds.). (1995). *Jewish Women Speak Out: Expanding the Boundaries of Psychology.* Seattle: Canopy Press.

Weiss, Avraham. (1990). *Women at Prayer: A Halakhic Analysis of Women's Prayer Groups.* Hoboken, N.J.: KTAV.

Weissler, Chava. (1998). *Voices of the Matriarchs: Listening to the Prayers of Early Modern Jewish Women.* Boston: Beacon Press.

Winkler, Gershon. (1991). *They Called Her Rebbe: The Maiden of Ludomir.* New York: Judaica Press.

Zakutinsky, Rivka. (1992). *Techinas: A Voice from the Heart.* Brooklyn, N.Y.: Aura Press.

Zemer, Moshe. (1999). *Evolving Halakhah: A Progressive Approach to Traditional Jewish Law.* Woodstock, Vt.: Jewish Lights.

Zornberg, Avivah Gottlieb. (1995). *Genesis: The Beginning of Desire.* Philadelphia: Jewish Publication Soceity.

————. (2001). *The Particulars of Rapture: Reflections on Exodus.* New York: Doubleday.

About the Contributors

Susan Alter has been a board member of ICWOW since its inception. She traveled to Israel to work with attorney Arnold Shpaer on the halakhic aspects of ICWOW's case. She served as a member of the New York City Council from 1978 to 1993 and was the first Orthodox elected official to it. For many years she was a member of Agunah, Inc., an organization she co-founded, and she remains involved in *agunah* activism.

Dr. Susan Aranoff is professor of economics at Kingsborough Community College in Brooklyn, New York. Her research and activism focus on gender inequality and its impact on the legal, economic, and political status of women. Among her articles are "Two Views of Women: Two Views of Marriage" and "Orthodox Jewish Divorce: An Imbalance in Bargaining Power." She is currently completing work on two books dealing with the struggle to free *agunot*, Orthodox Jewish women chained to dead marriages. She is a founding board member of ICWOW, Agunah, Inc., and the Jewish Orthodox Feminist Alliance. She has held numerous leadership positions in the New York UJA-Federation campaign and served for many years as a board member of Hebrew Immigrant Aid Society (HIAS). Dr. Aranoff has spoken across the United States and abroad on women and Judaism and is well known in her community for her classes in Judaica. She has six children and three grandchildren.

Chaia Beckerman is an editor and writer living in Jerusalem. She has been a member of Women of the Wall since its early days. She has a husband, daughter, and son.

Miriam Benson received her undergraduate education at the University of Pennsylvania. She then lived in Israel for six years, during which time she studied law at Hebrew University and worked as an attorney. Benson was an active member of WOW in 1989. Upon her return to the United States, she worked as an attorney in New York and Connecticut and is currently the executive director of the Connecticut Valley Region of United Synagogue of Conservative Judaism. She has maintained her connection with WOW by serving as legal liaison between ICWOW and the attorneys in Israel. Benson is married to Rabbi Jon-Jay Tilsen of Congregation Beth El-Keser Israel in New Haven. They have three children.

Danielle Bernstein was born in France in 1947, graduated in classical studies at the University of Strasbourg (France) and in Hebrew and Jewish studies at the Institut des Langues Orientales (Paris). Bernstein immigrated to Israel in 1975, married in California in 1981, and raised two sons and a daughter in the 1980s. When the children were well into school, she went back to school to realize an old dream and became a dance-movement therapist. At the same time, she became more involved in Torah learning in a women's study group in Yeruham, a small town in the Negev to which she later moved. In this framework her religious-feminist identity became more articulated, and as a result she helped to created the women's *tefillah* group in Yeruham. Upon resettling for family reasons in the Jerusalem area in 1995, she joined WOW and has been a board member ever since.

Rabbi Deborah J. Brin lives in a small town in Iowa with her partner, Lynn (Yael) McKeever, and their dog, Shayna. She is an avid backyard bird feeder and watcher who ends up feeding more squirrels than birds. She loves walking all over town with Shayna, an exceptionally well-behaved and beautiful dog who is better known than her owners. Rabbi Brin, the only rabbi for miles and miles, is the associate chaplain at Grinnell College, where she has created a vibrant community of students who love hanging out together and "doing Jewish." She is thrilled to be the rabbi for these men and women, the "future congregants, rabbis, and farmers of America." Before moving to Iowa, Rabbi Brin lived in Albuquerque, Toronto, Philadelphia, and Minneapolis, where she grew up.

Dr. Phyllis Chesler is an emerita professor of psychology and women's studies, a psychotherapist, and an expert courtroom witness. She is a founder of the Association for Women in Psychology (1969) and the National Women's Health Network (1974). She is on the advisory boards of the *Journal of Women and Therapy, Feminism and Psychology: An International Journal,* and *Nashim: A Journal of Jewish Women's Studies.* She is a charter member of the Women's Forum. Dr. Chesler has published hundreds of articles and ten books: *Women and Madness* (1972); *Women, Money and Power* (1976); *About Men* (1978); *With Child: A Diary of Motherhood* (1979); *Mothers on Trial: The Battle for Children and Custody* (1986); *Sacred Bond: The Legacy of Baby M* (1988); *Patriarchy: Notes of an Expert Witness* (1994); *Feminist Foremothers in Women's Studies, Psychology, and Mental Health* (1996); *Letters to a Young Feminist* (1998); and *Woman's Inhumanity to Woman* (2002). She had the honor of uncovering the Torah on December 1, 1988, in the historic women's prayer service at the Kotel and has been studying Torah ever since. She published her first *d'var Torah* in *Nashim* in 2000. She grew up in Borough Park, New York, now lives in Brooklyn, and is a member of the Park Slope Jewish Center. She has one son.

Karen Lee Erlichman is a licensed clinical social worker in private practice and the interfaith program coordinator at Jewish Family and Children's Services in San Francisco. She is also a spiritual direction trainee at the Mercy Center in Burlingame, California. She was in Jerusalem in 1988 with the first group of women who prayed together at the Wall, and she attended the International Jewish Feminist Conference. She has an article forthcoming in *Women and Therapy* entitled "Together We Build a *Mishkan*: Integrating Feminist Spirituality into Social Work Practice."

Rabbi Helene Ferris has been spiritual leader of Temple Israel of Northern Westchester in Croton, New York, since 1991. She has a bachelor of arts degree from Barnard College (1959), a master of arts in psychology from Columbia University (1962), a master of Hebrew letters from Hebrew Union College–Jewish Institute of Religion (1979), and was ordained in 1981. Before becoming the rabbi in Croton, she was the assistant rabbi at the Stephen Wise Free Synagogue in New York City, where she instituted a shelter for the homeless, founded an early childhood center, and organized the first conference on homosexuality in the Jewish community (1986). Rabbi Ferris was the first woman on the governing board of the New York Board of Rabbis and the first woman appointed to the Rabbinic Board of Overseers of HUC-JIR. Rabbi Ferris is married to Alan Ferris. They have three grown children, two grandchildren, and one on the way.

Rabbi Susan Grossman was a founding member of ICWOW. A member of the first class of women accepted for ordination at the Conservative movement's Jewish Theological Seminary, Rabbi Grossman serves as spiritual leader of Beth Shalom Congregation in Columbia, Maryland. She is one of the editors of *Etz Hayim Torah and Commentary: The Conservative Movement Humash*. She co-edited, along with Rivka Haut, *Daughters of the King: Women and the Synagogue*. She currently serves on the Committee for Jewish Law and Standards of the Conservative Movement. She lives in Maryland with her husband, David Boder, and their son, Yonatan.

Dr. Bonna Devora Haberman has taught on the faculty of the Harvard University Divinity School, Brandeis University, and Hebrew College. She founded Women of the Wall in Jerusalem. Currently she is resident scholar in women's studies at Brandeis University; founder and director of Mistabra: The Israel-Diaspora Institute for Jewish Textual Activism, housed at Brandeis University; and director of Education Initiative at the New Jewish High School of Greater Boston. Mistabra is mobilizing a Jewish movement against gender oppression and the trafficking of women into prostitution.

Rivka Haut is an Orthodox activist who has fought for the rights of religious women in the areas of Talmud study, marriage and divorce, and synagogue life. She was involved in the formation of halakhic women's prayer groups and the Women's Tefillah Network. She organized the first women's prayer service at the Kotel. Haut co-edited *Daughters of the King: Women in the Synagogue*, with Susan Grossman (JPS, 1992). She has worked to free *agunot*, women unable to obtain Jewish religious divorces, for many years.

She has been a director of Agunah, Inc., a caseworker for GET, and is presently director of the JOFA (Jewish Orthodox Feminist Alliance) task force on *agunot*. Haut was married to the late Rabbi Irwin H. Haut for thirty-seven years. They have two daughters, two sons-in-law, and three grandchildren: Ariel, Ayelet, and Esther Eleanna.

Anat Hoffman served three terms on the Municipal Council of Jerusalem and currently is head of the Reform movement in Israel. She is a leader of the movement fighting for women's right to pray at the Western Wall and in the battle for equal pay for equal work. She has pushed relentlessly for the provision of adequate municipal services for the more than 150,000 Palestinian citizens of Jerusalem. She has fought to see that the Jewish Orthodox bloc in the Council does not dictate lifestyle choices for the secular population of Jerusalem. She has fought for religious pluralism. Hoffman has represented the Civil Rights and Peace Movement on the Jerusalem City Council for the past ten years. She was born in Jerusalem and in her teens was an Israeli swimming champion. After army service studied for her bachelor of science degree in psychology at the University of California in Los Angeles and her masters at Bar Ilan University in Ramat Gan. Married and the mother of three, she was a founding member of Women of the Wall and Women in Black. She is a member of the executive board of the Israel Women's Network, an umbrella feminist organization.

Rahel Jaskow was born in New York State and moved to Israel in 1991. She has been active in Women of the Wall since 1995. She is a singer, and her first CD, *Day of Rest* (Argaman), was released in November 2000 and won the 2001 Just Plain Folks award for best CD in the ethnic music category. Jaskow serves as a prayer leader for Women of the Wall and her local women's prayer group in Jerusalem, Shirat Sara. She also participates regularly in the Leader Minyan as a Torah reader. Her film narration credits include *The Power of Hearing: The Story of Dr. Daniel Ling* and *I Am Joseph Your Brother* (Tal-El Productions). Jaskow's publishing credits include articles in *Horizons* magazine and the anthology *More of Our Lives* (Targum Press, 1993), and two stories in the forthcoming volume of the Small Miracles series, *Small Miracles for the Jewish Heart* (ed. Yitta Halberstam Mandelbaum, Adams Publishing). Jaskow created and coordinates the International Directory of Women's Tefillah Groups on the Internet (www.geocities.com/wtgdirectory), and she created the home page for the local women's prayer group in Jerusalem, Shirat Sara (www.geocities.com/shirat_sara). Her own website is at www.geocities.com/raheljaskow.

Dr. Norma Baumel Joseph is associate professor of religion at Concordia University. She is director of the women and religion specialization, and graduate program director of the doctoral program in religion. She is also an associate of the Concordia Institute for Canadian Jewish Studies. Her research areas include women and Judaism, Jewish law and ethics, and women and religion. Dr. Joseph appeared in and was consultant to the films *Half the Kingdom* and *Untying the Bonds: Jewish Divorce*. Her doctoral dissertation focused on the legal decisions of Rabbi Moses Feinstein as they describe and delineate separate spheres for women in the Jewish community. Since the early 1970s she has promoted women's greater participation in Jewish religious and communal life. Founding member of the Canadian Coalition of Jewish Women for the Get (Jewish divorce), Dr. Joseph successfully worked with the community and the federal government to pass a law in 1990 (Divorce Act, ch.18, 21.1) that would protect Jewish women in difficult divorce situations and aid them in their pursuit of a Jewish divorce. Author of many publications, Dr. Joseph was awarded the Jacob Zipper Education Award. She is currently a recipient of two Canadian research grants: one on gender and modern Jewish law and the other on gender and identity in the Iraqi Jewish community of Montreal.

Betsy (Batya) Kallus is originally from Boston, Massachusetts and has lived in Israel for the last twelve years. She works as the grants program director for The Abraham Fund, an organization promoting coexistence between Jewish and Arab citizens of Israel. She has been involved with Women of the Wall since arriving in Israel. She is married and the mother of Yochanon.

Leslie J. Klein is a studio artist now living in San Antonio, Texas. She has had many one-person shows, both in the United States and in Israel, including *The Eden Trilogy*, exhibited at the Artist's House in Jerusalem. Klein is also well known for her work in fabric-painting, dying, and constructing clothing and Judaic pieces such as challah covers and *tallitot*. She is currently a member of Textures Gallery, an art-to-wear-boutique in San Antonio. Klein has been active in feminist art for many years. In Miami she served as president of the Women's Caucus for Art of South Florida and on the board of the National WCA. She was southeastern regional chairwoman of the American Jewish Congress Commission for Women's Equality, and in 1988 she participated in the first Women's Torah Service at the Western Wall in Jerusalem, an earthshaking moment for her.

Rabbi Myriam Klotz is the former rabbinic director of the Kimmel-Spiller Jewish Healing Center of Jewish Family Services of Delaware. She directs the Miriam's Well Jewish Healing Rabbinic Internship program at the Reconstructionist Rabbinical College (RRC) and Germantown Jewish Centre in Philadelphia, and is a spiritual director at the RRC. Rabbi Klotz leads workshops nationally on *Torat HaGuf*, the Torah of the Body, and is a founding member of Shabbat Unplugged. She lives in Philadelphia with her partner, Margot Stein, and their three children, Raffi, Aryeh, and Sammy J.

Marion Krug was one of the Torah readers at the first women's *tefillah* at the Kotel in December 1988. A member of the women's *tefillah* movement for almost three decades, and one of the founders of the Teaneck Women's Tefillah, Krug is an Orthodox Jewish activist who is deeply committed to the survival of the Jewish people both physically and spiritually. Born in Germany and deported to Poland, she spent her formative years in England, where the family found refuge just prior to World War II. She has lived in the United States since 1952 and has spent forty years as a working professional in the Jewish community. As a layperson, Krug was actively involved in establishing three Orthodox synagogues and in fighting for the rights of *agunot* and the recognition of women within the framework of Halakhah. She is a member, founder, and past chairwoman of the Women's Chevrah Kadishah of Congregation Rinat Yisrael.

Dr. Gavrielle Levine is an active member of the Park Slope Jewish Center, an egalitarian Conservative synagogue in Brooklyn, New York. She was raised and educated in a Conservadox Jewish community, which did not honor women at the Torah. In the 1980s she was a founding member of the New York City P'nai Ohr community. She is an associate professor of education at the C. W. Post Campus of Long Island University. Her specialty is teacher preparation in mathematics instruction. She has had a strong interest in gender issues for many years, which has led her to the study of *ulpan* Hebrew, *haftarah* cantillation, and beginning Talmud study. She is looking forward to preparing for an adult bat mitzvah in the coming year.

Shulamit Magnus is associate professor of Jewish studies and history and chairwoman of Jewish studies at Oberlin College. She is the author of *Jewish Emancipation in a German City: Cologne 1798–1871* (Stanford University Press) and many articles about modern Jewish history, Jewish women's history, and gender in Jewish society. Her full, annotated translation of and critical introduction to the *Memoirs of Pauline Wengeroff* will shortly be in press; she is also writing a book about Wengeroff's memoirs and women's experience of Jewish modernity.

Aliza Michaels Metzner was raised in Brooklyn, New York. She graduated from Colgate University in 1975 with a bachelor of arts degree in social psychology and art, and from the University of Chicago with an MBA in 1979. Metzner's professional career spans banking, product and market development, management consulting, and art. Since her early student years, Metzner has derived a sense of purpose and meaning through social action and creative expression. Metzner currently works as a figurative sculptor and teaches religious school. She has developed a program that ignites the spark within children and their parents to understand and love the practice of Judaism and the teachings of Torah. Metzner enjoys introducing a history that includes women—some whose names have been lost but whose stories are important to our people. Metzner lives in Orinda, California, with her husband and two daughters.

Beryl Michaels attended the International Jewish Feminist Conference in 1988. She has been a supporter of WOW since its inception. Michaels' master's degree from the University of Chicago and bachelor's degree from the University of Illinois provide the academic foundation for her thirty-year career in the nonprofit sector, much of which has been as a Jewish communal professional. She is now the force behind JAYBEE Consultants, Sacramento, California, with three areas of concentration: executive search, executive coaching, and strategic development for nonprofits. She can be reached at jbconsultants@attbi.com. Michaels and her husband are members of the Jewish Reconstructionist Congregation, Evanston, Illinois, and the Mosaic Law Congregation, Sacramento, California. In 2001, Michaels organized the first Jewish women's feminist seder in Sacramento.

Haviva Ner-David has been an active member of WOW for many years. She is a doctoral candidate at Bar-Ilan University, and she is studying with an Orthodox rabbi in Jerusalem in order to receive *smichah*, rabbinic ordination. She authored *Life on the Fringes: A Feminist Journey Towards Traditional Rabbinic Ordination* (JFL Books, 2000). She also wrote "Parenting as a Religious Jewish Feminist," which appeared in *Yentl's Revenge* (Seal Press, 2001).

Dr. Vanessa L. Ochs is the Ida and Nathan Kolodiz Director of Jewish Studies and associate professor of religion at the University of Virginia in Charlottesville. She teaches courses in the anthropology of Judaism, religion and material culture, the literature of spirituality, women and Judaism, and Judaism and healing. Previously, she has taught at Colgate, Yale, Hebrew University, and Drew, and was a senior fellow at CLAL, the National Jewish Center for Learning and Leadership. She is a director of ICWOW, the author of *Words on Fire: One Woman's Journey into the Sacred* (Westview) and *Safe and Sound* (Penguin), and editor, with Rabbi Irwin Kula, of *The Book of Jewish Sacred Practices* (Jewish Lights). She has written for many newspapers and magazines, including *The New York Times, New York Newsday, New York Daily News, Tikkun, Moment, Lilith, Crosscurrents, Forward,* and Beliefnet.com. She was awarded a National Endowment for the Arts Fellowship in creative writing. Her new books are about new Jewish ritual and new midrash. Dr. Ochs earned her bachelor of arts in drama and French from Tufts University, a master of fine arts in theater from Sarah Lawrence College, and a doctorate in the anthropology of religion at Drew University.

Sharon Pikus is chairwoman of the Long Island Region of the American Jewish Congress Commission for Women's Equality. She is also on the board of directors and is the program chairwoman of US/Israel Women to Women.

Sue Polansky received a bachelor of science in occupational therapy from Columbia University and a master of science in psychology from the University of Bridgeport. She currently resides in Longmeadow, Massachusetts and serves on the executive committee of the Jewish Federation of Greater Springfield and on other committees, including those of Partnership 2000, the Jewish Endowment Foundation, Jewish Geriatrics Service, and the board of the western New England region of Hadassah. Marni Polansky is an undergraduate at Duke University and a life member of Hadassah. Both have traveled to Israel numerous times.

420

Dr. Frances Livingstone Raday is professor of law at the Hebrew University of Jerusalem and holds the Elias Lieberman Chair in Labour Law. She has held visiting professorships at University of East Africa at Dar-es Salaam, University of Southern California, University of Tulane, and University of Copenhagen. She is currently serving as an independent expert on the U. N. Committee for Elimination of All Forms of Discrimination Against Women. Dr. Raday was the founding chairwoman of the Legal Centre of the Israel Women's Network and has acted as lead counsel for litigants in precedent-setting sex discrimination, Palestinian rights, and labor rights cases. She is chief editor and coauthor of *Woman's Status in Law and Society* (in Hebrew) (Schocken, 1995), and author of numerous articles on equality rights, religion and human rights, labor rights, and feminist legal theory.

Rabbi Geela Rayzel Raphael is the rabbinic director of the Jericho Project, Interfaith Family Support of JFCS, Philadelphia. Rabbi Raphael also directs the Jewish Creativity Project—outreach through music and arts. She sings with the MIRAJ, an a cappella group, and with Shabbat Unplugged, and teaches in the Philadelphia area.

Lilly Rivlin, a seventh-generation Jerusalemite, was trained as a political scientist and has worked internationally and domestically as a journalist, writer-filmmaker, and foundation consultant for the last thirty-five years. A feminist and political activist most of her life, she is a creator of Jewish feminist ritual and midrash. Rivlin's career began as the chief researcher for the 1972 bestseller *O Jerusalem,* by Larry Collins and Dominique La Pierre (Simon & Schuster), followed by the development and writing of *The Jews,* a thirteen-part TV series commissioned in England. She published in numerous national magazines *(Ms., US),* before focusing on film and video. Her credits include *Gimme a Kiss* (2000), *We're Still Here! The Jews of Russia and Ukraine* (1999), *Miriam's Daughters Now* (1986), and *The Tribe* (1984). Rivlin wrote *Welcome to Israel* (Behrman House Press, 2000), co-edited and contributed to *Which Lilith? Feminist Writers Re-create the World's First Woman* (Jason Aronson, 1998), and conceived and shot *When Will the Fighting Stop? A Child's View of Jerusalem* (Atheneum, 1990). In addition to her artistic career, Rivlin was associate director of the New Israel Fund, executive coordinator of US/Israel Women to Women, and has consulted on Arab-Israeli coexistence projects. In addition to being on the board of ICWOW, she is a vice-president of Meretz USA and is on the board of the Counseling Center for Women. There is a biographical entry on Rivlin in the forthcoming *International Encyclopedia of Jewish Women.*

Celia Szterenfeld lives in Rio de Janeiro, Brazil, and joined in the women's first prayer service at the Kotel in 1988. She is active in the Jewish congregation of Brazil and is a member of its Bat Kol Rosh Chodesh group. In 1999, fifty-five women of this group celebrated an adult group bat mitzvah.

Index

Index

Index

Index

About JEWISH LIGHTS Publishing

People of all faiths and backgrounds yearn for books that attract, engage, educate, and spiritually inspire.

Our principal goal is to stimulate thought and help all people learn about who the Jewish People are, where they come from, and what the future can be made to hold. While people of our diverse Jewish heritage are the primary audience, our books speak to people in the Christian world as well and will broaden their understanding of Judaism and the roots of their own faith.

We bring to you authors who are at the forefront of spiritual thought and experience. While each has something different to say, they all say it in a voice that you can hear.

Our books are designed to welcome you and then to engage, stimulate, and inspire. We judge our success not only by whether or not our books are beautiful and commercially successful, but by whether or not they make a difference in your life.

We at Jewish Lights take great care to produce beautiful books that present meaningful spiritual content in a form that reflects the art of making high quality books. Therefore, we want to acknowledge those who contributed to the production of this book.

Stuart M. Matlins

Stuart M. Matlins, Publisher

PRODUCTION
Tim Holtz, Martha McKinney & Bridgett Taylor

EDITORIAL
Amanda Dupuis, Polly Short Mahoney,
Lauren Seidman & Emily Wichland

TEXT DESIGN
Chelsea Cloeter, Chelsea Designs, Tucson, Arizona

TYPESETTING
Susan Ramundo

JACKET DESIGN
Drena Fagen

JACKET / TEXT PRINTING & BINDING
Lake Book, Melrose Park, Illinois

The Way Into... Series

A major multi-volume series to be completed over the next several years, **The Way Into... provides an accessible and usable "guided tour" of the Jewish faith, its people, its history and beliefs—in total, an introduction to Judaism for adults that will enable them to understand and interact with sacred texts.** Each volume is written by a major modern scholar and teacher, and is organized around an important concept of Judaism.

The Way Into... will enable all readers to achieve a real sense of Jewish cultural literacy through guided study. Available volumes:

The Way Into Torah
by *Dr. Norman J. Cohen*

What is "Torah"? What are the different approaches to studying Torah? What are the different levels of understanding Torah? For whom is study intended? Explores the origins and development of Torah, why it should be studied and how to do it. An easy-to-use, easy-to-understand introduction to an ancient subject.
6 x 9, 176 pp, HC, ISBN 1-58023-028-8 **$21.95**

The Way Into Jewish Prayer
by *Dr. Lawrence A. Hoffman*

Opens the door to 3,000 years of the Jewish way to God by making available all you need to feel at home in Jewish worship. Provides basic definitions of the terms you need to know as well as thoughtful analysis of the depth that lies beneath Jewish prayer.
6 x 9, 224 pp, HC, ISBN 1-58023-027-X **$21.95**

The Way Into Encountering God in Judaism
by *Dr. Neil Gillman*

Explains how Jews have encountered God throughout history—and today—by exploring the many metaphors for God in Jewish tradition. Explores the Jewish tradition's passionate but also conflicting ways of relating to God as Creator, relational partner, and a force in history and nature.
6 x 9, 240 pp, HC, ISBN 1-58023-025-3 **$21.95**

The Way Into Jewish Mystical Tradition
by *Rabbi Lawrence Kushner*

Explains the principles of Jewish mystical thinking, their religious and spiritual significance, and how they relate to our lives. A book that allows us to experience and understand the Jewish mystical approach to our place in the world.
6 x 9, 224 pp, HC, ISBN 1-58023-029-6 **$21.95**

Or phone, fax, mail or e-mail to: **JEWISH LIGHTS** Publishing
Sunset Farm Offices, Route 4 • P.O. Box 237 • Woodstock, Vermont 05091
Tel: (802) 457-4000 • Fax: (802) 457-4004 • www.jewishlights.com
Credit card orders: **(800) 962-4544** (9AM–5PM ET Monday–Friday)
Generous discounts on quantity orders. SATISFACTION GUARANTEED. Prices subject to change.

Spirituality/Jewish Meditation

Aleph-Bet Yoga
Embodying the Hebrew Letters for Physical and Spiritual Well-Being
by *Steven A. Rapp;* Foreword by *Tamar Frankiel & Judy Greenfeld;* Preface by *Hart Lazer*

Blends aspects of hatha yoga and the shapes of the Hebrew letters. Connects yoga practice with Jewish spiritual life. Easy-to-follow instructions, b/w photos.

7 x 10, 128 pp, Quality PB, b/w photos, ISBN 1-58023-162-4 **$16.95**

The Rituals & Practices of a Jewish Life
A Handbook for Personal Spiritual Renewal
by *Rabbi Kerry M. Olitzky* and *Rabbi Daniel Judson;* Foreword by *Vanessa L. Ochs;* Illustrated by *Joel Moskowitz*

This easy-to-use handbook explains the why, what, and how of ten specific areas of Jewish ritual and practice: morning and evening blessings, covering the head, blessings throughout the day, daily prayer, tefillin, tallit and *tallit katan,* Torah study, kashrut, *mikvah,* and entering Shabbat.

6 x 9, 272 pp, Quality PB, Illus., 1-58023-169-1 **$18.95**

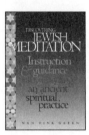    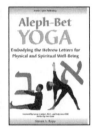

Discovering Jewish Meditation: *Instruction & Guidance for Learning an Ancient Spiritual Practice* by Nan Fink Gefen 6 x 9, 208 pp, Quality PB, ISBN 1-58023-067-9 **$16.95**

The Handbook of Jewish Meditation Practices: *A Guide for Enriching the Sabbath and Other Days of Your Life* by Rabbi David A. Cooper
6 x 9, 208 pp, Quality PB, ISBN 1-58023-102-0 **$16.95**

Meditation from the Heart of Judaism: *Today's Teachers Share Their Practices, Techniques, and Faith* Ed. by Avram Davis 6 x 9, 256 pp, Quality PB, ISBN 1-58023-049-0 **$16.95**

The Way of Flame: *A Guide to the Forgotten Mystical Tradition of Jewish Meditation* by Avram Davis 4½ x 8, 176 pp, Quality PB, ISBN 1-58023-060-1 **$15.95**

Minding the Temple of the Soul: *Balancing Body, Mind, and Spirit through Traditional Jewish Prayer, Movement, and Meditation* by Tamar Frankiel and Judy Greenfeld
7 x 10, 184 pp, Quality PB, Illus., ISBN 1-879045-64-8 **$16.95**

Entering the Temple of Dreams: *Jewish Prayers, Movements, and Meditations for the End of the Day* by Tamar Frankiel and Judy Greenfeld
7 x 10, 192 pp, Illus., Quality PB, ISBN 1-58023-079-2 **$16.95**

Children's Spirituality

Cain & Abel   AWARD WINNER!
Finding the Fruits of Peace
by *Sandy Eisenberg Sasso*
Full-color illus. by *Joani Keller Rothenberg*

For ages 5 & up

A sensitive recasting of the ancient tale shows we have the power to deal with anger in positive ways. Provides questions for kids and adults to explore together. "Editor's Choice"—American Library Association's *Booklist*

9 x 12, 32 pp, HC, Full-color illus., ISBN 1-58023-123-3 **$16.95**

For Heaven's Sake   AWARD WINNER!
For ages 4 & up

by *Sandy Eisenberg Sasso*; Full-color illus. by *Kathryn Kunz Finney*
Everyone talked about heaven, but no one would say what heaven was or how to find it. So Isaiah decides to find out. 9 x 12, 32 pp, HC, Full-color illus., ISBN 1-58023-054-7 **$16.95**

God Said Amen   AWARD WINNER!
For ages 4 & up

by *Sandy Eisenberg Sasso*; Full-color illus. by *Avi Katz*
Inspiring tale of two kingdoms: one overflowing with water but without oil to light its lamps; the other blessed with oil but no water to grow its gardens. The kingdoms' rulers ask God for help but are too stubborn to ask each other. Shows that we need only reach out to each other to find God's answer to our prayers. 9 x 12, 32 pp, HC, Full-color illus., ISBN 1-58023-080-6 **$16.95**

God in Between   AWARD WINNER!
For ages 4 & up

by *Sandy Eisenberg Sasso*; Full-color illus. by *Sally Sweetland*
If you wanted to find God, where would you look? This magical, mythical tale teaches that God can be found where we are: within all of us and the relationships between us.
9 x 12, 32 pp, HC, Full-color illus., ISBN 1-879045-86-9 **$16.95**

A Prayer for the Earth: *The Story of Naamah, Noah's Wife*
For ages 4 & up

by *Sandy Eisenberg Sasso*; Full-color illus. by *Bethanne Andersen* AWARD WINNER!
Opens religious imaginations to new ideas about the story of the Flood. When God tells Noah to bring the animals onto the ark, God also calls on Naamah, Noah's wife, to save each plant on Earth. 9 x 12, 32 pp, HC, Full-color illus., ISBN 1-879045-60-5 **$16.95**

But God Remembered   AWARD WINNER!
Stories of Women from Creation to the Promised Land
For ages 8 & up

by *Sandy Eisenberg Sasso*; Full-color illus. by *Bethanne Andersen*
Vibrantly brings to life four stories of courageous and strong women from ancient tradition; all teach important values through their actions and faith.
9 x 12, 32 pp, HC, Full-color illus., ISBN 1-879045-43-5 **$16.95**

Life Cycle/Grief/Divorce

Divorce Is a Mitzvah: *A Practical Guide to Finding Wholeness and Holiness When Your Marriage Dies*
by *Rabbi Perry Netter;*
Afterword—"Afterwards: New Jewish Divorce Rituals"—by *Rabbi Laura Geller*
What does Judaism tell you about divorce? This first-of-its-kind handbook provides practical wisdom from biblical and rabbinic teachings and modern psychological research, as well as information and strength from a Jewish perspective for those experiencing the challenging life-transition of divorce. 6 x 9, 224 pp, Quality PB, ISBN 1-58023-172-1 **$16.95**

Against the Dying of the Light
A Parent's Story of Love, Loss and Hope
by *Leonard Fein*
The sudden death of a child. A personal tragedy beyond description. Rage and despair deeper than sorrow. What can come from it? Raw wisdom and defiant hope. In this unusual exploration of heartbreak and healing, Fein chronicles the sudden death of his 30-year-old daughter and reveals what the progression of grief can teach each one of us.
5½ x 8½, 176 pp, HC, ISBN 1-58023-110-1 **$19.95**

Mourning & Mitzvah, 2nd Ed.: *A Guided Journal for Walking the Mourner's Path through Grief to Healing* with *Over 60 Guided Exercises*
by *Anne Brener, L.C.S.W.*
For those who mourn a death, for those who would help them, for those who face a loss of any kind, Brener teaches us the power and strength available to us in the fully experienced mourning process. Revised and expanded. 7½ x 9, 304 pp, Quality PB, ISBN 1-58023-113-6 **$19.95**

Grief in Our Seasons: *A Mourner's Kaddish Companion*
by *Rabbi Kerry M. Olitzky*
A wise and inspiring selection of sacred Jewish writings and a simple, powerful ancient ritual for mourners to read each day, to help hold the memory of their loved ones in their hearts. Offers a comforting, step-by-step daily link to saying Kaddish.
4½ x 6½, 448 pp, Quality PB, ISBN 1-879045-55-9 **$15.95**

 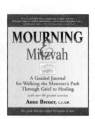   

Tears of Sorrow, Seeds of Hope
A Jewish Spiritual Companion for Infertility and Pregnancy Loss
by Rabbi Nina Beth Cardin   6 x 9, 192 pp, HC, ISBN 1-58023-017-2 **$19.95**

A Time to Mourn, A Time to Comfort
A Guide to Jewish Bereavement and Comfort
by Dr. Ron Wolfson 7 x 9, 336 pp, Quality PB, ISBN 1-879045-96-6 **$18.95**

When a Grandparent Dies
A Kid's Own Remembering Workbook for Dealing with Shiva and the Year Beyond
by Nechama Liss-Levinson, Ph.D.
8 x 10, 48 pp, HC, Illus., 2-color text, ISBN 1-879045-44-3 **$15.95**   For ages 7–13

Life Cycle & Holidays

The Jewish Family Fun Book: *Holiday Projects, Everyday Activities, and Travel Ideas with Jewish Themes*
by *Danielle Dardashti* & *Roni Sarig*; Illustrated by *Avi Katz*

With almost 100 easy-to-do activities to re-invigorate age-old Jewish customs and make them fun for the whole family, this complete sourcebook details activities for fun at home and away from home, including meaningful everyday and holiday crafts, recipes, travel guides, enriching entertainment and much, much more. Illustrated.
6 x 9, 288 pp, Quality PB, Illus., ISBN 1-58023-171-3 **$18.95**

The Book of Jewish Sacred Practices
CLAL's Guide to Everyday & Holiday Rituals & Blessings
Ed. by *Rabbi Irwin Kula* & *Vanessa L. Ochs, Ph.D.*

A meditation, blessing, profound Jewish teaching, and ritual for more than one hundred everyday events and holidays. 6 x 9, 368 pp, Quality PB, ISBN 1-58023-152-7 **$18.95**

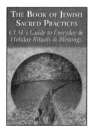

Celebrating Your New Jewish Daughter: *Creating Jewish Ways to Welcome Baby Girls into the Covenant—New and Traditional Ceremonies*
by Debra Nussbaum Cohen; Foreword by Rabbi Sandy Eisenberg Sasso
6 x 9, 272 pp, Quality PB, ISBN 1-58023-090-3 **$18.95**

The New Jewish Baby Book AWARD WINNER!
Names, Ceremonies & Customs—A Guide for Today's Families
by Anita Diamant 6 x 9, 336 pp, Quality PB, ISBN 1-879045-28-1 **$18.95**

Parenting As a Spiritual Journey
Deepening Ordinary & Extraordinary Events into Sacred Occasions
by Rabbi Nancy Fuchs-Kreimer 6 x 9, 224 pp, Quality PB, ISBN 1-58023-016-4 **$16.95**

Putting God on the Guest List, 2nd Ed. AWARD WINNER!
How to Reclaim the Spiritual Meaning of Your Child's Bar or Bat Mitzvah
by Rabbi Jeffrey K. Salkin 6 x 9, 224 pp, Quality PB, ISBN 1-879045-59-1 **$16.95**

The Bar/Bat Mitzvah Memory Book: *An Album for Treasuring the Spiritual Celebration* by Rabbi Jeffrey K. Salkin and Nina Salkin
8 x 10, 48 pp, Deluxe HC, 2-color text, ribbon marker, ISBN 1-58023-111-X **$19.95**

For Kids—Putting God on Your Guest List
How to Claim the Spiritual Meaning of Your Bar or Bat Mitzvah
by Rabbi Jeffrey K. Salkin 6 x 9, 144 pp, Quality PB, ISBN 1-58023-015-6 **$14.95**

Bar/Bat Mitzvah Basics, 2nd Ed.: *A Practical Family Guide to Coming of Age Together*
Ed. by Cantor Helen Leneman 6 x 9, 240 pp, Quality PB, ISBN 1-58023-151-9 **$18.95**

Hanukkah, 2nd Ed.: *The Family Guide to Spiritual Celebration*—The Art of Jewish Living
by Dr. Ron Wolfson 7 x 9, 240 pp, Quality PB, Illus., ISBN 1-58023-122-5 **$18.95**

Shabbat, 2nd Ed.: *Preparing for and Celebrating the Sabbath*—The Art of Jewish Living
by Dr. Ron Wolfson 7 x 9, 320 pp, Quality PB, Illus., ISBN 1-58023-164-0 **$19.95**

The Passover Seder—The Art of Jewish Living
by Dr. Ron Wolfson 7 x 9, 352 pp, Quality PB, Illus., ISBN 1-879045-93-1 **$16.95**

Spirituality—The Kushner Series
Books by Lawrence Kushner

The Way Into Jewish Mystical Tradition
Explains the principles of Jewish mystical thinking, their religious and spiritual significance, and how they relate to our lives. A book that allows us to experience and understand the Jewish mystical approach to our place in the world.
6 x 9, 224 pp, HC, ISBN 1-58023-029-6 **$21.95**

Jewish Spirituality: *A Brief Introduction for Christians*
Addresses Christian's questions, revealing the essence of Judaism in a way that people whose own tradition traces its roots to Judaism can understand and appreciate.
5½ x 8½, 112 pp, Quality PB, ISBN 1-58023-150-0 **$12.95**

Eyes Remade for Wonder: *The Way of Jewish Mysticism and Sacred Living*
A Lawrence Kushner Reader Intro. by *Thomas Moore*
Whether you are new to Kushner or a devoted fan, you'll find inspiration here. With samplings from each of Kushner's works, and a generous amount of new material, this book is to be read and reread, each time discovering deeper layers of meaning in our lives.
6 x 9, 240 pp, Quality PB, ISBN 1-58023-042-3 **$16.95**; HC, ISBN 1-58023-014-8 **$23.95**

   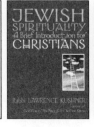 

Invisible Lines of Connection: *Sacred Stories of the Ordinary* **AWARD WINNER!**
5½ x 8½, 160 pp, Quality PB, ISBN 1-879045-98-2 **$15.95**

Honey from the Rock: *An Introduction to Jewish Mysticism* **SPECIAL ANNIVERSARY EDITION**
6 x 9, 176 pp, Quality PB, ISBN 1-58023-073-3 **$15.95**

The Book of Letters: *A Mystical Hebrew Alphabet* **AWARD WINNER!**
Popular HC Edition, 6 x 9, 80 pp, 2-color text, ISBN 1-879045-00-1 **$24.95**; *Deluxe Gift Edition,* 9 x 12, 80 pp, HC, 4-color text, ornamentation, slipcase, ISBN 1-879045-01-X **$79.95**; *Collector's Limited Edition,* 9 x 12, 80 pp, HC, gold-embossed pages, hand-assembled slipcase. With silkscreened print. Limited to 500 signed and numbered copies, ISBN 1-879045-04-4 **$349.00**

The Book of Words: *Talking Spiritual Life, Living Spiritual Talk* **AWARD WINNER!**
6 x 9, 160 pp, Quality PB, 2-color text, ISBN 1-58023-020-2 **$16.95**; HC, ISBN 1-879045-35-4 **$21.95**

God Was in This Place & I, i Did Not Know: *Finding Self, Spirituality and Ultimate Meaning*
6 x 9, 192 pp, Quality PB, ISBN 1-879045-33-8 **$16.95**

The River of Light: *Jewish Mystical Awareness* **SPECIAL ANNIVERSARY EDITION**
6 x 9, 192 pp, Quality PB, ISBN 1-58023-096-2 **$16.95**

Because Nothing Looks Like God
by Lawrence and Karen Kushner; Full-color illus. by Dawn W. Majewski
11 x 8½, 32 pp, HC, Full-color illus., ISBN 1-58023-092-X **$16.95** **For ages 4 & up**

Spirituality

My People's Prayer Book: *Traditional Prayers, Modern Commentaries*
Ed. by *Dr. Lawrence A. Hoffman*

Provides a diverse and exciting commentary to the traditional liturgy, helping modern men and women find new wisdom in Jewish prayer, and bring liturgy into their lives. Each book includes Hebrew text, modern translation, and commentaries *from all perspectives* of the Jewish world.
Vol. 1—*The Sh'ma and Its Blessings*, 7 x 10, 168 pp, HC, ISBN 1-879045-79-6 **$23.95**
Vol. 2—*The Amidah*, 7 x 10, 240 pp, HC, ISBN 1-879045-80-X **$23.95**
Vol. 3—*P'sukei D'zimrah* (Morning Psalms), 7 x 10, 240 pp, HC, ISBN 1-879045-81-8 **$24.95**
Vol. 4—*Seder K'riat Hatorah* (The Torah Service), 7 x 10, 264 pp, HC, ISBN 1-879045-82-6 **$23.95**
Vol. 5—*Birkhot Hashachar* (Morning Blessings), 7 x 10, 240 pp, HC, ISBN 1-879045-83-4 **$24.95**
Vol. 6—*Tachanun and Concluding Prayers*, 7 x 10, 240 pp, HC, ISBN 1-879045-84-2 **$24.95**

Six Jewish Spiritual Paths: *A Rationalist Looks at Spirituality*
by Rabbi Rifat Sonsino
6 x 9, 208 pp, Quality PB, ISBN 1-58023-167-5 **$16.95**; HC, ISBN 1-58023-095-4 **$21.95**

Becoming a Congregation of Learners
Learning as a Key to Revitalizing Congregational Life by Isa Aron, Ph.D.;
Foreword by Rabbi Lawrence A. Hoffman, Co-Developer, Synagogue 2000
6 x 9, 304 pp, Quality PB, ISBN 1-58023-089-X **$19.95**

Self, Struggle & Change
Family Conflict Stories in Genesis and Their Healing Insights for Our Lives
by Dr. Norman J. Cohen 6 x 9, 224 pp, Quality PB, ISBN 1-879045-66-4 **$16.95**

Voices from Genesis: *Guiding Us through the Stages of Life*
by Dr. Norman J. Cohen 6 x 9, 192 pp, Quality PB, ISBN 1-58023-118-7 **$16.95**

Ancient Secrets: *Using the Stories of the Bible to Improve Our Everyday Lives*
by Rabbi Levi Meier, Ph.D. 5½ x 8½, 288 pp, Quality PB, ISBN 1-58023-064-4 **$16.95**

The Business Bible: *10 New Commandments for Bringing Spirituality & Ethical Values into the Workplace*
by Rabbi Wayne Dosick 5½ x 8½, 208 pp, Quality PB, ISBN 1-58023-101-2 **$14.95**

Being God's Partner: *How to Find the Hidden Link Between Spirituality and Your Work*
by Rabbi Jeffrey K. Salkin; Intro. by Norman Lear AWARD WINNER!
6 x 9, 192 pp, Quality PB, ISBN 1-879045-65-6 **$16.95**; HC, ISBN 1-879045-37-0 **$19.95**

God & the Big Bang
Discovering Harmony Between Science & Spirituality AWARD WINNER!
by Daniel C. Matt 6 x 9, 224 pp, Quality PB, ISBN 1-879045-89-3 **$16.95**

Soul Judaism: *Dancing with God into a New Era*
by Rabbi Wayne Dosick 5½ x 8½, 304 pp, Quality PB, ISBN 1-58023-053-9 **$16.95**

Finding Joy: *A Practical Spiritual Guide to Happiness* AWARD WINNER!
by Rabbi Dannel I. Schwartz with Mark Hass
6 x 9, 192 pp, Quality PB, ISBN 1-58023-009-1 **$14.95**; HC, ISBN 1-879045-53-2 **$19.95**

Spirituality & More

The Jewish Lights Spirituality Handbook
A Guide to Understanding, Exploring & Living a Spiritual Life
Ed. by *Stuart M. Matlins, Editor in Chief, Jewish Lights Publishing*

Rich, creative material from over fifty spiritual leaders on every aspect of Jewish spirituality today: prayer, meditation, mysticism, study, rituals, special days, the everyday, and more.
6 x 9, 456 pp, Quality PB, ISBN 1-58023-093-8 **$18.95**; HC, ISBN 1-58023-100-4 **$24.95**

The Story of the Jews: *A 4,000-Year Adventure—A Graphic History Book*
Written and illustrated by *Stan Mack*

Through witty cartoons and accurate narrative, illustrates the major characters and events that have shaped the Jewish people and culture. For all ages.
6 x 9, 304 pp, Quality PB, Illus., ISBN 1-58023-155-1 **$16.95**

The Jewish Prophet: *Visionary Words from Moses and Miriam to Henrietta Szold and A. J. Heschel*
by *Rabbi Dr. Michael J. Shire*

This beautifully illustrated collection of Jewish prophecy features the lives and teachings of thirty men and women, from biblical times to modern day. Provides an inspiring and informative description of the role each played in their own time, and an explanation of why we should know about them in our time. Illustrated with illuminations from medieval Hebrew manuscripts.
6½ x 8½, 128 pp, HC, 123 full-color illus., ISBN 1-58023-168-3 **$25.00**

 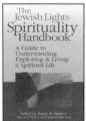 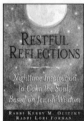  

The Enneagram and Kabbalah: *Reading Your Soul*
by Rabbi Howard A. Addison 6 x 9, 176 pp, Quality PB, ISBN 1-58023-001-6 **$15.95**

Cast in God's Image: *Discover Your Personality Type Using the Enneagram and Kabbalah*
by Rabbi Howard A. Addison 7 x 9, 176 pp, Quality PB, ISBN 1-58023-124-1 **$16.95**

Mystery Midrash: *An Anthology of Jewish Mystery & Detective Fiction* AWARD WINNER!
Ed. by Lawrence W. Raphael 6 x 9, 304 pp, Quality PB, ISBN 1-58023-055-5 **$16.95**

Criminal Kabbalah: *An Intriguing Anthology of Jewish Mystery & Detective Fiction*
Ed. by Lawrence W. Raphael; Foreword by Laurie R. King
6 x 9, 256 pp, Quality PB, ISBN 1-58023-109-8 **$16.95**

Sacred Intentions: *Daily Inspiration to Strengthen the Spirit, Based on Jewish Wisdom*
by Rabbi Kerry M. Olitzky & Rabbi Lori Forman
4½ x 6½, 448 pp, Quality PB, ISBN 1-58023-061-X **$15.95**

Restful Reflections: *Nighttime Inspiration to Calm the Soul, Based on Jewish Wisdom*
by Rabbi Kerry M. Olitzky & Rabbi Lori Forman
4½ x 6½, 448 pp, Quality PB, ISBN 1-58023-091-1 **$15.95**

Embracing the Covenant: *Converts to Judaism Talk About Why & How* Ed. by Rabbi Allan Berkowitz & Patti Moskovitz 6 x 9, 192 pp, Quality PB, ISBN 1-879045-50-8 **$16.95**

Wandering Stars: *An Anthology of Jewish Fantasy & Science Fiction* Ed. by Jack Dann; Intro. by Isaac Asimov 6 x 9, 272 pp, Quality PB, ISBN 1-58023-005-9 **$16.95**

Israel—A Spiritual Travel Guide: *A Companion for the Modern Jewish Pilgrim* AWARD WINNER!
by Rabbi Lawrence A. Hoffman 4¾ x 10, 256 pp, Quality PB, ISBN 1-879045-56-7 **$18.95**

Women's Spirituality

The Women's Torah Commentary: *New Insights from Women Rabbis on the 54 Weekly Torah Portions* Ed. by *Rabbi Elyse Goldstein*

For the first time, women rabbis provide a commentary on the entire Five Books of Moses. More than twenty-five years after the first woman was ordained a rabbi in America, these inspiring teachers bring their rich perspectives to bear on the biblical text. In a week-by-week format; a perfect gift for others, or for yourself. 6 x 9, 496 pp, HC, ISBN 1-58023-076-8 **$34.95**

Moonbeams: *A Hadassah Rosh Hodesh Guide*
Ed. by *Carol Diament, Ph.D.*

This hands-on "idea book" focuses on *Rosh Hodesh*, the festival of the new moon, as a source of spiritual growth for Jewish women. A complete sourcebook that will initiate or rejuvenate women's study groups, it is also perfect for women preparing for *bat mitzvah*, or for anyone interested in learning more about *Rosh Hodesh* observance and what it has to offer. 8½ x 11, 240 pp, Quality PB, ISBN 1-58023-099-7 **$20.00**

 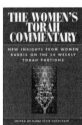   

Lifecycles In Two Volumes **AWARD WINNERS!**
V. 1: *Jewish Women on Life Passages & Personal Milestones*
Ed. and with Intros. by Rabbi Debra Orenstein
V. 2: *Jewish Women on Biblical Themes in Contemporary Life*
Ed. and with Intros. by Rabbi Debra Orenstein and Rabbi Jane Rachel Litman
V. 1: 6 x 9, 480 pp, Quality PB, ISBN 1-58023-018-0 **$19.95**
V. 2: 6 x 9, 464 pp, Quality PB, ISBN 1-58023-019-9 **$19.95**

ReVisions: *Seeing Torah through a Feminist Lens* **AWARD WINNER!**
by Rabbi Elyse Goldstein 5½ x 8½, 224 pp, Quality PB, ISBN 1-58023-117-9 **$16.95**;
208 pp, HC, ISBN 1-58023-047-4 **$19.95**

The Year Mom Got Religion: *One Woman's Midlife Journey into Judaism*
by Lee Meyerhoff Hendler 6 x 9, 208 pp, Quality PB, ISBN 1-58023-070-9 **$15.95**

Ecology

Torah of the Earth: *Exploring 4,000 Years of Ecology in Jewish Thought*
In 2 Volumes Ed. by *Rabbi Arthur Waskow*

An invaluable key to understanding the intersection of ecology and Judaism. Leading scholars provide a guided tour of Jewish ecological thought.
Vol. 1: *Biblical Israel & Rabbinic Judaism*, 6 x 9, 272 pp, Quality PB, ISBN 1-58023-086-5 **$19.95**
Vol. 2: *Zionism & Eco-Judaism*, 6 x 9, 336 pp, Quality PB, ISBN 1-58023-087-3 **$19.95**

Ecology & the Jewish Spirit: *Where Nature & the Sacred Meet* Ed. and with Intros.
by Ellen Bernstein 6 x 9, 288 pp, Quality PB, ISBN 1-58023-082-2 **$16.95**

The Jewish Gardening Cookbook: *Growing Plants & Cooking for Holidays & Festivals*
by Michael Brown 6 x 9, 224 pp, Illus., Quality PB, ISBN 1-58023-116-0 **$16.95**;
HC, ISBN 1-58023-004-0 **$21.95**

Spirituality

The Dance of the Dolphin
Finding Prayer, Perspective and Meaning in the Stories of Our Lives
by *Karyn D. Kedar*

Helps you decode the three "languages" we all must learn—prayer, perspective, meaning—to weave the seemingly ordinary and extraordinary together.
6 x 9, 176 pp, HC, ISBN 1-58023-154-3 **$19.95**

Does the Soul Survive?
A Jewish Journey to Belief in Afterlife, Past Lives & Living with Purpose
by *Rabbi Elie Kaplan Spitz;* Foreword by *Brian L. Weiss, M.D.*

Spitz relates his own experiences and those shared with him by people he has worked with as a rabbi, and shows us that belief in afterlife and past lives, so often approached with reluctance, is in fact true to Jewish tradition.
6 x 9, 288 pp, Quality PB, ISBN 1-58023-165-9 **$16.95**; HC, ISBN 1-58023-094-6 **$21.95**

The Gift of Kabbalah
Discovering the Secrets of Heaven, Renewing Your Life on Earth
by *Tamar Frankiel, Ph.D.*

Makes accessible the mysteries of Kabbalah. Traces Kabbalah's evolution in Judaism and shows us its most important gift: a way of revealing the connection between our "everyday" life and the spiritual oneness of the universe. 6 x 9, 256 pp, HC, ISBN 1-58023-108-X **$21.95**

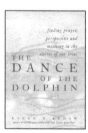 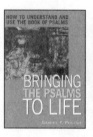   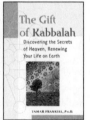

God Whispers: *Stories of the Soul, Lessons of the Heart*
by Karyn D. Kedar 6 x 9, 176 pp, Quality PB, ISBN 1-58023-088-1 **$15.95**

Bringing the Psalms to Life: *How to Understand and Use the Book of Psalms*
by Rabbi Daniel F. Polish
6 x 9, 208 pp, Quality PB, ISBN 1-58023-157-8 **$16.95**; HC, ISBN 1-58023-077-6 **$21.95**

The Empty Chair: *Finding Hope and Joy—*
Timeless Wisdom from a Hasidic Master, Rebbe Nachman of Breslov AWARD WINNER!
4 x 6, 128 pp, Deluxe PB, 2-color text, ISBN 1-879045-67-2 **$9.95**

The Gentle Weapon: *Prayers for Everyday and Not-So-Everyday Moments*
Adapted from the Wisdom of Rebbe Nachman of Breslov
4 x 6, 144 pp, Deluxe PB, 2-color text, ISBN 1-58023-022-9 **$9.95**

Or phone, fax, mail or e-mail to: **JEWISH LIGHTS Publishing**
Sunset Farm Offices, Route 4 • P.O. Box 237 • Woodstock, Vermont 05091
Tel: (802) 457-4000 • Fax: (802) 457-4004 • www.jewishlights.com
Credit card orders: (800) 962-4544 (9AM–5PM ET Monday–Friday)
Generous discounts on quantity orders. SATISFACTION GUARANTEED. Prices subject to change.